Award-Winning Recipes Showcase An Entire Year of Great Eating

WELCOME to *2001 Taste of Home Annual Recipes*, a cookbook you're sure to reach for again and again because it's *packed* with favorite recipes shared by cooks across the country.

Here you'll find each of the 539 recipes published during the year 2000 in *Taste of Home*—North America's most popular cooking magazine—plus 46 *bonus* recipes. That's 585 in all!

Whether you're making dinner for your family, baking a dish to pass at a potluck supper or whipping up something wonderful just for yourself, there's a home-style recipe that will really "hit the spot".

2000 was a fabulous year for *Taste of Home*, so don't be surprised if you have a hard time deciding which recipe to try first. Why not sample some winners from our national recipe contests to get you started?

• **A Sunny Selection of Citrus.** Orange Walnut Chicken (p. 90), a zesty main course that's impressive yet not tricky to prepare, earned the Grand Prize. Runners-up ranged from a colorful, crunchy salad, Mandarin Avocado Toss (p. 33), to an unbeatable dessert classic, Shortbread Lemon Bars (p. 124).

• **Luscious Lasagna Lineup.** Traditional Lasagna (p. 82), with its baked Italian cheeses and tasty beef and pork mix, deservedly won this contest, but those that broke with tradition offered an eclectic mix of superb eating.

Check out Chicken Chili Lasagna (p. 83), German Lasagna (p. 88), Turkey Ravioli Lasagna (p. 86), Seafood Tortilla Lasagna (p. 95) or Very Veggie Lasagna (p. 83).

• **Pork on Parade.** The judges awarded the blue ribbon to Fruit-Pecan Pork Roast (p. 80), which looks and tastes great wrapped in a rosy cranberry and apricot sauce. Comfort foods like Calgary Stampede Ribs (p. 74), Potato Pork Pie (p. 96) and Chops with Mushroom Gravy (p. 86) won big here.

• **Sheer Pleasure of Pears.** This fruit's amazing versatility is proven by the winners. Top honors went to Pear Custard Bars (p. 132), while runners-up included Pear-Stuffed Tenderloin (p. 104), Pecan-Pear Tossed Salad (p. 36) and Cinnamon-Swirl Pear Bread (p. 114).

• **Sweetheart Treats.** By the time they had tasted all of the finalists, our judges were humming *Let Me Call You Sweetheart* and singing the praises of chocolate. Grand Prize winner Valentine Berries and Cream (p. 163) and second-place Sweetheart Walnut Torte (p. 155) would come out on top whether the competition was a beauty contest *or* a taste test. Wow!

• **Thanksgiving Side Dishes.** From Curried Pumpkin Soup (p. 54), Carrots in Almond Sauce (p. 60) and Two-Tone Baked Potatoes (p. 62) to Mushroom Wild Rice (p. 65), Sweet Potato Crescents (p. 116) and Parmesan Onion Bake (p. 70), these award-winners refuse to let a stuffed turkey upstage them on the buffet table. They're dressed in their holiday best.

Inside this book, you'll also find feature pages on prime Nebraska beef (p. 102), crunchy popcorn treats from Indiana (p. 22), super summer fruit salads (p. 40), tantalizing chicken wings (p. 14) and delectable dips and satisfying spreads (p. 10) for your next family get-together.

With 585 recipes to try, you're bound to find something for everyone!

PAIR OF WINNERS. Pear Custard Bars (p. 132) took Grand Prize and Pork and Pear Stir-Fry (p. 80) earned second place in our national pear recipe contest.

2001 Taste of Home Annual Recipes

Editors: Heidi Reuter Lloyd, Julie Schnittka
Art Director: Claudia Wardius
Food Editor: Janaan Cunningham
Associate Editors: Jean Steiner, Susan Uphill, Kristine Krueger
Assistant Art Director: Linda Dzik
Production: Mandi Schuldt, Erin Brauer, Cliff Muehlenberg

Taste of Home®

Executive Editor: Kathy Pohl
Food Editor: Janaan Cunningham
Associate Food Editors: Coleen Martin, Diane Werner
Senior Recipe Editor: Sue A. Jurack
Test Kitchen Director: Karen Johnson
Senior Editor: Bob Ottum
Managing Editor: Ann Kaiser
Assistant Managing Editor: Faithann Stoner
Associate Editors: Kristine Krueger, Sharon Selz
Test Kitchen Home Economists: Sue Draheim, Julie Herzfeldt, Pat Schmeling, Wendy Stenman, Karen Wright
Test Kitchen Assistants: Sue Hampton, Kris Lehman
Editorial Assistants: Barb Czysz, Mary Ann Koebernik
Design Director: Jim Sibilski
Art Director: Vicky Marie Moseley
Food Photography: Dan Roberts
Food Photography Artist: Stephanie Marchese
Photo Studio Manager: Anne Schimmel
Production: Ellen Lloyd, Claudia Wardius
Publisher: Roy Reiman

Taste of Home Books
©2000 Reiman Publications, LLC
5400 S. 60th St., Greendale WI 53129

International Standard Book Number:
0-89821-291-X
International Standard Serial Number:
1094-3463

PICTURED AT RIGHT. Clockwise from upper right: Four-Cheese Spinach Lasagna (p. 75); Rhubarb-Topped Cheesecake (p. 154); Cinnamon-Swirl Pear Bread (p. 114); Cottage Cheese Crab Salad, Moist Bran Muffins and Peach Strawberry Smoothie (pp. 202 and 203); Strudel Sticks (p. 164); Coffee Mallow Pie (p. 137); Lemon Schaum Torte (p. 175).

Taste of Home 2001
Annual Recipes

PICTURED ON FRONT COVER. Top to bottom: Roasted Garlic Mashed Potatoes (p. 69), Ham with Pineapple Sauce (p. 224), Glazed Raspberry Pie (p. 140) and Steamed Lemon Broccoli (p. 61).

PICTURED ON BACK COVER. Top to bottom: Valentine Berries and Cream, Raspberry White Chocolate Mousse and True Love Truffles (pp. 162 and 163).

FOR ADDITIONAL COPIES of this book, write *Taste of Home* Books, P.O. Box 908, Greendale WI 53129.

To order by credit card, call toll-free 1-800/344-2560 or visit our Web site at www.reimanpub.com.

Snacks & Beverages

When midday munchies or late-night hunger strikes, turn to this sweet and savory selection of spreads, dips, appetizers and beverages.

❦ ❦ ❦

MMM-MUNCHIES! Clockwise from upper left: Cranberry Popcorn Bars (p. 23), Corny Chocolate Crunch (p. 22), Caramel Popcorn Balls (p. 23), Wontons with Sweet-Sour Sauce (p. 12), Hot Corn Dip (p. 16), Puffs with Honey Butter (p. 17) and Six-Vegetable Juice (p. 20).

Strawberry Smoothies

We dreamed up this drink one afternoon when we were hungry and wanted something sweet. It's thick, creamy and absolutely heavenly.
—Rachel Brown and Andrea Perry
Jonesboro, Arkansas

     3 cups crushed ice
     1 cup powdered nondairy creamer
   3/4 cup whipping cream
    16 small strawberries, hulled
   1/2 cup sugar
   1/4 cup milk
   1/4 cup honey

Place half of each ingredient in a blender; cover and process on high until smooth. Pour into a pitcher. Repeat. Refrigerate for 30 minutes. Stir before serving. **Yield:** 5 servings.

—— 🍷 🍷 🍷 ——

Shrimp-Stuffed Celery

My family is proud to produce celery on the beautiful island of Maui. As you can guess, we take a lot of "ribbing" for working so hard in a tropical paradise. This appealing appetizer has a creamy filling that blends nicely with crunchy, fresh celery.
—Shirley Watanabe, Kula, Hawaii

     1 bunch celery, separated into ribs
     1 package (3 ounces) cream cheese, softened
     2 tablespoons mayonnaise
     1 can (6 ounces) tiny shrimp, rinsed and finely chopped
     1 tablespoon *each* finely chopped onion, green pepper and stuffed olives
     1 tablespoon minced fresh parsley
     1 to 2 drops hot pepper sauce
   1/4 teaspoon salt
   1/8 teaspoon pepper
   1/8 teaspoon Worcestershire sauce

Cut celery ribs into 2-in. pieces. Finely chop one piece; set aside. In a mixing bowl, beat cream cheese and mayonnaise until smooth. Stir in the remaining ingredients and reserved chopped celery. Stuff into celery ribs. Refrigerate until serving. **Yield:** about 3 dozen appetizers.

—— 🍷 🍷 🍷 ——

Crisp Potato Skins

Here's a great late-night snack, appetizer or after-school treat from the Potato Board. The potato skins pack plenty of crunchy goodness...and just think of

Clam-Ups

(Pictured above)

These appetizers can be assembled ahead and frozen before baking. I keep them on hand for snacking.
—Patricia Kile, Greentown, Pennsylvania

       1 can (6-1/2 ounces) minced clams
       2 tablespoons diced onion
       5 tablespoons butter *or* margarine, *divided*
   3-1/2 teaspoons all-purpose flour
     1/2 teaspoon prepared horseradish
     1/4 teaspoon garlic powder
     1/4 teaspoon Worcestershire sauce
Dash salt
       9 slices bread, crusts removed
Paprika

Drain clams, reserving juice; set aside. In a skillet, saute onion in 1 tablespoon butter until tender. Stir in flour until blended. Gradually add horseradish, garlic powder, Worcestershire sauce, salt and reserved clam juice. Bring to a boil; cook and stir for 2 minutes or until thickened. Remove from heat; stir in clams. Flatten bread with a rolling pin. Melt remaining butter; brush one side of each slice of bread. Spread with clam mixture; roll up. Brush with remaining butter; sprinkle with paprika. Cut rolls into thirds; place on a greased baking sheet. Bake at 425° for 5-8 minutes or until lightly browned. Serve warm. **Yield:** 27 appetizers.

all the soup, mashed potatoes, fried patties and casseroles you'll be able to make from the "insides".

6 medium potatoes (about 2 pounds)
1/4 cup butter *or* margarine, melted
1 teaspoon soy sauce
Coarse salt, sour cream, chopped chives *and/or* bacon bits

Bake potatoes at 400° for 45 minutes or until tender. Cool, then cut into quarters lengthwise. Scoop out the pulp, leaving 1/8-in. shells. Refrigerate pulp for use in other recipes. Increase oven temperature to 500°. Combine the butter and soy sauce; brush on both sides of potato skins. Place on a baking sheet. Bake for 10-12 minutes or until crisp. Top with salt, sour cream, chives and/or bacon bits. **Yield:** 6 servings.

━━━ 🍽 🍽 🍽 ━━━

Orange Pineapple Punch

This concoction is as quick to fix as it is to refresh. Simply stir together the easy-to-find ingredients and serve. With its orange color, it suited our "Halloween Hoedown" perfectly. It made quite a splash among our guests. But we've found it's great any time of year.
—Connie Brueggeman, Sparta, Wisconsin

1 envelope unsweetened orange drink mix
1 cup sugar
2 cups pineapple juice, chilled
3 cups cold water
2 cups ginger ale *or* lemon-lime soda, chilled

In a blender, blend drink mix, sugar and pineapple juice until sugar is dissolved and mixture is frothy. Pour into a punch bowl; add water and soda. Serve immediately. **Yield:** 2 quarts.

━━━ 🍽 🍽 🍽 ━━━

Crunchy Cheese Nibblers

With five ingredients, these savory bites are easy to make. *—Janis Plourde, Smooth Rock Falls, Ontario*

1 cup (4 ounces) finely shredded cheddar cheese
1 cup crushed potato chips
1/2 cup all-purpose flour
1/4 cup butter *or* margarine, softened
1 teaspoon ground mustard

In a bowl, combine all ingredients. Shape dough into 3/4-in. balls. Place on ungreased baking sheets and flatten slightly. Bake at 375° for 5-8 minutes or until golden brown. Remove to a wire rack. Serve warm. **Yield:** about 3 dozen.

Tangy Texas Salsa
(Pictured below)

I'm a "transplant" here from Wisconsin. Even after some 20 years, I still can't get enough of our wonderful local citrus. The combination of tangy fruit, spicy jalapeno and distinctive cilantro is perfect with chips. We also serve it over any meat, poultry or fish. It's a great way to work citrus into a main dish.
—Lois Kildahl, McAllen, Texas

1 medium grapefruit
1 large navel orange
1 *each* medium green, sweet red and yellow pepper, chopped
1 medium tomato, seeded and chopped
1 jalapeno pepper, seeded and chopped*
3 tablespoons chopped red onion
1 tablespoon minced fresh cilantro *or* parsley
1-1/2 teaspoons sugar
1/2 teaspoon salt

Peel, section and dice grapefruit and orange, removing all membrane. Place in a bowl; add remaining ingredients and mix well. Cover and refrigerate for at least 2 hours. **Yield:** about 5 cups. ***Editor's Note:** When cutting or seeding hot peppers, use rubber or plastic gloves to protect your hands. Avoid touching your face.

Dazzle Family and Friends with Festive Dips and Spreads

DIP into this appealing array of appetizer recipes from fellow cooks, and you'll surely spread goodwill and good taste during the holiday season.

🎺 🎺 🎺

Christmas Cheese Ball

(Pictured below)

This rich cheese spread is delicious and wonderfully attractive. —Esther Shank, Harrisonville, Virginia

2 **packages (8 ounces *each*) cream cheese, softened**
2 **cups (8 ounces) shredded sharp cheddar cheese**
1 **tablespoon finely chopped onion**
1 **tablespoon diced pimientos**
1 **tablespoon diced green pepper**
2 **teaspoons Worcestershire sauce**
1 **teaspoon lemon juice**
Chopped pecans, toasted
Assorted crackers

MERRY MUNCHIES sure to spread good cheer are Ruby-Red Pretzel Dip, Southwestern Star Dip and Christmas Cheese Ball (shown above, clockwise from upper right).

In a mixing bowl, combine the first seven ingredients; mix well. Shape into two balls; roll in pecans. Cover and chill. Remove from the refrigerator 15 minutes before serving. Serve with crackers. **Yield:** 2 cheese balls (1-1/2 cups each).

—— 🍴 🍴 🍴 ——

Ruby-Red Pretzel Dip

(Pictured below left)

Plain pretzels get a pretty coating and tangy taste from this thick, festive blend. —*Grace Yaskovic*
Branchville, New Jersey

> 1 can (16 ounces) jellied cranberry sauce
> 3/4 cup sugar
> 1/4 cup vinegar
> 1 teaspoon ground ginger
> 1 teaspoon ground mustard
> 1/4 teaspoon ground cinnamon
> 1/8 teaspoon pepper
> 1 tablespoon all-purpose flour
> 1 tablespoon cold water

Red food coloring, optional
Pretzels

In a saucepan, combine the first seven ingredients; whisk over medium heat until smooth. Combine flour and cold water until smooth; add to cranberry mixture. Bring to a boil; cook and stir for 2 minutes. Transfer to a bowl; stir in food coloring if desired. Cover and chill overnight. Serve with pretzels. **Yield:** 2 cups.

—— 🍴 🍴 🍴 ——

Southwestern Star Dip

(Pictured at left)

I enjoyed this sensational dip at a holiday party and begged for the recipe. —*Joan Hallford*
North Richland Hills, Texas

> 2 cups (8 ounces) shredded sharp cheddar cheese
> 1 cup mayonnaise*
> 1 can (4-1/2 ounces) chopped ripe olives, drained, *divided*
> 1 can (4 ounces) chopped green chilies, undrained
> 1/4 teaspoon garlic powder
> 1/8 teaspoon hot pepper sauce
> 1 medium tomato, chopped
> 1/4 cup chopped green onions

Tortilla chips

In a bowl, combine cheese, mayonnaise, 1/3 cup olives, chilies, garlic powder and hot pepper sauce.

Transfer to an ungreased 9-in. pie plate. Bake, uncovered, at 350° for 20 minutes or until hot and bubbly. Sprinkle tomato on top in the shape of a star; outline with remaining olives. Sprinkle onions around the star. **Yield:** 2-2/3 cups. ***Editor's Note:** Light or fat-free mayonnaise may not be substituted for regular mayonnaise in this recipe.

—— 🍴 🍴 🍴 ——

Mushroom Liver Pate

It's easy to make this smooth, zippy spread. And it tastes so good! —*Linda Rock, Stratford, Wisconsin*

> 1/4 pound fresh mushrooms, finely chopped
> 1 tablespoon butter *or* margarine
> 1 package (8 ounces) braunschweiger
> 1/2 cup sour cream
> 1 tablespoon finely chopped green onion
> 1/2 teaspoon Dijon mustard

Dash cayenne pepper
Minced fresh parsley

In a skillet, saute mushrooms in butter until tender. Remove from the heat. Stir in the braunschweiger, sour cream, onion, mustard and cayenne; mix well. Press into a 1-1/2-cup bowl lined with plastic wrap. Cover and refrigerate until serving. Invert onto a plate; garnish with parsley. **Yield:** 1-1/2 cups.

—— 🍴 🍴 🍴 ——

Fiesta Crab Dip

I often fix a batch of this mild, fresh-tasting crab dip that tempts taste buds. —*Patricia Walls*
Aurora, Minnesota

> 1 package (8 ounces) cream cheese, softened
> 1 cup picante sauce
> 1 package (8 ounces) imitation crabmeat, chopped
> 1 cup (4 ounces) shredded cheddar cheese
> 1/3 cup thinly sliced green onions
> 2 tablespoons sliced ripe olives
> 2 tablespoons diced fresh tomato
> 2 tablespoons minced fresh cilantro *or* parsley

Tortilla chips, assorted crackers *or* fresh vegetables

In a mixing bowl, combine the cream cheese and picante sauce. Add the crab, cheese and onions; mix well. Cover and refrigerate. Transfer to a serving bowl. Sprinkle with the olives, tomato and cilantro. Serve with chips, crackers or vegetables. **Yield:** 3 cups.

cornstarch; gradually stir in pineapple juice, vinegar and soy sauce until smooth. Bring to a boil; cook and stir for 2 minutes or until thickened. Reduce heat; stir in green pepper and pineapple. Cover and simmer for 5 minutes; set aside and keep warm. In a bowl, combine pork, cabbage, sprouts, onion, eggs, salt and pepper. Place about 1 tablespoonful in the center of each wrapper. Moisten edges with water; fold opposite corners together over filling and press to seal. In an electric skillet, heat 1 in. of oil to 375°. Fry wontons for 2-1/2 minutes or until golden brown, turning once. Drain on paper towels. Serve with sauce. **Yield:** about 8-1/2 dozen (2-1/2 cups sauce). ***Editor's Note:** Fill wonton wrappers a few at a time, keeping others covered until ready to use.

— ▼ ▼ ▼ —

Sweet Onion Cheese Spread

People rave over this rich-tasting, buttery onion spread. —Shirley Glaab, Hattiesburg, Mississippi

✓ Uses less fat, sugar or salt. Includes Nutritional Analysis and Diabetic Exchanges.

   3 **large sweet onions, coarsely chopped**
   1 **garlic clove, minced**
   2 **tablespoons butter *or* margarine**
   2 **cups (8 ounces) shredded sharp cheddar cheese**
   1 **cup mayonnaise**
1/2 **teaspoon hot pepper sauce**
Assorted crackers

In a large skillet, saute onions and garlic in butter until tender. Remove from the heat; stir in cheese, mayonnaise and hot pepper sauce. Transfer to an ungreased 1-1/2-qt. baking dish. Bake at 375° for 20-25 minutes or until lightly browned. Serve with crackers. **Yield:** about 5 cups. **Nutritional Analysis:** One 2-tablespoon serving (prepared with reduced-fat margarine, light mayonnaise and reduced-fat cheddar cheese) equals 34 calories, 72 mg sodium, 3 mg cholesterol, 3 gm carbohydrate, 2 gm protein, 2 gm fat, trace fiber. **Diabetic Exchange:** 1/2 meat.

— ▼ ▼ ▼ —

Salsa Guacamole

I've never tasted better guacamole than this. If there's time, I make homemade tortilla chips by frying 1-inch strips of flour tortillas in oil and salting them. —Lauren Heyn, Oak Creek, Wisconsin

✓ Uses less fat, sugar or salt. Includes Nutritional Analysis and Diabetic Exchanges.

Wontons with Sweet-Sour Sauce

(Pictured above and on page 6)

This simple finger food makes an awesome appetizer and is perfect for potlucks. I serve these crispy pork rolls with sweet-and-sour sauce, and they disappear in a hurry—folks can't seem to get enough of them. —Korrin Grigg, Neenah, Wisconsin

   1 **can (14 ounces) pineapple tidbits**
1/2 **cup packed brown sugar**
   1 **tablespoon cornstarch**
1/3 **cup cider vinegar**
   1 **tablespoon soy sauce**
1/2 **cup chopped green pepper**
1/2 **pound ground pork**
   2 **cups finely shredded cabbage**
3/4 **cup finely chopped fresh bean sprouts**
   1 **small onion, finely chopped**
   2 **eggs, lightly beaten**
1/2 **teaspoon salt**
1/4 **teaspoon pepper**
   2 **packages (12 ounces *each*) wonton wrappers***
Oil for frying

Drain pineapple, reserving juice. Set pineapple aside. In a saucepan, combine brown sugar and

6 small ripe avocados, halved, pitted and peeled
1/4 cup lemon juice
1 cup salsa
2 green onions, finely chopped
1/4 teaspoon salt *or* salt-free seasoning blend
1/4 teaspoon garlic powder
Tortilla chips

In a bowl, mash avocados with lemon juice. Stir in the salsa, onions, salt and garlic powder. Serve immediately with tortilla chips. **Yield:** 4 cups. **Nutritional Analysis:** 2 tablespoons (prepared with salt-free seasoning blend; calculated without tortilla chips) equals 10 calories, 55 mg sodium, 0 cholesterol, 1 gm carbohydrate, trace protein, 1 gm fat, trace fiber. **Diabetic Exchange:** Free food.

Pepperoni Pizza Dip

We used to grow a lot of bell peppers on my parents' farm. We once grossed 23 tons of peppers—that's a lot of handpicking! This dip is a hearty party snack that always goes quickly. —Connie Bryant
Wallingford, Kentucky

1 package (8 ounces) cream cheese, softened
1/2 cup sour cream
1/8 teaspoon dried oregano
1/8 teaspoon garlic powder
1/8 teaspoon cayenne pepper
1/2 cup pizza sauce
3/4 cup chopped green pepper
10 pepperoni slices, quartered
1/4 cup sliced green onions
1/2 cup shredded mozzarella cheese
Toasted bread rounds *or* breadsticks

In a mixing bowl, combine the first five ingredients. Spread into an ungreased 9-in. pie plate or serving plate. Cover with pizza sauce; top with green pepper, pepperoni and onions. Bake at 350° for 10 minutes. Sprinkle with cheese. Bake 5-8 minutes longer or until cheese is melted. Serve with bread rounds or breadsticks. **Yield:** 8-10 servings.

Shelling Pecans

Try this simple strategy to get the most meat from pecans: Before shelling, put the pecans in a pot and cover them with water. Bring the water to a boil. Remove the pot from the stove and let the pecans stand for about 5 minutes. Drain, rinse, then pat the nuts dry. Shell the nuts immediately.

Hot Ginger Coffee
(Pictured below)

When we lived in New Hampshire, I'd sit by the fire and sip this coffee on a cold winter day. It's a great warm-up after shoveling snow, skiing, skating or snow-mobiling. —Audrey Thibodeau, Gilbert, Arizona

6 tablespoons ground coffee (not instant)
1 tablespoon grated orange peel
1 tablespoon chopped crystallized *or* candied ginger*
1/2 teaspoon ground cinnamon
6 cups cold water
Whipped cream, cinnamon sticks *and/or* additional orange peel, optional

Combine the coffee, orange peel, ginger and cinnamon; pour into a coffee filter. Brew according to manufacturer's directions. Pour into mugs; garnish with whipped cream, cinnamon sticks and orange peel if desired. **Yield:** 6 servings. ***Editor's Note:** Look for crystallized or candied ginger in the spice or baking section of your grocery store.

For Good Eating, Just 'Wing It'!

BIRDS of a feather flock together, especially when there's a heaping platter of seasoned chicken wings to munch. These savory varieties are definitely something to cluck about!

— ▽ ▽ ▽ —

Zesty Chicken Wings

(Pictured below)

These spicy barbecue wings are so easy to make. I fix a double batch since my family thinks they're great. You should see them disappear!
—Joan Rose
Langley, British Columbia

    1/2 **cup corn syrup**
    1/2 **cup ketchup**
    1/4 **cup cider vinegar**
    1/4 **cup Worcestershire sauce**
    1/4 **cup Dijon mustard**
      1 **small onion, chopped**
      3 **garlic cloves, minced**
      1 **tablespoon chili powder**
   16 **whole chicken wings (about 3 pounds)**

In a saucepan, combine the first eight ingredients. Bring to a boil. Reduce heat; simmer, uncovered, for 15-20 minutes or until thickened. Meanwhile, cut chicken wings into three sections; discard wing tips. Place wings in a well-greased 15-in. x 10-in. x 1-in. baking pan. Bake at 375° for 30 minutes, turning once. Brush with sauce. Bake 20-25 minutes longer, turning and basting once, or until chicken juices run clear. Serve with additional sauce if desired. **Yield:** 10-12 servings.

— ▽ ▽ ▽ —

Raspberry Glazed Wings

These fruity glazed wings are a staple at our house. They're a super finger food when entertaining and also make a tasty entree.
—Sue Seymour
Valatie, New York

    3/4 **cup seedless raspberry jam**
    1/4 **cup cider vinegar**
    1/4 **cup soy sauce**
      3 **garlic cloves, minced**
      1 **teaspoon pepper**
   16 **whole chicken wings (about 3 pounds)**

In a saucepan, combine jam, vinegar, soy sauce, garlic and pepper. Bring to a boil; boil for 1 minute. Cut chicken wings into three sections; discard wing tips. Place wings in a large bowl; add raspberry mixture and toss to coat. Cover and refrigerate for 4 hours. Line a 15-in. x 10-in. x 1-in. baking pan with foil and heavily grease the foil. Using a slotted spoon and reserving the marinade, place wings in pan. Bake at 375° for 30 minutes, turning once. Meanwhile, in a saucepan, bring marinade to a rolling boil; boil for 1 minute. Reduce heat; simmer, uncovered for 10-15 minutes or until thickened. Brush over wings. Bake 20-25 minutes longer, turning and basting once, or until chicken juices run clear. **Yield:** 10-12 servings.

— ▽ ▽ ▽ —

Spicy Hot Wings

Friends and family go wild when I serve these tongue-tingling baked chicken wings. The creamy dipping sauce is a mild accompaniment.
—Anna Free
Loudonville, Ohio

   10 **whole chicken wings (about 2 pounds)**
    1/2 **cup butter *or* margarine, melted**
    2 to 5 **teaspoons hot pepper sauce**

3/4 teaspoon garlic salt
1/4 teaspoon paprika
ROQUEFORT SAUCE:
  3/4 cup sour cream
    1 tablespoon dried minced onion
    1 tablespoon milk
  1/2 cup crumbled Roquefort *or* blue cheese
  1/4 teaspoon garlic salt
  1/8 teaspoon ground mustard
Paprika, optional
Celery sticks, optional

Cut chicken wings into three sections; discard wing tips. Place wings in a greased 15-in. x 10-in. x 1-in. baking pan. Combine butter, hot pepper sauce, garlic salt and paprika; pour over wings. Bake at 375° for 30 minutes. Turn; bake 20-25 minutes longer or until chicken juices run clear. Meanwhile, for sauce, combine the sour cream, onion, milk, cheese, garlic salt and mustard in a blender. Cover and process until smooth. Pour into a bowl; sprinkle with paprika if desired. Cover and refrigerate until serving. Drain wings. Serve with sauce and celery if desired. **Yield:** 6-8 servings.

Taco Party Wings

Even though winter doesn't cool down all that much in this part of the country, I still like to serve snacks with added warmth, like these zesty party wings. Friends sure do enjoy 'em.   —*Betty Riley, Phoenix, Arizona*

2-1/2 pounds chicken wings
  1/4 cup cornmeal
    1 envelope taco seasoning mix
    2 teaspoons dried parsley flakes
  3/4 teaspoon salt

Separate sections of chicken wings at the joints, discarding wing tip portion. Combine remaining ingredients in a bowl or plastic bag; add chicken wings and stir or shake to coat. Place in a single layer on two greased 15-in. x 10-in. x 1-in. baking pans. Bake at 350° for 25 minutes; turn and bake 10 minutes longer or until chicken juices run clear. **Yield:** 6-8 servings. **Editor's Note:** Recipe may easily be doubled.

Sesame Chicken Wings

(Pictured above right)

Many times I've taken this dish to church dinners and I'm always asked for the recipe. It's a super appetizer for any gathering.   —*Mrs. John Nydegger*
Wellsville, New York

  1/2 cup soy sauce
  1/3 cup water
  1/4 cup sugar
    2 tablespoons sesame *or* olive oil
    4 green onions with tops, sliced
  1/2 medium onion, sliced
    2 garlic cloves, minced
    1 to 2 tablespoons sesame seeds
Dash pepper
2-1/2 pounds chicken wings

In a large plastic bag or glass dish, combine the first nine ingredients. Add the chicken wings; coat well. Cover and refrigerate for 2-3 hours or overnight, turning occasionally. Remove chicken to a shallow rack in a baking pan; discard the marinade. Bake, uncovered, at 350° for 30 minutes. Turn and bake about 20 minutes longer or until tender. **Yield:** 6-8 servings.

Cool the Heat

Cool blue cheese salad dressing and celery sticks pair well with spicy hot chicken wings. But experiment with a variety of dressings (like ranch) and vegetables (like cucumber slices).

LATE-NIGHT SNACKING begins with Puffs with Honey Butter, Tortilla Snack Strips and Hot Corn Dip (shown above, clockwise from bottom).

Hot Corn Dip

(Pictured above and on page 6)

This dip is a flavorful hot mixture of vegetables and cheese. I assemble it in the morning and serve it later.
—Pam Gauld, Watkinsville, Georgia

> 1 can (15-1/4 ounces) whole kernel corn, drained
> 2 cans (4 ounces *each*) chopped green chilies, drained
> 1/2 cup chopped sweet red pepper
> 1 cup (4 ounces) shredded Monterey Jack cheese
> 2 tablespoons chopped jalapeno pepper*
> 1 cup mayonnaise*
> 1/2 cup grated Parmesan cheese
> 2 tablespoons sliced ripe olives
> Tortilla chips

In a bowl, combine the corn, chilies, red pepper, Monterey Jack cheese and jalapeno. Stir in mayonnaise and Parmesan cheese. Transfer to an ungreased 2-qt. baking dish. Cover and bake at 350° for 30 minutes or until heated through. Sprinkle with olives. Serve with tortilla chips. **Yield:** about 3 cups. *****Editor's Note:** When cutting or seeding hot peppers, use rubber or plastic gloves to protect your hands. Avoid touching your face. Light or low-fat mayonnaise is not recommended for this recipe.

Puffs with Honey Butter

(Pictured at left and on page 6)

A priest shared the recipe for these delicious dough-nut-like puffs. Honey butter is yummy on top.
—*Ruth Plaushin, Swiftwater, Pennsylvania*

1/4 cup plus 3 tablespoons butter (no substitutes), softened, *divided*
1/4 cup honey
3 eggs
1 carton (8 ounces) plain yogurt
2 cups all-purpose flour
2 teaspoons baking powder
1 teaspoon baking soda
1/2 teaspoon ground nutmeg
1/4 teaspoon salt
Oil for deep-fat frying

In a bowl, combine 1/4 cup butter and honey until smooth; set aside. In a mixing bowl, beat the eggs until lemon-colored. Add the yogurt and remaining butter. Combine the flour, baking powder, baking soda, nutmeg and salt; stir into yogurt mixture. In a deep-fat fryer or electric skillet, heat oil to 360°. Drop batter by teaspoonfuls into oil. Fry until golden, about 2 minutes. Drain on paper towels. Serve warm with the honey butter. **Yield:** 5 dozen.

———— 🍸 🍸 🍸 ————

Tortilla Snack Strips

(Pictured at left)

These crisp strips are a super homemade alternative to commercial snack chips. They go great with many different kinds of dip or salsa. —*Karen Riordan Fern Creek, Kentucky*

☑ Uses less fat, sugar or salt. Includes Nutritional Analysis and Diabetic Exchanges.

2 tablespoons butter *or* margarine, melted
6 flour tortillas (7 inches)
1/2 teaspoon ground cumin
1/2 teaspoon garlic powder
1/2 teaspoon onion salt *or* onion powder
Dash to 1/8 teaspoon cayenne pepper, optional

Brush butter over one side of each tortilla. Combine the seasonings; lightly sprinkle 1/4 teaspoon over each tortilla. Make two stacks of tortillas, with three in each stack. Using a serrated knife, cut each stack into nine thin strips. Place in an ungreased 15-in. x 10-in. x 1-in. baking pan. Bake at 400° for 8-10 minutes or until lightly browned. Serve warm. **Yield:** 1-1/2 dozen. **Nutritional Analysis:** Two strips (prepared with onion powder, reduced-fat margarine and fat-free tortillas) equals 88 calories, 256

mg sodium, 0 cholesterol, 16 gm carbohydrate, 2 gm protein, 2 gm fat, 1 gm fiber. **Diabetic Exchange:** 1 starch.

———— 🍸 🍸 🍸 ————

Oat Snack Mix

Kids of all ages seem to enjoy the creative combination of ingredients in this not-so-sweet mix. My three children would rather munch on this than on candy.
—*Patti Brandt, Reedsburg, Wisconsin*

1/2 cup butter *or* margarine
1/3 cup honey
1/4 cup packed brown sugar
1 teaspoon ground cinnamon
1/2 teaspoon salt
3 cups square oat cereal
1-1/2 cups old-fashioned oats
1 cup chopped walnuts
1/2 cup dried cranberries
1/2 cup chocolate-covered raisins

In a saucepan or microwave-safe bowl, combine the first five ingredients; heat until the butter is melted. Stir until the sugar is dissolved. In a large bowl, combine cereal, oats and nuts. Drizzle with butter mixture and mix well. Place in a greased 15-in. x 10-in. x 1-in. baking pan. Bake, uncovered, at 275° for 45 minutes, stirring every 15 minutes. Cool for 15 minutes, stirring occasionally. Stir in cranberries and chocolate-covered raisins. Store in an airtight container. **Yield:** about 6 cups.

———— 🍸 🍸 🍸 ————

Crab Triangles

I love to entertain friends and family from our rural community. Satisfying appetizers like these crisp golden wedges are fun to make and serve.
—*Jane Summers, Laddonia, Missouri*

1 can (6 ounces) crabmeat, drained, flaked and cartilage removed
1 jar (5 ounces) sharp American cheese spread
1/4 cup butter *or* margarine, softened
1 tablespoon mayonnaise
1 teaspoon garlic powder
1/2 teaspoon seasoned salt
6 English muffins, split

In a bowl, combine crab, cheese spread, butter, mayonnaise, garlic powder and salt. Spread over muffins. Broil 4-6 in. from the heat for 2 minutes or until golden brown. Cut each muffin into quarters. **Yield:** 6 servings.

Garden Salsa
(Pictured below)

In this recipe, ripe garden ingredients and subtle seasonings make a mouth-watering salsa that's a real summer treat. —*Michelle Beran, Claflin, Kansas*

✓ Uses less fat, sugar or salt. Includes Nutritional Analysis and Diabetic Exchanges.

  6 medium tomatoes, finely chopped
3/4 cup finely chopped green pepper
1/2 cup finely chopped onion
1/2 cup thinly sliced green onions
  6 garlic cloves, minced
  2 teaspoons cider vinegar
  2 teaspoons lemon juice
  2 teaspoons vegetable oil
  1 to 2 teaspoons minced jalapeno pepper*
  1 to 2 teaspoons ground cumin
1/2 teaspoon salt
1/4 to 1/2 teaspoon cayenne pepper
Tortilla chips

In a large bowl, combine the first 12 ingredients. Cover and refrigerate until serving. Serve with chips. **Yield:** 5 cups. **Nutritional Analysis:** 2 tablespoons of salsa equals 17 calories, 62 mg sodium, 0 cholesterol, 3 gm carbohydrate, trace protein, trace fat, trace fiber. **Diabetic Exchange:** Free food. ***Editor's Note:** When cutting or seeding hot peppers, use rubber or plastic gloves to protect your hands. Avoid touching your face.

Hot Cranberry Cider

Adding colorful appeal to a wintertime meal is easy—just turn to this tasty cider. The cranberry juice gives it lots of flavor, too. —*Anna Mary Beiler, Strasburg, Pennsylvania*

  3 quarts unsweetened apple juice *or* cider
  1 quart cranberry juice
  2 to 3 whole cloves
  1 cinnamon stick (3-1/2 inches)

Combine all the ingredients in a large kettle; bring to a boil. Boil for 5 minutes. Reduce heat; cover and simmer for 30 minutes. Remove the cloves and cinnamon stick. Serve warm. **Yield:** 25-30 servings (1 gallon).

— 🍷 🍷 🍷 —

Italian Pretzels

These super-easy, microwave-quick munchies are always a hit at parties. They disappear so fast, I have to make a double-batch to ensure there will be enough! —*Carrie Rogers, North Wilkesboro, North Carolina*

  2 cups miniature pretzel twists
  1 tablespoon butter *or* margarine, melted
1-1/2 teaspoons spaghetti sauce mix
1-1/2 teaspoons grated Parmesan cheese

Place pretzels in a microwave-safe bowl. Combine butter and spaghetti sauce mix; pour over pretzels and toss to coat evenly. Microwave on high for 2-3 minutes or until pretzels are toasted, stirring every 30 seconds. Immediately sprinkle with cheese; toss to coat. Cool. **Yield:** 2 cups. **Editor's Note:** This recipe was tested in an 850-watt microwave oven.

— 🍷 🍷 🍷 —

Low-Fat Eggnog

Everyone can enjoy a traditional taste of the season with this smooth, creamy eggnog. Our kids love it. —*Paula Zsiray, Logan, Utah*

✓ Uses less fat, sugar or salt. Includes Nutritional Analysis and Diabetic Exchanges.

  11 cups cold skim milk
  2 teaspoons vanilla extract
  2 packages (1.5 ounces *each*) instant sugar-free vanilla pudding mix
Artificial sweetener equivalent to 1/3 cup sugar
1/2 teaspoon ground nutmeg

In a large bowl, combine the milk and vanilla. In another bowl, combine the dry pudding mix, sweetener and nutmeg. Whisk into the milk mixture until smooth. Refrigerate until serving. **Yield:**

12 servings. **Nutritional Analysis:** One 1-cup serving equals 105 calories, 408 mg sodium, 4 mg cholesterol, 17 gm carbohydrate, 8 gm protein, trace fat, 0 fiber. **Diabetic Exchanges:** 1 skim milk, 1/2 starch.

— 🝝 🝝 🝝 —

Chili Cheese Tidbits

When I had three active teenagers at home, I heard, "Mom, what's for a snack?" 365 days a year. We all love spicy finger foods, and this recipe fills the bill.
—*Karen Ann Bland, Gove, Kansas*

> 3 cans (4 ounces *each*) chopped green
>   chilies, drained
> 3 eggs, lightly beaten
> 2 cups (8 ounces) shredded cheddar cheese
Triscuits *or* other crackers

Spread chilies onto the bottom of a greased 8-in. square baking pan. Pour eggs over chilies; sprinkle with cheese. Bake, uncovered, at 350° for 20-25 minutes or until cheese is melted. Cool slightly; cut into squares and serve on crackers. Refrigerate leftovers. **Yield:** 3 dozen.

— 🝝 🝝 🝝 —

Herbed Cheese Dip

(Pictured above)

This savory cheese dip is a fresh-tasting and excellent replacement for expensive gourmet dips.
—*Patricia Kile, Greentown, Pennsylvania*

✓ Uses less fat, sugar or salt. Includes Nutritional Analysis and Diabetic Exchanges.

> 1 package (8 ounces) nonfat cream cheese,
>   softened
> 1/4 cup skim milk
> 1 tablespoon nonfat sour cream
> 1 tablespoon minced fresh parsley
> 1 teaspoon grated Parmesan cheese
> 1 teaspoon olive *or* vegetable oil
> 1 teaspoon lemon juice
> 1 teaspoon reduced-fat margarine, softened
> 3/4 teaspoon garlic powder
> 1/2 teaspoon dried tarragon
> 1/4 teaspoon celery seed
> 1/8 teaspoon dill weed
Fresh vegetables

In a small mixing bowl, combine the first 12 ingredients; beat until smooth. Serve with vegetables. Store in the refrigerator. **Yield:** 1-1/2 cups. **Nutritional Analysis:** 2 tablespoons equals 28 calories, 114 mg sodium, 2 mg cholesterol, 2 gm carbohydrate, 3 gm protein, 1 gm fat, trace fiber. **Diabetic Exchange:** 1/2 very lean meat.

╱ *Comforting Coffee*

Looking for a way to make ordinary coffee extra special for company? Try these flavorful additions. Before brewing your coffee, add to the grounds 1 to 2 teaspoons ground cinnamon, 1 to 2 teaspoons brown sugar and a dash or two of ground cardamom.

Six-Vegetable Juice

(Pictured above and on page 6)

Our family and friends enjoy my vegetable garden by the glassfuls. My husband likes spicy foods, and after one sip, he proclaimed this juice perfect. For more delicate palates, you can leave out the hot peppers.
—Deborah Moyer, Liberty, Pennsylvania

> **5 pounds ripe tomatoes, peeled and chopped**
> **1/2 cup water**
> **1/4 cup chopped green pepper**
> **1/4 cup chopped carrot**
> **1/4 cup chopped celery**
> **1/4 cup lemon juice**
> **2 tablespoons chopped onion**
> **1 tablespoon salt**
> **1 to 1-1/2 small serrano peppers***

In a large Dutch oven or soup kettle, combine the first eight ingredients. Remove stems and seeds if desired from peppers; add to tomato mixture. Bring to a boil; reduce heat. Cover and simmer for 30 minutes or until vegetables are tender. Cool. Press mixture through a food mill or fine sieve. Refrigerate or freeze. Shake or stir juice well before serving. **Yield:** 2 quarts. ***Editor's Note:** When cutting or seeding hot peppers, use rubber or plastic gloves to protect your hands. Avoid touching your face.

Treasure-Filled Apples

On the way home from church each Sunday, granddaughter Regan and I plan a cooking project. One week she chose red-hot candies to stuff inside these apples, calling her "treasures" bright shiny rubies.
—Bobbi Liston, Arlington, Texas

> **6 medium tart apples**
> **1/2 cup sugar**
> **1/4 cup red-hot candies**
> **1/4 teaspoon ground cinnamon**

Cut tops off apples and set tops aside. Core apples to within 1/2 in. of bottom. Place in a greased 8-in. square baking dish. In a bowl, combine sugar, candies and cinnamon; spoon 2 tablespoons into each apple. Replace tops. Spoon any remaining sugar mixture over the apples. Bake, uncovered, at 350° for 30-35 minutes or until apples are tender, basting occasionally. **Yield:** 6 servings.

— 🍷 🍷 🍷 —

Roasted Mixed Nuts

It's impossible to stop eating these savory nuts once you start. We love to munch on them as an evening snack.   *—Carolyn Zimmerman, Fairbury, Illinois*

> **1 pound mixed nuts**
> **1/4 cup maple syrup**
> **2 tablespoons brown sugar**
> **1 envelope ranch salad dressing mix**

In a bowl, combine the nuts and maple syrup; mix well. Sprinkle with brown sugar and salad dressing mix; stir gently to coat. Spread in a greased 15-in. x 10-in. x 1-in. baking pan. Bake at 300° for 20-25 minutes or until lightly browned. Cool. Store in an airtight container. **Yield:** 3 cups.

— 🍷 🍷 🍷 —

Layered Fiesta Dip

For a fun party dip, try this colorful version. It's like guacamole, but with peas instead of avocado.
—Iola Egle, McCook, Nebraska

✓ Uses less fat, sugar or salt. Includes Nutritional Analysis and Diabetic Exchanges.

> **2 cans (16 ounces *each*) fat-free refried beans**
> **1 can (4 ounces) chopped green chilies, undrained**
> **2 cups (16 ounces) nonfat sour cream**
> **1 envelope reduced-sodium taco seasoning mix**
> **2 cups frozen peas, thawed**
> **1/4 cup chopped onion**

1 tablespoon lime juice
1/2 teaspoon chili powder
2 garlic cloves, minced
Dash hot pepper sauce
1/2 cup *each* shredded reduced-fat cheddar
    and Monterey Jack cheeses
1 cup chopped tomatoes
1/3 cup sliced green onions
Baked tortilla chips

In a bowl, combine beans and chilies; mix well. Spread onto a 12-in. round serving platter. Combine the sour cream and taco seasoning; spoon and spread evenly over the bean mixture. Set aside. In a food processor or blender, combine peas, onion, lime juice, chili powder, garlic and hot pepper sauce; cover and process until smooth. Spread evenly over sour cream layer. Sprinkle with cheeses, tomatoes and green onions. Serve with chips. **Yield:** 14 servings. **Nutritional Analysis:** One serving (calculated without chips) equals 143 calories, 510 mg sodium, 6 mg cholesterol, 22 gm carbohydrate, 9 gm protein, 1 gm fat, 5 gm fiber. **Diabetic Exchanges:** 1-1/2 starch, 1/2 lean meat.

Fruity Mint Punch

This sweet, refreshing drink has tea as its base. The mint is mild but lingers on the tongue.
—*Linnea Rein, Topeka, Kansas*

8 tea bags
1/2 to 3/4 cup chopped fresh mint
4 cups boiling water
1-1/2 cups sugar
6 ounces lemonade concentrate
6 ounces limeade concentrate
3/4 cup orange juice
3 quarts cold water

Place the tea bags and mint in a heat-resistant pitcher or bowl; add the boiling water. Let stand for 5 minutes; strain. Stir in the sugar, concentrates and orange juice; refrigerate. Just before serving, place mint mixture in a large punch bowl; stir in cold water. **Yield:** 4-1/2 quarts.

Fresh from the Freezer

After you squeeze an orange or lemon for juice, put the peel in a resealable plastic bag and freeze. When recipes call for peel, you'll have a ready supply, which grates very easily when frozen. Grate what you need and pop the peel back in the freezer for future use.

Garlic-Mushroom Appetizer
(Pictured below)

My grandfather, who was a hotel chef for many years, created this recipe. He prepared these mushrooms for big family gatherings, and they always were gone quickly. Everyone knew that if he made a dish, it was guaranteed to be good.
—*Rosanna Houlton*
Fort Collins, Colorado

1 cup chopped onion
1/2 cup vegetable *or* olive oil
3 tablespoons butter *or* margarine
2 pounds fresh mushrooms, sliced
1 can (28 ounces) crushed tomatoes in
    puree, undrained
1 teaspoon salt
1/4 teaspoon pepper
1/2 cup cider *or* red wine vinegar
1 bunch fresh parsley, finely chopped
    (about 1-1/2 cups)
3 garlic cloves, minced
Sliced French bread

In a saucepan, saute the onion in oil and butter until transparent. Add the mushrooms; cook for 2 minutes. Add the tomatoes, salt and pepper; cover and simmer for 20-30 minutes. Add the vinegar, parsley and garlic; mix well. Cover and simmer for 10 minutes. Chill several hours or overnight. To serve, spoon onto slices of French bread. **Yield:** 12-16 servings.

Getting Down to Crunch Time

IN INDIANA, where popcorn is a top crop, the concept of "crunch time" takes on a whole new meaning.

Growing popcorn is an important job since Americans eat 16 billion quarts of popcorn each year.

The pop in popcorn comes from a small amount of moisture (13-1/2% to 14%) inside each kernel. As kernels are heated, the moisture changes to steam. The hard outer hull resists the increasing pressure until it finally bursts. The soft starch inside puffs up as the steam is released, and the kernel turns inside out.

Fun times are sure to pop up when you try the following recipes!

— ▼ ▼ ▼ —

Corny Chocolate Crunch
(Pictured below and on page 6)

This sweet treat tastes almost like candy—and it's gone just about as fast! —Delores Ward, Decatur, Indiana

LEAN YOUR EARS THIS WAY! Caramel Popcorn Balls, Corny Chocolate Crunch and Cranberry Popcorn Bars (shown above, top to bottom) are endorsed by Indiana cooks for satisfying popcorn snacking.

3 quarts popped popcorn
3 cups Corn Chex
3 cups broken corn chips
1 package (11 ounces) butterscotch chips
3/4 pound dark chocolate candy coating

In a large bowl, combine the popcorn, cereal and corn chips; set aside. In a saucepan over medium-low heat, melt butterscotch chips and candy coating; stir until smooth. Pour over popcorn mixture and toss to coat. Spread into two greased 15-in. x 10-in. x 1-in. baking pans. When cool enough to handle, break into pieces. **Yield:** about 5 quarts.

Caramel Popcorn Balls

(Pictured at left and on page 6)

I've been a fan of popcorn since my mother used to grow corn in our garden. I've shared this special treat for years. Friends and family often request it during the holidays. —Anne Welsh, Greenwood, Indiana

2 quarts popped popcorn
3 cups crisp rice cereal
42 caramels
3 tablespoons water
1 cup salted peanuts
1/8 teaspoon salt

Combine popcorn and cereal in a large bowl; set aside. In a heavy saucepan over low heat or in a microwave-safe dish, heat caramels and water until the caramels are melted. Stir in peanuts and salt; mix well. Pour over popcorn mixture and toss to coat. With buttered hands, shape into 3-in. balls. Reshape if necessary when partially cooled. **Yield:** 10 popcorn balls.

Cranberry Popcorn Bars

(Pictured at left and on page 6)

Between work and home, I eat popcorn every day. Our company makes old-fashioned stovetop popcorn poppers. We're in the heart of popcorn country and are always trying new popcorn varieties and seasonings. These snack bars are crisp and tangy.
—Steve Dold, Monon, Indiana

6 cups popped popcorn
3 cups miniature marshmallows
1 tablespoon butter _or_ margarine
1 cup dried cranberries, chopped
1 cup chopped walnuts
2 tablespoons grated orange peel
1/4 teaspoon salt

Place popcorn in a large bowl; set aside. In a heavy saucepan over low heat, cook and stir marshmallows and butter until smooth. Stir in cranberries, walnuts, orange peel and salt; mix well. Pour over popcorn and toss to coat. Press into a greased 11-in. x 7-in. x 2-in. baking pan. Cool. Cut into bars with a serrated knife. **Yield:** 1 dozen.

Chili Popcorn

I came up with this fun, deliciously different seasoned popcorn to provide a snack for my extended family of high school actors when I was teaching drama. It's inexpensive and easy—a great way to take the edge off hearty appetites. This is a savory, irresistible snack.
—Patsie Ronk, Galveston, Indiana

☑ Uses less fat, sugar or salt. Includes Nutritional Analysis and Diabetic Exchanges.

3 quarts popped popcorn
2 tablespoons butter _or_ margarine, melted
1 tablespoon Dijon mustard
2 teaspoons chili powder
1/4 teaspoon salt
1/4 teaspoon ground cumin

Place popcorn in a large bowl. Combine the remaining ingredients; drizzle over the popcorn and toss until well coated. **Yield:** 3 quarts. **Nutritional Analysis:** One 1-cup serving (prepared with reduced-fat margarine) equals 68 calories, 204 mg sodium, 0 cholesterol, 7 gm carbohydrate, 1 gm protein, 4 gm fat. **Diabetic Exchanges:** 1/2 starch, 1/2 fat.

Popcorn Pointers

Here are a few kernels of wisdom that will steer you toward perfect popcorn and an earful of compliments:

To pop popcorn on the stove, use a 3- or 4-quart pan with a loose-fitting lid to allow the steam to escape. Add 1/3 cup vegetable oil for every cup of kernels.

Heat the oil to between 400° and 460° (if the oil smokes, it's too hot). Drop in one kernel, and when it pops, add the rest—just enough to cover the bottom of the pan with a single layer.

Cover the pan and shake to spread the oil. When the popping begins to slow, remove the pan from the heat. The hot oil will pop the remaining kernels.

Don't pre-salt the kernels—this toughens popcorn. If desired, salt the corn after it's popped.

Layered Vegetable Cheesecake

(Pictured above)

A cake that's savory instead of sweet? Absolutely! Everyone who tastes this cheesy concoction, topped with a dilly of a cucumber sauce, will relish its richness and come back for more. It's a family favorite.
—Donna Cline, Pensacola, Florida

1-1/3 cups dry bread crumbs
   1/3 cup butter *or* margarine, melted
     2 packages (8 ounces *each*) cream cheese, softened
     2 eggs
     1 cup (8 ounces) sour cream
   1/3 cup all-purpose flour
   1/4 cup finely chopped onion
   1/4 teaspoon salt
   1/4 teaspoon white pepper
   3/4 cup shredded carrots
   3/4 cup diced green pepper
   3/4 cup diced sweet red pepper
Optional garnishes: carrots and sweet red pepper cut into flowers, green pepper cut into leaves, green onions, fresh savory and bay leaves
CUCUMBER DILL SAUCE:
     1 cup (8 ounces) plain yogurt
   1/3 cup mayonnaise *or* salad dressing

   1/2 cup finely chopped unpeeled cucumber
   1/4 teaspoon salt
   1/4 teaspoon dill weed

Combine bread crumbs and butter; press onto the bottom and 1 in. up the sides of an ungreased 9-in. springform pan. In a mixing bowl, beat cream cheese until fluffy. Add eggs, one at a time, beating well after each addition. Add sour cream, flour, onion, salt and pepper; mix well. Pour 1 cup into the crust; sprinkle with carrots. Continue layering with 1 cup cream cheese mixture, green pepper, another cup of cream cheese mixture, red pepper, then remaining cream cheese mixture. Bake at 300° for 1 hour or until set. Turn oven off; cool cheesecake in oven for 1 hour with door propped open. Carefully run a knife between crust and sides of pan. Cool completely at room temperature. Chill at least 8 hours. Just before serving, remove sides of pan. Garnish as desired with vegetables and herbs. Serve cool or warm. To serve warm, remove from the refrigerator 1 hour before serving. Let cheesecake come to room temperature for 30 minutes, then reheat at 300° for 20-25 minutes or until warm. Combine sauce ingredients in a small bowl; chill. Serve with the cheesecake. **Yield:** 12-14 appetizer servings; 10-12 main-dish servings. **Editor's Note:** Cheesecake may be baked a day ahead and refrigerated.

— 🍷 🍷 🍷 —

Avocado Taco Dip

This attractive dip is guaranteed to disappear in a hurry. It is simple to make and so tasty.
—Ruth Ann Stelfox, Raymond, Alberta

     1 can (16 ounces) refried beans
     1 cup (8 ounces) sour cream
   2/3 cup mayonnaise
     1 envelope taco seasoning
     1 can (4 ounces) chopped green chilies, drained
     4 medium ripe avocados, halved, pitted and peeled
     2 teaspoons lime juice
   1/4 teaspoon salt
   1/4 teaspoon garlic powder
     1 cup (4 ounces) shredded sharp cheddar cheese
   1/2 cup thinly sliced green onions
   1/2 cup chopped fresh tomato
     1 can (2-1/4 ounces) sliced ripe olives, drained
Tortilla chips

Spread beans in a shallow 2-1/2-qt. dish. In a bowl, combine sour cream, mayonnaise and taco seasoning; spread over beans. Sprinkle with chilies. In a bowl, mash avocados with lime juice, salt and garlic powder. Spread over the chilies. Sprinkle with the cheese, onions, tomato and olives. Cover and refrigerate until serving. Serve with tortilla chips. **Yield:** 12-14 servings.

— 🍶 🍶 🍶 —

Festive Apple-Cheese Log

With apples, pecans and cinnamon, this fun spread is almost like dessert. —Anna Mayer
Fort Branch, Indiana

      1 **package (8 ounces) cream cheese,**
        softened
  1/2 **cup finely chopped tart apple**
  1/4 **cup chopped pecans**
  1/4 **teaspoon ground cinnamon**
Additional chopped pecans, toasted
Vanilla wafers, sugar cookies *or* assorted
    crackers

In a bowl, combine the cream cheese, apple, pecans and cinnamon. Shape into a log; roll in toasted pecans. Cover and refrigerate. Remove from the refrigerator 20 minutes before serving. Serve with vanilla wafers, cookies or crackers. **Yield:** 1 cheese log.

— 🍶 🍶 🍶 —

Corn Bread Pizza Wheels

This hearty, colorful snack looks like you fussed, but it's simple to make. —Patrick Lucas
Cochran, Georgia

    1 **pound ground beef**
    1 **can (16 ounces) kidney beans, rinsed and**
      drained
    1 **can (8 ounces) tomato sauce**
    4 **teaspoons chili powder**
    1 **jar (4 ounces) diced pimientos, drained**
    1 **can (4 ounces) chopped green chilies,**
      drained
    1 **cup (4 ounces) shredded cheddar cheese**
    2 **tablespoons cornmeal**
    2 **tubes (11-1/2 ounces *each*) refrigerated**
      corn bread twists
Shredded lettuce, sliced tomatoes and sour
    cream

In a skillet, cook the beef over medium heat until no longer pink; drain. Add the beans, tomato sauce and chili powder. Simmer, uncovered, until liquid has evaporated. Remove from the heat; cool. Stir in the pimientos, chilies and cheese; set aside. Sprinkle two greased 14-in. pizza pans with cornmeal.

Pat corn bread dough into a 14-in. circle on each pan. With a sharp knife, cut a 7-in. "X" in the center of the dough. Cut another 7-in. "X" to form eight pie-shaped wedges in the center. Spoon the filling around edge of dough. Fold points of dough over filling; tuck under ring and pinch to seal (filling will be visible). Bake at 400° for 15-20 minutes or until pizza wheels are golden brown. Fill the center with lettuce, tomatoes and sour cream. **Yield:** 2 pizzas (8 servings each).

— 🍶 🍶 🍶 —

Maple Hot Chocolate
(Pictured below)

When I first developed this version of hot chocolate, my husband was quite skeptical. But after one taste, his doubts were erased. It really hits the spot on a chilly morning, especially when served with cinnamon rolls or doughnuts. —Darlene Miller, Linn, Missouri

  1/4 **cup sugar**
    1 **tablespoon baking cocoa**
  1/8 **teaspoon salt**
  1/4 **cup hot water**
    1 **tablespoon butter *or* margarine**
    4 **cups milk**
    1 **teaspoon maple flavoring**
    1 **teaspoon vanilla extract**
  12 **large marshmallows**

In a large saucepan, combine sugar, cocoa and salt. Stir in hot water and butter; bring to a boil. Add the milk, maple flavoring, vanilla and 8 marshmallows. Heat through, stirring occasionally, until marshmallows are melted. Ladle into mugs and top each with a marshmallow. **Yield:** 4 servings.

Refreshing Raspberry Cooler

This drink is a super change of pace from iced tea or punch. My aunt gave me this recipe when our children were little. Now they're all adults, but we still enjoy this pretty beverage when we get together.
—Doreen Patterson
Qualicum Beach, British Columbia

    8 cups fresh *or* frozen raspberries, thawed
1-1/2 cups sugar
   2/3 cup cider vinegar
   1/2 cup water
     2 liters ginger ale, chilled
     2 cups cold water

In a large saucepan, crush the berries. Stir in sugar, vinegar and water. Bring to a boil; reduce heat. Simmer, uncovered, for 20 minutes. Strain to remove seeds; refrigerate. Just before serving, stir in ginger ale and cold water. Serve over ice. **Yield:** about 3-1/2 quarts.

— 🍺 🍺 🍺 —

Bacon-Cheese Appetizer Pie

(Pictured below)

I first made this for an open house years ago and everybody liked it. It's very easy to make and tastes delicious. Cheesecake is popular in these parts—it's fun to have it for an appetizer instead of dessert.
—Joanie Elbourn, Gardner, Massachusetts

Pastry for a single-crust pie
    3 packages (8 ounces *each*) cream cheese, softened
    4 eggs, lightly beaten
  1/4 cup milk
    1 cup (4 ounces) shredded Swiss cheese
  1/2 cup sliced green onions
    6 bacon strips, cooked and crumbled
  1/2 teaspoon salt
  1/8 teaspoon pepper
  1/8 teaspoon cayenne pepper

Roll the pastry into a 13-1/2-in. circle. Fit into the bottom and up the sides of an ungreased 9-in. springform pan. Lightly prick the bottom. Bake at 450° for 8-10 minutes or until lightly browned. Cool slightly. In a mixing bowl, beat cream cheese until fluffy. Add eggs and milk; beat until smooth. Add the Swiss cheese, onions, bacon, salt, pepper and cayenne; mix well. Pour into the crust. Bake at 350° for 40-45 minutes or until a knife inserted near the center comes out clean. Cool for 20 minutes. Remove sides of pan. Cut into thin slices; serve warm. **Yield:** 16-20 servings.

Iced Tea Trick

When making a pitcher of iced tea, add fruit juice (pineapple or citrus juice). It tastes refreshing, delicious and saves on the amount of tea you use.

Taco Appetizer Platter

A crowd usually gathers when I set out my barbecue-flavored taco dip. It's gone before I know it!
—Iola Egle, McCook, Nebraska

1-1/2 **pounds ground beef**
  1/2 **cup water**
    1 **envelope taco seasoning**
    2 **packages (8 ounces *each*) cream cheese,**
      softened
  1/4 **cup milk**
    1 **can (4 ounces) chopped green chilies,**
      drained
    2 **medium tomatoes, seeded and chopped**
    1 **cup chopped green onions**
1-1/2 **cups chopped lettuce**
  1/2 **to 3/4 cup honey barbecue sauce**
    1 **to 1-1/2 cups shredded cheddar cheese**
Large corn chips

In a skillet, cook the beef over medium heat until no longer pink; drain. Add water and taco seasoning; simmer for 5 minutes. In a bowl, combine the cream cheese and milk; spread on a 14-in. serving platter or pizza pan. Top with the meat mixture. Sprinkle with chilies, tomatoes, onions and lettuce. Drizzle with barbecue sauce. Sprinkle with cheddar cheese. Serve with the corn chips. **Yield:** 8-10 servings.

— 🍷 🍷 🍷 —

Vegetable Tortilla Stack

These tasty layered tortillas are a hit with my children and grandchildren. Nutritious vegetables are deliciously disguised in this snack.   *—Irene Muller*
Wray, Colorado

  3/4 **cup chopped green pepper**
  3/4 **cup chopped sweet red pepper**
    1 **small onion, chopped**
    2 **tablespoons vegetable oil**
  1/2 **cup picante sauce**
    1 **package (16 ounces) frozen broccoli-**
      cauliflower blend
    6 **flour tortillas (8 inches)**
    1 **can (16 ounces) refried beans**
    2 **cups (8 ounces) shredded Monterey Jack**
      cheese
    2 **cups (8 ounces) shredded cheddar cheese**
Minced fresh cilantro *or* parsley, sliced ripe
  olives, sour cream and additional picante
  sauce

In a skillet, saute peppers and onion in oil until tender. Stir in picante sauce; set aside. Cook frozen vegetables according to package directions; drain. Cool slightly and coarsely chop. Place two tortillas on an ungreased baking sheet. Spread each with 1/3 cup refried beans and sprinkle with 1/3 cup pepper mixture. Top each with another tortilla. Spoon 1-1/2 cups vegetable blend over each tortilla and sprinkle with Monterey Jack cheese. Top the last two tortillas with remaining beans and pepper mixture; place one on each stack. Sprinkle with cheddar cheese. Bake at 375° for 10-15 minutes or until heated through and cheese is melted. Garnish with cilantro and olives. Cut into wedges. Serve with sour cream and picante sauce. **Yield:** 2 stacks (4-6 servings each).

Cheesy Olive Snacks
(Pictured above)

Olive lovers will snap up these chewy, delicious appetizers. They're easy since the topping can be made ahead and they bake only 7 minutes.
—Dorothy Anderson, Ottawa, Kansas

  1 **cup (4 ounces) shredded mozzarella**
    cheese
  1 **cup (4 ounces) shredded cheddar cheese**
  1 **can (4-1/4 ounces) chopped ripe olives,**
    drained
1/2 **cup mayonnaise**
1/3 **cup chopped green onions**
Triscuit crackers

In a bowl, combine the first five ingredients. Spread on crackers. Place on an ungreased baking sheet. Bake at 375° for 7 minutes. Serve immediately. **Yield:** about 4 dozen.

Salads & Dressings

Cool and crunchy or warm and wonderful, salads can be the first, second or main course. Add a homemade dressing for a memorable meal.

——— 🥄 🥄 🥄 ———

SUPER SELECTIONS. Clockwise from upper left: Tossed Spinach Salad (p. 35), Seven-Layer Gelatin Salad (p. 34), Ham 'n' Spuds Salad (p. 42) and Cucumber Tuna Boats (p. 37).

pineapple juice. Chill until partially set. Stir in apple and nuts if desired. Pour into six 1/2-cup molds or a 1-qt. bowl coated with nonstick cooking spray. Chill until set. Unmold onto lettuce leaves if desired and top with a dollop of mayonnaise. **Yield:** 6 servings. **Nutritional Analysis:** One serving (prepared with sugar-free strawberry gelatin and spreadable strawberry fruit, and without nuts and mayonnaise) equals 96 calories, 33 mg sodium, 0 cholesterol, 24 gm carbohydrate, 1 gm protein, trace fat, 1 gm fiber. **Diabetic Exchange:** 1-1/2 fruit.

Fruity Banana Freeze

It's easy to double or triple this refreshing recipe for a luncheon or shower. —Dixie Terry, Marion, Illinois

> 2 cups (16 ounces) sour cream
> 1-2/3 cups mashed ripe bananas (about 4 medium)
> 1 can (8 ounces) crushed pineapple, undrained
> 3/4 cup sugar
> 1/2 cup chopped pecans
> 1/4 cup quartered maraschino cherries
> 1 tablespoon lemon juice
> 1/2 teaspoon salt

In a bowl, combine all ingredients. Pour into a 9-in. square dish. Freeze until firm. Remove from the freezer 15 minutes before serving. **Yield:** 12 servings.

Pork Fajita Salad

For a refreshing take on fajitas, try this salad. Your crowd will love the festive layers and creamy guacamole. —Iola Egle, McCook, Nebraska

> 1/4 cup olive *or* vegetable oil
> 2 tablespoons lime juice
> 1 teaspoon dried oregano
> 1 teaspoon chili powder
> 4 boneless pork loin chops (1 inch thick, about 1-1/2 pounds)
> 2-1/4 cups chicken broth
> 1 cup uncooked long grain rice
> 2 ripe avocados, peeled
> 1 tablespoon lemon juice
> 1 medium tomato, seeded and chopped
> 1 jalapeno pepper, seeded and chopped*
> 2 tablespoons minced fresh cilantro *or* parsley
> 1 tablespoon finely chopped onion
> 1 head iceberg lettuce, shredded

Strawberry-Rhubarb Gelatin

(Pictured above)

The tangy flavor of this favorite salad comes through with every refreshing bite. It's a quick, simple salad and an excellent addition to any meal. Our family and friends look forward to this rose-colored dish when joining us for dinner on the farm. —Kathy Flowers, Burkesville, Kentucky

✓ Uses less fat, sugar or salt. Includes Nutritional Analysis and Diabetic Exchanges.

> 1 cup chopped fresh *or* frozen rhubarb
> 3/4 cup water
> 1 package (3 ounces) strawberry gelatin
> 1/3 cup sugar
> 1 tablespoon strawberry jam *or* spreadable strawberry fruit
> 1 cup unsweetened pineapple juice
> 1 medium tart apple, diced
> 1/2 cup chopped walnuts, optional
> Lettuce leaves and mayonnaise, optional

In a saucepan over medium heat, bring rhubarb and water to a boil. Reduce heat; cover and simmer for 8-10 minutes or until rhubarb is tender. Remove from the heat. Add the gelatin powder, sugar and jam; stir until gelatin is dissolved. Add

1 can (15 ounces) black beans, rinsed and drained
1 cup (4 ounces) shredded sharp cheddar cheese
1 jar (11 ounces) salsa
2 cups (16 ounces) sour cream
Sliced ripe olives and green onions

In a large resealable plastic bag, combine the first four ingredients. Add pork chops. Seal and turn to coat; refrigerate for 8 hours or overnight, turning occasionally. Drain, discarding marinade. Grill chops, uncovered, over medium heat for 12-14 minutes or until juices run clear, turning once. Thinly slice pork; set aside. In a saucepan, bring broth to a boil; stir in rice. Return to a boil. Reduce heat; cover and simmer for 15 minutes or until rice is tender. Cool. Meanwhile, for guacamole, mash avocados with lemon juice. Stir in the tomato, jalapeno, cilantro and onion. In a 5-qt. glass salad bowl, layer lettuce, beans, cheese, pork and guacamole. Spread with salsa. Combine rice and sour cream; spread over salsa. Garnish with olives and green onions. **Yield:** 6 servings. ***Editor's Note:** When cutting or seeding hot peppers, use rubber or plastic gloves to protect your hands. Avoid touching your face.

— 🥣 🥣 🥣 —

Marinated Sweet Potato Salad

My dad, Carter, has been growing sweet potatoes for 20 years. My brother, P.K., and I have been partners in the operation for the last 2. This recipe, from our mom, Bettye, and our wives, Stephanie and Mary, is a terrific way to serve our favorite vegetable.
        —*Tim Jack Edmondson, Vardaman, Mississippi*

8 medium sweet potatoes (about 3-1/2 pounds)
1 cup tarragon *or* cider vinegar
1/2 cup vegetable oil
1 tablespoon honey
2 garlic cloves, minced
2 bay leaves
1/2 teaspoon salt
1/4 teaspoon pepper
1/4 teaspoon dried oregano
1/4 teaspoon dried thyme
1 medium onion, halved and thinly sliced
1 medium green pepper, julienned

In a large saucepan, cook sweet potatoes in boiling salted water just until tender, about 20 minutes. Cool completely. Meanwhile, in a small bowl, combine the next nine ingredients; set aside. Peel potatoes; cut in half lengthwise, then into 1/4-in. slices. In a large bowl, combine the sweet potatoes,

onion and green pepper. Add dressing and gently toss to coat. Cover and refrigerate for at least 3 hours. Discard bay leaves before serving. **Yield:** 14-16 servings.

— 🥣 🥣 🥣 —

Parsley Tortellini Toss
(Pictured below)

Two ladies from our church brought this over after I had my first child. Every time I make it, I think of those two dear sisters who made my initial days as a mom easier. —*Jacqueline Graves, Lawrenceville, Georgia*

1 package (16 ounces) frozen cheese tortellini
1-1/2 cups cubed provolone cheese
1-1/2 cups cubed mozzarella cheese
1 cup cubed fully cooked ham
1 cup cubed cooked turkey
1 cup frozen peas, thawed
2 medium carrots, shredded
1/2 medium sweet red pepper, diced
1/2 medium green pepper, diced
1 cup minced fresh parsley
1/2 cup olive *or* vegetable oil
3 tablespoons cider *or* red wine vinegar
2 tablespoons grated Parmesan cheese
2 garlic cloves, minced

Cook tortellini according to package directions; rinse in cold water and drain. Place in a large bowl; add the next eight ingredients. In a jar with a tight-fitting lid, combine the remaining ingredients; shake well. Pour over salad and toss to coat. Cover and chill until serving. **Yield:** 12-15 servings.

Salmon Potato Salad

(Pictured below)

For a deluxe side dish, I whip up this recipe featuring salmon and potatoes in a creamy dill dressing. The trick is to fix enough—people are bound to come back for seconds!
—*Shirley Awood Glaab
Hattiesburg, Mississippi*

6 cups cubed cooked red potatoes
1 cup chopped cucumber
1 cup chopped celery
3/4 cup sliced green onions
2 tablespoons minced fresh parsley
1 teaspoon dill weed
1 teaspoon dried basil
1 can (14-3/4 ounces) salmon, drained, bones and skin removed
DRESSING:
1-3/4 cups mayonnaise
2 tablespoons lemon juice
1/2 teaspoon salt
1/2 teaspoon garlic salt
1/2 teaspoon lemon-pepper seasoning

In a large bowl, combine the first seven ingredients. Add salmon; toss lightly. In a small bowl, combine the dressing ingredients; mix well. Pour over the salad and stir gently. Cover and refrigerate for 1 hour. **Yield:** 8 servings.

Warm Apricot Chicken Salad

This colorful salad is topped with marinated sauteed chicken. It's hearty, refreshing and nutritious. Even our kids like the sweet and tangy flavor.
—*Carolyn Popwell, Lacey, Washington*

✓ Uses less fat, sugar or salt. Includes Nutritional Analysis and Diabetic Exchanges.

1 pound boneless skinless chicken breasts, cut into strips
2 tablespoons orange marmalade
1 tablespoon soy sauce
6 fresh apricots, sliced
2 teaspoons grated orange peel
1/2 pound fresh spinach, stems removed
1 medium sweet red pepper, julienned
1 tablespoon vegetable oil
1/4 cup ranch salad dressing
1/4 cup slivered almonds, toasted

In a large bowl, combine the chicken, marmalade and soy sauce. Cover and refrigerate for 20-30 minutes. Meanwhile, toss apricots and orange peel. Place spinach on a serving platter or four salad plates; top with apricots. In a skillet, saute red pepper and chicken mixture in oil until chicken juices run clear. Remove from the heat; stir in salad dressing. Spoon over spinach and apricots; sprinkle with almonds. **Yield:** 4 servings. **Nutritional Analysis:** One serving (prepared with light soy sauce, orange marmalade fruit spread and fat-free ranch dressing) equals 303 calories, 388 mg sodium, 63 mg cholesterol, 24 gm carbohydrate, 28 gm protein, 11 gm fat, 3 gm fiber. **Diabetic Exchanges:** 3-1/2 meat, 1 vegetable, 1 fruit.

———— 🥄 🥄 🥄 ————

Greens with Citrus Dressing

You don't miss the oil in this light and tangy dressing. It's a festive and refreshing way to top salad greens.
—*Suzanne Schreiber, Keno, Oregon*

✓ Uses less fat, sugar or salt. Includes Nutritional Analysis and Diabetic Exchanges.

1/3 cup orange juice
1/4 cup cider *or* red wine vinegar
3 tablespoons honey
3 tablespoons water
2 tablespoons lemon juice
1-1/2 teaspoons grated orange peel
1 tablespoon finely chopped raisins, optional
Torn salad greens

In a jar with a tight-fitting lid, combine orange juice, vinegar, honey, water, lemon juice, orange peel and raisins if desired; shake well. Serve over salad greens. **Yield:** 1 cup. **Nutritional Analysis:** 2 tablespoons of dressing (prepared without raisins) equals 31 calories, 1 mg sodium, 0 cholesterol, 9 gm carbohydrate, trace protein, trace fat, trace fiber. **Diabetic Exchange:** 1/2 fruit.

— 🥄 🥄 🥄 —

Cabbage Parsley Slaw

This recipe was given to me 40 years ago by my Aunt Claire. She was a fantastic cook. I still have many of her handwritten recipes and use them often.
—_Lucille Taylor, Luverne, Minnesota_

✓ Uses less fat, sugar or salt. Includes Nutritional Analysis and Diabetic Exchanges.

- **1 medium head cabbage, shredded (about 6 cups)**
- **2 cups minced fresh parsley**
- **1 celery rib, chopped**
- **6 bacon strips, cooked and crumbled**
- **1-1/2 cups mayonnaise _or_ salad dressing**
- **2 tablespoons plus 1 teaspoon Worcestershire sauce**
- **3/4 teaspoon onion powder**

In a large bowl, toss the cabbage, parsley, celery and bacon. In a small bowl, combine the mayonnaise, Worcestershire sauce and onion powder. Pour over cabbage mixture and toss to coat. Cover and refrigerate for at least 2 hours. **Yield:** 10 servings. **Nutritional Analysis:** One 3/4-cup serving (prepared with turkey bacon and fat-free mayonnaise) equals 75 calories, 428 mg sodium, 7 mg cholesterol, 12 gm carbohydrate, 3 gm protein, 2 gm fat, 3 gm fiber. **Diabetic Exchanges:** 2-1/2 vegetable, 1/2 fat.

— 🥄 🥄 🥄 —

Mandarin Avocado Toss

(Pictured above right)

A perky blend of colors, shapes and textures makes this salad appealing to adults and children alike. My family requests it for its juicy oranges, smooth avocado slices and crunchy almonds and sunflower kernels. It's a breeze to prepare and an ideal luncheon item.
—_Colleen Weisberg, Minot, North Dakota_

- **1/2 cup sunflower kernels**
- **1/2 cup slivered almonds**
- **2 tablespoons butter _or_ margarine**
- **1/2 cup vegetable oil**
- **3 tablespoons cider _or_ red wine vinegar**
- **1 tablespoon lemon juice**

- **2 teaspoons sugar**
- **1/2 teaspoon salt**
- **1/2 teaspoon ground mustard**
- **1 garlic clove, minced**
- **4 cups torn leaf lettuce**
- **1 can (11 ounces) mandarin oranges, drained**
- **1 ripe avocado, peeled and cubed**
- **1 to 2 green onions, chopped**

In a small skillet, saute sunflower kernels and almonds in butter. Cool. Meanwhile, in a jar with tight-fitting lid, combine the oil, vinegar, lemon juice, sugar, salt, mustard and garlic; shake well. In a large salad bowl, toss the lettuce, oranges, avocado, onions and sunflower kernel mixture. Drizzle with dressing. Serve immediately. **Yield:** 6-8 servings.

🥄 _Versatile Vinegar_

To make your own tarragon vinegar, fill a glass bottle with 1 cup fresh tarragon leaves. Add a quart of warm vinegar. Store in a cool, dry place for 2 to 4 weeks; strain out the leaves for a flavorful, versatile vinegar. For a simple salad dressing, mix the vinegar with oil or mayonnaise.

Seven-Layer Gelatin Salad

(Pictured above and on page 28)

This is a very pretty salad that my mother always makes for Christmas dinner. You can choose different flavors to make other color combinations to match up with specific holidays.
— *Jan Hemness*
Stockton, Missouri

    7 packages (3 ounces *each*) assorted
        flavored gelatin
4-1/2 cups boiling water, *divided*
4-1/2 cups cold water, *divided*
    1 can (12 ounces) evaporated milk, *divided*
    1 carton (8 ounces) frozen whipped
        topping, thawed

In a bowl, dissolve 1 package of gelatin in 3/4 cup boiling water. Add 3/4 cup cold water; stir. Spoon into a 13-in. x 9-in. x 2-in. dish coated with non-stick cooking spray. Refrigerate until almost set, about 40 minutes. In a bowl, dissolve another package of gelatin in 1/2 cup boiling water. Add 1/2 cup cold water and 1/2 cup milk; stir. Spoon over the first layer. Refrigerate until almost set, about 40 minutes. Repeat five times, alternating plain gelatin with creamy gelatin, refrigerating between layers. Just before serving, spread top with whipped topping. **Yield:** 15-20 servings. **Editor's Note:** This salad takes time to prepare since each layer must be set before the next one is added.

Cranberry Compote

This best-of-the-season dish adds to the beauty and bounty of any holiday spread. Whether served warm or cold, it's a delectable fruity feast for the eyes when it's presented in a clear glass bowl.
— *Carole Dishman, Hampton, Virginia*

    2 medium tart apples, peeled and sliced
    1 package (12 ounces) fresh *or* frozen
        cranberries
1-1/4 cups sugar
    1 cup golden raisins
    1/4 cup orange juice
    1 teaspoon grated orange peel
    1 teaspoon salt
    1/4 teaspoon ground allspice
    1/4 teaspoon ground cinnamon
    1 can (15-1/4 ounces) sliced peaches,
        drained
    1 can (15 ounces) apricot halves, drained
    1 cup chopped pecans

In a saucepan, combine the first nine ingredients. Bring to a boil. Reduce heat; simmer, uncovered, for 10 minutes or until cranberries pop and apples are tender. Add the peaches and apricots; heat through. Stir in pecans; serve warm or chilled. Store in the refrigerator. **Yield:** 6 cups.

Basil Bean Salad

A light herb vinaigrette makes this tangy salad so refreshing for a warm summer evening. —*Marian Platt*
Sequim, Washington

✓ Uses less fat, sugar or salt. Includes Nutritional Analysis and Diabetic Exchanges.

    2 pounds fresh green *or* wax beans,
        trimmed
    3 green onions, sliced
2/3 cup minced fresh basil
    2 to 4 tablespoons olive *or* vegetable oil
    2 tablespoons cider *or* red wine vinegar
1/2 teaspoon salt
Pepper to taste
2/3 cup grated Romano cheese

Cut beans into 1-1/4-in. pieces. Place in a saucepan and cover with water; bring to a boil. Cook, uncovered, for 10 minutes or until crisp-tender. Rinse with cold water and drain well. In a bowl, combine the beans, onions, basil, oil, vinegar, salt and pepper. Sprinkle with Romano cheese and toss to coat. **Yield:** 10 servings. **Nutritional Analysis:** One 3/4-cup serving (prepared with 2 tablespoons oil) equals 66 calories, 165 mg sodium, 3 mg cholesterol, 7 gm carbohydrate, 3 gm protein, 4 gm fat, 1 gm fiber. **Diabetic Exchanges:** 1 vegetable, 1/2 fat.

Tossed Spinach Salad

(Pictured on page 28)

From-scratch French-style dressing is a bold topping that suits the hearty ingredients in this salad. When I make it to share at a get-together, I never have any left over. I take the salad and dressing in disposable containers and come home happily empty-handed.
—*Myra Innes, Auburn, Kansas*

- 1 package (10 ounces) fresh spinach, torn
- 1 pound fresh mushrooms, sliced
- 1/2 pound sliced bacon, cooked and crumbled
- 3 celery ribs, sliced
- 1 cup (4 ounces) shredded cheddar cheese
- 3 hard-cooked eggs, chopped
- 3 green onions, sliced
- 1 cup ketchup
- 3/4 cup vinegar
- 3/4 cup vegetable oil
- 1/2 cup sugar
- 1 teaspoon salt
- 1 teaspoon Worcestershire sauce

In a large salad bowl, combine the first seven ingredients. In a jar with a tight-fitting lid, combine the remaining ingredients; shake until sugar is dissolved. Drizzle over salad and toss to coat. Serve immediately. **Yield:** 12 servings.

Greens with Herb Dressing

This light, savory herb dressing is a refreshing topper for mixed salad greens. —*Marian Platt Sequim, Washington*

✓ Uses less fat, sugar or salt. Includes Nutritional Analysis and Diabetic Exchanges.

- 6 tablespoons olive *or* vegetable oil
- 2 tablespoons cider *or* red wine vinegar
- 2 teaspoons Dijon mustard
- 1 teaspoon *each* minced fresh tarragon and thyme *or* 2 teaspoons minced fresh herbs of your choice
- 2 teaspoons lemon *or* lime juice
- 2 garlic cloves, minced
- 1/4 teaspoon salt
- Dash pepper
- 8 cups mixed salad greens

In a jar with a tight-fitting lid, combine the first eight ingredients; shake well. Place the greens in a salad bowl. Drizzle with dressing and toss to coat. Serve immediately. **Yield:** 8 servings. **Nutritional Analysis:** One serving equals 102 calories, 119 mg sodium, 0 cholesterol, 2 gm carbohydrate, 1 gm protein, 10 gm fat, 1 gm fiber. **Diabetic Exchange:** 2 fat.

'I Wish I Had That Recipe...'

"I HAD LUNCH with a church group at Mary Ellen's Tea Room in Dallas, Texas," says Andra Kunkle of Lenoir, North Carolina.

"We especially enjoyed the sweet Poppy Seed Dressing on fresh fruit. I'd love to add that tasty recipe to my collection."

Contacting tea room owner Mary Ellen Robich, we learned that she is an avid *Taste of Home* subscriber. "I'm happy—and honored—to share the Poppy Seed Dressing recipe with fellow readers," she said enthusiastically.

"It's served with all our fruit salad choices, including the popular Three Salad Plate that features Chicken Walnut Apple Salad, Spinach Salad and Fresh Fruit Salad. In addition to salads, other favorites we serve include sandwiches, soups, entrees and desserts, all served in four cheerful dining rooms and an outdoor courtyard."

Located at 138 Spring Creek Village on the northwest corner of Coit and Belt Line in Dallas, Mary Ellen's Tea Room is open Monday through Saturday from 11 a.m. to 2:30 p.m. Phone 1-972/386-9080.

Poppy Seed Dressing

- 2 cups sugar
- 3/4 teaspoon salt
- 3/4 teaspoon onion powder
- 3/4 teaspoon ground mustard
- 3/4 cup vinegar
- 1 cup vegetable oil
- 3/4 teaspoon poppy seeds

In a mixing bowl, combine the first four ingredients. Add the vinegar and beat for 4 minutes. Add the oil; beat for 10 minutes. Add poppy seeds; beat for 5 minutes. **Yield:** 2-3/4 cups.

Pecan-Pear Tossed Salad

(Pictured below)

To save time, I prepare the ingredients and dressing the day before, then combine them just before serving. This salad has become a star at family gatherings. Once, when I forgot to bring it, dinner was postponed so I could go home and get it! —Marjean Claassen Sedgwick, Kansas

    2 tablespoons fresh raspberries
  3/4 cup olive *or* vegetable oil
    3 tablespoons cider vinegar
    2 tablespoons plus 1 teaspoon sugar
  1/4 to 1/2 teaspoon pepper
SALAD:
    4 medium ripe pears, thinly sliced
    2 teaspoons lemon juice
    8 cups torn salad greens
  2/3 cup pecan halves, toasted
  1/2 cup fresh raspberries
  1/3 cup (2 ounces) crumbled feta *or* blue
        cheese

Press raspberries through a sieve, reserving juice. Discard seeds. In a jar with a tight-fitting lid, combine oil, vinegar, sugar, pepper and reserved raspberry juice; shake well. Toss pear slices with lemon juice; drain. In a salad bowl, combine the salad greens, pears, pecans and raspberries. Sprinkle with cheese. Drizzle with dressing. **Yield:** 8 servings.

Cinnamon Fruit Salad

Cinnamon in the dressing on this refreshing fruit salad brings a holiday touch to breakfast or brunch. You'll never eat plain fruit salad again! —Nancy Johnson, Laverne, Oklahoma

✓ Uses less fat, sugar or salt. Includes Nutritional Analysis and Diabetic Exchanges.

    1 medium navel orange, peeled, sectioned
        and halved
    1 kiwifruit, peeled, sliced and quartered
    1 medium ripe banana, sliced
    1 medium apple, sliced
    6 seedless grapes, halved
    2 tablespoons sunflower kernels
  1/4 cup nonfat orange *or* vanilla yogurt
Artificial sweetener equivalent to 4 teaspoons
    sugar
  1/8 teaspoon ground cinnamon

In a large bowl, combine fruit and sunflower kernels. In a small bowl, combine yogurt, sweetener and cinnamon; mix well. Pour over fruit and toss to coat. Serve immediately. **Yield:** 8 servings. **Nutritional Analysis:** One 1/2-cup serving equals 63 calories, 6 mg sodium, trace cholesterol, 13 gm carbohydrate, 1 gm protein, 1 gm fat, 2 gm fiber. **Diabetic Exchange:** 1 fruit.

Festive Tossed Salad

With its unique medley of fruits and its festive look, this salad is a holiday tradition at our house. Our three daughters have come to expect it. One forkful reminds us of all the things we can be thankful for. —Jauneen Hosking, Greenfield, Wisconsin

  1/2 cup sugar
  1/3 cup cider *or* red wine vinegar
    2 tablespoons lemon juice
    2 tablespoons finely chopped onion
  1/2 teaspoon salt
  2/3 cup vegetable oil
    2 to 3 teaspoons poppy seeds
   10 cups torn romaine
    1 cup (4 ounces) shredded Swiss cheese
    1 medium apple, cored and cubed
    1 medium pear, cored and cubed
  1/4 cup dried cranberries
  1/2 to 1 cup chopped cashews

In a blender or food processor, combine the sugar, vinegar, lemon juice, onion and salt. Cover and process until blended. With blender running, gradually add oil. Add poppy seeds and blend. In a salad bowl, combine the romaine, Swiss cheese, apple, pear and cranberries. Drizzle with desired amount of dressing. Add cashews; toss to coat. Serve immediately. **Yield:** 8-10 servings.

— ⚑ ⚑ ⚑ —

Nutty Carrot Salad

With the sunflower kernels and a peanutty dressing, this is a new twist on carrot-raisin salad. My family loves this delightfully different combination, and I'm positive your family will, too.
— *Tami Escher, Dumont, Minnesota*

  2 **cups shredded carrots**
  1 **can (8 ounces) crushed pineapple, drained**
1/4 **to 1/2 cup raisins**
1/4 **to 1/2 cup sunflower kernels**
1/4 **cup salted peanuts**
1/4 **cup peanut butter**
1/4 **cup vanilla yogurt**
1/4 **cup mayonnaise**
1/8 **teaspoon salt**
Lettuce leaves

In a bowl, toss the carrots, pineapple, raisins, sunflower kernels and peanuts. In a small bowl, combine the peanut butter, yogurt, mayonnaise and salt; mix well. Pour over carrot mixture and stir gently to coat. Serve in a lettuce-lined bowl. **Yield:** 4 servings.

— ⚑ ⚑ ⚑ —

Cucumber Tuna Boats

(Pictured above right and on page 28)

For a refreshing summer meal, you can't beat this creamy tuna salad mounded into cucumber halves. Hard-cooked eggs make the salad extra hearty, and the crispness of the cucumber is delightful. It's an extra-special luncheon entree or light supper.
— *Mildred Stubbs, Hamlet, North Carolina*

  3 **medium cucumbers**
  1 **can (6 ounces) tuna, flaked**
  2 **hard-cooked eggs, chopped**
1/2 **cup shredded cheddar cheese**
1/2 **cup diced celery**
1/4 **cup mayonnaise *or* salad dressing**
  2 **tablespoons sweet pickle relish**
  1 **tablespoon finely chopped onion**
  1 **teaspoon lemon juice**
1/2 **teaspoon salt**

Cut cucumbers in half lengthwise; remove and discard seeds. Cut a thin slice from bottom of cucumber if necessary so each sits flat. In a bowl, combine the remaining ingredients. Spoon into the cucumbers. Serve immediately. **Yield:** 3 servings.

— ⚑ ⚑ ⚑ —

Honey-Lime Fruit Plate

This sweet-tart salad is simple yet elegant. I can easily assemble it for a family dinner, and it's special enough for company. — *Joan Hallford*
North Richland Hills, Texas

  2 **medium nectarines, sliced**
  2 **medium navel oranges, peeled and sliced**
  2 **kiwifruit, peeled and sliced**
  1 **cup fresh *or* frozen blueberries**
Leaf lettuce
  2 **tablespoons honey**
  1 **tablespoon limeade concentrate**
  1 **tablespoon vegetable oil**
1/4 **teaspoon grated orange peel**
Dash ground mustard

Arrange the fruit on lettuce-lined salad plates. In a jar with tight-fitting lid, combine the remaining ingredients; shake well. Drizzle over salads; serve immediately. **Yield:** 4 servings.

1/2 cup olive *or* vegetable oil, *divided*
1/4 cup minced fresh basil
  1 tablespoon vinegar
  1 tablespoon plus 1/2 cup grated Parmesan cheese, *divided*
1/2 teaspoon sugar
  1 pound large uncooked shrimp, peeled and deveined
1/4 cup butter *or* margarine
Lettuce leaves

For dressing, combine 1/4 cup oil, basil, vinegar, 1 tablespoon Parmesan and sugar in a saucepan over low heat. Meanwhile, combine shrimp and remaining Parmesan. In a skillet, heat butter and remaining oil. Add shrimp and saute until they turn pink, about 4 minutes. Drain on paper towels. Serve on lettuce; drizzle with warm dressing. **Yield:** 4-6 servings.

Thousand Island Dressing

(Pictured above)

This creamy dressing has a fresh taste that complements any tossed salad. —Elizabeth Hunter
Prosperity, South Carolina

✓ Uses less fat, sugar or salt. Includes Nutritional Analysis and Diabetic Exchanges.

3/4 cup plain nonfat yogurt
  3 tablespoons chili sauce
  1 tablespoon sweet pickle relish
Artificial sweetener equivalent to 3/4 teaspoon sugar

In a small bowl, whisk together all ingredients. Refrigerate until serving. **Yield:** 1 cup. **Nutritional Analysis:** One 2-tablespoon serving equals 18 calories, 24 mg sodium, trace cholesterol, 2 gm carbohydrate, 2 gm protein, trace fat, trace fiber. **Diabetic Exchange:** Free food.

Basil Parmesan Shrimp

This is a simple, elegant dish using fresh basil. Our university women's gourmet group raved about it, and due to its simplicity, it has become my favorite entertaining dish. —Laura Hamilton, Belleville, Ontario

Walnut Pear Salad

This nutty salad is absolutely beautiful with mixed types and colors of lettuce. Pears and apricot nectar add fruity sweetness. —Marian Platt
Sequim, Washington

1/3 cup apricot nectar
  2 tablespoons olive *or* vegetable oil
  2 tablespoons cider *or* red wine vinegar
  1 teaspoon chopped fresh mint *or* 1/4 teaspoon dried mint flakes
1/8 teaspoon salt
1/8 teaspoon ground mustard
  3 medium pears, peeled, halved and sliced
12 cups mixed salad greens
3/4 chopped walnuts, toasted

In a jar with a tight-fitting lid, combine the first six ingredients; shake well. Combine pears and dressing in a large serving bowl. Cover and refrigerate until chilled. Just before serving, add greens to pear mixture; toss to coat. Sprinkle with walnuts. **Yield:** 6 servings.

Rainbow Fruit Salad

To entice my children to eat fruit when they were young, I often "disguised" it in this easy-to-prepare salad. I still make it today—and I'm a great-grandmother. The salad goes well with barbecued meats or cold sandwiches. —Jonnie Adams Sisler
Stevensville, Montana

  2 large firm bananas, sliced
  2 tablespoons lemon juice

2 cups seeded cubed watermelon
2 cups fresh *or* canned pineapple chunks
1 pint fresh strawberries, halved
1 pint fresh blueberries
3 kiwifruit, peeled and sliced
2 packages (3 ounces *each*) cream cheese, softened
1/3 cup confectioners' sugar
2 tablespoons fresh lime juice
1/2 teaspoon grated lime peel
1 cup whipping cream, whipped

Toss bananas and lemon juice; place in a 4-qt. glass serving bowl. Add remaining fruit in layers. In a mixing bowl, beat cream cheese until smooth. Gradually add sugar, lime juice and peel. Stir in a small amount of whipped cream; mix well. Fold in remaining whipped cream. Spread over fruit. Chill until serving. **Yield:** 16-20 servings.

Minty Pasta Salad

Mint apple jelly provides sweetness and chopped mint brings out the herb's flavor in this refreshing pasta salad. —Nina Hall, Citrus Heights, California

3 tablespoons mint apple jelly
1/4 cup mayonnaise
2 tablespoons cider *or* white wine vinegar
1 to 2 tablespoons chopped fresh mint *or* 1 to 2 teaspoons dried mint flakes
1/2 teaspoon salt
1/4 teaspoon pepper
8 ounces small pasta, cooked and drained
2 cups cubed cooked chicken
1 sweet yellow pepper, cut into 1-inch pieces
1 cup chopped cucumber
1/4 cup sliced green onions

In a microwave-safe bowl, heat jelly, uncovered, on high for 20-30 seconds or until melted; cool slightly. Stir in the mayonnaise, vinegar, mint, salt and pepper until blended. In a salad bowl, combine the remaining ingredients. Add dressing and toss to coat. Cover and chill for at least 1 hour before serving. **Yield:** 4-8 servings. **Editor's Note:** This recipe was tested in an 850-watt microwave.

Simple Salad

If you're asked to bring a salad for a dinner, try this pretty change from traditional tossed salad ingredients: lettuce greens with chopped carrot, celery and apple, plus raisins and sliced almonds.

Patio Potato Salad

(Pictured below)

A sweet and creamy cooked dressing lends old-fashioned goodness to this side dish. It goes well with most any entree. Since the flavors need time to blend, this is a nice make-ahead salad for family barbecues, potlucks and picnics. —Romaine Wetzel
Lancaster, Pennsylvania

1/3 cup sugar
1 tablespoon cornstarch
1 to 1-1/2 teaspoons ground mustard
1 teaspoon salt
1/2 teaspoon celery seed
1/2 cup milk
1/4 cup vinegar
1 egg, beaten
1/4 cup butter *or* margarine, cubed
1/4 cup chopped onion
1/4 cup mayonnaise
7 medium red potatoes, cubed and cooked
3 hard-cooked eggs, chopped
Lettuce leaves and paprika, optional

In a saucepan, combine sugar, cornstarch, mustard, salt and celery seed. Stir in the milk, vinegar and egg until smooth. Add butter. Bring to a boil; cook and stir for 2 minutes or until thickened and bubbly. Cool. Stir in onion and mayonnaise. In a large bowl, combine potatoes and hard-cooked eggs. Add dressing and toss gently to coat. Cover and refrigerate for at least 1 hour. If desired, serve in a lettuce-lined bowl and sprinkle with paprika. **Yield:** 8-10 servings.

Fruit Salads Say 'Summer!'

FRUIT SALADS delight the eyes and dazzle the taste buds with vivid colors and refreshing flavors. The luscious lineup here is sure to result in lots of compliments and few leftovers. You'll find new ways to enjoy the juicy melons and ripe berries that summer brings, plus all-season standbys like apples and bananas.

Fruit Salad with Apricot Dressing
(Pictured below)

When I serve this lovely, refreshing salad for picnics and holidays, the bowl empties fast. —Carol Lambert El Dorado, Arkansas

SENSATIONAL SALADS. Bursting with natural sweetness, Fruit Salad with Apricot Dressing, Avocado Citrus Toss and Chilly Melon Cups (shown above, clockwise from top) present fresh fruits at their best.

1 cup sugar
1 tablespoon cornstarch
2 cans (5-1/2 ounces *each*) apricot nectar
1 teaspoon vanilla extract
6 large red apples, coarsely chopped
8 medium firm bananas, sliced
1 medium fresh pineapple, peeled, cored
   and cut into chunks (about 5 cups)
1 quart fresh strawberries, quartered
2 cups green grapes

In a microwave-safe bowl, stir the sugar, cornstarch and apricot nectar until smooth. Microwave, uncovered, on high for 6-8 minutes or until slightly thickened, stirring every 2 minutes. Stir in the vanilla. Refrigerate. In a large bowl, combine the fruit. Drizzle with dressing; gently toss to coat. Cover and refrigerate until serving. **Yield:** 26 (1-cup) servings. **Editor's Note:** This recipe was tested in an 850-watt microwave.

— 🝓 🝓 🝓 —

Chilly Melon Cups

(Pictured at left)

This cool treat is stored in the freezer so it's always handy. It's a great way to use what's left from a fruit platter or melon boat.
—*Katie Koziolek*
Hartland, Minnesota

1 cup water
1 cup sugar
1/2 cup lemonade concentrate
1/2 cup orange juice concentrate
4 cups watermelon balls *or* cubes
2 cups cantaloupe balls *or* cubes
2 cups honeydew balls *or* cubes
2 cups pineapple chunks
2 cups fresh raspberries

In a large bowl, combine the water, sugar and concentrates; stir until the sugar is dissolved. Add fruit and stir gently to coat. Spoon into foil-lined muffin cups or 3-oz. plastic cups. Freeze for up to 3 months. Before serving, thaw overnight in the refrigerator or at room temperature for 30-45 minutes until mixture is slushy. **Yield:** 12-14 servings.

— 🝓 🝓 🝓 —

Avocado Citrus Toss

(Pictured at left)

The light dressing doesn't mask the goodness of sweet citrus sections, crisp lettuce, crunchy almonds and mellow avocados.
—*Marie Hattrup*
The Dalles, Oregon

6 cups torn salad greens
2 medium grapefruit, peeled and sectioned
3 navel oranges, peeled and sectioned
1 ripe avocado, peeled and sliced
1/4 cup slivered almonds, toasted
DRESSING:
1/2 cup vegetable oil
1/3 cup sugar
3 tablespoons vinegar
2 teaspoons poppy seeds
1 teaspoon finely chopped onion
1/2 teaspoon ground mustard
1/2 teaspoon salt

In a large salad bowl, toss the greens, grapefruit, oranges, avocado and almonds. In a jar with tight-fitting lid, combine the dressing ingredients; shake well. Drizzle over the salad and toss to coat. **Yield:** 6 servings.

— 🝓 🝓 🝓 —

Honeydew Fruit Bowls

Melon puree served over sweet, colorful fruit is a welcome, refreshing dish, especially in the warm summer months. Melon halves make fun "bowls" for this treat. Children and adults alike will enjoy the creative combination of flavors and the unusual presentation.
—*Isabel Fowler, Fairbanks, Alaska*

✓ Uses less fat, sugar or salt. Includes Nutritional Analysis and Diabetic Exchanges.

1 large honeydew, halved
1 large red apple, diced
1 large navel orange, sectioned
1 medium firm banana, sliced
1 kiwifruit, peeled and sliced
1/2 cup blueberries, *divided*
2 tablespoons orange juice concentrate
1 tablespoon lemon juice
1 cup unsweetened raspberries
2 tablespoons half-and-half cream

Remove the fruit from the honeydew; set the melon bowls and fruit aside. In a bowl, combine the apple, orange, banana, kiwi, 1/4 cup of blueberries, orange juice concentrate and lemon juice. Spoon into the melon bowls and set aside. In a blender or food processor, combine the honeydew, raspberries and remaining blueberries; cover and process until blended. Stir in the cream. Pour over the fruit. Set the bowls in a bed of ice; serve immediately. **Yield:** 16 servings (served in 2 fruit bowls). **Nutritional Analysis:** One 2/3-cup serving equals 58 calories, 9 mg sodium, 1 mg cholesterol, 14 gm carbohydrate, 1 gm protein, trace fat, 2 gm fiber. **Diabetic Exchange:** 1 fruit.

Roquefort Pear Salad

(Pictured above)

Guests at a barbecue we hosted last summer brought this cool, refreshing salad. Now it's a mainstay at most all our cookouts. The mingling of zesty tastes and textures instantly wakes up the taste buds.
—*Sherry Duval, Baltimore, Maryland*

    10 cups torn salad greens
     3 large ripe pears, peeled and cut into large
       pieces
    1/2 cup thinly sliced green onions
     4 ounces crumbled Roquefort *or* blue
       cheese
    1/4 cup slivered almonds, toasted
MUSTARD VINAIGRETTE:
    1/3 cup olive *or* vegetable oil
     3 tablespoons cider *or* red wine vinegar
1-1/2 teaspoons sugar
1-1/2 teaspoons Dijon mustard
     1 garlic clove, minced
    1/2 teaspoon salt
Pepper to taste

In a large bowl, combine the salad greens, pears, onions, cheese and almonds. In a jar with a tight-fitting lid, combine the vinaigrette ingredients; shake well. Pour over salad; toss to coat. Serve immediately. **Yield:** 8-10 servings.

Luncheon Spinach Salad

A friend served this colorful salad at a church dinner but wouldn't reveal the ingredients. My daughter and I created our own version. The subtle curry flavor brings folks back for seconds. —*Evy Fitzgerald Sun Lakes, Arizona*

     3 packages (6 ounces *each*) fresh
       baby spinach, stems removed
     2 medium tart apples, chopped
     1 cup cubed cooked turkey
    2/3 cup peanuts
    1/2 cup raisins
    1/4 thinly sliced green onions
     2 tablespoons sesame seeds, toasted
    2/3 cup vegetable oil
    1/3 cup honey
    1/4 cup vinegar
     1 tablespoon grated orange peel
     1 teaspoon salt
     1 teaspoon curry powder
     1 teaspoon ground mustard

In a salad bowl, combine the spinach, apples, turkey, peanuts, raisins, onions and sesame seeds. In a jar with a tight-fitting lid, combine the remaining ingredients; shake well. Drizzle over the salad and toss to coat; serve immediately. **Yield:** 10 servings.

——— 🥛 🥛 🥛 ———

Ham 'n' Spuds Salad

(Pictured on page 28)

Not only does this make a hearty salad that's a family favorite—it's good for carrying to picnics and church suppers and a tasty way to use up ham!
—*Jo Baker, Litchfield, Illinois*

     2 cups cubed cooked potatoes
     2 cups cubed fully cooked ham
     4 hard-cooked eggs, chopped
    1/2 cup pitted ripe olives
    1/2 cup sliced celery
    1/4 cup finely chopped green pepper
    1/4 cup finely chopped onion
    1/2 cup mayonnaise
    1/4 cup sweet pickle relish
     2 tablespoons minced pimientos
     1 tablespoon prepared spicy brown *or*
       yellow mustard
     2 teaspoons cider vinegar
Lettuce leaves, optional

In a bowl, combine potatoes, ham, eggs, olives, celery, green pepper and onion. In a small bowl, combine mayonnaise, relish, pimientos, mustard and vinegar; pour over potato mixture. Toss lightly to coat. Chill for several hours. Serve in a lettuce-lined bowl if desired. **Yield:** 6-8 servings.

— 🥄 🥄 🥄 —

Fennel Green Salad

Fennel is a hardy plant with many uses. One favorite is this crisp salad. The subtle fennel dressing has wonderful homemade flavor. —_Mary Sisson Eibs_
Tucson, Arizona

   3 **cups torn salad greens**
1/4 **cup sliced fennel bulb**
   3 **tablespoons chopped red onion**
   3 **fresh mushrooms, sliced**
   2 **tablespoons chopped sweet red pepper**
1/3 **cup vegetable oil**
1/4 **cup cider vinegar**
1/4 **cup finely chopped fennel fronds**
1/2 **teaspoon honey**
1/8 **teaspoon salt**

In a salad bowl, combine greens, fennel bulb, onion, mushrooms and red pepper. In a jar with a tight-fitting lid, combine the oil, vinegar, fennel fronds, honey and salt; shake well. Drizzle over salad and toss to coat. **Yield:** 4 servings.

— 🥄 🥄 🥄 —

Spiral Shrimp Salad

With lots of vegetables and delightful fresh flavor, this colorful salad makes a wonderful summer lunch or light dinner. —_Anne Day, Pilot Grove, Missouri_

☑ Uses less fat, sugar or salt. Includes Nutritional Analysis and Diabetic Exchanges.

2-1/2 **cups frozen cooked salad shrimp, thawed**
   2 **cups broccoli florets**
1-1/2 **cups cooked spiral pasta**
1/3 **cup** _each_ **chopped green, sweet red and yellow pepper**
1/3 **cup sliced green onions**
1/4 **cup fat-free mayonnaise**
1/2 **cup fat-free Italian salad dressing**
1/4 **teaspoon dill weed**

In a bowl, combine the shrimp, broccoli, pasta, peppers and onions. In a bowl, combine mayonnaise, salad dressing and dill. Pour over shrimp mixture; toss to coat. Cover and chill at least 2 hours. **Yield:** 6 servings. **Nutritional Analysis:** One (1-cup) serving equals 125 calories, 378 mg sodium, 92 mg cholesterol, 16 gm carbohydrate, 12 gm protein, 1 gm fat, 2 gm fiber. **Diabetic Exchanges:** 1 starch, 1 very lean meat, 1/2 vegetable.

Fruited Lemon Gelatin Salad

(Pictured below)

As light and pleasant as a summer breeze—that's how I would describe this sunny salad. With oranges, grapes and pineapple peeking out of every spoonful, it's a fun, fruity addition to any meal.
—_Erla Burkholder, Ewing, Illinois_

   1 **package (6 ounces) lemon gelatin**
   2 **cups boiling water**
   1 **can (12 ounces) lemon-lime soda**
   1 **can (20 ounces) crushed pineapple**
   1 **can (15 ounces) mandarin oranges, drained**
   2 **cups halved green grapes**
   1 **egg**
1/2 **cup sugar**
   2 **tablespoons all-purpose flour**
   1 **tablespoon butter** _or_ **margarine**
   1 **cup whipping cream, whipped**
Lettuce leaves, optional

Dissolve gelatin in boiling water. Stir in soda. Refrigerate until partially set. Drain pineapple, reserving juice; set pineapple aside. Add water to pineapple juice, if necessary, to measure 1 cup; set aside. Stir pineapple, oranges and grapes into gelatin. Pour into a 13-in. x 9-in. x 2-in. dish. Refrigerate. In a saucepan over medium heat, combine egg, sugar, flour, butter and reserved pineapple juice. Bring to a boil; cook and stir for 2 minutes or until thickened. Cool completely. Fold in whipped cream. Spread over gelatin. Refrigerate until firm. Cut into squares; serve on lettuce if desired. **Yield:** 15-18 servings.

Soups & Sandwiches

Nothing beats the classic combination of soup and a sandwich. Here are oodles of options. Just mix and match to suit your taste.

—— 🍴 🍴 🍴 ——

PERFECT PAIRS. Clockwise from upper left: Curried Chicken Pockets (p. 51), Chili with Potato Dumplings (p. 50), Apple-Ham Grilled Cheese (p. 55) and Butternut Squash Soup (p. 53).

Waldorf Turkey Sandwiches

(Pictured below)

Apples, celery and raisins give this special turkey salad a great flavor and tempting texture.
—Meghan Bodas, Rapid City, South Dakota

✓ Uses less fat, sugar or salt. Includes Nutritional Analysis and Diabetic Exchanges.

1-1/4 cups cubed cooked turkey breast
    1 small apple, chopped
  1/4 cup diced celery
    3 tablespoons fat-free mayonnaise
    2 tablespoons plain nonfat yogurt
    2 tablespoons chopped walnuts
    1 tablespoon raisins
  1/8 teaspoon ground nutmeg
  1/8 teaspoon ground cinnamon
    8 slices raisin bread, toasted
    4 lettuce leaves

In a bowl, combine the first nine ingredients. Cover and refrigerate for 1 hour. Spoon 3/4 cup turkey mixture onto four slices of bread; top with a lettuce leaf and remaining bread. **Yield:** 4 servings. **Nutritional Analysis:** One serving (calculated without bread) equals 127 calories, 114 mg sodium, 26 mg cholesterol, 9 gm carbohydrate, 12 gm protein, 5 gm fat, 1 gm fiber. **Diabetic Exchanges:** 1-1/2 lean meat, 1/2 fruit.

Split Pea Soup

My husband has always loved split pea soup, but I never cared for it—until I came across this recipe. The combination of flavors is so tasty that even I have to admit to liking it. —Holly Dow, Chapman, Maine

    1 small onion, diced
    1 tablespoon vegetable oil
    4 cups water
    1 can (14-1/2 ounces) chicken broth
1-1/2 cups dry split peas, rinsed
    1 cup cubed fully cooked ham
    3 bay leaves
1-1/2 teaspoons salt
  1/2 teaspoon dried rosemary, crushed
  1/4 teaspoon dried thyme
  1/4 teaspoon pepper

In a large saucepan, saute onion in oil until tender. Add remaining ingredients. Bring to a boil; reduce heat. Cover and simmer for 1 hour or until peas are tender. Discard bay leaves. **Yield:** 6 servings.

— 🍽 🍽 🍽 —

Provolone Pepper Burgers

I'm known around our neighborhood as the "grill sergeant". These burgers are one of my most-requested entrees. They're a flavorful change from plain ground beef patties. —Nick Mescia, Surprise, Arizona

  1/3 cup finely cubed provolone cheese
  1/4 cup diced roasted red peppers
  1/4 cup finely chopped onion
Salt and pepper to taste
    1 pound ground beef
    4 hamburger buns, split

In a bowl, combine the cheese, red peppers, onion, salt and pepper. Add beef and mix well. Shape into four patties. Grill, covered, over medium-hot heat for 4-5 minutes on each side or until meat is no longer pink. Serve on buns. **Yield:** 4 servings.

— 🍽 🍽 🍽 —

Rosemary Mushroom Soup

This recipe comes from an herb farm where I worked for 30 years. Although it starts with canned mushroom soup, it tastes rich and from scratch when it's done. —Sandra Burrows, Coventry, Connecticut

    1 cup sliced fresh mushrooms
    2 garlic cloves, minced
  1/4 cup butter *or* margarine
    1 can (10-3/4 ounces) condensed cream of mushroom soup, undiluted
    1 cup half-and-half cream

1 tablespoon minced fresh rosemary *or*
1 teaspoon dried rosemary, crushed
1/2 teaspoon paprika
2 tablespoons minced chives

In a large saucepan, saute the mushrooms and garlic in butter until tender. Stir in the mushroom soup, cream, rosemary and paprika; heat through but do not boil. Sprinkle with minced chives. **Yield:** 3 servings.

Shrimp Egg Salad

My family loves this change-of-pace sandwich filling. It has a tasty blend of ingredients.
—*Ruth Ann Stelfox, Raymond, Alberta*

1 can (4-1/4 ounces) tiny shrimp, rinsed and drained
2 hard-cooked eggs, chopped
1/4 cup finely chopped celery
3 tablespoons mayonnaise
1 teaspoon lemon juice
1/4 teaspoon onion powder
1/4 teaspoon salt
1/8 to 1/4 teaspoon lemon-pepper seasoning
Bread *or* crackers

Combine the first eight ingredients; mix well. Use as a sandwich spread or serve on crackers. **Yield:** 1-1/2 cups.

Poor Boy Loaf

A zesty spread flavors this hot loaf. Hearty appetites will appreciate this savory, satisfying sandwich.
—*Marcia Orlando, Boyertown, Pennsylvania*

1 unsliced loaf (12 ounces) Italian bread
1/4 cup butter *or* margarine, softened
1 tablespoon prepared mustard
1 tablespoon minced fresh parsley
1 garlic clove, minced
1/8 to 1/4 teaspoon crushed red pepper flakes
2 medium tomatoes, thinly sliced
6 ounces sliced mozzarella cheese
6 ounces thinly sliced hard salami
1/3 cup pickled sweet pepper rings

Cut bread into 1/2-in. slices, leaving slices attached at the bottom. In a small bowl, combine the butter, mustard, parsley, garlic and red pepper flakes. Spread on every other slice. Place tomatoes, mozzarella, salami and pepper rings between the buttered slices. Wrap in foil. Bake at 350° for 10-12 minutes or until cheese is melted. **Yield:** 8 servings.

Cream of Vegetable Soup

(Pictured above)

When I needed to come up with a soup for a potluck years ago, this was the result. I adapted a cream of broccoli recipe I'd used often and put in plenty of vegetables left over from a dinner party. Now I make extra vegetables just so I can prepare this soup.
—*Mary Parker, Copperas Cove, Texas*

1 medium onion, chopped
3/4 cup butter *or* margarine
1/2 cup all-purpose flour
3 cans (10-1/2 ounces *each*) condensed chicken broth *or* 4 cups chicken broth
2 cups milk
2 cups half-and-half cream
1 teaspoon dried basil
1/2 teaspoon salt
1/2 teaspoon pepper
1/4 teaspoon garlic powder
5 cups chopped cooked mixed vegetables (such as broccoli, carrots and cauliflower)

In a large kettle or Dutch oven, saute onion in butter until tender. Add flour; cook and stir until bubbly. Gradually add chicken broth; cook and stir until thickened, about 5 minutes. Stir in the milk, cream, basil, salt, pepper and garlic powder. Add the vegetables; cook gently until heated through. **Yield:** 8-10 servings (about 3 quarts).

♨ ♨ ♨

'I Wish I Had That Recipe...'

"I'D LOVE to make the Pork BBQ Sandwich I enjoyed for lunch at The Sherwood Inn in Skaneateles, New York," says Julie Fella of Rochester. "It was the best I have ever had!"

Nestled on the shores of Skaneateles Lake (one of the Finger Lakes), The Sherwood Inn was originally a stagecoach stop for travelers in 1807.

Inn operations director Linda Hartnett kindly shared the recipe, saying, "Pork BBQ is a favorite in this region, and our chef developed this tasty version. The meat is very tender, and caramelized onions add a touch of sweetness."

Located at 26 W. Genessee St. in Skaneateles, The Sherwood Inn serves lunch daily from 11 a.m. to 2 p.m., dinner from 5 to 10 p.m. 1-800/374-3796. Web site: www.thesherwoodinn.com.

Pork BBQ Sandwiches

     1 bone-in pork shoulder roast (about 4 pounds)
     1 cup water
     1 teaspoon salt
     2 cups finely chopped celery
   1/3 cup steak sauce
   1/4 cup cider *or* white wine vinegar
   1/4 cup packed brown sugar
     2 teaspoons lemon juice
     2 teaspoons chili sauce
     1 teaspoon ketchup
     2 medium onions, sliced
     2 teaspoons sugar
     1 tablespoon olive *or* vegetable oil
     1 tablespoon butter *or* margarine
    16 hoagie buns, split

Place pork roast, water and salt in a Dutch oven. Cover and simmer for 3-1/2 to 4 hours or until the meat is very tender. Remove meat and discard bone; shred meat with two forks. Skim fat from pan juices. Stir in the celery, steak sauce, vinegar, brown sugar, lemon juice, chili sauce, ketchup and shredded pork. Cover and simmer for 1 hour. In a large skillet over low heat, saute onions and sugar in oil and butter for 20-30 minutes or until golden brown and tender, stirring occasionally. Serve pork and onions on buns. **Yield:** 16 servings.

♨ ♨ ♨

Cream of Asparagus Soup

My best friend and I enjoy this smooth soup so much we had to share it. Pepper gives it zip.
—Hilda Magnuson, Whittier, California

✓ Uses less fat, sugar or salt. Includes Nutritional Analysis and Diabetic Exchanges.

     1 medium onion, chopped
     1 garlic clove, minced
     3 cups cut fresh asparagus (1-inch pieces)
 2-1/2 cups low-sodium chicken broth
   1/8 teaspoon crushed red pepper flakes
     3 ounces fat-free cream cheese, cubed
     2 tablespoons light sour cream
     1 tablespoon snipped fresh dill *or* 1 teaspoon dill weed
   1/2 teaspoon ground nutmeg

In a large saucepan coated with nonstick cooking spray, saute onion and garlic until tender. Add asparagus, broth and red pepper flakes. Bring to a boil. Reduce heat; cover and simmer for 10-15 minutes or until asparagus is tender. Place a third of mixture in a blender; add cream cheese, sour cream and dill. Cover; process until smooth. Return to pan; cook over medium heat until heated through. Sprinkle with nutmeg. **Yield:** 4 servings.
Nutritional Analysis: One serving equals 91 calories, 192 mg sodium, 7 mg cholesterol, 11 gm carbohydrate, 8 gm protein, 2 gm fat, 3 gm fiber.
Diabetic Exchanges: 1 vegetable, 1/2 starch, 1/2 fat.

♨ ♨ ♨

Italian Venison Sandwiches

I became interested in cooking while taking a foods class in high school. An avid hunter and fisherman, I like to prepare what I catch. I started by helping my dad, who is a great cook. I still ask for his opinion on new dishes. The slow cooker makes easy work of these flavorful, tender venison sandwiches.
—Andrew Henson, Morrison, Illinois

     2 cups water
     1 envelope onion soup mix
     1 tablespoon dried basil
     1 tablespoon dried parsley flakes
     1 teaspoon beef bouillon granules
   1/2 teaspoon celery salt
   1/4 teaspoon garlic powder
   1/4 teaspoon cayenne pepper
   1/4 teaspoon pepper
     1 boneless venison roast (3 to 4 pounds), cut into 1-inch cubes
    10 to 12 sandwich rolls, split
Green pepper rings, optional

In a slow cooker, combine the first nine ingredients. Add venison and stir. Cover and cook on low for 8 hours or until meat is tender. Using a slotted spoon, spoon into rolls. Top with pepper rings if desired. **Yield:** 10-12 servings.

Favorite Fennel Soup

For an interesting first course, try this delicate soup. The light broth has a mild fennel taste.
—*Nanette Cheramie, Oklahoma City, Oklahoma*

  4 fennel bulbs, sliced
  1 large onion, chopped
  2 tablespoons butter *or* margarine
  2 cans (14-1/2 ounces *each*) vegetable *or* chicken broth
  2 cups milk
  1 bay leaf
Salt and pepper to taste
  2 egg yolks
1/2 cup half-and-half cream

In a large saucepan, saute fennel and onion in butter until tender. Add the broth, milk and seasonings. Cover and simmer for 30 minutes. Strain, reserving broth. Discard fennel, onion and bay leaf. In a small bowl, beat egg yolks and cream. Gradually add a small amount of hot soup. Return all to the pan. Cook and stir until slightly thickened. Simmer 10-15 minutes longer (do not boil). **Yield:** 5 servings.

Mushroom Bisque

The subtle taste of parsley comes through in this rich, creamy broth. It has great flavor, plus it's so easy.
—*Emily Chaney, Penobscot, Maine*

1/2 pound fresh mushrooms, sliced
  1 medium onion, sliced
  1 cup minced fresh parsley
1/4 cup butter *or* margarine
  1 tablespoon all-purpose flour
  1 can (14-1/2 ounces) beef broth
  1 cup (8 ounces) sour cream

In a large saucepan, saute mushrooms, onion and parsley in butter until tender. Stir in flour until blended; gradually add broth. Bring to a boil; cook and stir for 2 minutes or until thickened. Cool slightly. Transfer to a blender; cover and process until pureed. Return to pan. Stir in sour cream; heat through, stirring occasionally (do not boil). **Yield:** 4 servings.

Pear Waldorf Pitas

(Pictured below)

Here's a guaranteed table-brightener for a shower, luncheon or party. Just stand back and watch these sandwiches vanish. For an eye-catching presentation, I tuck each one into a colorful folded napkin.
—*Roxann Parker, Dover, Delaware*

✓ Uses less fat, sugar or salt. Includes Nutritional Analysis and Diabetic Exchanges.

  2 medium ripe pears, diced
1/2 cup thinly sliced celery
1/2 cup halved seedless red grapes
  2 tablespoons finely chopped walnuts
  2 tablespoons lemon yogurt
  2 tablespoons mayonnaise
1/8 teaspoon poppy seeds
 10 miniature pita pockets, halved
Lettuce leaves

In a bowl, combine pears, celery, grapes and walnuts. In another bowl, combine yogurt, mayonnaise and poppy seeds; mix well. Add to pear mixture; toss to coat. Refrigerate for 1 hour or overnight. To serve, line pita halves with lettuce and add 2 tablespoons pear mixture. **Yield:** 10 servings. **Nutritional Analysis:** One serving (prepared with non-fat yogurt and light mayonnaise) equals 117 calories, 165 mg sodium, 1 mg cholesterol, 23 gm carbohydrate, 4 gm protein, 2 gm fat, 2 gm fiber. **Diabetic Exchanges:** 1 starch, 1/2 fruit.

Chili with Potato Dumplings

(Pictured below and on page 45)

I've been making this chili, with a few ingredients added or changed, most of my married life.
—Shirley Marshall, Michigantown, Indiana

- **1 pound ground beef**
- **1 pound ground turkey**
- **1/2 cup chopped onion**
- **1 can (16 ounces) kidney beans, rinsed and drained**
- **1 can (15-1/2 ounces) mild chili beans, undrained**
- **1/2 cup chopped green pepper**
- **4 teaspoons chili powder**
- **1 teaspoon salt**
- **1 teaspoon paprika**
- **1 teaspoon cumin seed**
- **1/2 teaspoon garlic salt**
- **1/2 teaspoon dried oregano**
- **1/4 teaspoon crushed red pepper flakes**
- **3 cups V-8 juice**

DUMPLINGS:
- **1 cup mashed potato flakes**
- **1 cup all-purpose flour**
- **1 tablespoon minced fresh parsley**
- **2 teaspoons baking powder**
- **1/2 teaspoon salt**
- **1 cup milk**
- **1 egg, beaten**

In a 5-qt. Dutch oven over medium heat, cook beef, turkey and onion until meat is no longer pink; drain. Add the next 11 ingredients; bring to a boil. Reduce heat; cover and simmer for 30 minutes, stirring occasionally. In a bowl, combine the first five dumpling ingredients. Stir in milk and egg just until moistened. Let rest for 3 minutes. Drop by tablespoonfuls onto simmering chili. Cover and cook for 15 minutes. **Yield:** 8 servings (2 quarts).

Low-Fat Potato Soup

My husband usually doesn't care for low-fat dishes. So after finishing a bowl of this rich-tasting soup, he was surprised to learn that it's very low in fat.
—Natalie Warf, Spring Lake, North Carolina

✓ Uses less fat, sugar or salt. Includes Nutritional Analysis and Diabetic Exchanges.

- **1-3/4 cups diced peeled potatoes**
- **1 medium onion, chopped**
- **1/4 cup chopped celery**
- **1 can (14-1/2 ounces) low-sodium chicken broth**
- **1/8 teaspoon pepper**
- **3 tablespoons cornstarch**
- **1 can (12 ounces) evaporated skim milk, *divided***
- **1 cup (4 ounces) shredded reduced-fat cheddar cheese**

In a large saucepan, combine the potatoes, onion, celery, broth and pepper. Bring to a boil. Reduce heat; cover and simmer for 15-18 minutes or until the vegetables are tender. Combine cornstarch and 1/4 cup of milk until smooth; stir into potato mixture. Add the remaining milk. Bring to a boil; cook and stir for 2 minutes or until thickened. Remove from the heat. Stir in the cheese until melted. **Yield:** 5 servings. **Nutritional Analysis:** One serving equals 178 calories, 274 mg sodium, 9 mg cholesterol, 26 gm carbohydrate, 14 gm protein, 2 gm fat, 2 gm fiber. **Diabetic Exchanges:** 1-1/2 starch, 1 lean meat, 1 vegetable.

Fiddlehead Soup

My family loves this delicious soup made with fiddleheads (the tightly curled young fronds from bracken, ostrich and cinnamon ferns). We have been hunting for and harvesting wild edible plants for a number of years now. Fiddleheads are one of the first plants to sprout in the spring. *—Karen Grasley, Quadeville, Ontario*

1 cup fiddleheads* *or* sliced fresh asparagus

1 cup sliced fresh mushrooms
3/4 cup sliced leeks
1/4 cup sliced green onions
1/2 cup butter _or_ margarine
1/4 cup all-purpose flour
1/2 teaspoon salt
1/8 teaspoon cayenne pepper
3 cups milk
1 cup chicken broth
1 teaspoon lemon juice

In a saucepan, cook fiddleheads, mushrooms, leeks and onions in butter until the onions are tender, about 4 minutes. Remove from the heat; stir in the flour, salt and cayenne. Gradually add the milk and broth, stirring until blended. Bring to a gentle boil; cook and stir for 10 minutes. Reduce heat; simmer, uncovered, for 10 minutes. Stir in lemon juice. **Yield:** 4 servings. ***Editor's Note:** As with any wild ingredient, be certain of what you're picking and that it's edible. If you're unsure, check with your county Extension agent.

Betty's Burgers

I dreamed up these cheese- and vegetable-stuffed burgers for a family barbecue years ago. They're delicious grilled or pan-fried. You bite into a surprise.
—_Betty Canoles, Atascadero, California_

1-1/2 pounds ground beef
6 thin slices cheddar cheese
1 large green pepper, julienned
1 medium onion, thinly sliced
1 medium tomato, thinly sliced
6 thin slices Swiss cheese
Salt and pepper to taste
Lettuce leaves
6 hamburger buns, split

Shape beef into 12 thin patties. Top six patties with a slice of cheddar cheese, green pepper strips, and a slice of onion, tomato and Swiss cheese. Top each with another patty and seal edges. Season to taste. Broil, grill or pan-fry burgers until meat is no longer pink. Serve on lettuce-lined buns. **Yield:** 6 servings.

Curried Chicken Pockets

(Pictured above right and on page 44)

I served these fluffy homemade pitas stuffed with zippy chicken filling for a picnic the day my husband and I got engaged. Now our children enjoy them!
—_Lisa Scandrette, Eveleth, Minnesota_

1/2 cup mayonnaise _or_ salad dressing
1/2 cup chutney
1 tablespoon curry powder
6 cups cubed cooked chicken
PITA BREAD:
1 package (1/4 ounce) active dry yeast
1-1/3 cups warm water (110° to 115°), _divided_
3 to 3-1/2 cups all-purpose flour
1 tablespoon vegetable oil
1 teaspoon salt
1/4 teaspoon sugar
3 tablespoons cornmeal
Lettuce leaves

In a bowl, combine the mayonnaise, chutney, curry powder and chicken; refrigerate until serving. In a mixing bowl, dissolve yeast in 1/3 cup warm water. Add 1-1/2 cups of flour, oil, salt, sugar and remaining water; beat until smooth. Add enough remaining flour to form a soft dough. Turn onto a floured surface; knead until smooth and elastic, about 10 minutes. Place in a greased bowl, turning once to grease top. Cover and let rise in a warm place until doubled, about 1 hour. Punch dough down; shape into six balls. Let rise for 30 minutes. Sprinkle three ungreased baking sheets with cornmeal. Roll each ball into a 7-in. circle. Place two circles on each baking sheet. Let rise for 30 minutes. Bake at 500° for 10 minutes or until lightly browned. Cool. Cut pitas in half. Line each with lettuce; fill with 1/3 cup of chicken mixture. **Yield:** 12 sandwiches.

about 1 hour. Meanwhile, in a skillet, cook sausage until no longer pink; drain and cool. Stir in mozzarella, 2 eggs and basil; set aside. Punch dough down; divide in half. Roll one portion into a 15-in. x 10-in. rectangle on a greased baking sheet. Spoon half of the sausage mixture lengthwise down one side of rectangle to within 1 in. of edges. Fold dough over filling; pinch edges to seal. Cut four diagonal slits on top of stromboli. Repeat with remaining dough and filling. Beat remaining egg; brush over loaves. Sprinkle with Parmesan. Cover and let rise until doubled, about 45 minutes. Bake at 375° for 20-25 minutes or until golden brown. Slice; serve warm. **Yield:** 2 loaves.

— 🍷 🍷 🍷 —

Cream of Basil Soup

I really enjoy creating my own recipes. This one evolved one afternoon when I had an abundance of basil in my garden. I served it to the ladies' reading club, and everyone wanted the recipe!
— *Aida Von Babbel, Coquitlam, British Columbia*

      3 cups chicken broth
      1 cup minced fresh basil
  1/4 cup butter *or* margarine
      3 tablespoons all-purpose flour
White pepper to taste
      3 cups milk
  1/2 cup sour cream

In a saucepan, simmer broth and basil, uncovered, for 15 minutes. In another saucepan, melt butter. Stir in flour and pepper until smooth; gradually add milk. Bring to a boil; cook and stir 2 minutes or until thickened. Reduce heat; slowly stir in broth and sour cream (do not boil). **Yield:** 8 servings.

— 🍷 🍷 🍷 —

Zesty Turkey Chili

My family loves chili, but I wanted to cut some of its calories and fat. This recipe features ground turkey, fat-free broth and unbeatable flavor.
— *Margareta Thorner, Carlsbad, California*

✓ Uses less fat, sugar or salt. Includes Nutritional Analysis and Diabetic Exchanges.

      1 large onion, chopped
      3 garlic cloves, minced
      1 teaspoon vegetable oil
      1 can (4 ounces) chopped green chilies
      2 teaspoons ground cumin
  1-1/2 teaspoons dried oregano
  1/4 teaspoon ground cloves
  1/8 teaspoon hot pepper sauce

Cheesy Sausage Stromboli

(Pictured above)

I've had a hundred requests for this recipe over the years. Perfect for brunch or as an evening snack, this sausage-filled bread is not tricky to make...and I never have to worry about storing leftovers!
— *Vada McRoberts, Silver Lake, Kansas*

      5 cups all-purpose flour
      2 tablespoons sugar
      2 teaspoons salt
      2 packages (1/4 ounce *each*) active dry yeast
  1-1/2 cups warm water (120° to 130°)
  1/2 cup warm milk (120° to 130°)
      2 tablespoons butter *or* margarine, melted
      2 pounds bulk pork sausage
      4 cups (16 ounces) shredded mozzarella cheese
      3 eggs
      1 teaspoon minced fresh basil *or* 1/4 teaspoon dried basil
      2 tablespoons grated Parmesan cheese

In a mixing bowl, combine flour, sugar, salt and yeast. Add water, milk and butter; beat on low until well combined. Turn onto a well-floured surface; knead until smooth and elastic, 6-8 minutes. Place in a greased bowl, turning once to grease top. Cover and let rise in a warm place until doubled,

1/8 teaspoon cayenne pepper
2 cans (15-1/2 ounces *each*) great northern beans, rinsed and drained
3 cups reduced-sodium fat-free chicken broth
3 cups cubed cooked turkey breast

In a large saucepan, saute the onion and garlic in oil for 5 minutes. Add chilies and seasonings; cook and stir 3 minutes. Stir in beans, broth and turkey; simmer for 15 minutes. **Yield:** 8 servings. **Nutritional Analysis:** One serving (1 cup) equals 219 calories, 554 mg sodium, 32 mg cholesterol, 31 gm carbohydrate, 17 gm protein, 3 gm fat. **Diabetic Exchanges:** 2 starch, 1 lean meat, 1 vegetable.

— 🥄 🥄 🥄 —

Corn and Bean Soup

For lunch or dinner on a chilly day, this fresh-tasting colorful vegetable soup really hits the spot. It's quick and easy to make. —*Betty Andrzejewski Chino, California*

☑ Uses less fat, sugar or salt. Includes Nutritional Analysis and Diabetic Exchanges.

1 can (10-1/2 ounces) low-sodium chicken broth
2 medium carrots, diced
2 celery ribs, diced
1 small potato, peeled and diced
1 small onion, chopped
1-1/2 cups frozen corn
1 can (15 ounces) white kidney *or* cannellini beans, rinsed and drained
1 cup skim milk
1 teaspoon dried thyme
1/4 teaspoon garlic powder
Pepper to taste

In a large saucepan, combine the broth, carrots, celery, potato and onion. Bring to a boil. Reduce heat; cover and simmer for 10-12 minutes or until vegetables are tender. Stir in the remaining ingredients; simmer 5-7 minutes longer or until corn is tender. **Yield:** 5 servings. **Nutritional Analysis:** One serving equals 185 calories, 330 mg sodium, 3 mg cholesterol, 35 gm carbohydrate, 11 gm protein, 2 gm fat, 7 gm fiber. **Diabetic Exchanges:** 2 starch, 1 vegetable.

— 🥄 🥄 🥄 —

Butternut Squash Soup

(Pictured at right and on page 44)

With pureed butternut squash, this deep golden soup is especially delicious in autumn. If you'd like, you can intensify the garlic flavor by adding one extra bulb. —*Lynn Proudfoot, Huntington, Connecticut*

3 pounds unpeeled butternut squash, halved and seeded
2 large unpeeled onions
1 small garlic bulb
1/4 cup olive *or* vegetable oil
2 tablespoons minced fresh thyme *or* 2 teaspoons dried thyme
3 to 3-1/2 cups chicken broth
1/2 cup whipping cream
3 tablespoons minced fresh parsley
1/2 teaspoon salt
1/4 teaspoon pepper
Fresh thyme sprigs, optional

Cut squash into eight large pieces. Place cut side up in a 15-in. x 10-in. x 1-in. baking pan. Cut 1/4 in. off tops of onion and garlic bulbs (the end that comes to a closed point). Place cut side up in the baking pan. Brush with oil; sprinkle with thyme. Cover tightly and bake at 350° for 1-1/2 to 2 hours or until vegetables are very tender. Uncover and let stand until lukewarm. Remove peel from squash and onions; remove soft garlic from skins. Combine vegetables, broth and cream. Puree in small batches in a blender or food processor until smooth; transfer to a large saucepan. Add parsley, salt and pepper; heat through (do not boil). Garnish with thyme if desired. **Yield:** 8 servings (2 quarts).

Curried Pumpkin Soup

(Pictured below)

I whipped up this satisfying soup last Thanksgiving for my family, and everyone was crazy about it! Even my brother, one of the pickiest eaters I know, passed his bowl for seconds. —Kimberly Knepper, Euless, Texas

  1/2 **pound fresh mushrooms, sliced**
  1/2 **cup chopped onion**
    2 **tablespoons butter *or* margarine**
    2 **tablespoons all-purpose flour**
  1/2 **to 1 teaspoon curry powder**
    3 **cups vegetable broth**
    1 **can (15 ounces) solid-pack pumpkin**
    1 **can (12 ounces) evaporated milk**
    1 **tablespoon honey**
  1/2 **teaspoon salt**
  1/4 **teaspoon pepper**
  1/4 **teaspoon ground nutmeg**
Sour cream and chives, optional

In a large saucepan, saute the mushrooms and onion in butter until tender. Stir in flour and curry powder until blended. Gradually add the broth. Bring to a boil; cook and stir for 2 minutes or until thickened. Add the pumpkin, milk, honey, salt, pepper and nutmeg; heat through. Garnish individual servings with sour cream and chives if desired. **Yield:** 7 servings.

— 🛒 🛒 🛒 —

Veggie Pockets

Even our five children enjoy the crunchy vegetable filling in these handy meatless sandwiches. It's a great way to use a variety of garden produce.
—June Ballard, Weston, Idaho

✓ Uses less fat, sugar or salt. Includes Nutritional Analysis and Diabetic Exchanges.

    3 **medium onions, thinly sliced**
    2 **tablespoons vegetable oil**
    2 **tablespoons barbecue sauce**
    4 **cups broccoli florets, cooked and drained**
    2 **cups cauliflowerets, cooked and drained**
  1/4 **cup reduced-fat mayonnaise**
  1/2 **cup *each* grated carrot, red cabbage and yellow summer squash**
    6 **pita breads (6 inches), halved and warmed**
    2 **cups shredded lettuce**

In a saucepan, cook onions in oil until tender. Add barbecue sauce; cook and stir for 2 minutes. Add broccoli and cauliflower; heat through. Stir in mayonnaise, carrot, cabbage and squash; heat through. Fill each pita half with about 2 tablespoons lettuce and 1/2 cup vegetable mixture. **Yield:** 12 servings. **Nutritional Analysis:** One serving equals 143 calories, 218 mg sodium, 1 mg cholesterol, 24 gm carbohydrate, 4 gm protein, 4 gm fat, 3 gm fiber. **Diabetic Exchanges:** 1 starch, 1 vegetable, 1 fat.

— 🛒 🛒 🛒 —

Cincinnati Chili

Cinnamon and cocoa give a rich brown color to this hearty chili. This dish will warm you up on a cold day.
—Edith Joyce, Parkman, Ohio

    1 **pound ground beef**
    1 **pound ground pork**
    4 **medium onions, chopped**
    6 **garlic cloves, minced**
    2 **cans (16 ounces *each*) kidney beans, rinsed and drained**
    1 **can (28 ounces) crushed tomatoes**
  1/4 **cup vinegar**
  1/4 **cup baking cocoa**
    2 **tablespoons chili powder**
    2 **tablespoons Worcestershire sauce**
    4 **teaspoons ground cinnamon**
    3 **teaspoons dried oregano**

2 teaspoons ground cumin
2 teaspoons ground allspice
2 teaspoons hot pepper sauce
3 bay leaves
1 teaspoon sugar
Salt and pepper to taste
Hot cooked spaghetti
Shredded cheddar cheese, sour cream, chopped
    tomatoes and green onions

In a Dutch oven or soup kettle, cook beef, pork, onions and garlic over medium heat until meat is no longer pink; drain. Add the beans, tomatoes, vinegar, cocoa and seasonings; bring to a boil. Reduce heat; cover and simmer for 1-1/2 hours or until heated through. Discard bay leaves. Serve over spaghetti. Garnish with cheese, sour cream, tomatoes and onions. **Yield:** 6-8 servings.

——— ▼ ▼ ▼ ———

Apple-Ham Grilled Cheese

(Pictured above and on page 45)

After finding this recipe years ago, I altered it to fit our tastes by adding the apples. Our whole family loves it! We look forward to fall when we go out to the orchards to gather the fresh-picked ingredients for pies, cobblers, salads…and, of course, this sandwich.
    —*Shirley Brazel, Rocklin, California*

1 cup chopped tart apples
1/3 cup mayonnaise
1/4 cup finely chopped walnuts
8 slices process American cheese
8 slices sourdough bread
4 slices fully cooked ham
1/4 cup butter *or* margarine, softened

Combine apples, mayonnaise and walnuts. Place a slice of cheese on four slices of bread. Layer each with 1/3 cup of the apple mixture, a slice of ham and another slice of cheese; cover with remaining bread. Butter the outsides of the sandwiches. Cook in a large skillet over medium heat on each side until bread is golden brown and cheese is melted. **Yield:** 4 servings.

——— ▼ ▼ ▼ ———

10-Minute Tomato Soup

No one can believe this great-tasting soup only has four ingredients. It really does go from start to sipping in 10 minutes, so why bother with canned soup?
    —*Ada Ryger, Beresford, South Dakota*

2 cups crushed canned tomatoes
1/2 teaspoon baking soda
2 cups milk
2 tablespoons butter *or* margarine

In a large heavy saucepan, heat tomatoes until boiling. Remove from the heat; add remaining ingredients. Return to heat and cook on medium until butter is melted and the soup is heated through. **Yield:** 3-4 servings (1 quart).

Side Dishes & Condiments

Whether you're looking for an accompaniment to a meal or a topping for a favorite food, you and your family will relish these recipes.

SIDE SHOWS. Clockwise from upper left: Fabulous Fettuccine (p. 63), Brussels Sprouts Supreme (p. 71), Special Squash Casserole (p. 62), Carrots in Almond Sauce (p. 60) and Creamy Herb Dressing (p. 64).

Almost Raspberry Jam

I hesitate to tell folks that this "raspberry" jam actually features green tomatoes flavored with gelatin. But after a taste, they're begging me to share the recipe.
—*Sue Ellen Dillard, El Dorado, Arkansas*

5-1/2 cups chopped green tomatoes
5-1/2 cups sugar
1 package (6 ounces) raspberry gelatin

In a large kettle, combine tomatoes and sugar. Simmer for 25 minutes, stirring occasionally. Remove from the heat; stir in gelatin until dissolved, about 1 minute. Pour into jars or plastic containers; cool, stirring occasionally to prevent floating fruit. Top with lids. Refrigerate up to 3 weeks. **Yield:** 7 cups.

Company Potato Casserole

Swiss cheese lends distinctive flavor to this rich, creamy potato casserole. Since it tastes wonderful and looks so lovely, this side dish is perfect for serving company or as part of a special holiday meal.
—*Mrs. Sylvester Socolovitch, Cheboygan, Michigan*

5 cups cooked cubed peeled potatoes
1-1/2 cups (12 ounces) sour cream
1-1/4 cups shredded Swiss cheese, *divided*
1/2 cup shredded carrot
1/4 cup chopped onion
2 tablespoons minced fresh parsley
1 teaspoon salt
1/2 teaspoon dill weed
1/4 teaspoon pepper
1/4 teaspoon paprika

In a bowl, combine the potatoes, sour cream, 1 cup of cheese, carrot, onion, parsley, salt, dill and pepper. Transfer to a greased 8-in. square baking dish. Sprinkle with the paprika and remaining cheese. Bake, uncovered, at 350° for 25-35 minutes or until bubbly. **Yield:** 8 servings.

Wild Rice Stuffing

(Pictured above)

Since trying this stuffing recipe from my sister, I've never made any other kind. It's so moist and tasty. When a big bowlful starts circulating around the table, happy holiday smiles get even bigger! —*Connie Olson Green River, Wyoming*

Turkey giblets
4 cups water
1 package (6 ounces) long grain and wild rice
1 celery rib, chopped
1 small onion, chopped
1/2 cup butter *or* margarine
2-1/2 cups crushed seasoned stuffing
1-1/2 cups chicken broth

Remove the liver from giblets if desired. Place giblets and water in a saucepan. Cover and simmer for 2 hours or until tender. Meanwhile, prepare the rice according to package directions. In a small skillet, saute the celery and onion in butter; add to the rice. Drain and dice giblets. Stir the stuffing, broth and giblets into rice. Spoon into an ungreased 1-1/2-qt. baking dish. Bake, uncovered, at 350° for 25-30 minutes or until heated through. **Yield:** 8-10 servings.

Peppery Black Bean Salsa

I love foods that surprise the senses with a tempting mix of textures and colors—like this one. Use this as a topping for grilled meat or serve it as a relish on the side. —*Gary Maly, West Chester, Ohio*

✓ Uses less fat, sugar or salt. Includes Nutritional Analysis and Diabetic Exchanges.

4 jalapeno peppers*
2 cans (15 ounces *each*) black beans, rinsed and drained

2 cups fresh *or* frozen corn
1 medium sweet red *or* orange pepper, diced
1 cup chopped seeded tomato
1 medium red onion, chopped
1/3 cup lime juice
2 tablespoons minced fresh cilantro *or* parsley
1 garlic clove, minced

Place jalapenos on a broiler pan; broil 4 in. from the heat until skins blister, about 2 minutes. With tongs, rotate jalapenos a quarter turn. Broil and rotate until all sides are blistered and blackened. Immediately place jalapenos in a brown paper bag; close bag and let stand 15-20 minutes. Peel off and discard charred skin. Remove stems and seeds. Finely chop jalapenos. In a bowl, combine remaining ingredients. Add jalapenos; mix well. Cover and chill for several hours. **Yield:** 12 servings. **Nutritional Analysis:** One 1/2-cup serving (prepared with frozen corn) equals 90 calories, 222 mg sodium, 0 cholesterol, 18 gm carbohydrate, 5 gm protein, 1 gm fat, 5 gm fiber. **Diabetic Exchanges:** 1 starch, 1/2 vegetable. *Editor's Note:** When handling hot peppers, use rubber or plastic gloves to protect your hands. Avoid touching your face.

—— 🥄 🥄 🥄 ——

Cheesy Cauliflower

I couldn't "sell" cauliflower to my daughters until I came up with this saucy casserole. Then they requested it. It appeals to kids' tastes, even with vegetables they don't usually eat. —Barbara Jaggers
Colorado Springs, Colorado

1 large head cauliflower (about 2 pounds), broken into florets
1/3 cup butter *or* margarine
1/3 cup all-purpose flour
3/4 teaspoon salt
1/4 teaspoon pepper
2-1/2 cups milk
1 cup frozen peas
1/2 cup sliced fresh mushrooms
1-1/2 cups (6 ounces) shredded cheddar cheese, *divided*

In a covered saucepan, cook cauliflower in a small amount of water until crisp-tender. Meanwhile, in another saucepan, melt butter. Stir in flour, salt and pepper until smooth. Gradually stir in milk. Bring to a boil; cook and stir for 2 minutes or until thickened. Remove from the heat. Drain the cauliflower. Add peas, mushrooms, 1 cup of cheese and cauliflower to the milk mixture; stir gently. Transfer to a greased 2-1/2-qt. baking dish. Sprinkle with re-

maining cheese. Cover and bake at 350° for 15 minutes. Uncover; bake 10 minutes longer or until heated through. **Yield:** 8 servings.

—— 🥄 🥄 🥄 ——

Summer Berry Salsa

(Pictured below)

Other fruits are often used in relishes and sauces, but I decided to make one with my favorites—strawberries and blueberries. I get rave reviews when I serve this fruity, distinctive salsa over meat. It's also delicious atop a spinach or lettuce salad. —Diane Hixon
Niceville, Florida

✓ Uses less fat, sugar or salt. Includes Nutritional Analysis and Diabetic Exchanges.

1 pint fresh blueberries
1 pint fresh strawberries, chopped
1/4 cup sugar
2 tablespoons finely chopped onion
1 tablespoon lemon juice
1/2 teaspoon pepper
2 drops hot pepper sauce
1/4 cup slivered *or* sliced almonds, toasted

In a bowl, combine the first seven ingredients. Cover and refrigerate for 1 hour. Just before serving, stir in almonds. Serve with chicken, pork or fish. **Yield:** 4 cups. **Nutritional Analysis:** One 1/4-cup serving equals 42 calories, 2 mg sodium, 0 cholesterol, 8 gm carbohydrate, 1 gm protein, 1 gm fat, 1 gm fiber. **Diabetic Exchange:** 1/2 fruit.

Minted Butter

I prefer to serve this mint butter with scones, but it goes well with other breads, too. When I make the butter, it's only with mint fresh from our garden.
—Sherry Smeltzer, Osage Beach, Missouri

- 1 cup butter, softened
- 3 tablespoons confectioners' sugar
- 2 tablespoons chopped fresh mint *or* 2 teaspoons dried mint flakes
- 1 tablespoon grated lemon peel
- 1 tablespoon lemon juice

In a mixing bowl, cream butter. Beat in remaining ingredients. Cover and refrigerate. **Yield:** 1 cup.

Carrots in Almond Sauce

(Pictured below and on page 56)

Here's an easy way to add elegance and flavor to plain carrots. The combination of tender vegetables and crunchy nuts is different and delightful. Plus, the touch of dill lends just the right "zip". *—Carol Anderson*
Salt Lake City, Utah

- 1 pound carrots, julienned
- 1/2 cup thinly sliced green onions
- 1/4 cup butter *or* margarine
- 1 teaspoon cornstarch
- 1/2 cup water
- 1/2 teaspoon chicken bouillon granules

- 1/2 teaspoon dill weed
- 1/8 teaspoon pepper
- 1/4 cup sliced almonds, toasted

In a saucepan, cook carrots in a small amount of water until crisp-tender; drain. Transfer to a serving bowl and keep warm. In the same pan, saute onions in butter until tender. Combine cornstarch and water until smooth; stir into onions. Add bouillon, dill and pepper. Bring to a boil over medium heat; cook and stir for 1 minute or until thickened and bubbly. Stir in almonds. Pour over carrots; stir to coat. **Yield:** 6 servings.

Green Pepper Saute

I created this recipe one summer when I had an abundance of green peppers in my garden. This spicy recipe is a great companion for any meat dish. It's also delicious served over rice. When I take it to potlucks, many people want the recipe.
—Joyce Turley
Slaughters, Kentucky

- 3 large green peppers, cut into 1/2-inch strips
- 1 cup sliced celery
- 1 small onion, thinly sliced
- 1 garlic clove, minced
- 2 tablespoons vegetable oil
- 1 can (15 ounces) tomato sauce
- 1/2 teaspoon dried basil
- Salt and pepper to taste
- 1/2 cup crushed seasoned salad croutons

In a large skillet, saute the peppers, celery, onion and garlic in oil until tender. Stir in the tomato sauce, basil, salt and pepper. Simmer, uncovered, for 8-10 minutes or until vegetables are tender and mixture is thickened. Sprinkle with croutons. **Yield:** 4 servings.

Fancy French Beans

I serve this when I'm entertaining because so many people tell me they like it. Water chestnuts, bean sprouts and almonds add crunch. If you'd like the mixture a little creamier, use only 4 teaspoons of flour.
—June Mullins, Livonia, Missouri

- 4 cups frozen French-style green beans
- 1 cup bean sprouts
- 1 can (8 ounces) sliced water chestnuts, drained
- 2 tablespoons butter *or* margarine
- 2 tablespoons all-purpose flour
- 1/4 teaspoon salt

1/8 teaspoon pepper
Dash cayenne pepper
1-1/2 cups half-and-half cream
1/2 teaspoon Worcestershire sauce
1/2 cup sliced almonds
1/4 cup shredded Swiss cheese
1/4 cup grated Parmesan cheese

Cook beans according to package directions. Add bean sprouts and water chestnuts; heat through. Drain well and set aside. In a saucepan, melt butter. Stir in flour, salt, pepper and cayenne until smooth. Gradually add cream. Bring to a boil; cook and stir for 2 minutes or until thickened. Add Worcestershire sauce and bean mixture; toss to coat. Pour into a greased 2-qt. baking dish. Combine almonds and cheeses; sprinkle over the top. Broil 4-6 in. from the heat for 5 minutes or until almonds are golden brown and cheese is bubbly. **Yield:** 6-8 servings.

Sweet Potato Fries

Just because you're watching your waistline doesn't mean you can't indulge in some french fries. In this recipe, sweet potatoes are sprinkled with zesty seasonings and baked in the oven for a low-fat treat.
—Elvera Dallman, Franklin, Nebraska

Uses less fat, sugar or salt. Includes Nutritional Analysis and Diabetic Exchanges.

1 pound sweet potatoes
1 egg white
2 teaspoons chili powder
1/4 teaspoon garlic powder
1/4 teaspoon onion powder

Peel and cut potatoes into 1/4-in. x 1/2-in. strips. In a bowl, combine egg white and seasonings; beat well. Add potatoes; toss to coat. Place in a single layer on two baking sheets coated with nonstick cooking spray. Bake, uncovered, at 450° for 20-25 minutes or until golden brown. **Yield:** 8 servings. **Nutritional Analysis:** One 1/2-cup serving equals 40 calories, 20 mg sodium, 0 cholesterol, 9 gm carbohydrate, 1 gm protein, trace fat. **Diabetic Exchange:** 1/2 starch.

Better Beets

To dress up sliced cooked beets, try drizzling a bit of bottled sweet-and-sour sauce over them before serving. You'll be amazed at just how quickly this colorful vegetable disappears.

Steamed Lemon Broccoli

(Pictured above and on front cover)

I first tried this sunny side dish because it seemed to be a fresh, nutritious and easy combination. Now it's the only way my husband will eat broccoli. I love to pair it with grilled meat on hot days. —Michelle Hanson
Oacoma, South Dakota

Uses less fat, sugar or salt. Includes Nutritional Analysis and Diabetic Exchanges.

1 large bunch broccoli, cut into spears
1 medium onion, halved and thinly sliced
1 cup thinly sliced celery
3 garlic cloves, minced
3 tablespoons butter *or* margarine
2 teaspoons grated lemon peel
1-1/2 teaspoons lemon juice
1/2 teaspoon salt, optional
1/4 teaspoon pepper

Place broccoli in a basket over 1 in. of boiling water in a saucepan. Cover; steam for 5-6 minutes or until crisp-tender. Rinse in cold water; drain and set aside. In a skillet, saute the onion, celery and garlic in butter until vegetables are tender, about 5 minutes. Add the lemon peel and juice, salt if desired, pepper and broccoli; heat through. **Yield:** 4 servings. **Nutritional Analysis:** One serving (prepared with reduced-fat margarine and without salt) equals 105 calories, 149 mg sodium, 0 cholesterol, 12 gm carbohydrate, 5 gm protein, 6 gm fat, 5 gm fiber. **Diabetic Exchanges:** 2 vegetable, 1 fat.

Rosemary Asparagus

This is a nice alternative to plain asparagus. It's a simple, flavorful way to dress them up. —Mavis Diment
Marcus, Iowa

- 1/2 cup chicken broth
- 1 to 2 tablespoons minced fresh rosemary *or* 1 to 2 teaspoons dried rosemary, crushed
- 1 garlic clove, halved
- 1 bay leaf
- 1 pound fresh asparagus, trimmed
- 1/3 cup chopped onion
- 1 tablespoon minced fresh parsley

In a skillet, combine the broth, rosemary, garlic and bay leaf. Add asparagus and onion. Bring to a boil. Reduce heat; cover and simmer for 3-5 minutes or until crisp-tender. Discard bay leaf. Garnish with parsley. **Yield:** 4 servings.

Creamy Mint Carrots

I grow a lot of mint, so I'm always looking for creative ways to cook with it. This delicious recipe is my son's favorite way to eat carrots. —Sue Gronholz
Beaver Dam, Wisconsin

- 2 to 2-1/2 pounds carrots, thinly sliced
- 1 teaspoon cornstarch
- 2 teaspoons cold water
- 1 cup whipping cream
- 1/4 cup packed brown sugar
- 2 to 3 tablespoons fresh mint *or* 2 to 3 teaspoons dried mint flakes
- 2 tablespoons butter *or* margarine
- 1 teaspoon salt
- 1/2 teaspoon pepper

Place carrots in a saucepan; cover with water. Bring to a boil; reduce heat. Cover and simmer for 10 minutes or until crisp-tender; drain. In a small bowl, combine cornstarch and water until smooth. In a small saucepan over medium heat, bring cream to a boil. Stir in cornstarch mixture. Cook and stir for 2 minutes or until thickened. Stir in the remaining ingredients. Pour over carrots. **Yield:** 8 servings.

Special Squash Casserole

(Pictured on page 56)

Squash has never topped our family's list of favorite foods, but this luscious casserole is an exception.
—Kathleen Cox, Wyoming, Michigan

Two-Tone Baked Potatoes

(Pictured above)

One potato...two potato...this recipe is doubly wonderful as far as spud lovers are concerned. I have a reputation at home and at work for trying new recipes. Everyone's glad I took a chance on this one.
—Sherree Stahn, Central City, Nebraska

- 6 medium russet potatoes
- 6 medium sweet potatoes
- 2/3 cup sour cream, *divided*
- 1/3 cup milk
- 3/4 cup shredded cheddar cheese
- 4 tablespoons minced chives, *divided*
- 1-1/2 teaspoons salt, *divided*

Pierce russet and sweet potatoes with a fork. Bake at 400° for 60-70 minutes or until tender. Set sweet potatoes aside. Cut a third off the top of each russet potato; scoop out pulp, leaving skins intact. Place the pulp in a bowl; mash with 1/3 cup sour cream, milk, cheese, 2 tablespoons chives and 3/4 teaspoon of salt. Set aside. Cut off the top of each sweet potato; scoop out pulp, leaving skins intact. Mash pulp with remaining sour cream, chives and salt. Stuff mixture into half of each potato skin; spoon russet potato filling into other half. Place on a baking sheet. Bake at 350° for 15-20 minutes or until heated through. **Yield:** 12 servings.

3 pounds butternut squash, peeled, seeded
  and cubed
3/4 cup milk
6 tablespoons butter *or* margarine, melted
3 eggs, beaten
1/2 teaspoon vanilla extract
3/4 cup sugar
3 tablespoons all-purpose flour
1/2 teaspoon ground cinnamon
1/8 teaspoon ground cloves
1/8 teaspoon ground nutmeg
TOPPING:
1/2 cup vanilla wafer crumbs (about 15
  wafers)
1/4 cup packed brown sugar
2 tablespoons butter *or* margarine, melted

Place squash in a large saucepan or Dutch oven; cover with water. Bring to a boil; cover and cook for 25-30 minutes or until tender. Drain and place in a mixing bowl; beat just until smooth. Add the milk, butter, eggs and vanilla; mix well. Combine the dry ingredients; add to squash mixture and mix well. Transfer to a greased 2-qt. baking dish. Cover and bake at 350° for 45 minutes. Meanwhile, in a small bowl, combine topping ingredients until crumbly; sprinkle over squash. Bake, uncovered, for 12-15 minutes or until heated through. **Yield:** 8-10 servings.

— 🍵 🍵 🍵 —

Microwave Salsa

I love the salsa served at my favorite Mexican restaurant, so I set out to match the flavor. I think I've achieved my goal. It's so easy to make in the microwave. Now we can enjoy salsa anytime. We eat it with tortilla chips as a snack or as a topping for grilled poultry. It's great hot or cold. —Pamela Schroeder
Santee, California

3 medium tomatoes, chopped
1 green onion, sliced
1 to 2 garlic cloves, minced
3 tablespoons finely chopped green pepper
1 tablespoon lemon juice
1-1/2 teaspoons minced fresh basil *or* 1/2
  teaspoon dried basil
1/2 teaspoon chili powder
1/2 teaspoon salt
1/8 teaspoon pepper

In a microwave-safe bowl, combine the tomatoes, onion and garlic. Add green pepper, lemon juice and seasonings; mix well. Microwave on high for 45-60 seconds or until heated through. Salsa can be stored in the refrigerator for up to 3 days. **Yield:** 4 cups.

Fabulous Fettuccine

(Pictured below and on page 56)

My mother-in-law is from Italy, so my husband, Bob, grew up eating pasta dishes. I've been preparing this fresh-tasting version for several years. Bob requests it often, and even his mom thinks it's very good.
—Mary Kay Morris, Cokato, Minnesota

1/2 pound sliced bacon, diced
3 tablespoons olive *or* vegetable oil
2 large onions, chopped
3 pounds fresh tomatoes, peeled, seeded
  and chopped *or* 2 cans (14-1/2 ounces
  each) diced tomatoes, undrained
3 garlic cloves, minced
2 tablespoons minced fresh tarragon *or* 2
  teaspoons dried tarragon
1/2 teaspoon salt
1/4 teaspoon pepper
Pinch to 1/8 teaspoon cayenne pepper
1/4 cup minced fresh parsley
1 pound fettuccine
Shredded Parmesan cheese

In a skillet, cook bacon until crisp. Remove to paper towels. Drain, reserving 1 tablespoon drippings. Add oil and onions to drippings; saute until tender, about 5 minutes. Add tomatoes and garlic; simmer, uncovered, for 5 minutes. Stir in tarragon, salt, pepper and cayenne; cover and simmer for 20 minutes, stirring occasionally. Meanwhile, cook fettuccine according to package directions. Add parsley to the tomato mixture; simmer 5 minutes longer. Stir in bacon. Drain fettuccine; top with tomato mixture. Sprinkle with Parmesan cheese. **Yield:** 4-6 servings.

Maple Glazed Squash

Squash gets a pleasant sweet and spicy flavor from maple syrup and cinnamon in this recipe.
— *Betty Sitzman, Wray, Colorado*

  2 medium acorn squash
Salt and pepper to taste
  1 cup maple syrup
  1 medium tart apple, peeled and chopped
  2 tablespoons raisins, optional
  1 teaspoon ground cinnamon

Cut squash into 1-in. rings and remove seeds. Place squash in a greased 13-in. x 9-in. x 2-in. baking dish. Sprinkle with salt and pepper. In a bowl, combine remaining ingredients; pour over squash. Cover and bake at 350° for 50-60 minutes or until tender. **Yield:** 6 servings.

------- 🥄 🥄 🥄 -------

Creamy Herb Dressing

(Pictured below and on page 56)

This dressing for vegetables is so easy. I make it the night before Thanksgiving to save time on such a busy day. I use asparagus, green beans or broccoli for an eye-pleasing, hunger-satisfying side dish.
— *Brigitte Hinz, Des Plaines, Illinois*

1-1/2 cups mayonnaise *or* salad dressing
  2/3 cup whipping cream
  1/2 cup chopped green onions
  1/2 cup minced fresh parsley

  1 can (2 ounces) anchovy fillets, drained, optional
  2 tablespoons minced chives
  2 tablespoons lemon juice
  2 pounds fresh asparagus spears, trimmed

In a blender, combine the first seven ingredients; cover and process until smooth. Cover and refrigerate for at least 1 hour. In a skillet, cook asparagus in a small amount of water for 3-4 minutes or until crisp-tender; drain well. Spoon dressing over asparagus. Store dressing in the refrigerator. **Yield:** 6 servings (2-1/2 cups dressing).

------- 🥄 🥄 🥄 -------

Vegetable Rice Medley

I keep an herb garden and plant several seasonal vegetables each spring. I can't wait until the farmer's market opens each summer so I can see what tasty squash, beans and greens the real farmers are offering up. Then I can head home and make this recipe.
— *Andy Anderson, Graham, Washington*

✓ Uses less fat, sugar or salt. Includes Nutritional Analysis and Diabetic Exchanges.

  1 medium leek (white portion only), minced
  2 garlic cloves, minced
  2 teaspoons vegetable oil
4-1/2 cups chicken broth
  2 cups uncooked long grain rice
  1 cup raisins *or* dried cranberries
  2 cups cubed zucchini, yellow summer squash *and/or* butternut squash
  3/4 cup frozen baby lima beans, thawed
  1 teaspoon ground turmeric
  1/2 teaspoon ground ginger
Dash cayenne pepper
  1 cup peeled seeded chopped plum tomatoes
  3/4 cup frozen peas, thawed
  1/4 cup minced fresh cilantro *or* parsley
Lemon wedges *or* hot pepper sauce, optional

In a Dutch oven, saute the leek and garlic in oil until tender. Add broth, rice, raisins, squash, lima beans and seasonings. Bring to a boil. Reduce heat; cover and simmer for 15 minutes. Add the tomatoes and peas; cover and cook 5 minutes longer or until liquid is absorbed and the rice is tender. Serve with lemon or hot pepper sauce if desired. **Yield:** 14 servings. **Nutritional Analysis:** One serving (prepared with raisins, zucchini and low-sodium broth) equals 182 calories, 54 mg sodium, 1 mg cholesterol, 38 gm carbohydrate, 5 gm protein, 2 gm fat, 2 gm fiber. **Diabetic Exchanges:** 2 starch, 1 vegetable.

Basil Parsley Pesto

Pesto is an uncooked Italian sauce traditionally made from basil, olive oil, garlic, Parmesan cheese and sometimes pinenuts. This recipe comes from another Reiman Publications magazine, Birds and Blooms.

> 1 **cup tightly packed fresh basil *or* cilantro leaves**
> 1 **cup tightly packed fresh parsley leaves**
> 1 **to 2 garlic cloves**
> 1/2 **cup olive *or* vegetable oil**
> 1/2 **cup grated Parmesan cheese**
> 1/4 **teaspoon salt**

Combine all ingredients in a food processor; cover and puree until smooth. Toss with hot cooked pasta or vegetables, spread on French bread or use in any recipe calling for pesto. Can be refrigerated for several weeks or frozen in a tightly covered container. **Yield:** 3/4 cup.

Mushroom Wild Rice

(Pictured at right)

This colorful casserole is a standout from my mother's collection of family recipes. With its great texture and taste, it doesn't play second fiddle to either the pumpkin pie or the turkey at Thanksgiving!
—Charlene Baert, Winnipeg, Manitoba

> 4 **cups water**
> 1 **cup uncooked wild rice**
> 1 **teaspoon butter *or* margarine**
> 1-1/2 **teaspoons salt, *divided***
> 1/2 **cup uncooked brown rice**
> 8 **bacon strips, diced**
> 2 **cups sliced fresh mushrooms**
> 1 **large onion, chopped**
> 1 **medium green pepper, chopped**
> 1 **medium sweet red pepper, chopped**
> 1 **celery rib, thinly sliced**
> 1 **can (14-1/2 ounces) beef broth**
> 2 **tablespoons cornstarch**
> 1/4 **cup cold water**
> 1/2 **cup slivered almonds**

In a large saucepan, bring water, wild rice, butter and 1/2 teaspoon salt to a boil. Reduce heat; cover and simmer for 40 minutes. Stir in brown rice. Cover and simmer 25-30 minutes longer or until rice is tender. Meanwhile, in a large skillet, cook bacon until crisp. Remove bacon to paper towels; drain, reserving 2 tablespoons drippings. In the drippings, saute mushrooms, onion, peppers and celery until tender. Stir in broth and remaining salt. Bring to a boil. Combine cornstarch and cold water until smooth; stir into mushroom mixture. Cook and stir for 2 minutes or until thickened and bubbly; stir in almonds and bacon. Drain rice; add mushroom mixture. Transfer to a greased 13-in. x 9-in. x 2-in. baking dish. Cover and bake at 350° for 25 minutes. Uncover; bake 5-10 minutes longer or until heated through. **Yield:** 12 servings.

Horseradish Sauce

As delicious as ham is by itself, horseradish greatly enhances the fabulous flavor. We enjoy this simple horseradish sauce on a variety of ham recipes.
—Edna Duffield, Lineville, Iowa

> 1/4 **cup prepared horseradish**
> 1-1/2 **teaspoons vinegar**
> 1 **tablespoon prepared mustard**
> 1/2 **teaspoon salt**
> 1/2 **teaspoon Worcestershire sauce**
> 4 **drops hot pepper sauce**
> 1 **cup whipping cream, whipped**

In a small bowl, combine the first six ingredients. Mix well. Gently fold in whipped cream. Chill. Serve with sliced ham, ham loaf or ham balls. **Yield:** about 2 cups.

1 cup skim milk
1-1/4 cups shredded reduced-fat cheddar
   cheese
   2/3 cup fat-free cottage cheese
Pepper to taste
2-1/2 cups cooked elbow macaroni
   1 tablespoon grated onion
Paprika

In a blender or food processor, combine the milk, cheeses and pepper. Cover and process until creamy. Pour into a bowl; stir in macaroni and onion. Transfer to a 1-1/2-qt. baking dish coated with nonstick cooking spray. Sprinkle with paprika. Bake, uncovered, at 350° for 1 hour or until heated through. **Yield:** 4 servings. **Nutritional Analysis:** One 3/4-cup serving equals 233 calories, 372 mg sodium, 12 mg cholesterol, 30 gm carbohydrate, 20 gm protein, 3 gm fat, 1 gm fiber. **Diabetic Exchanges:** 2 starch, 2 very lean meat.

🥣 🥣 🥣

Strawberry Rhubarb Compote

At the height of rhubarb season, I make a big batch of this compote. My family especially likes to warm it up for a fruity breakfast treat. —Fay Bellgardt
Montrose, Colorado

1/2 cup water
   5 cups chopped fresh *or* frozen rhubarb
   2 to 4 tablespoons sugar
   2 cups fresh strawberries, halved
1/8 teaspoon ground ginger

In a medium saucepan, bring water to a boil. Add rhubarb and sugar. Cook for 5-10 minutes or until rhubarb is tender, stirring occasionally. Remove the rhubarb from heat; stir in strawberries and ginger. Serve warm or cold. **Yield:** 6 servings.

🥣 🥣 🥣

Broccoli-Nut Stuffing Bake

Many years ago, a co-worker brought this great vegetable side dish to a potluck luncheon. Made with stuffing mix and accented with walnuts, it's appropriate for a holiday dinner or any meal. —Georgia Hennings
Alliance, Nebraska

3 pounds fresh broccoli, cut into spears
   or 3 packages (10 ounces *each*) frozen
   broccoli spears, thawed and drained
1/2 cup plus 6 tablespoons butter *or*
   margarine, *divided*
1/4 cup all-purpose flour
4-1/2 teaspoons chicken bouillon granules
   2 cups milk

Cheddar Potato Strips

(Pictured above)

I like this dish because it's something you can feed family and friends and win compliments. It's very pretty, with parsley sprinkled over melted cheese. The mild flavor pairs well with any meat. —Lucinda Walker
Somerset, Pennsylvania

3 large potatoes, cut into 1/2-inch strips
1/2 cup milk
   1 tablespoon butter *or* margarine
Salt and pepper to taste
1/2 cup shredded cheddar cheese
   1 tablespoon minced fresh parsley

In a greased 13-in. x 9-in. x 2-in. baking dish, arrange potatoes in a single layer. Pour milk over potatoes. Dot with butter; sprinkle with salt and pepper. Cover and bake at 425° for 30 minutes or until potatoes are tender. Sprinkle with cheese and parsley. Bake, uncovered, 5 minutes longer or until cheese is melted. **Yield:** 4 servings.

🥣 🥣 🥣

Low-Fat Macaroni and Cheese

When I want a side dish that's real old-fashioned comfort food, I make a batch of this macaroni and cheese.
—Joanie Elbourn, Gardner, Massachusetts

✓ Uses less fat, sugar or salt. Includes Nutritional Analysis and Diabetic Exchanges.

1-1/2 cups crushed seasoned stuffing
2/3 cup chopped walnuts
2/3 cup water

Place broccoli in a saucepan; add 1 in. of water. Bring to a boil. Reduce heat; cover and simmer for 5-6 minutes or until crisp-tender. Drain and place in a greased 13-in. x 9-in. x 2-in. baking dish. In a saucepan, melt 1/2 cup butter; stir in flour and bouillon until blended. Gradually add milk. Bring to a boil; cook and stir for 2 minutes. Pour over broccoli. Combine stuffing and walnuts. Heat water and remaining butter until melted; toss with stuffing mixture. Sprinkle over casserole. Bake, uncovered, at 400° for 15-18 minutes or until golden brown. **Yield:** 7 servings.

— 🝙 🝙 🝙 —

Baked Stuffed Carrots

(Pictured below)

The preparation makes this side dish much more impressive than plain cooked carrots—and it tastes better, too! —Roma Steckling, Aitkin, Minnesota

12 medium carrots, peeled
1/4 cup mayonnaise
4 teaspoons grated onion
2 teaspoons prepared horseradish
1/8 teaspoon ground nutmeg
Salt and pepper to taste
1/4 cup dry bread crumbs
2 tablespoons butter *or* margarine, melted, *divided*
1/8 teaspoon paprika

Place carrots in a skillet; add 1 in. of water. Bring to a boil. Reduce heat; cover and simmer for 10-15 minutes or until crisp-tender. Drain. Cut a thin lengthwise slice out of each carrot. Scoop out carrot, leaving a 1/4-in. shell; set shells aside. Process the removed carrot in a food processor or blender until finely chopped. Transfer to a bowl; add mayonnaise, onion, horseradish, nutmeg, salt and pepper. Spoon into carrot shells. Place in a greased 13-in. x 9-in. x 2-in. baking dish. Combine crumbs, 1 tablespoon butter and paprika; sprinkle over carrots. Drizzle with remaining butter. Bake, uncovered, at 375° for 20-25 minutes or until tender. **Yield:** 6 servings.

— 🝙 🝙 🝙 —

Steak Sauce

This savory recipe is just the thing for folks who think a steak dinner is only complete when each meaty morsel is dripping with sauce. —Patricia Yurcisin Barnesboro, Pennsylvania

2 cups ketchup
2 garlic cloves, minced
2/3 cup chopped onion
1/2 cup *each* lemon juice, water, Worcestershire sauce and vinegar
1/4 cup soy sauce
1/4 cup packed dark brown sugar
2 tablespoons prepared mustard

Combine all of the ingredients in a 3-qt. saucepan; bring to a boil over medium heat. Reduce heat and simmer, uncovered, for 30 minutes. Strain if desired. Cover and refrigerate. **Yield:** about 3 cups.

Mixed Beans with Lime Butter

(Pictured below)

This is a simple yet delicious way to showcase green beans. It's best with beans fresh from your garden or the farmer's market. —Lois Fetting
Nelson, Wisconsin

- 1/2 pound *each* fresh green and wax beans, trimmed
- 2 tablespoons butter *or* margarine
- 2 teaspoons snipped fresh dill
- 2 teaspoons lime juice
- 1 teaspoon grated lime peel
- 1/2 teaspoon salt
- 1/4 teaspoon pepper

Place beans in a saucepan and cover with water; bring to a boil. Cook, uncovered, for 10 minutes or until crisp-tender; drain. Melt butter in a skillet; add the dill, lime juice and peel, salt, pepper and beans. Stir to coat and cook until heated through. **Yield:** 4 servings.

Pear Cranberry Chutney

One day as a kid, I told my parents I didn't like what we were having for breakfast. They told me to make my own, and I've been cooking ever since. I love cranberries, and the sweet-sour taste of this chutney goes very well with fall foods. —Andy Anderson
Graham, Washington

- 4 cups fresh *or* frozen cranberries
- 1 cup raisins
- 1 medium onion, finely chopped
- 3/4 cup packed brown sugar
- 1/3 cup cider vinegar
- 2 garlic cloves, minced
- 3 teaspoons mustard seed
- 1/4 teaspoon ground mustard
- 1/4 teaspoon *each* ground ginger, allspice and cloves
- 1/4 teaspoon crushed red pepper flakes
- 1 large pear, peeled and coarsely chopped

In a saucepan, combine the cranberries, raisins, onion, brown sugar, vinegar, garlic and seasonings. Bring to a boil. Reduce heat; cook, uncovered, for 30-35 minutes, stirring occasionally. Add pear. Cook 10 minutes longer or until tender. Serve warm or cold. Store in the refrigerator. **Yield:** 3 cups.

Cornmeal Mushroom Casserole

Everyone knows I can never bring just one dish to a potluck—I usually prepare several. This is one of my most requested dishes. —Gary Maly
West Chester, Ohio

- 7 cups milk *or* water
- 2 cups cornmeal
- 2 pounds fresh mushrooms, coarsely chopped
- 1 medium onion, chopped
- 3/4 cup chopped sweet red pepper
- 2 garlic cloves, minced
- 2 tablespoons olive *or* vegetable oil
- 1/4 cup soy sauce
- 1/3 cup all-purpose flour
- 4 cups half-and-half cream
- 1 cup (4 ounces) shredded Monterey Jack cheese
- 1 cup (4 ounces) shredded cheddar cheese
- 1 cup grated Parmesan cheese

In a large saucepan, bring milk to a boil. Slowly whisk in cornmeal until blended. Cook and stir until thickened. Spread into two greased 13-in. x 9-in. x 2-in. baking pans. Cover and refrigerate overnight. In a skillet, saute the mushrooms, onion, red pepper and garlic in oil until tender. Add soy sauce; cook for 8-10 minutes or until liquid is absorbed. Sprinkle with flour; cook and stir until blended. Gradually stir in cream; cook and stir until thickened. Remove cornmeal crusts from pans; place one in a greased 4-qt. baking dish (lasagna pan). Top with half of the mushroom mixture; sprinkle with half of the cheeses. Top with the second cornmeal crust and remaining mushroom mixture and cheeses. Cover and bake at 350° for 35 minutes. Uncover; bake 15 minutes longer or until lightly browned. Let stand 15-20 minutes before cutting. **Yield:** 14-16 servings.

♦ ♦ ♦

Creamy Broccoli Casserole

This saucy side dish was named "grand champion" in the Heart Healthy Contest at a local fair one year. Its tempting appearance makes folks want to dig in.
—*Rhonda Sells, Strafford, Missouri*

✓ Uses less fat, sugar or salt. Includes Nutritional Analysis and Diabetic Exchanges.

> 2 **packages (10 ounces *each*) frozen chopped broccoli, thawed and drained**
> 1 **can (10-3/4 ounces) condensed low-fat cream of chicken soup, undiluted**
> 2 **teaspoons lemon juice**
> 1/2 **cup crushed seasoned stuffing**
> 1 **tablespoon reduced-fat margarine, melted**
> 1/4 **cup reduced-fat shredded cheddar cheese**

Place the broccoli in an 8-in. square baking dish coated with nonstick cooking spray. Combine soup and lemon juice; pour over broccoli. Toss stuffing and margarine; sprinkle over soup mixture. Cover and bake at 350° for 25-30 minutes. Uncover; sprinkle with cheese. Bake 5 minutes longer or until cheese is melted. **Yield:** 7 servings. **Nutritional Analysis:** One serving equals 81 calories, 289 mg sodium, 4 mg cholesterol, 11 gm carbohydrate, 4 gm protein, 2 gm fat, 3 gm fiber. **Diabetic Exchanges:** 1 vegetable, 1/2 starch, 1/2 fat.

♦ ♦ ♦

Chunky Rhubarb Applesauce

Our backyard was filled with rhubarb when I was growing up in Illinois, and Mom would always add some to her applesauce.
—*Cheryl Miller*
Fort Collins, Colorado

> 1 **pound rhubarb, trimmed and cut into 1/2-inch chunks**
> 2 **pounds baking apples, peeled, cored and cut into 1/2-inch chunks**
> 1/2 **to 1 cup sugar**
> 1/4 **teaspoon ground cinnamon**
> 1/8 **teaspoon ground nutmeg**

Place rhubarb, apples and sugar to taste in a large saucepan. Cover and simmer until fruit is soft, about 40-45 minutes. Stir in cinnamon and nutmeg. Serve warm or cold. **Yield:** 3-4 cups.

Roasted Garlic Mashed Potatoes

(Pictured above and on front cover)

My family loves potatoes and considers this dressed-up version a favorite. Mouth-watering flavor comes from roasted garlic and rosemary. These fluffy, pleasing potatoes make a standout side dish for any meat.
—*Rita Wenrich, La Luz, New Mexico*

> 2 **whole garlic heads**
> 1 **tablespoon olive *or* vegetable oil**
> 6 **medium baking potatoes, peeled and cubed**
> 1 **cup plus 2 tablespoons milk**
> 2 **tablespoons butter *or* margarine**
> 1 **tablespoon minced fresh rosemary *or* 1 teaspoon dried rosemary, crushed**
> 1 **teaspoon salt**

Cut the top off garlic heads so each clove is exposed. Brush with oil; wrap in foil. Bake at 350° for 45 minutes or until garlic is very soft. Cool for 5 minutes. Remove garlic from skins; mash and set aside. Place potatoes in a saucepan and cover with water. Bring to a boil; cover and cook for 20-25 minutes or until very tender. Drain well. Add milk, butter, rosemary, salt and garlic; mash until light and fluffy. **Yield:** 6 servings.

Nick's Corn Pudding

I've always enjoyed cooking and experimenting with recipes. My corn pudding is a variation of a recipe from a friend. It's a comforting, buttery side dish with lots of corn. —Nick Mescia, Surprise, Arizona

>   3 eggs
>   1 cup whipping cream
>   2 cans (one 15-1/4 ounces, one 8-3/4 ounces) whole kernel corn, drained
>   1/2 cup butter *or* margarine, melted
>   2 tablespoons sugar
> 4-1/2 teaspoons all-purpose flour
>   1 teaspoon baking powder
>   1/2 teaspoon salt
>   1/4 teaspoon pepper

In a large bowl, beat the eggs and cream. Add the corn and butter. Combine the remaining ingredients; stir into corn mixture. Pour into a greased 1-1/2-qt. baking dish. Bake, uncovered, at 350° for 45-55 minutes or until set and golden brown. **Yield:** 4-6 servings.

Herbed Potatoes 'n' Peas

This side dish makes a winner out of any meal. Red potatoes and green peas add color to the table, and the herbs add zing to garden vegetables. —Gail Buss, Westminster, Maryland

>   1 pound small red potatoes
>   2 bay leaves
>   1/4 cup butter *or* margarine
>   3/4 teaspoon salt
>   1/4 teaspoon dried marjoram
>   1/4 teaspoon dried thyme
> Dash pepper
>   1 package (10 ounces) frozen peas, thawed

Place potatoes and bay leaves in a saucepan; cover with water. Bring to boil. Cover and cook for 8-10 minutes or just until tender; drain. Cut the potatoes into quarters; return to pan. Add butter and seasonings. Cover and cook for 5-8 minutes or until potatoes are tender, stirring occasionally. Stir in peas; heat through. Discard bay leaves. **Yield:** 4-6 servings.

Parmesan Onion Bake

(Pictured above)

Dinner guests in my home know to expect the unexpected! I love experimenting with unusual combinations of ingredients. This cheesy onion bake always adds excitement to a meal. —Linda Vail, Ballwin, Missouri

>   6 medium onions, sliced
>   1 cup diced celery
>   8 tablespoons butter *or* margarine, *divided*
>   1/4 cup all-purpose flour
>   1 teaspoon salt
>   1/8 teaspoon pepper
> 1-1/2 cups milk
>   1/3 cup grated Parmesan cheese
>   1/2 cup chopped pecans

In a large skillet, saute onions and celery in 3 tablespoons butter until tender; drain and set aside. In a saucepan, melt the remaining butter; stir in flour, salt and pepper until smooth. Gradually stir in milk. Bring to a boil; cook and stir for 2 minutes or until thickened. Pour over vegetables; toss to coat. Pour into an ungreased 2-qt. baking dish. Sprinkle with cheese and pecans. Bake, uncovered, at 350° for 20-25 minutes or until heated through. **Yield:** 6-8 servings.

Rhubarb Blueberry Jam

I appreciate the convenience of this recipe because it calls for canned blueberries. Spoon some on toast, biscuits or even pancakes and waffles. —Dorothea Cleveland, Loveland, Colorado

5 cups diced fresh *or* frozen rhubarb
1 cup water
5 cups sugar
1 can (21 ounces) blueberry pie filling
1 package (6 ounces) raspberry gelatin

In a large kettle, combine rhubarb and water. Cook over medium-high heat for 4 minutes or until the rhubarb is tender. Add sugar and bring to a boil for 2 minutes. Stir in pie filling. Remove from the heat; cool for 10 minutes. Add gelatin and mix well. Pour hot jam into hot jars, leaving 1/4-in. headspace. Adjust caps. Process for 15 minutes in a boiling-water bath. **Yield:** about 8 half-pints.

— ▼ ▼ ▼ —

Gingered Lime Carrots

The produce manager at my grocery store suggested this memorable mixture of lightly sweet carrots, zesty ginger and tart lime. It's easy to fall in love with this recipe, which now has a permanent place among my favorites. My husband and I especially enjoy it with poultry or fish. —Dorothy Swanson
St. Louis, Missouri

1 pound carrots, cut into 1/2-inch slices
1 tablespoon water
1 tablespoon lime juice
1 tablespoon butter *or* margarine
1 tablespoon honey
1 teaspoon grated lime peel
1/4 teaspoon ground ginger *or* 1 teaspoon grated fresh gingerroot
Lime slices

In a 1-1/2-qt. microwave-safe bowl, combine carrots and water. Cover and cook on high for 7-8 minutes or until crisp-tender, stirring once. Let stand for 5 minutes. Meanwhile, in a small bowl, combine lime juice, butter, honey, peel and ginger. Cover and microwave on high for 1 minute. Drain carrots; stir in the lime mixture. Cover and cook on high for 1 minute. Garnish with lime. **Yield:** 4 servings. **Editor's Note:** This recipe was tested in an 850-watt microwave.

Tasty Veggies

Jazz up mashed potatoes by stirring in some horse-radish, crumbled bacon and cheddar cheese.

When making chicken dumplings, stir in a pinch of curry powder to the dry ingredients.

Add a little chopped onion when cooking carrots.

Brussels Sprouts Supreme

(Pictured below and on page 56)

A zippy cheese sauce is the perfect accompaniment for the bold flavor of brussels sprouts. Even those who don't care for this vegetable may enjoy it served this way. Plus, it looks so appealing on the table.
—Edna Hoffman, Hebron, Indiana

1 pound fresh brussels sprouts, trimmed
1 cup chopped celery
2 tablespoons butter *or* margarine
2 tablespoons all-purpose flour
1 cup milk
1/2 cup shredded process American cheese
1/4 teaspoon salt
Pinch cayenne pepper, optional

Place brussels sprouts, celery and a small amount of water in a saucepan; cover and cook for 8 minutes or until crisp-tender. Meanwhile, in another saucepan, melt butter. Stir in flour until smooth. Gradually add milk; bring to a boil. Reduce heat; cook and stir for 2 minutes or until thickened. Add cheese, salt and cayenne if desired; stir until cheese is melted. Drain sprouts and celery; top with cheese sauce. **Yield:** 4-6 servings.

Main Dishes

From beef, game and seafood to pasta, chicken and pork, this featured fare is sure to please.

ENJOYABLE ENTREES. Clockwise from upper left: Creamy Beef Lasagna (p. 81), Steak with Citrus Salsa (p. 84), Herbed Chicken Quarters (p. 89), Whole Wheat Veggie Pizza (p. 105) and Mandarin Pork Roast (p. 96).

Calgary Stampede Ribs
(Pictured below)

"More, please!" is what I hear when I serve these robust, finger-licking ribs to family or guests. The first time my husband and I tried them, we pronounced them "the best ever". The recipe has its roots in the Calgary Stampede, an annual Western and agricultural fair and exhibition in our province. —Marian Misik Sherwood Park, Alberta

> 4 pounds pork back ribs, cut into serving-size pieces
> 3 garlic cloves, minced
> 1 tablespoon sugar
> 1 tablespoon paprika
> 2 teaspoons *each* salt, pepper, chili powder and ground cumin

BARBECUE SAUCE:
> 1 small onion, finely chopped
> 2 tablespoons butter *or* margarine
> 1 cup ketchup
> 1/4 cup packed brown sugar
> 3 tablespoons lemon juice
> 3 tablespoons Worcestershire sauce
> 2 tablespoons vinegar
> 1-1/2 teaspoons ground mustard
> 1 teaspoon celery seed
> 1/8 teaspoon cayenne pepper

Rub ribs with garlic; place in a shallow roasting pan. Cover and bake at 300° for 2 hours. Cool slightly. Combine the seasonings and rub over ribs. Cover and refrigerate for 8 hours or overnight. In a saucepan, saute onion in butter until tender. Stir in the remaining sauce ingredients. Bring to a boil. Reduce heat; cook and stir until thickened, about 10 minutes. Remove from the heat; set aside 3/4 cup. Brush ribs with some of the remaining sauce. Grill, covered, over medium heat for 12 minutes, turning and basting with sauce. Serve with reserved sauce. **Yield:** 4 servings.

Venison Pot Roast

This dish has tender meat and wonderful seasonings. Game is plentiful around our home—and that's a good thing—since my family could eat this satisfying meal every week. —Debbie Phillips, Pittsburg, Texas

> 3 tablespoons all-purpose flour
> 1/2 teaspoon salt
> 1/2 teaspoon pepper
> 1 boneless shoulder venison roast (3 pounds)
> 2 tablespoons vegetable oil
> 1 cup apple juice *or* cider
> 1 cup beef broth
> 1 medium onion, sliced
> 1 teaspoon dried thyme
> 1 bay leaf
> 8 small potatoes, peeled
> 6 medium carrots, cut into 2-inch pieces
> 4 celery ribs, cut into 2-inch pieces

Combine the first three ingredients; rub over roast. In a Dutch oven, brown roast on all sides in oil. Add apple juice, broth, onion, thyme and bay leaf. Bring to a boil; reduce heat. Cover and simmer for 2 hours. Add potatoes, carrots and celery; cover and simmer for 1 hour or until meat and vegetables are tender. Discard bay leaf. Thicken pan juices if desired. **Yield:** 6-8 servings.

Steak Fajitas

A zesty tomato and jalapeno relish and tender strips of steak make these traditional fajitas extra special. —Rebecca Baird, Salt Lake City, Utah

> 2 medium tomatoes, seeded and diced
> 1/2 cup diced red onion
> 1/4 cup lime juice
> 3 tablespoons minced fresh cilantro *or* parsley
> 1 jalapeno pepper, seeded and chopped*
> 2 teaspoons ground cumin
> 1/2 teaspoon salt
> 1 beef flank steak (about 1-1/2 pounds)
> 1 large onion, halved and sliced
> 1 tablespoon vegetable oil
> 6 flour tortillas (6 inches), warmed

Canned black beans and guacamole

In a bowl, combine the first seven ingredients. Cover and refrigerate. Broil or grill steak over medium-hot heat for 6-8 minutes on each side or until meat reaches desired doneness (for rare, a meat thermometer should read 140°; medium, 160°; well-done, 170°). Meanwhile, in a skillet, saute onion in oil until crisp-tender. Slice steak into thin strips across the grain; place on tortillas. Top with onion and the reserved tomato relish. Serve with black beans and guacamole. **Yield:** 6 servings. ***Editor's Note:** When cutting or seeding hot peppers, use rubber or plastic gloves to protect your hands. Avoid touching your face.

— 🏺 🏺 🏺 —

Four-Cheese Spinach Lasagna

(Pictured at right)

This rich cheesy lasagna has become one of my specialties. It's packed with fresh-tasting vegetables like spinach, carrots, red pepper and broccoli. I love to serve the colorful casserole to guests, since it's always a huge success.
— *Kimberly Kneisly*
Englewood, Ohio

   2 **cups chopped fresh broccoli**
1-1/2 **cups julienned carrots**
   1 **cup sliced green onions**
1/2 **cup chopped sweet red pepper**
   3 **garlic cloves, minced**
   2 **teaspoons vegetable oil**
1/2 **cup all-purpose flour**
   3 **cups milk**
1/2 **cup grated Parmesan cheese,** *divided*
1/2 **teaspoon salt**
1/4 **teaspoon pepper**
   1 **package (10 ounces) frozen chopped spinach, thawed and well drained**
1-1/2 **cups small-curd cottage cheese**
   1 **cup (4 ounces) shredded mozzarella cheese**
1/2 **cup shredded Swiss cheese**
  12 **lasagna noodles, cooked and drained**

In a skillet, saute the vegetables and garlic in oil until crisp-tender. Remove from the heat; set aside. In a heavy saucepan, whisk the flour and milk until smooth. Bring to a boil; cook and stir for 2 minutes. Reduce heat; add 1/4 cup Parmesan cheese, salt and pepper. Cook 1 minute longer or until cheese is melted. Remove from the heat; stir in spinach. Set 1 cup aside. In a bowl, combine the cottage cheese, mozzarella and Swiss. Spread 1/2 cup of the spinach mixture in a greased 13-in. x 9-in. x 2-in. baking dish. Layer with four noodles, half of the cheese mixture and vegetables and 3/4 cup spinach mixture. Repeat layers. Top with re-

maining noodles, reserved spinach mixture and remaining Parmesan cheese. Cover and bake at 375° for 35 minutes. Uncover; bake 15 minutes longer or until bubbly. Let stand 15 minutes before cutting. **Yield:** 12 servings.

Curried Red Snapper

My husband and daughter don't usually care for fish, but they love it prepared this way. A tasty curry sauce baked over the fish makes the delicious difference.
— *Lynette Kerslake, Corbett, Oregon*

1-1/2 **pounds fresh** *or* **frozen red snapper***
   2 **medium onions, chopped**
   2 **celery ribs, chopped**
   1 **tablespoon butter** *or* **margarine**
   1 **teaspoon curry powder**
3/4 **teaspoon salt**
1/4 **cup milk**

Place the fish in a greased 13-in. x 9-in. x 2-in. baking dish. In a skillet, saute onions and celery in butter until tender. Add curry powder and salt; mix well. Remove from the heat; stir in milk. Spoon over fish. Bake, uncovered, at 350° for 25 minutes or until fish flakes easily with a fork. **Yield:** 6 servings. ***Editor's Note:** Cod, flounder, haddock, ocean perch or any other lean fish can be substituted for the red snapper.

Roasted Pork Loin

(Pictured above)

This roast is great holiday fare, with incredible seasoning. But it's too good to save just for special occasions. It makes a warm, satisfying supper.
—Grace Yaskovic, Branchville, New Jersey

　1/2　cup finely chopped onion
　1/2　cup finely chopped celery
　1/2　cup finely chopped green pepper
　　3　tablespoons butter *or* margarine
　　6　garlic cloves, minced
　　1　teaspoon salt
　　1　teaspoon pepper
　　1　teaspoon onion powder
　　1　teaspoon dried thyme
　　1　teaspoon paprika
　　1　teaspoon ground mustard
　1/2　teaspoon garlic powder
　　1　boneless pork loin roast (4 to 5 pounds)

In a skillet, combine the first 12 ingredients; saute until the vegetables are tender. Untie roast and separate. Randomly cut 20 deep slits, 1 in. wide, on inside surface of roast. Fill slits with some of the vegetable mixture; retie roast. Place on a rack in a shallow baking pan. Spread remaining vegetable mixture over the roast. Bake, uncovered, at 325° for 2-3 hours or until a meat thermometer reaches 160°-170°. Let stand for 10 minutes before slicing. **Yield:** 12-15 servings.

Cheesy Beef Casserole

This hearty casserole tastes like lasagna and makes a satisfying meal when served with a green salad and crusty garlic bread.　—Ardyce Piehl
Wisconsin Dells, Wisconsin

　　4　cups uncooked medium egg noodles
　　1　pound ground beef
　3/4　cup chopped onion
　　2　cans (8 ounces *each*) tomato sauce
　1/2　teaspoon garlic powder
　1/2　teaspoon salt
　1/4　teaspoon pepper
　　1　package (8 ounces) cream cheese, softened
　　1　cup small-curd cottage cheese
　1/2　cup grated Parmesan cheese
　1/3　cup sliced green onions
　1/4　cup chopped green pepper
Additional Parmesan cheese, optional

Cook noodles according to package directions. Meanwhile, in a skillet, cook beef and onion over medium heat until meat is no longer pink; drain. Add tomato sauce, garlic powder, salt and pepper. In a mixing bowl, combine the cream cheese, cottage cheese, Parmesan, onions and green pepper. Drain the noodles; place half in a greased 13-in. x 9-in. x 2-in. baking dish. Top with half of the meat and cheese mixtures. Repeat layers. Sprinkle with additional Parmesan if desired. Cover and bake at 350° for 30-35 minutes or until heated through. **Yield:** 6 servings.

Franks 'n' Cabbage

Getting my kids to eat cabbage is a challenge, so I dress it up with this recipe. The kids like the franks and the creamy, mild mustard sauce. It's an easy, fun meal for the whole family.　—Precious Owens
Elizabethtown, Kentucky

　　1　medium head cabbage, cut into 1-inch pieces
　　1　package (1 pound) hot dogs
　　2　tablespoons butter *or* margarine
　　2　tablespoons all-purpose flour
　1/2　teaspoon salt
1-1/2　cups milk
　　2　tablespoons prepared mustard

Place cabbage in a saucepan; add 1 in. of water. Bring to a boil. Reduce heat; cover and simmer for 6-8 minutes or until crisp-tender. Meanwhile, place 1 in. of water in a skillet. Bring to a boil; add the hot dogs. Remove from the heat; cover and let stand for 7 minutes. For mustard sauce, melt butter in a small saucepan over low heat. Stir in flour and salt until smooth. Gradually add milk and mustard. Bring to a boil; cook and stir for 2 minutes. Drain cabbage and hot dogs; top with the mustard sauce. **Yield:** 4-6 servings.

— ▼ ▼ ▼ —

Mashed Potato Sausage Bake

Sausage and savory seasonings like onion and garlic taste great in this casserole. It's especially satisfying during the colder months. —*Jennifer Seevers*
North Bend, Oregon

☑ Uses less fat, sugar or salt. Includes Nutritional Analysis and Diabetic Exchanges.

  5 medium potatoes, peeled and quartered
1/2 cup light sour cream
1/4 cup low-sodium chicken broth
  1 pound fully cooked light kielbasa *or* Polish sausage, sliced
  8 ounces fresh mushrooms, sliced
  1 cup chopped onion
  1 garlic clove, minced
1/4 cup reduced-fat shredded cheddar cheese
  1 teaspoon dried parsley flakes
  1 teaspoon dried oregano

Place potatoes in a saucepan; cover with water. Bring to a boil; reduce heat. Cover and simmer for 20-25 minutes or until very tender; drain. Transfer to a mixing bowl. Add sour cream and broth; beat on low speed until smooth. In a skillet, cook sausage, mushrooms, onion and garlic until vegetables are tender. Spread half of the potato mixture into a 9-in. x 5-in. x 3-in. loaf pan coated with nonstick cooking spray. Top with sausage mixture and remaining potatoes. Sprinkle with cheese, parsley and oregano. Bake at 350° for 10-15 minutes or until cheese is melted. Serve with a spoon. **Yield:** 7 servings. **Nutritional Analysis:** One serving equals 210 calories, 616 mg sodium, 49 mg cholesterol, 22 gm carbohydrate, 15 gm protein, 7 gm fat, 2 gm fiber. **Diabetic Exchanges:** 1-1/2 meat, 1 starch, 1 vegetable.

— ▼ ▼ ▼ —

Turkey Lime Kabobs

(Pictured at right)

My husband loves to grill these deliciously different turkey kabobs, and everyone gets a kick out of the zingy taste from the limes and jalapenos. Its tongue-tingling combination of flavors makes this one company dish that always draws compliments.
—*Shelly Johnston, Rochester, Minnesota*

  3 cans (6 ounces *each*) orange juice concentrate, thawed
1-1/4 cups lime juice
  1 cup honey
  4 to 5 jalapeno peppers, seeded and chopped*
 10 garlic cloves, minced
  3 tablespoons ground cumin
  2 tablespoons grated lime peel
  1 teaspoon salt
  2 pounds boneless turkey, chicken *or* pork, cut into 1-1/4-inch cubes
  4 medium sweet red *or* green peppers, cut into 1-inch pieces
  1 large red onion, cut into 1-inch pieces
  3 small zucchini, cut into 3/4-inch slices
  8 ounces fresh mushrooms
  3 medium limes, cut into wedges

In a bowl, combine the first eight ingredients; mix well. Pour half of marinade into a large resealable plastic bag; add meat and turn to coat. Pour remaining marinade into another large resealable plastic bag. Add vegetables and turn to coat. Seal and refrigerate for 8 hours or overnight, turning occasionally. Drain meat, discarding marinade. Drain vegetables, reserving marinade for basting. On metal or soaked bamboo skewers, alternate meat, vegetables and lime wedges. Grill, uncovered, over medium heat for 4-5 minutes on each side. Baste with reserved marinade. Continue turning and basting for 10-12 minutes or until meat juices run clear and vegetables are tender. **Yield:** 8 servings. ***Editor's Note:** When cutting or seeding hot peppers, use rubber or plastic gloves to protect your hands. Avoid touching your face.

Sausage Potato Lasagna

(Pictured below)

I decided to pair up two of my favorites—lasagna and potatoes—in this scrumptious dish. Sliced potatoes take the place of noodles, and the comforting blend of flavors is sure to please anyone with a hearty appetite.
—Melissa Pokorny, Abbotsford, British Columbia

       1/2 **pound bulk Italian sausage**
         2 **cups sliced fresh mushrooms**
         4 **medium potatoes, peeled and thinly sliced**
         1 **package (10 ounces) frozen chopped spinach, thawed and well drained**
   1-1/2 **cups ricotta cheese**
       1/4 **cup grated Parmesan cheese**
         1 **egg, beaten**
         1 **medium onion, chopped**
         2 **garlic cloves, minced**
         2 **tablespoons butter *or* margarine**
         2 **tablespoons all-purpose flour**
Salt and pepper to taste
       1/4 **teaspoon ground nutmeg**
   1-1/2 **cups milk**
         1 **cup (4 ounces) shredded mozzarella cheese, *divided***
Additional nutmeg, optional

In a skillet, cook sausage and mushrooms over medium heat until meat is no longer pink; drain and set aside. Place potatoes in a saucepan; cover with water. Bring to a boil. Reduce heat; cover and cook for 5 minutes or until crisp-tender. Drain and set aside. In a bowl, combine the spinach, ricotta, Parmesan and egg; set aside. In a saucepan, saute onion and garlic in butter until tender. Stir in flour, salt, pepper and nutmeg until blended. Gradually add milk. Bring to a boil; cook and stir for 2 minutes. Remove from the heat. Layer half of the potatoes in a greased 11-in. x 7-in. x 2-in. baking dish. Top with half of the spinach mixture, sausage mixture, white sauce and mozzarella. Layer with the remaining potatoes, spinach mixture, sausage mixture and white sauce. Cover and bake at 350° for 30-35 minutes or until potatoes are tender. Sprinkle with the remaining mozzarella. Bake, uncovered, 5 minutes longer or until cheese is melted. Let stand 15 minutes before cutting. **Yield:** 6-8 servings.

— 🍵 🍵 🍵 —

Gingered Pork Tenderloin

Ginger, onions and garlic pack a flavorful punch paired with pork tenderloin. These tasty medallions smothered in golden caramelized onions are a simple and satisfying main dish. *—Rebecca Evanoff Holden, Massachusetts*

         2 **large onions, thinly sliced**
         4 **teaspoons olive *or* vegetable oil**
       1/4 **cup water**
         1 **teaspoon ground ginger *or* 4 teaspoons minced fresh gingerroot**
         2 **garlic cloves, minced**
       1/2 **cup apple jelly**
         1 **pork tenderloin (1 pound)**
       1/4 **teaspoon salt**
Hot cooked rice pilaf *or* rice

In a skillet, saute onions in oil and water for 5-6 minutes. Stir in ginger and garlic. Cover and cook for 8-12 minutes or until onions are tender, stirring occasionally. Reduce heat; stir in apple jelly until melted. Cut tenderloin into eight slices; flatten each to 1/2-in. thickness. Sprinkle with salt. In a skillet coated with nonstick spray, saute pork for 4 minutes; turn. Top with reserved onions; cover and cook for 5-7 minutes or until meat juices run clear. Serve with rice pilaf. **Yield:** 2-3 servings.

— 🍵 🍵 🍵 —

Tropical Turkey Meat Loaf

I modified another recipe to come up with this wonderful, moist meat loaf. The pineapple-jalapeno picante is a sweet and tangy topping. *—Frances Page Ontario, California*

✓ Uses less fat, sugar or salt. Includes Nutritional Analysis and Diabetic Exchanges.

Egg substitute equivalent to 2 eggs
         1 **can (8 ounces) unsweetened crushed pineapple, undrained, *divided***

3 tablespoons light soy sauce
1 teaspoon sugar
3/4 teaspoon ground ginger
1/2 teaspoon ground mustard
1/4 teaspoon garlic powder
1 cup dry bread crumbs
1-1/2 pounds ground turkey breast
1 tablespoon finely chopped onion
1 green onion, finely chopped
2 teaspoons finely chopped jalapeno pepper*
1 teaspoon honey
1 teaspoon lime juice
Pinch pepper

In a bowl, combine egg substitute, 1/3 cup pineapple and the seasonings. Add bread crumbs; mix well. Crumble meat over mixture; mix well. Press into an 8-in. x 4-in. x 2-in. loaf pan coated with nonstick cooking spray. Top with 1 tablespoon pineapple. Bake at 350° for 1-1/4 hours or until a meat thermometer reads 180°. Let stand 5 minutes before serving. Meanwhile, in a small bowl, combine onions, jalapeno, honey, lime juice, pepper and remaining pineapple. Serve with the meat loaf. **Yield:** 8 servings (2/3 cup sauce). **Nutritional Analysis:** One serving equals 174 calories, 387 mg sodium, 25 mg cholesterol, 15 gm carbohydrate, 24 gm protein, 2 gm fat, 1 gm fiber. **Diabetic Exchanges:** 3 very lean meat, 1 fruit. ***Editor's Note:** When cutting or seeding hot peppers, use rubber or plastic gloves to protect your hands. Avoid touching your face.

Pat chicken dry with paper towels. Combine the oregano, seasoned salt and pepper; rub over chicken. In a skillet over medium heat, brown the chicken in butter; transfer to a 5-qt. slow cooker. Add water, lemon juice, garlic and bouillon to the skillet; bring to a boil, stirring to loosen browned bits. Pour over chicken. Cover and cook on low for 3-4 hours. Baste the chicken. Add parsley. Cover and cook 15-30 minutes longer or until meat juices run clear. If desired, thicken cooking juices and serve over chicken and rice. **Yield:** 6 servings.

Slow-Cooked Lemon Chicken

(Pictured above right)

Garlic, oregano and lemon juice give spark to this memorable main dish. It's easy to fix—just brown the chicken in a skillet, then let the slow cooker do the work. I like to serve this dish to company.
—Walter Powell, Wilmington, Delaware

6 bone-in chicken breast halves (about 3 pounds), skin removed
1 teaspoon dried oregano
1/2 teaspoon seasoned salt
1/4 teaspoon pepper
2 tablespoons butter *or* margarine
1/4 cup water
3 tablespoons lemon juice
2 garlic cloves, minced
1 teaspoon chicken bouillon granules
2 teaspoons minced fresh parsley
Hot cooked rice

Homemade Egg Substitute

This tasty alternative to whole eggs is perfect for folks who need to watch their diets. It scrambles up fluffy and delicious.
—June Formanek
Belle Plaine, Iowa

✓ Uses less fat, sugar or salt. Includes Nutritional Analysis and Diabetic Exchanges.

3 egg whites
2 tablespoons instant nonfat dry milk powder
1 teaspoon water
2 to 3 drops yellow food coloring, optional

In a small bowl, combine all ingredients; mix well. Use as a substitute for eggs. **Yield:** 1 serving (equivalent to 2 eggs). **Nutritional Analysis:** One serving equals 64 calories, 156 mg sodium, 2 mg cholesterol, 5 gm carbohydrate, 10 gm protein, trace fat, 0 fiber. **Diabetic Exchanges:** 1 very lean meat, 1/2 skim milk.

ginger in oil for 2 minutes. Add the pears; stir-fry for 1 minute or until pepper is crisp-tender. Remove and keep warm. Stir-fry half of the pork at a time for 1-2 minutes or until meat is no longer pink. Return the pear mixture and all of the pork to pan. Add water chestnuts and reserved sauce. Bring to a boil; cook and stir for 2 minutes. Add the peas and heat through. Sprinkle with almonds. Serve over rice. **Yield:** 4 servings. **Nutritional Analysis:** One serving (prepared with light soy sauce and reduced-sugar apricot fruit spread instead of plum preserves; calculated without rice) equals 368 calories, 563 mg sodium, 67 mg cholesterol, 45 gm carbohydrate, 28 gm protein, 9 gm fat, 8 gm fiber. **Diabetic Exchanges:** 3 lean meat, 1-1/2 fruit, 1 starch, 1 vegetable.

Pork and Pear Stir-Fry

(Pictured above)

I've served this full-flavored stir-fry for years, always to rave reviews. Tender pork and ripe pears make a sweet combination, and a spicy sauce adds plenty of zip. This dish is a must for help-yourself luncheons or fellowship dinners. —Betty Phillips
French Creek, West Virginia

✓ Uses less fat, sugar or salt. Includes Nutritional Analysis and Diabetic Exchanges.

   1/2 cup plum preserves
    3 tablespoons soy sauce
    2 tablespoons lemon juice
    1 tablespoon prepared horseradish
    2 teaspoons cornstarch
   1/4 teaspoon crushed red pepper flakes
    1 medium sweet yellow *or* green pepper, julienned
   1/8 to 1/4 teaspoon ground ginger *or* 1/2 to 1 teaspoon minced fresh gingerroot
    1 tablespoon vegetable oil
    3 medium ripe pears, peeled and sliced
    1 pound pork tenderloin, cut into 1/4-inch strips
    1 can (8 ounces) sliced water chestnuts, drained
1-1/2 cups fresh *or* frozen snow peas
    1 tablespoon sliced almonds, toasted
Hot cooked rice

In a bowl, combine the first six ingredients; set aside. In a skillet or wok, stir-fry yellow pepper and

Fruit-Pecan Pork Roast

This spectacular roast was a huge hit with members of the cooking club I belong to. The sweet, tangy fruit glaze looks lovely and is a wonderful complement to the juicy pork. It's a family favorite for holidays.
—Gay Flynn, Bellevue, Nebraska

    1 rolled boneless pork loin roast (3-1/2 pounds)
   1/2 cup chopped green onions
    4 tablespoons butter *or* margarine, *divided*
   1/4 cup orange juice
    1 bay leaf
    1 can (16 ounces) whole-berry cranberry sauce
   1/2 cup chicken broth
   1/2 cup chopped pecans
    1 tablespoon cider *or* red wine vinegar
   1/4 teaspoon salt
   1/8 teaspoon pepper
   1/8 teaspoon sugar
   1/4 cup apricot preserves

Place roast on a rack in a shallow roasting pan. Bake, uncovered, at 350° for 1 hour. Meanwhile, in a skillet, saute onions in 1 tablespoon of butter for 1 minute. Add orange juice and bay leaf; cook and stir over medium-high heat until thickened, about 4 minutes. Add the cranberry sauce, broth, pecans and vinegar; cook and stir until slightly thickened, about 5 minutes. Reduce heat; stir in the salt, pepper, sugar and remaining butter until butter is melted. Discard bay leaf. Remove 1/4 cup sauce and stir in preserves; spoon over roast. Set remaining sauce aside. Bake roast 45 minutes longer or until a meat thermometer reads 160°-170°. Let stand 10-15 minutes before slicing. Serve with reserved sauce. **Yield:** 10-12 servings.

Golden Game Hens

I served game hens at a diplomatic dinner when my wife, Ruth, was the defense attaché at the American Embassy in Budapest, Hungary. They were an appealing choice because they filled a plate and garnered many fine comments.
—Andy Anderson
Graham, Washington

  6 **Cornish game hens (20 ounces** *each***)**
  1 **medium tart apple, sliced**
  1 **medium onion, sliced**
  1/4 **cup butter** *or* **margarine, melted**
  1/4 **cup soy sauce**

Loosely stuff hens with apple and onion. Place on a rack in a shallow baking pan. Combine butter and soy sauce; brush over hens. Bake, uncovered, at 350° for 50-60 minutes or until a meat thermometer reads 165° and juices run clear, basting occasionally. **Yield:** 6 servings.

——— 🥤 🥤 🥤 ———

Creamy Beef Lasagna

(Pictured on page 72)

The creamy Stroganoff-like filling in this distinctive lasagna makes it a stick-to-your-ribs entree.
—Jane Frawley, Charles Town, West Virginia

1-1/2 **pounds ground beef**
  2 **cans (15 ounces** *each***) tomato sauce**
  1/4 **cup chopped onion**
  2 **teaspoons sugar**
  2 **teaspoons salt**
  2 **teaspoons Worcestershire sauce**
  1/2 **teaspoon garlic salt**
  2 **packages (8 ounces** *each***) cream cheese, softened**
  1 **cup (8 ounces) sour cream**
  1/4 **cup milk**
  18 **lasagna noodles, cooked and drained**
  1 **cup (4 ounces) shredded cheddar cheese**
Minced fresh parsley, optional

In a skillet, cook beef over medium heat until no longer pink; drain. Stir in tomato sauce, onion, sugar, salt, Worcestershire sauce and garlic salt. In a mixing bowl, beat cream cheese, sour cream and milk until smooth. In a greased 13-in. x 9-in. x 2-in. baking dish, layer a fourth of the meat sauce, six noodles and a third of the cream cheese mixture. Repeat layers twice. Top with the remaining meat sauce. Cover and bake at 350° for 40 minutes. Uncover; sprinkle with cheddar cheese. Bake 5 minutes or until the cheese is melted. Let stand 15 minutes before cutting. Sprinkle with parsley if desired. **Yield:** 12 servings.

Rabbit Gumbo

(Pictured below)

My husband's family has enjoyed this satisfying gumbo for many years. Bold seasonings and savory sausage slices enhance the mild meat. John doesn't do much hunting anymore, but we still enjoy this Cajun dish on cool evenings.
—Marie Reine
St. Amant, Louisiana

  1 **small onion, chopped**
  1 **small green pepper, chopped**
  1/4 **cup vegetable oil**
  1 **dressed rabbit (about 3 pounds), cut into pieces**
  1/2 **pound smoked sausage, halved and cut into 1/4-inch slices**
  1 **teaspoon salt**
  1/2 **teaspoon dried thyme**
  1/4 **teaspoon pepper**
  1/4 **teaspoon cayenne pepper**
  1/2 **cup sliced okra**
Hot cooked rice

In a Dutch oven, saute the onion and green pepper in oil until tender. Add rabbit and enough water to cover. Cover and simmer for 1-1/2 to 2 hours or until meat is very tender. Add the sausage, salt, thyme, pepper and cayenne. Simmer, uncovered, for 15-20 minutes. Remove rabbit; cool. Debone and cut into bite-size pieces; return to pan. Stir in okra; bring to a boil. Serve in bowls over hot cooked rice. **Yield:** 4-6 servings.

Traditional Lasagna

(Pictured below)

My family first tasted this rich, classic lasagna at a friend's home on Christmas Eve. We were so impressed that it became our own holiday tradition as well. I also prepare it other times of the year. It's requested often by my sister's Italian in-laws—I consider that the highest compliment!
—Lorri Foockle
Granville, Illinois

   1 pound ground beef
3/4 pound bulk pork sausage
   3 cans (8 ounces *each*) tomato sauce
   2 cans (6 ounces *each*) tomato paste
   2 garlic cloves, minced
   2 teaspoons sugar
   1 teaspoon Italian seasoning
   1 teaspoon salt
1/2 teaspoon pepper
   3 eggs
   3 tablespoons minced fresh parsley
   3 cups (24 ounces) small-curd cottage cheese
   1 carton (8 ounces) ricotta cheese
1/2 cup grated Parmesan cheese
   9 lasagna noodles, cooked and drained
   6 slices provolone cheese
   3 cups (12 ounces) shredded mozzarella cheese, *divided*

In a skillet, cook beef and sausage over medium heat until no longer pink; drain. Add the next seven ingredients. Simmer, uncovered, for 1 hour, stir-

LOVE THAT LASAGNA! Chicken Chili Lasagna and Traditional Lasagna (shown above, top to bottom) stack up well when you need to feed a hungry crowd.

ring occasionally. In a bowl, combine the eggs, parsley, cottage cheese, ricotta and Parmesan. Spread 1 cup of meat sauce in an ungreased 13-in. x 9-in. x 2-in. baking dish. Layer with three noodles, provolone cheese, 2 cups cottage cheese mixture, 1 cup mozzarella, three noodles, 2 cups meat sauce, remaining cottage cheese mixture and 1 cup mozzarella. Top with the remaining noodles, meat sauce and mozzarella (dish will be full). Cover and bake at 375° for 50 minutes. Uncover; bake 20 minutes longer. Let stand 15 minutes before cutting. **Yield:** 12 servings.

———— 🥄 🥄 🥄 ————

Chicken Chili Lasagna

(Pictured at left)

This saucy lasagna is my adaptation of a chicken enchilada recipe. My husband and I enjoy the mild blend of seasonings, cheeses and tender chicken. The dish has become very popular with my co-workers after I shared leftovers one day for lunch. —Cindee Rolston
St. Marys, West Virginia

  2 packages (3 ounces *each*) cream cheese, softened
  1 medium onion, chopped
  8 green onions, chopped
  2 cups (8 ounces) shredded Mexican-cheese blend, *divided*
  2 garlic cloves, minced
  3/4 teaspoon ground cumin, *divided*
  1/2 teaspoon minced fresh cilantro *or* parsley
  3 cups cubed cooked chicken
  1/4 cup butter *or* margarine
  1/4 cup all-purpose flour
1-1/2 cups chicken broth
  1 cup (4 ounces) shredded Monterey Jack cheese
  1 cup (8 ounces) sour cream
  1 can (4 ounces) chopped green chilies, drained
  1/8 teaspoon dried thyme
  1/8 teaspoon salt
  1/8 teaspoon pepper
 12 flour tortillas (6 inches), halved

In a mixing bowl, combine cream cheese, onions, 1-1/2 cups Mexican-cheese blend, garlic, 1/4 teaspoon cumin and cilantro. Stir in chicken; set aside. In a saucepan, melt butter. Stir in flour until smooth; gradually add broth. Bring to a boil; cook and stir for 2 minutes or until thickened. Remove from the heat. Stir in Monterey Jack cheese, sour cream, chilies, thyme, salt, pepper and remaining cumin. Spread 1/2 cup of the cheese sauce in a greased 13-in. x 9-in. x 2-in. baking dish. Top with six tortilla halves, a third of the chicken mixture and a fourth of the cheese sauce. Repeat tortilla, chicken and cheese sauce layers twice. Top with remaining tortillas, cheese sauce and Mexican cheese. Cover and bake at 350° for 30 minutes. Uncover; bake 10 minutes longer or until heated through. Let stand 5 minutes before cutting. **Yield:** 12 servings.

———— 🥄 🥄 🥄 ————

Very Veggie Lasagna

I concocted this quick and easy recipe to use up some of the abundant fresh produce from my garden. When I made a batch to share at a church potluck, I received lots of compliments. —Berniece Baldwin
Glennie, Michigan

  2 medium carrots, julienned
  1 medium zucchini, cut into 1/4-inch slices
  1 yellow summer squash, cut into 1/4-inch slices
  1 medium onion, sliced
  1 cup broccoli florets
  1/2 cup sliced celery
  1/2 cup julienned sweet red pepper
  1/2 cup julienned green pepper
  2 garlic cloves, minced
  1 teaspoon salt
  2 tablespoons vegetable oil
  1 jar (28 ounces) spaghetti sauce
 14 lasagna noodles, cooked and drained
  4 cups (16 ounces) shredded mozzarella cheese

In a large skillet, stir-fry the vegetables, garlic and salt in oil until crisp-tender. Spread 3/4 cup spaghetti sauce in a greased 13-in. x 9-in. x 2-in. baking dish. Arrange seven noodles over sauce, overlapping as needed. Layer with half of the vegetables, spaghetti sauce and cheese. Repeat layers. Cover and bake at 350° for 60-65 minutes or until bubbly. Let stand for 15 minutes before cutting. **Yield:** 12 servings.

🥄 *Lasagna Lessons*

Try replacing a quarter of the mozzarella cheese in your lasagna recipe with shredded sharp cheddar.

When covering cheese-topped lasagna with foil before baking, coat the underside of the foil with nonstick cooking spray. That way the melted cheese won't come off with the foil.

Freeze individual pieces of leftover lasagna in an airtight container for a quick lunch or dinner later.

In a large resealable plastic bag, combine the first six ingredients; add beef. Seal and refrigerate for 2 hours or overnight, turning occasionally. Drain and discard marinade. Broil or grill steak, uncovered, over medium heat for 4-6 minutes on each side or until meat reaches desired doneness (for rare, a meat thermometer should read 140°; medium, 160°; well-done, 170°). Combine salsa ingredients in a bowl. Cut steak across the grain into thin slices. Serve with salsa. **Yield:** 4-6 servings. ***Editor's Note:** When cutting or seeding hot peppers, use rubber or plastic gloves to protect your hands. Avoid touching your face.

Steak with Citrus Salsa

(Pictured above and on page 72)

A lime juice marinade really perks up grilled steaks. This snappy, light citrus salsa is a super change from the usual heavy steak sauce. I brighten up winter meals by broiling the meat and serving it this way.
—*Kathleen Smith, Pittsburgh, Pennsylvania*

- 1/2 cup soy sauce
- 1/4 cup chopped green onions
- 3 tablespoons lime juice
- 2 tablespoons brown sugar
- 1/8 teaspoon hot pepper sauce
- 1 garlic clove, minced
- 1-1/2 pounds boneless sirloin steak (about 1 inch thick)

SALSA:
- 2 navel oranges, peeled, sectioned and chopped
- 1/4 cup chopped green onions
- 2 tablespoons orange juice
- 2 tablespoons cider *or* red wine vinegar
- 2 tablespoons chopped lemon
- 1 tablespoon chopped lime
- 1 tablespoon sugar
- 1 tablespoon minced fresh cilantro *or* parsley
- 1 teaspoon minced jalapeno pepper*
- 1/2 teaspoon grated lemon peel
- 1/2 teaspoon grated lime peel
- 1/8 teaspoon salt

Orange-Glazed Pork Loin

This is one of the best pork recipes I've tried. My family looks forward to this roast for dinner, and guests always want the recipe. The flavorful rub and a glaze sparked with orange juice are also good on pork chops.
—*Lynnette Miete, Alna, Maine*

- 1 teaspoon salt
- 1 garlic clove, minced
- 1/4 teaspoon dried thyme
- 1/4 teaspoon ground ginger
- 1/4 teaspoon pepper
- 1 rolled boneless pork loin roast (about 5 pounds)

GLAZE:
- 1/4 cup packed brown sugar
- 1 tablespoon cornstarch
- 1 cup orange juice
- 1/3 cup water
- 1 tablespoon Dijon mustard

Combine the salt, garlic, thyme, ginger and pepper; rub over entire roast. Place roast with fat side up on a rack in a shallow roasting pan. Bake, uncovered, at 350° for 2 hours. Meanwhile, in a saucepan, combine brown sugar and cornstarch. Stir in the remaining glaze ingredients until smooth. Bring to a boil; cook and stir for 2 minutes. Brush some of the glaze over roast. Bake 1 hour longer or until a meat thermometer reads 160°, brushing occasionally with glaze. Let stand for 10 minutes before slicing; serve with remaining glaze. **Yield:** 12-16 servings.

Sweet 'n' Sour Meat Loaf

I found this down-home recipe in a cookbook published by patrons and friends of the small independent school where I teach third grade.
—*Tia Yeatts Tappahannock, Pennsylvania*

2 cups water
5 tablespoons brown sugar
5 tablespoons vinegar
2 tablespoons cornstarch
2 tablespoons corn syrup
2 tablespoons soy sauce
1 teaspoon salt
MEAT LOAF:
2 eggs
2 teaspoons Worcestershire sauce
1 cup dry bread crumbs
1/2 cup chopped onion
2 teaspoons salt
1/2 teaspoon pepper
2 pounds lean ground beef
1/2 pound ground pork

In a saucepan, combine the first seven ingredients; bring to a boil. Cook and stir for 2 minutes or until thickened; set aside. In a large bowl, combine the first six meat loaf ingredients; add 2/3 cup of the reserved sauce and mix well. Crumble beef and pork over mixture and mix well. Pat into two greased 8-in. x 4-in. x 2-in. loaf pans. Pour the remaining sauce over loaves. Bake, uncovered, at 350° for 50 minutes or until meat is no longer pink and a meat thermometer reads 160°-170°. Let stand for 10 minutes before slicing. **Yield:** 2 loaves (5 servings each).

Nutty Turkey Slices

This is a flavorful way to dress up turkey breast slices. You can really taste the walnuts in the crunchy golden coating, and there's just a hint of lemon.
—Nancy Schmidt, Center, Colorado

3/4 cup ground walnuts
1/4 cup grated Parmesan cheese
1/2 teaspoon Italian seasoning
1/2 teaspoon paprika
6 turkey breast slices (about 1 pound)
3 tablespoons butter *or* margarine
1 teaspoon cornstarch
1/2 cup chicken broth
2 teaspoons lemon juice

In a shallow bowl, combine the walnuts, Parmesan cheese, Italian seasoning and paprika. Coat both sides of turkey slices with crumb mixture. In a large skillet over medium heat, brown half of the turkey at a time in butter for 6-8 minutes or until juices run clear; remove and keep warm. Combine the cornstarch, broth and lemon juice until smooth; add to skillet. Stir to loosen browned bits and bring to a boil; cook and stir for 1 minute. Serve with turkey slices. **Yield:** 3-6 servings.

Chicken in Pear Sauce

(Pictured below)

Pairing poultry with pears brought applause from my husband and four children. Simple enough for everyday meals and ideal for company, this dish is a year-round standout. We enjoy it with boiled potatoes.
—Andrea Lunsford, Spokane, Washington

4 boneless skinless chicken breast halves
1/2 teaspoon salt
1/8 teaspoon white pepper
2 tablespoons vegetable oil
5 thick-cut bacon strips, diced
1 can (14-1/2 ounces) chicken broth
2 to 3 medium ripe pears, peeled and diced
2 tablespoons cornstarch
2 tablespoons cold water
1/4 cup snipped chives

Sprinkle chicken with salt and pepper. In a skillet over medium heat, cook chicken in oil on both sides for about 10 minutes or until juices run clear. Meanwhile, in a saucepan, cook bacon until crisp. Drain, reserving 1 tablespoon drippings; set bacon aside. Gradually stir broth into the drippings, scraping pan to loosen browned bits. Bring to a boil. Boil, uncovered, for 5 minutes. Add pears; return to a boil. Boil, uncovered, for 5 minutes or until pears are tender. Combine cornstarch and water until smooth; add the chives. Gradually stir into pear sauce; bring to a boil. Cook and stir for 2 minutes or until thickened and bubbly. Stir in bacon. Serve over the chicken. **Yield:** 4 servings.

Turkey Ravioli Lasagna

(Pictured below)

I came up with this "shortcut" lasagna one day when the dinner hour was fast approaching and all I had in the freezer was some frozen ravioli. Now I make it often, and my husband and son devour it.
—Anne Plesmid, Sagamore Hills, Ohio

- 1 pound ground turkey *or* beef
- 1/2 teaspoon garlic powder
- Salt and pepper to taste
- 1 cup grated carrots
- 1 cup sliced fresh mushrooms
- 1 tablespoon olive *or* vegetable oil
- 1 jar (28 ounces) spaghetti sauce
- 1 package (25 ounces) frozen cheese ravioli, cooked and drained
- 3 cups (12 ounces) shredded mozzarella cheese
- 1/2 cup grated Parmesan cheese
- Minced fresh parsley, optional

In a skillet, cook turkey over medium heat until no longer pink; drain. Sprinkle with garlic powder, salt and pepper; set aside. In a saucepan, cook carrots and mushrooms in oil until tender. Stir in the spaghetti sauce. Spread 1/2 cup sauce in a greased 13-in. x 9-in. x 2-in. baking dish. Layer with half of the ravioli, spaghetti sauce mixture, turkey and cheeses. Repeat layers. Sprinkle with parsley if desired. Cover and bake at 375° for 25-30 minutes or until bubbly. Uncover; bake 10 minutes longer. Let stand 15 minutes before serving. **Yield:** 12 servings.

———— 🥄 🥄 🥄 ————

Avocado Chicken Casserole

Avocados look luscious in this easy layered casserole, and they melt in your mouth. —Martha Sue Stroud
Clarksville, Texas

- 1/4 cup butter *or* margarine
- 1/4 cup all-purpose flour
- 1/2 teaspoon salt
- 1/4 teaspoon *each* garlic powder, onion powder, dried basil, marjoram and thyme
- 1-1/2 cups milk
- 1 cup half-and-half cream
- 8 ounces medium egg noodles, cooked and drained
- 3 medium ripe avocados, peeled and sliced
- 3 cups cubed cooked chicken
- 2 cups (8 ounces) shredded cheddar cheese

In a large saucepan, melt butter; stir in flour and seasonings until smooth. Gradually add milk and cream. Bring to a boil; cook and stir for 2 minutes. Remove from the heat. In a greased 13-in. x 9-in. x 2-in. baking dish, layer half of the noodles, avocados, chicken, white sauce and cheese. Repeat layers. Cover and bake at 350° for 20-25 minutes. Uncover; bake 5 minutes longer or until bubbly. **Yield:** 6 servings.

———— 🥄 🥄 🥄 ————

Chops with Mushroom Gravy

After driving my family crazy trying new recipes, I always return to this standby. These moist, comforting pork chops come out great every time. We love the rich gravy over the chops and mashed potatoes.
—Loraine Van Broeck, Geneva, Illinois

- 1/2 cup all-purpose flour
- 1 to 2 teaspoons paprika
- 1-1/2 teaspoons salt
- 1/4 teaspoon pepper
- 6 to 8 boneless pork loin chops (1 inch thick)
- 1/4 cup butter *or* margarine
- 1 medium onion, chopped
- 1/2 cup chopped green pepper
- 1 can (4 ounces) mushroom stems and pieces, drained
- 2 cups milk
- 2 tablespoons lemon juice
- Hot mashed potatoes

In a large resealable plastic bag, combine the first four ingredients. Add pork chops, one at a time; toss to coat. Set remaining flour mixture aside. In a large skillet, saute chops in butter until golden brown; transfer to a greased 13-in. x 9-in. x 2-in. baking dish. In the same skillet, saute the onion, green pepper and mushrooms until tender. Stir in reserved flour mixture; gradually add milk until blended. Bring to a boil; cook and stir for 2 minutes or until thickened. Remove from the heat; stir in lemon juice. Pour over chops. Cover and bake at 350° for 50-60 minutes or until the meat is no longer pink. Serve with mashed potatoes. **Yield:** 6-8 servings.

———— 🍵 🍵 🍵 ————

Canadian Meat Pie

(Pictured at right)

This hearty meat pie has a filling seasoned with a tasty combination of herbs and spices and is topped with a flaky golden crust. Called tourtiere, it's a dish traditionally served by French Canadians following midnight Mass on Christmas Eve. —_Sue Paquin_
Waterbury, Connecticut

> 2 cups all-purpose flour
> 1 teaspoon salt
> 2/3 cup plus 2 tablespoons shortening
> 1 egg, beaten
> 2 to 3 tablespoons cold water
> Milk
> FILLING:
> 3/4 pound ground beef
> 3/4 pound ground pork
> 1 medium onion, chopped
> 1 garlic clove, minced
> 1/4 cup water
> 1 teaspoon salt
> 1/2 teaspoon rubbed sage
> 1/2 teaspoon dried thyme
> 1/4 teaspoon ground allspice
> 1/4 teaspoon pepper
> 1/8 teaspoon ground cloves

In a bowl, combine flour and salt. Cut in shortening until the mixture resembles coarse crumbs. Add egg and water; toss lightly with a fork until dough forms a ball. Divide dough in half; refrigerate. In a skillet over medium heat, cook beef, pork, onion and garlic until meat is no longer pink; drain. Stir in remaining ingredients; heat through. On a floured surface, roll out one portion of dough. Line a 9-in. pie plate with bottom pastry. Spoon filling into crust. Roll out remaining dough to fit top of pie. Place over filling. Seal and flute edges. Brush pastry with milk; cut slits in top. Bake at 375° for

30-35 minutes or until golden brown, covering edges loosely with foil if necessary. Let stand for 15 minutes before cutting. **Yield:** 8 servings.

Pork and Onion Kabobs

A sweet and savory marinade brings out the best in pork, as these grilled kabobs prove. They're a super supper, easy to prepare and fun to serve to company. The pork is so tasty grilled with onion wedges.
—_Mary Lou Wayman, Salt Lake City, Utah_

> 1/2 cup soy sauce
> 1/4 cup chili sauce
> 1/4 cup honey
> 2 tablespoons olive _or_ vegetable oil
> 2 teaspoons curry powder
> 2 tablespoons finely chopped onion
> 2 pounds boneless pork, cut into cubes
>   (1-inch pieces)
> 3 medium onions, cut into 1-inch wedges

In a bowl, combine the first six ingredients. Remove half for basting; cover and refrigerate. Add pork to the remaining marinade; toss to coat. Cover and refrigerate for 3 hours or overnight. Drain and discard the marinade. Alternately thread pork cubes and onion wedges on metal or soaked bamboo skewers. Grill, uncovered, over medium heat for 5 minutes; turn. Baste with reserved marinade. Continue turning and basting for 15 minutes or until meat juices run clear. **Yield:** 6 servings.

Polynesian Kabobs

With their explosion of flavors and textures, these kabobs make a quick, satisfying entree. I've also served them as a fun appetizer. —*Chris Anderson*
Morton, Illinois

✓ Uses less fat, sugar or salt. Includes Nutritional Analysis and Diabetic Exchanges.

> 1 can (8 ounces) unsweetened pineapple chunks
> 1 package (12 ounces) light pork breakfast sausage links
> 1 can (8 ounces) whole water chestnuts, drained
> 1 large sweet red pepper, cut into 1-inch chunks
> 2 tablespoons honey
> 2 teaspoons light soy sauce
> 1/8 teaspoon ground nutmeg
> Dash pepper

Drain pineapple, reserving 1 tablespoon juice (discard remaining juice or save for another use). Thread sausages, water chestnuts, pineapple and red pepper alternately onto 12 metal or soaked bamboo skewers. Grill kabobs, uncovered, over medium-hot heat for 7 minutes. In a small bowl, combine honey, soy sauce, nutmeg, pepper and reserved pineapple juice. Turn kabobs; brush with honey mixture. Grill 5-6 minutes longer or until the sausages are browned. **Yield:** 6 servings (2 kabobs each). **Nutritional Analysis:** One serving equals 147 calories, 531 mg sodium, 43 mg cholesterol, 14 gm carbohydrate, 11 gm protein, 6 gm fat, 2 gm fiber. **Diabetic Exchanges:** 1 meat, 1 vegetable, 1/2 fruit.

Sausage Bean Burritos

(Pictured above)

Like my mother and grandmother, I'm a frugal cook. I purchase meats in bulk, including sausage. This is one creative way I've found to use sausage in a main dish. Our children often request these burritos.
—*Eleanor Chlan, Ellicott City, Maryland*

> 3/4 pound bulk pork sausage
> 1/2 cup chopped green pepper
> 1/3 cup chopped onion
> 1 can (15 ounces) black beans, rinsed and drained
> 1-1/2 cups cooked long grain rice
> 1-1/2 cups salsa, *divided*
> 10 flour tortillas (7 inches)
> 1 cup (4 ounces) shredded cheddar cheese, *divided*

In a large saucepan, cook sausage, green pepper and onion over medium heat until meat is no longer pink; drain. Stir in beans, rice and 1 cup salsa; mix well. Spread about 1/2 cup sausage mixture down the center of each tortilla; sprinkle with 1 tablespoon cheese. Roll up and place, seam side down, in a greased 13-in. x 9-in. x 2-in. baking dish. Top with remaining salsa. Cover and bake at 350° for 30 minutes. Uncover; sprinkle with remaining cheese. Bake 5-10 minutes longer or until cheese is melted. **Yield:** 10 burritos.

German Lasagna

Sausage and sauerkraut are a palate-pleasing pair, especially in lasagna. My once skeptical family now clamors for second helpings of this hearty entree.
—*Naomi Hochstetler, Woodburn, Indiana*

> 3/4 cup butter *or* margarine
> 3/4 cup all-purpose flour
> 1 tablespoon beef bouillon granules
> 2 teaspoons onion salt
> 2 teaspoons pepper, *divided*
> 1/2 teaspoon white pepper, optional
> 2-1/4 cups milk
> 1 can (14-1/2 ounces) chicken broth
> 1 pound smoked kielbasa *or* Polish sausage, chopped
> 2 eggs
> 1 carton (12 ounces) small-curd cottage cheese

9 lasagna noodles, cooked and drained
1 jar (16 ounces) sauerkraut, rinsed and squeezed dry
2 cups (8 ounces) shredded Monterey Jack cheese, *divided*

In a saucepan, melt butter. Stir in the flour, bouillon, onion salt, 1 teaspoon pepper and white pepper if desired until smooth. Gradually stir in milk and broth. Bring to a boil; cook and stir for 2 minutes or until thickened. Add sausage; heat through. Combine the eggs, cottage cheese and remaining pepper. Spread 1 cup sausage mixture in a greased 13-in. x 9-in. x 2-in. baking dish. Layer with three noodles, a third of the sausage mixture, half of the cottage cheese mixture and sauerkraut and 3/4 cup Monterey Jack. Repeat layers. Top with the remaining noodles and sausage mixture (dish will be full). Cover and bake at 350° for 50-60 minutes or until bubbly. Sprinkle with the remaining Monterey Jack. Bake 5 minutes longer or until cheese is melted. Let stand for 15 minutes before cutting. **Yield:** 12 servings.

———— 🝙 🝙 🝙 ————

Baked Seafood Avocados

Everyone who tastes this wonderful dish is surprised that the avocados are baked. I especially enjoy making this for a luscious luncheon.
—Marian Platt, Sequim, Washington.

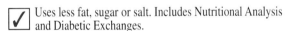 Uses less fat, sugar or salt. Includes Nutritional Analysis and Diabetic Exchanges.

1 cup mayonnaise
3/4 cup chopped celery
1/2 cup thinly sliced green onions
1/8 teaspoon salt, optional
1/8 teaspoon pepper
1 can (4-1/2 ounces) crabmeat, drained, flaked and cartilage removed
1 can (4 ounces) medium shrimp, rinsed and drained
4 large ripe avocados, halved and pitted
1 to 2 tablespoons lemon juice
1/4 cup crushed potato chips, optional

In a bowl, combine the mayonnaise, celery, onions, salt if desired and pepper. Add crab and shrimp; mix well. Peel avocados if desired. Sprinkle avocados with lemon juice; fill with seafood mixture. Sprinkle with potato chips if desired. Place in an ungreased 13-in. x 9-in. x 2-in. baking dish. Bake, uncovered, at 350° for 25-30 minutes or until bubbly. **Yield:** 8 servings. **Nutritional Analysis:** One serving (prepared with light mayonnaise and without salt and potato chips) equals 269 calories,

247 mg sodium, 46 mg cholesterol, 13 gm carbohydrate, 9 gm protein, 22 gm fat, 5 gm fiber. **Diabetic Exchanges:** 3 fat, 1 meat, 1 fruit.

———— 🝙 🝙 🝙 ————

Herbed Chicken Quarters
(Pictured below and on page 72)

I often grill chicken in the summer, and this herbed version is a big hit with our three daughters. A salad and seasoned potatoes make scrumptious complements to the plump, juicy chicken.
—Erika Aylward
Clinton, Michigan

4 medium lemons, cut into wedges
1/2 cup vegetable oil
8 garlic cloves, minced
4 teaspoons minced fresh basil
2 teaspoons minced fresh thyme
2 teaspoons salt
1/2 teaspoon cayenne pepper
1 broiler/fryer chicken (about 3 pounds), quartered

Gently squeeze juice from lemons into a large resealable plastic bag; leave lemon wedges in the bag. Add oil, garlic, basil, thyme, salt and cayenne. Add the chicken and turn to coat. Seal bag and refrigerate for 24 hours, turning frequently. Drain and discard marinade. Grill chicken, covered, over medium heat, turning every 15 minutes, for 1 hour or until juices run clear. **Yield:** 4 servings.

Orange Walnut Chicken

(Pictured below)

For an impressive main dish that's not tricky to prepare, try this mouth-watering chicken. With orange juice concentrate, lemon juice and orange marmalade, the pretty sauce has a zesty taste. —TerryAnn Moore
Haddon Township, New Jersey

- 3 tablespoons orange juice concentrate
- 3 tablespoons vegetable oil, *divided*
- 1 tablespoon soy sauce
- 1 garlic clove, minced
- 4 boneless skinless chicken breast halves
- 1/2 cup coarsely chopped walnuts
- 1 tablespoon butter *or* margarine
- 4 green onions, thinly sliced, *divided*
- 1/2 cup orange marmalade
- 1/2 cup orange juice
- 1/4 cup lemon juice
- 2 tablespoons honey
- 1 to 2 tablespoons grated orange peel
- 2 to 3 teaspoons grated lemon peel
- 1/2 teaspoon salt
- 1/8 teaspoon pepper
Hot cooked rice

In a large resealable plastic bag, combine orange juice concentrate, 2 tablespoons oil, soy sauce and garlic. Add chicken; seal bag and turn to coat. Refrigerate for 2-3 hours. Remove chicken; reserve marinade. In a skillet, cook chicken in remaining oil until juices run clear. Meanwhile, in a saucepan, saute walnuts in butter until lightly browned; remove and set aside. Set aside 1/4 cup green onions for garnish. Add remaining onions to saucepan; saute until tender. Add reserved marinade and the next eight ingredients. Bring to a rolling boil; boil for 2 minutes. Reduce heat; simmer, uncovered, for 5-10 minutes or until sauce reaches desired consistency. Serve chicken over rice; top with sauce and reserved walnuts and onions. **Yield:** 4 servings.

— 🍷 🍷 🍷 —

Golden Catfish Fillets

My grandparents lived on a canal along the Ohio River. When we visited, we couldn't wait for Dad and Grandfather to catch a boatload of catfish so we could have this terrific dinner. This is Grandmother's recipe. —Sharon Stevens, Weirton, West Virginia

- 3 eggs
- 3/4 cup all-purpose flour
- 3/4 cup cornmeal
- 1 teaspoon garlic powder
- 1/2 teaspoon salt
- 1/2 teaspoon pepper
- 5 catfish fillets (4 to 8 ounces *each*)
Oil for frying

In a shallow bowl, beat eggs until foamy. In another shallow bowl, combine flour, cornmeal and seasonings. Dip fillets in eggs, then coat with cornmeal mixture. Heat 1/4 in. of oil in a large skillet; fry fish over medium-high heat for 3-4 minutes on each side or until fish flakes easily with a fork. **Yield:** 6-8 servings.

— 🍷 🍷 🍷 —

Leg of Lamb Dinner

Rosemary and currant jelly give this tender, juicy roast a wonderful flavor. Your house will be filled with the savory aroma of this dinner. —Ruth Andrewson
Peck, Idaho

- 1 leg of lamb (5 to 7 pounds)
- 8 garlic cloves, cut into slivers
- 4 teaspoons minced fresh rosemary, *divided*
- 2 teaspoons ground mustard
- 1-1/2 teaspoons salt, *divided*
- 1 teaspoon chopped fresh mint *or* 1/4 teaspoon dried mint flakes
- 1/4 teaspoon pepper
- 1 tablespoon water
- 3 pounds red potatoes, cut into 1-inch slices
- 1 package (16 ounces) baby carrots
- 2 tablespoons olive *or* vegetable oil
- 3 cups fresh *or* frozen peas
- 3 tablespoons cornstarch
- 1 cup beef broth
- 1/2 cup cold water
- 1/3 to 1/2 cup currant jelly

Remove thin fat layer from roast. Make deep cuts in the meat; insert a garlic sliver in each. Combine 3 teaspoons rosemary, mustard, 1 teaspoon of salt, mint and pepper. Add water; mix well. Rub over meat. Place on a rack in a large roasting pan. Bake, uncovered, at 350° for 1-1/2 hours. Meanwhile, in a bowl, toss potatoes, carrots, oil and remaining rosemary and salt. Place in another greased roasting pan. Bake, uncovered, for 1 to 1-3/4 hours. Baste roast with pan drippings; bake 30 minutes to 2 hours longer or until meat reaches desired doneness (160° for medium-well, 170° for well-done). Add peas to vegetable mixture; bake 10 minutes longer or until vegetables are browned and tender. Remove roast and vegetables to a warm serving platter and keep warm. Strain pan drippings into a saucepan; skim fat. In a small bowl, combine cornstarch, broth and cold water until smooth; add to drippings. Stir in jelly. Bring to a boil; cook and stir for 2 minutes or until thickened. Serve with roast and vegetables. **Yield:** 10-12 servings.

Pork with Mustard Sauce

This is a dressy way to serve pork tenderloin. It has a subtle mint flavor. —Mildred Sherrer, Bay City, Texas

- 3/4 **pound pork tenderloin**
- 1 **tablespoon all-purpose flour**
- 3/4 **cup milk**
- 2 **to 3 teaspoons finely chopped fresh mint**
  or 1/2 to 3/4 teaspoon dried mint flakes
- 3 **tablespoons Dijon mustard**
- 2 **tablespoons chicken broth**
- 1/4 **cup sour cream**
- 1/8 **teaspoon pepper**

Place pork on a greased rack in a roasting pan. Bake, uncovered, at 375° for 40-45 minutes or until a meat thermometer reads 160°-170°. Let stand 5 minutes before slicing. Meanwhile, combine flour, milk and mint in a small saucepan until blended. Bring to a boil over medium heat; cook and stir for 2 minutes. Stir in mustard and broth; remove from the heat. Whisk in sour cream and pepper. Serve with the pork. **Yield:** 2-3 servings.

Easter Brunch Lasagna

(Pictured above right)

Ham, broccoli and hard-cooked eggs are terrific together in this unique brunch lasagna. I came up with the recipe for a family gathering. Muffins and fresh fruit are all I add to nicely round out the meal.
—Sarah Larson, La Farge, Wisconsin

- 1/2 **cup butter *or* margarine**
- 1/3 **cup all-purpose flour**
- 1/4 **teaspoon salt**
- Dash white pepper
- 3 **cups milk**
- 1/4 **cup finely chopped green onions**
- 1 **teaspoon lemon juice**
- 1/4 **teaspoon hot pepper sauce**
- 9 **lasagna noodles, cooked and drained**
- 2 **cups diced fully cooked ham**
- 1 **package (10 ounces) frozen chopped broccoli, thawed**
- 1/2 **cup grated Parmesan cheese**
- 3 **cups (12 ounces) shredded cheddar cheese**
- 4 **hard-cooked eggs, finely chopped**

In a heavy saucepan, melt butter over medium heat. Stir in flour, salt and pepper until smooth. Gradually add milk. Bring to a boil; cook and stir for 2 minutes or until thickened. Remove from the heat; stir in onions, lemon juice and hot pepper sauce. Spread a fourth of the white sauce in a greased 13-in. x 9-in. x 2-in. baking dish. Top with three noodles, half of the ham and broccoli, 3 tablespoons Parmesan cheese, 1 cup cheddar cheese, half of the eggs and a fourth of the white sauce. Repeat layers. Top with the remaining noodles, white sauce and cheeses. Bake, uncovered, at 350° for 40-45 minutes or until bubbly. Let stand 15 minutes before cutting. **Yield:** 12 servings.

Corn-Stuffed Butterfly Chops

(Pictured above)

Corn stuffing is a delicious twist in this old family recipe from an aunt. I fix these chops for special meals with scalloped potatoes, coleslaw and pickled beets. My family and friends always compliment my cooking when I make them. —Marie Dragwa Simpson, Pennsylvania

1-1/2 cups frozen corn, thawed
1-1/2 cups soft bread crumbs
1 tablespoon minced fresh parsley
1 tablespoon finely chopped onion
3/4 teaspoon rubbed sage
3/4 teaspoon salt
1/4 teaspoon pepper
1 egg
3 tablespoons milk
4 bone-in pork loin chops (1-1/2 inches thick)
2 tablespoons vegetable oil
1/4 cup water

In a bowl, combine the first seven ingredients. In another bowl, lightly beat the egg and milk; stir into the corn mixture. Cut a pocket in each chop almost to the bone. Stuff about 1/4 cup corn mixture into each chop; secure with toothpicks. In a large skillet, cook the chops in oil until browned on both sides. Transfer to a greased 13-in. x 9-in. x 2-in. baking dish; add water. Cover and bake at 350° for 1 hour or until a thermometer inserted into the stuffing reads 160°-170°. Discard toothpicks. **Yield:** 4 servings.

Cranberry Chicken

In this tasty recipe, tender baked chicken gets dressed up for the holidays with a chunky spiced fruit sauce. —Linda Rock, Stratford, Wisconsin

✓ Uses less fat, sugar or salt. Includes Nutritional Analysis and Diabetic Exchanges.

6 boneless skinless chicken breast halves (1-1/2 pounds)
1 can (16 ounces) whole-berry cranberry sauce
1 large tart apple, peeled and chopped
1/2 cup raisins
1/4 cup chopped walnuts
1 teaspoon curry powder

Place chicken in a 13-in. x 9-in. x 2-in. baking dish coated with nonstick cooking spray. Bake, uncovered, at 350° for 20 minutes. Meanwhile, combine the remaining ingredients. Spoon over chicken. Bake, uncovered, 20-25 minutes longer or until chicken juices run clear. **Yield:** 6 servings. **Nutritional Analysis:** One serving equals 334 calories, 81 mg sodium, 73 mg cholesterol, 42 gm carbohydrate, 28 gm protein, 6 gm fat, 2 gm fiber. **Diabetic Exchanges:** 4 very lean meat, 3 fruit.

Zucchini Beef Lasagna

This fresh-tasting and mildly seasoned Italian entree is a real crowd-pleaser. —Brenda Tumasone Newhall, California

✓ Uses less fat, sugar or salt. Includes Nutritional Analysis and Diabetic Exchanges.

1 pound lean ground beef
2 garlic cloves, minced
2 cans (8 ounces *each*) no-salt-added tomato sauce
1/2 cup water
1 can (6 ounces) tomato paste
2 bay leaves
1 teaspoon minced fresh parsley
1 teaspoon Italian seasoning
1 package (16 ounces) lasagna noodles, cooked, rinsed and drained
1 cup fat-free cottage cheese
1 small zucchini, sliced and cooked
1 cup (8 ounces) light sour cream

In a skillet, cook the beef and garlic over medium heat until meat is no longer pink; drain. Add the tomato sauce, water, tomato paste, bay leaves, parsley and Italian seasoning; mix well. Bring to a boil; reduce heat. Simmer, uncovered, for 30-40 minutes. Discard bay leaves. Spread 1/2 cup meat sauce in a 13-in. x 9-in. x 2-in. baking dish coated with nonstick cooking spray. Arrange five noodles over sauce, cutting to fit. Spread with cottage cheese. Cover with five noodles, half of the meat sauce and the zucchini. Cover with five noodles and sour cream. Top with the remaining noodles and meat sauce. Bake, uncovered, at 350° for 30-35 minutes or until heated through. Let stand for 15 minutes before cutting. **Yield:** 12 servings. **Nutritional Analysis:** One serving equals 187 calories, 270 mg sodium, 21 mg cholesterol, 19 gm carbohydrate, 14 gm protein, 8 gm fat, 2 gm fiber. **Diabetic Exchanges:** 1 starch, 1 lean meat, 1 vegetable, 1/2 fat.

——— 🍵 🍵 🍵 ———

Jambalaya Pasta

My husband liked this dish at a restaurant, so we decided to re-create it at home. Guests frequently comment on how appetizing it looks and how great it tastes.
—*Christy Leonhard, Durham, North Carolina*

✓ Uses less fat, sugar or salt. Includes Nutritional Analysis and Diabetic Exchanges.

- 1/2 cup *each* chopped onion, green pepper and sweet red pepper
- 1/3 cup chopped celery
- 1 tablespoon butter *or* margarine
- 1 can (14-1/2 ounces) Italian diced *or* stewed tomatoes, undrained
- 1 can (14-1/2 ounces) chicken broth
- 2/3 cup sliced fresh mushrooms
- 1 teaspoon dried basil *or* thyme
- 3 to 4 bay leaves
- 1/4 teaspoon garlic powder
- 1/4 teaspoon pepper
- 1/8 teaspoon cayenne pepper
- 8 ounces spiral pasta
- 2 cups cubed cooked chicken, turkey *or* pork

In a skillet, saute onion, peppers and celery in butter until tender. Stir in tomatoes, broth, mushrooms and seasonings. Bring to a boil; reduce heat. Cover and simmer for 15-20 minutes. Meanwhile, cook pasta according to package directions. Add chicken to tomato mixture; heat through. Drain pasta; add to chicken mixture. Discard bay leaves. **Yield:** 8 servings (2 quarts). **Nutritional Analysis:** One serving (prepared with reduced-fat margarine, no-salt-added stewed tomatoes, low-sodium broth and chicken) equals 167 calories, 62 mg sodium, 22 mg cholesterol, 25 gm carbohydrate, 10 gm protein, 3 gm fat, 2 gm fiber. **Diabetic Exchanges:** 1-1/2 vegetable, 1 starch, 1 lean meat.

——— 🍵 🍵 🍵 ———

'I Wish I Had That Recipe...'

"A FEW YEARS back, I enjoyed the beef Stroganoff at The Founders Inn in Virginia Beach, Virginia," recalls Elizabeth Deguit of Richmond Hill, Georgia. "I can't forget how delicious it was—I hope *Taste of Home* can get the recipe."

Bob Zappatelli, executive chef at The Founders Inn, was happy to comply. "The Stroganoff is occasionally featured as a special entree at the inn's Swan Terrace Restaurant," he says.

"It's easy to prepare and a good dish to serve company. Using tenderloin makes it special."

Situated on 26 acres at I-64 and East Indian River Road, The Founders Inn includes a 240-room hotel, two restaurants and a dinner theater.

The Swan Terrace Restaurant serves from 7 a.m. to 9:30 p.m. daily and features Sunday brunch from 11:30 a.m. to 2 p.m., 1-800/926-4466.

Beef Tenderloin Stroganoff

- 1-1/2 pounds beef tenderloin, cut into thin strips
- 2 tablespoons all-purpose flour
- 2 tablespoons butter *or* margarine
- 2 tablespoons olive *or* vegetable oil
- 1-1/2 cups beef broth
- 1/4 cup sour cream
- 2 tablespoons tomato paste
- 1/2 teaspoon paprika
- Salt to taste
- Hot cooked noodles

In a shallow bowl or resealable plastic bag, toss beef in flour. In a large skillet, brown beef in butter and oil. Gradually stir in broth. In a bowl, combine the sour cream, tomato paste, paprika and salt. Bring beef mixture to a boil. Reduce heat; slowly stir in sour cream mixture (do not boil). Cook, uncovered, over low heat for 15-20 minutes, stirring frequently. Serve over noodles. **Yield:** 4-6 servings.

——— 🍵 🍵 🍵 ———

Parsley Pesto Spaghetti

This is a fun and tasty way to serve traditional pasta. I adapted it from a recipe I came across years ago.
        —Christine Wilson, Sellersville, Pennsylvania

  1 package (1 pound) spaghetti
  3 cups packed fresh parsley sprigs
  1 cup blanched almonds
  2 to 3 garlic cloves, minced
1-1/4 cups grated Parmesan cheese
  1/2 cup butter *or* margarine, melted
Salt and pepper to taste

Cook spaghetti according to package directions. Meanwhile, place the parsley, almonds and garlic in a food processor or blender; cover and process until finely chopped. Transfer to a large serving bowl; stir in cheese and butter. Drain spaghetti and add to pesto with salt and pepper; toss to coat. **Yield:** 10 servings.

——— 🝆 🝆 🝆 ———

Chicken Wings Fricassee

(Pictured below)

This comforting, old-fashioned dish with flavorful gravy uses inexpensive chicken wings for an impressive dinner that will please everyone.
        —Sundra Lewis, Bogalusa, Louisiana

 12 whole chicken wings (about 2-1/2
      pounds)
  1/3 to 1/2 cup all-purpose flour
  1 teaspoon seasoned salt
  3/4 teaspoon pepper, *divided*
  3 tablespoons vegetable oil

  2 medium onions, chopped
  1 garlic clove, minced
1-1/4 cups water
  1 teaspoon salt
Hot cooked rice

Cut chicken wings into three sections; discard wing tips. In a resealable plastic bag or shallow bowl, combine flour, seasoned salt and 1/2 teaspoon pepper. Add wings; toss to coat evenly. In a large skillet, brown wings on all sides in oil. Add onions and garlic; cook until tender. Stir in the water, salt and remaining pepper; mix well. Bring to a boil; reduce heat. Simmer, uncovered, for 30-35 minutes or until chicken juices run clear. Serve over rice. **Yield:** 4 servings.

——— 🝆 🝆 🝆 ———

Curry Chicken

I discovered this recipe while in college. I used a large-scale version to feed 20 hungry students. Everyone complimented the tasty combination of tomato and spices.   —Tim Buckmaster, Millsboro, Delaware

  1 cup dry bread crumbs
  3/4 teaspoon salt
  1/2 teaspoon paprika
  1/4 teaspoon pepper
  1/8 teaspoon ground ginger
  1 broiler/fryer chicken (3 to 4 pounds),
      cut up
  1/4 cup butter *or* margarine
  1/2 cup chopped green pepper
  1/4 cup chopped onion
  1 garlic clove, minced
  1 can (14-1/2 ounces) stewed tomatoes
  1 to 1-1/2 teaspoons curry powder
  1/2 teaspoon dried thyme
Hot cooked rice

In a shallow bowl, combine the bread crumbs, salt, paprika, pepper and ginger; coat chicken pieces. In a large skillet, brown chicken in butter. Transfer to a greased 13-in. x 9-in. x 2-in. baking dish; set aside. In the same skillet, saute the green pepper, onion and garlic until tender. Stir in tomatoes, curry and thyme. Pour over chicken. Bake, uncovered, at 350° for 30-35 minutes or until juices run clear. Serve over rice. **Yield:** 4-6 servings.

——— 🝆 🝆 🝆 ———

Fennel Stuffed Cod

Moist fish, a super stuffing and a creamy sauce make for a memorable main dish.   —Mary Ellen Wilcox
                          Scotia, New York

☑ Uses less fat, sugar or salt. Includes Nutritional Analysis and Diabetic Exchanges.

1 cup (8 ounces) plain yogurt
2-1/4 cups finely chopped fennel fronds, *divided*
1 teaspoon lemon juice
1 teaspoon snipped chives
1/8 teaspoon salt, optional
1/8 teaspoon pepper
2 celery ribs, chopped
1/4 cup chopped onion
2 to 4 tablespoons vegetable oil
4 cups stuffing croutons
1 cup chicken broth
2 eggs, beaten
4 cod or flounder fillets (1-1/2 pounds)
1 medium lemon, sliced

For sauce, combine yogurt, 1/4 cup of fennel, lemon juice, chives, salt if desired and pepper in a bowl. Cover and refrigerate for 2 hours or overnight. In a skillet, saute celery and onion in oil until tender. Remove from the heat. Stir in croutons, broth, eggs and remaining fennel. Spoon about 1 cup stuffing mixture onto each fillet; roll fish around stuffing. Transfer to a greased 2-qt. baking dish. Top each with a lemon slice. Bake at 350° for 30-35 minutes or until fish flakes easily with a fork and a thermometer inserted into stuffing reads 160°. Serve with the fennel sauce. **Yield:** 4 servings. **Nutritional Analysis:** One serving (prepared with 2 tablespoons oil, low-sodium broth and low-fat yogurt) equals 371 calories, 411 mg sodium, 142 mg cholesterol, 33 gm carbohydrate, 30 gm protein, 13 gm fat, 4 gm fiber. **Diabetic Exchanges:** 4 lean meat, 2 starch.

— 🥄 🥄 🥄 —

Seafood Tortilla Lasagna

(Pictured above right)

My husband and I enjoy lasagna, seafood and Mexican fare. One evening, I combined all three into this deliciously different entree. It certainly is a tempting, memorable change of pace from traditional Italian-style lasagnas. —Sharon Sawicki, Carol Stream, Illinois

1 jar (20 ounces) picante sauce
1-1/2 pounds uncooked medium shrimp, peeled and deveined
4 to 6 garlic cloves, minced
1/8 teaspoon cayenne pepper
1 tablespoon olive *or* vegetable oil
1/3 cup butter *or* margarine
1/3 cup all-purpose flour
1 can (14-1/2 ounces) chicken broth
1/2 cup whipping cream

15 corn tortillas (6 inches), warmed
1 package (16 ounces) imitation crabmeat, flaked
3 cups (12 ounces) shredded Colby/ Monterey Jack cheese

Place the picante sauce in a blender or food processor; cover and process until smooth. Set aside. In a skillet, cook the shrimp, garlic and cayenne in oil until shrimp turn pink, about 3 minutes; remove and set aside. In the same skillet, melt the butter. Stir in flour until smooth. Gradually add the broth. Bring to a boil; cook and stir for 2 minutes or until thickened. Reduce heat. Stir in cream and picante sauce; heat through. Spread 1/2 cup of sauce in a greased 13-in. x 9-in. x 2-in. baking dish. Layer with six tortillas, half of the shrimp, crab and white sauce and 1-1/4 cups cheese. Repeat layers. Tear or cut the remaining tortillas; arrange over cheese. Sprinkle with remaining cheese. Bake, uncovered, at 375° for 30-35 minutes or until bubbly. Let stand 15 minutes before cutting. **Yield:** 12 servings.

🥄 *Keen on Quiche?*

Before filling the pastry shell for quiche, lightly brush the inside with honey mustard. It makes each slice sweet and spicy—especially in a ham, Swiss cheese and spinach quiche.

let, saute onion and garlic in remaining butter until tender. Stir in flour until blended. Gradually stir in broth, mustard, thyme and 2 tablespoons parsley. Bring to a boil; cook and stir for 2 minutes or until thickened. Stir in pork; heat through. Pour over the potato crust. Pipe or spoon remaining mashed potatoes over top. Bake, uncovered, at 375° for 35-40 minutes or until the potatoes are lightly browned. Sprinkle with remaining parsley. **Yield:** 6 servings.

— 🍴 🍴 🍴 —

Mandarin Pork Roast

(Pictured on page 72)

I've taught university-level English for more than 40 years, but cooking is my first love. This spectacular roast is juicy and tender with delightful seasonings and a beautiful glaze. —*Grady Walker*
Tulsa, Oklahoma

  2 teaspoons dried rosemary, crushed
  4 garlic cloves, minced
  1 teaspoon pepper
  1 bone-in pork loin roast (about 5 pounds)
  1 can (11 ounces) mandarin oranges, drained
GLAZE:
  1/2 cup orange marmalade
  6 tablespoons orange juice concentrate
  1/4 cup soy sauce
  1/4 cup ketchup
  2 tablespoons honey
2-1/4 teaspoons ground mustard
1-1/2 teaspoons ground ginger
  2 garlic cloves, minced

Combine rosemary, garlic and pepper; rub over roast. Place roast, fat side up, on a rack in a shallow roasting pan. Bake, uncovered, at 350° for 1-1/4 to 1-1/2 hours. Arrange oranges over roast. Combine glaze ingredients; brush over roast. Bake 30 minutes longer or until a meat thermometer reads 160°-170°, brushing often with glaze. Let stand 10 minutes before slicing. **Yield:** 10-12 servings.

— 🍴 🍴 🍴 —

Chicken Bean Casserole

I love to make this hearty casserole with crisp-tender green beans. It's perfect for leftover chicken. Served with a thick slice of bread, it makes a satisfying meal. —*Darlene Markel, Mt. Hood, Oregon*

  6 tablespoons butter *or* margarine
  6 tablespoons all-purpose flour

Potato Pork Pie

(Pictured above)

A true comfort food that's impossible to resist, this main dish is hearty and saucy with flavors that blend so nicely together. Many shepherd's pie recipes call for beef, so this pork version is a tasty change of pace. —*Michelle Ross, Stanwood, Washington*

  2 pounds potatoes, peeled and cubed
1/3 cup whipping cream
  4 tablespoons butter *or* margarine, *divided*
3/4 teaspoon salt
1/8 teaspoon pepper
  1 medium onion, chopped
  1 garlic clove, minced
1/4 cup all-purpose flour
  1 can (14-1/2 ounces) beef broth
  1 tablespoon Dijon mustard
  1 teaspoon dried thyme
  4 tablespoons minced fresh parsley, *divided*
2-1/2 cups cubed cooked pork

Place potatoes in a saucepan and cover with water; bring to a boil. Cover and cook for 20-25 minutes or until very tender. Drain well. Mash potatoes with cream, 2 tablespoons butter, salt and pepper. Spread 1-1/2 cups of mashed potatoes into a greased shallow 1-1/2-qt. baking dish. In a skil-

1-1/2 cups chicken broth
  1/2 cup milk
    1 to 2 teaspoons soy sauce
  1/2 teaspoon salt
Dash pepper
  2/3 cup shredded Parmesan cheese, *divided*
    8 cups fresh cut green *or* wax beans,
      cooked and drained
    2 cups cubed cooked chicken

In a medium saucepan, melt butter. Stir in the flour until smooth. Gradually add the broth, milk, soy sauce, salt and pepper. Bring to a boil; cook and stir for 2 minutes or until thickened. Remove from the heat. Stir in 1/3 cup of the Parmesan cheese until melted. Add the beans and chicken; toss to coat. Transfer to a greased 2-qt. baking dish; sprinkle with the remaining cheese. Bake, uncovered, at 375° for 15-18 minutes or until golden brown. **Yield:** 6-8 servings.

———— 🎀 🎀 🎀 ————

Crab-Stuffed Sole

We live far from the ocean, which makes seafood special to my cattle-ranching family. —*Judie Anglen*
Riverton, Wyoming

    1 cup soft bread crumbs
    1 cup cooked *or* canned crabmeat, drained,
      flaked and cartilage removed
    1 small onion, finely chopped
    1 egg, lightly beaten
  1/2 teaspoon salt
Dash cayenne pepper
    4 sole, flounder *or* pike fillets (about 1
      pound)
    3 tablespoons butter *or* margarine, melted,
      divided
    1 tablespoon all-purpose flour
  1/2 cup chicken broth
Grated Parmesan cheese
Sliced almonds

In a bowl, combine bread crumbs, crab, onion, egg, salt and cayenne. Spoon onto fillets; roll up and secure with a toothpick. Place in a greased 2-qt. broiler-proof dish; drizzle with 2 tablespoons butter. Bake, uncovered, at 350° for 25-30 minutes or until fish flakes easily with a fork. Meanwhile, for sauce, place remaining butter in a saucepan. Stir in flour until smooth. Gradually add broth. Bring to a boil; cook and stir for 2 minutes or until thickened and bubbly. Drain liquid from baking dish. Spoon sauce over fillets; sprinkle with cheese and almonds. Broil 5 in. from the heat until cheese is melted and almonds are lightly browned. Discard toothpicks. **Yield:** 4 servings.

Italian Chicken Skillet

(Pictured below)

Hearty and well-seasoned, this delicious chicken is sure to appeal to all palates. —*Shirley Thompson*
Lane, Oklahoma

✓ Uses less fat, sugar or salt. Includes Nutritional Analysis and Diabetic Exchanges.

    8 bone-in chicken breast halves, skin
      removed
  3/4 cup sliced celery
  3/4 cup chopped green pepper
  1/4 cup chopped onion
    1 can (4 ounces) mushroom stems and
      pieces, drained
    2 cans (14-1/2 ounces *each*) no-salt-added
      stewed tomatoes
    1 teaspoon dried parsley flakes
    1 teaspoon vinegar
  1/2 teaspoon garlic powder
  1/2 teaspoon dried basil
  1/2 teaspoon dried oregano
  1/4 teaspoon pepper

In a large skillet coated with nonstick cooking spray, saute chicken over medium heat until browned. Remove and keep warm. In the same skillet, saute celery, green pepper, onion and mushrooms until tender. Return chicken to pan. Combine the remaining ingredients; pour over chicken and vegetables. Cover and simmer for 30 minutes. Uncover; simmer 10 minutes longer or until chicken juices run clear. **Yield:** 8 servings. **Nutritional Analysis:** One serving equals 184 calories, 147 mg sodium, 73 mg cholesterol, 9 gm carbohydrate, 28 gm protein, 3 gm fat, 3 gm fiber. **Diabetic Exchanges:** 3 very lean meat, 2 vegetable.

Pesto Pizza

Once a week, a good friend of mine fixes supper for me, my husband and our two daughters. We always request the same thing—her great pizza! —Arlyn Kantz
Fort Worth, Texas

1/2 cup olive *or* vegetable oil
4 whole garlic cloves
1-1/2 cups lightly packed fresh basil leaves
1 prebaked Italian bread shell crust
Shredded mozzarella cheese, sliced tomato, ripe olives and fresh mushrooms *or* toppings of your choice

In a blender, combine oil and garlic; cover and process until smooth. Add basil and blend thoroughly. Spread over crust. Sprinkle with toppings. Bake at 425° for 10 minutes. **Yield:** 6-8 servings.

Pepperoni Lasagna

(Pictured below)

I've served this satisfying lasagna for years—when our children were small, they preferred it more than a steak dinner! Now I bring a pan when I visit my grandkids. —Barbara McIntosh, Midland, Texas

1-1/2 pounds ground beef
1 small onion, chopped
2-1/2 cups water
1 can (8 ounces) tomato sauce
1 can (6 ounces) tomato paste
1 teaspoon beef bouillon granules
1 tablespoon dried parsley flakes
2 teaspoons Italian seasoning
1 teaspoon salt
1/4 teaspoon garlic salt
2 eggs
1 carton (12 ounces) small-curd cottage cheese
1/2 cup sour cream
8 lasagna noodles, cooked and drained
1 package (3-1/2 ounces) sliced pepperoni
2 cups (8 ounces) shredded mozzarella cheese
1/2 cup grated Parmesan cheese

In a skillet, cook beef and onion over medium heat until meat is no longer pink; drain. Add water, tomato sauce, tomato paste, bouillon and seasonings. Bring to a boil. Reduce heat; simmer, uncovered, for 30 minutes. In a bowl, combine eggs, cottage cheese and sour cream. Spread 1/2 cup meat sauce into a greased 13-in. x 9-in. x 2-in. baking dish. Layer with four noodles, the cottage cheese mixture and pepperoni. Top with remaining noodles and meat sauce. Sprinkle with mozzarella and Parmesan cheeses. Cover and bake at 350° for 35 minutes. Uncover; bake 10 minutes longer or until heated through. Let stand 15 minutes before cutting. **Yield:** 12 servings.

Scallops with Spinach Noodles

This delightful dish lets the delicate taste of the scallops come through. —Audrey Thibodeau
Gilbert, Arizona

1 pound bay scallops
1/4 cup milk
3 large tomatoes, peeled and diced
1 bay leaf
1/4 teaspoon salt
Dash pepper
8 ounces spinach noodles
3/4 cup all-purpose flour
2 garlic cloves, minced
3 tablespoons butter *or* margarine
2 tablespoons minced fresh parsley

Place scallops and milk in a bowl; set aside. In a saucepan, simmer tomatoes for 3 minutes. Remove tomatoes with a slotted spoon and set aside. Bring tomato liquid to a boil; cook, uncovered, until liquid is reduced by half. Add bay leaf, salt, pepper and tomatoes; set aside. Cook noodles according to package directions. Meanwhile, drain scallops; pat with paper towels until dry. Lightly coat scallops in flour. In a large skillet, cook scallops and garlic in butter until scallops are opaque, about 4 minutes. Discard bay leaf from tomato sauce; add

to scallops. Drain noodles; toss with scallops. Sprinkle with parsley. **Yield:** 5 servings. **Nutritional Analysis:** One serving (prepared with skim milk and reduced-fat margarine) equals 358 calories, 375 mg sodium, 30 mg cholesterol, 52 gm carbohydrate, 24 gm protein, 6 gm fat, 6 gm fiber. **Diabetic Exchanges:** 3-1/2 starch, 2 lean meat.

Prime Rib of Beef

This roast made its debut a few years back at Christmastime, when I made it instead of our traditional turkey dinner. Now we have a new tradition everyone looks forward to. —Tim Buckmaster
Millsboro, Delaware

  1/3 **cup _each_ chopped onion, carrot and**
       celery
    2 **teaspoons salt**
  1/2 **teaspoon pepper**
  1/2 **teaspoon garlic powder**
    1 **beef rib roast (6 to 8 pounds)**
    1 **can (14-1/2 ounces) beef broth**

Combine onion, carrot and celery; place in a greased roasting pan. Combine salt, pepper and garlic powder; rub over the roast. Place fat side up over vegetables. Bake, uncovered, at 350° for 2-1/2 to 3-1/2 hours or until meat reaches desired doneness (medium-rare, 145°; medium, 160°; well-done, 170°). Let stand for 10-15 minutes before carving. Skim fat from pan drippings; add beef broth, stirring to remove browned bits. Strain, discarding vegetables. Serve au jus with the roast. **Yield:** 8-10 servings.

Fluffy Scrambled Eggs

When our son, Chris, is hungry for something other than cold cereal in the morning, he whips up these eggs. Cheese and evaporated milk make them especially good. He also makes them when we go camping.
—Terry Pfleghaar, Elk River, Minnesota

  6 **eggs**
  1/4 **cup evaporated milk _or_ half-and-half**
       cream
  1/4 **teaspoon salt**
  1/8 **teaspoon pepper**
    1 **tablespoon vegetable oil**
    2 **tablespoons process cheese sauce**

In a bowl, beat eggs, milk, salt and pepper. In a skillet, heat oil; add egg mixture. Stir in cheese sauce. Cook and stir gently over medium heat until eggs are completely set. **Yield:** 3 servings.

Chicken Fajitas

(Pictured above)

The marinated chicken in these popular wraps is mouth-watering. They go together in a snap and always get raves! —Julie Sterchi, Harrisburg, Illinois

    4 **tablespoons vegetable oil, _divided_**
    2 **tablespoons lemon juice**
 1-1/2 **teaspoons seasoned salt**
 1-1/2 **teaspoons dried oregano**
 1-1/2 **teaspoons ground cumin**
    1 **teaspoon garlic powder**
  1/2 **teaspoon chili powder**
  1/2 **teaspoon paprika**
  1/2 **teaspoon crushed red pepper flakes,**
       optional
 1-1/2 **pounds boneless skinless chicken breasts,**
       cut into thin strips
  1/2 **medium sweet red pepper, julienned**
  1/2 **medium green pepper, julienned**
    4 **green onions, thinly sliced**
  1/2 **cup chopped onion**
    6 **flour tortillas (8 inches), warmed**
Shredded cheddar cheese, taco sauce _or_ salsa
  and guacamole _or_ sour cream

In a large resealable plastic bag, combine 2 tablespoons oil, lemon juice and seasonings. Add chicken. Seal and turn to coat; refrigerate for 1-4 hours. In a large skillet, saute peppers and onions in remaining oil until crisp-tender. Remove and keep warm. In the same skillet, cook chicken and marinade over medium-high heat for 5-6 minutes or until meat is no longer pink. Return pepper mixture to pan; heat through. Spoon filling down the center of tortillas; fold in half. Serve with cheese, taco sauce and guacamole. **Yield:** 6 servings.

stir-fry for 2 minutes. Add the corn and peas; stir-fry until vegetables are crisp-tender. Remove and keep warm. Stir-fry pork in remaining oil for 2 minutes. Add the onions, garlic, ginger and chili powder; cook and stir until pork is no longer pink. Remove and keep warm. Combine the water, soy sauce, honey and bouillon in the same pan. Combine cornstarch and cold water; gradually add to pan. Bring to a boil; cook and stir for 2 minutes or until thickened. Return the vegetables and pork mixture to pan; heat through. Stir in the peanuts. Serve over rice. **Yield:** 6 servings. **Nutritional Analysis:** One serving (prepared with frozen corn, light soy sauce, low-sodium bouillon and unsalted dry roasted peanuts; calculated without rice) equals 279 calories, 411 mg sodium, 45 mg cholesterol, 21 gm carbohydrate, 22 gm protein, 13 gm fat, 4 gm fiber. **Diabetic Exchanges:** 2 lean meat, 1-1/2 fat, 1 starch, 1 vegetable. ***Editor's Note:** Whole baby corn may be found in the Oriental food section of many grocery stores.

Pork Veggie Stir-Fry

(Pictured above)

A colorful combination of vegetables, tender pork strips, flavorful seasonings and crunchy peanuts makes this main dish appealing even to kids. Over rice, it's a fresh-tasting complete meal. —Laurel Reisinger Saskatoon, Saskatchewan

✓ Uses less fat, sugar or salt. Includes Nutritional Analysis and Diabetic Exchanges.

    3 cups sliced cauliflower
    3 tablespoons vegetable oil, *divided*
    2 medium carrots, julienned
    1 can (15 ounces) whole baby corn,* rinsed and drained *or* 1-1/2 cups frozen corn, thawed
1/2 cup frozen peas, thawed
    1 pound boneless pork, cut into thin strips
    2 green onions, thinly sliced
    2 garlic cloves, minced
3/4 teaspoon ground ginger *or* 1 tablespoon minced fresh gingerroot
1/2 to 1 teaspoon chili powder
    1 cup water
1/4 cup soy sauce
    4 teaspoons honey
    2 teaspoons chicken bouillon granules
    4 teaspoons cornstarch
    2 tablespoons cold water
1/4 cup salted peanuts
Hot cooked rice

In a large skillet or wok, stir-fry cauliflower in 2 tablespoons oil for 3 minutes. Add the carrots;

Basil Cream Chicken

My family likes basil, and this dish is our favorite. The basil flavor complements the rich, creamy sauce. —Billie Vaughan, Slinger, Wisconsin

1-1/2 pounds boneless skinless chicken breasts, cubed
1-1/3 cups finely chopped green onions
    1 pound fresh mushrooms, sliced
    2 tablespoons vegetable oil
1/2 cup butter *or* margarine
1/4 cup all-purpose flour
    2 cups chicken broth
    1 cup whipping cream
    2 tablespoons minced fresh basil *or* 2 teaspoons dried basil
1/4 teaspoon white pepper
Hot cooked fettuccine

In a skillet, saute chicken, onions and mushrooms in oil until the chicken is no longer pink. Meanwhile, in a large saucepan, melt butter. Stir in flour until smooth. Gradually add broth and cream. Stir in basil and pepper. Bring to a boil; cook and stir for 2 minutes or until thickened. Stir in chicken mixture. Serve over fettuccine. **Yield:** 6-8 servings.

Smoked Sausage and Beans

Kielbasa gives this dish a hearty flavor, and you don't have to spend hours in the kitchen preparing it. —Honore Hudson, Glenwood, Illinois

  2 medium onions, chopped
  2 garlic cloves, minced
  1 tablespoon olive *or* vegetable oil
  1 pound fully cooked smoked sausage, cut into 1/4-inch slices
  3 to 4 cups chicken broth
  1 can (16 ounces) kidney beans, rinsed and drained
  1 can (15-1/2 ounces) great northern beans, rinsed and drained
  1 can (15 ounces) garbanzo beans *or* chickpeas, rinsed and drained
  5 to 6 bay leaves
  1 teaspoon minced fresh parsley
  1 teaspoon ground cumin
Dash hot pepper sauce
Hot cooked rice *or* pasta

In a large skillet, saute onions and garlic in oil until tender. Add sausage; cook and stir until lightly browned. Add broth, beans and seasonings. Cover and simmer for 1 hour, stirring occasionally. Discard bay leaves. Serve in a bowl over rice or pasta. **Yield:** 8 servings. **Nutritional Analysis:** One serving (prepared with low-fat smoked turkey sausage and low-sodium broth; calculated without rice) equals 326 calories, 716 mg sodium, 36 mg cholesterol, 42 gm carbohydrate, 21 gm protein, 9 gm fat, 11 gm fiber. **Diabetic Exchanges:** 2-1/2 starch, 1 meat.

— 🦃 🦃 🦃 —

Barbecued Wild Duck

(Pictured at right)

Our three grown sons still request this finger-licking duck each fall. Basting with the homemade barbecue sauce keeps the meat nice and moist. I've also used this recipe with chicken. —Gloria Wedo
Slayton, Minnesota

  2 wild ducks (1 pound *each*), split in half
1/4 cup butter *or* margarine
1/2 cup ketchup
1/2 cup chopped onion
  1 garlic clove, minced
  5 teaspoons lemon juice
  1 tablespoon brown sugar
  1 tablespoon Worcestershire sauce
  1 teaspoon salt
1/2 teaspoon hot pepper sauce

Place ducks in a 13-in. x 9-in. x 2-in. baking dish. Cover and bake at 350° for 1-3/4 to 2 hours or until tender. Meanwhile, combine the remaining ingredients in a saucepan; bring to a boil. Reduce heat; cover and simmer for 5 minutes. Baste ducks with sauce during the last 30 minutes of baking time. **Yield:** 4 servings.

— 🦃 🦃 🦃 —

Grilled Pork Chops

I enjoy cooking because Mom taught me...now I take pleasure in teaching my son, José. This is a special family recipe with a flavorful marinade. The mouth-watering chops are so easy to make.
—Tim Buckmaster, Millsboro, Delaware

  1 medium onion, finely chopped
1/2 cup water
1/2 cup soy sauce
1/3 cup packed brown sugar
1/4 cup lemon juice
  1 garlic clove, minced
  6 loin pork chops (about 1 inch thick)

In a large heavy-duty resealable plastic bag or shallow glass container, combine the first six ingredients. Set aside 1/3 cup for basting; add pork chops to the remaining marinade. Seal or cover and refrigerate for several hours or overnight. Drain and discard marinade. Grill chops, covered, over medium-hot heat for 4 minutes. Turn; baste with reserved marinade. Grill 4-7 minutes longer or until juices run clear. **Yield:** 6 servings.

Round Up Your Family for Nebraska Beef Dishes

SINCE there are more head of cattle in Nebraska than people, it's no surprise that cattle ranching is the state's largest industry and that beef is a menu mainstay in most kitchens there.

Beef easily lends itself to a wide variety of cooking methods. The best method to use depends on the cut of meat. Here are some quick tips:

High heat can overcook or char the outside of beef cuts while leaving the inside underdone. Use medium heat for dry cooking methods (grilling, roasting, broiling, pan-frying) on tender cuts.

Moderate heat is also used for moist cooking methods (braising and cooking in liquid) on less tender cuts.

Roast Beef with Peppers
(Pictured below)

Having eaten home-raised beef all of my life, I've learned to cook all the various cuts. This flavorful roast gets Italian flair from oregano and garlic.
—*Jeanne Murray, Scottsbluff, Nebraska*

3 tablespoons vegetable oil
1 boneless rump roast (3 pounds)
3 cups hot water
4 teaspoons beef bouillon granules
1 tablespoon dried oregano
1 to 2 garlic cloves, minced

TRAILBLAZIN' TASTES. Rustle up a delicious dinner by serving Sticky Bones, Roast Beef with Peppers or Peppered Steaks with Salsa (shown above, top to bottom).

   1/2 **teaspoon salt**
   1/2 **teaspoon pepper**
     3 **medium bell peppers, julienned**
     3 **tablespoons butter** *or* **margarine**

In a Dutch oven, heat the oil over medium-high heat. Brown roast on all sides; drain. Combine the water, bouillon, oregano, garlic, salt and pepper; pour over roast. Cover and bake at 350° for 3 hours or until meat is tender. Remove roast to a warm serving platter. Let stand 10 minutes before slicing. Meanwhile, in a skillet, saute peppers in butter until tender. Serve peppers and pan juices with the roast. **Yield:** 8-10 servings.

------ 🍴 🍴 🍴 ------

Peppered Steaks with Salsa

(Pictured at left)

We grill all year, and beef is so good cooked outdoors. The simple marinade makes the steaks very juicy. We enjoy them with the refreshing salsa and tortillas. —*Robin Hyde, Lincoln, Nebraska*

   1/2 **cup cider** *or* **red wine vinegar**
     2 **tablespoons lime juice**
     2 **tablespoons olive** *or* **vegetable oil**
     2 **teaspoons chili powder**
     1 **garlic clove, minced**
     1 **to 2 teaspoons crushed red pepper flakes**
     1 **teaspoon salt**
   1/2 **teaspoon pepper**
     4 **boneless chuck eye steaks (about 8 ounces** *each***)**
SALSA:
     1 **large tomato, seeded and chopped**
     1 **medium ripe avocado, chopped**
     2 **green onions, thinly sliced**
     1 **tablespoon lime juice**
     1 **tablespoon minced fresh cilantro** *or* **parsley**
     1 **garlic clove, minced**
   1/4 **to 1/2 teaspoon salt**
   1/4 **teaspoon pepper**

In a large resealable plastic bag or shallow glass container, combine the first eight ingredients; mix well. Remove 1/4 cup for basting; refrigerate. Add steaks to the remaining marinade; turn to coat. Cover and refrigerate 8 hours or overnight. Meanwhile, combine salsa ingredients; cover and chill. Drain steaks, discarding marinade. Grill, covered, over medium heat for 7-8 minutes on each side, basting with reserved marinade, or until meat reaches desired doneness (for rare, a meat thermometer should read 140°; medium, 160°; well-done, 170°). Serve with salsa. **Yield:** 4 servings.

Nebraska Beef Rolls

Cheese and bacon add flavor and moisture to this memorable meat loaf. It will satisfy the whole family.
   —*Marjorie McClun, Louisville, Nebraska*

     2 **eggs, beaten**
   1/4 **cup ketchup**
     2 **tablespoons Worcestershire sauce**
     1 **cup (4 ounces) shredded cheddar cheese**
   1/4 **cup finely chopped onion**
     2 **tablespoons grated Parmesan cheese**
     1 **teaspoon salt**
   1/4 **teaspoon pepper**
     2 **pounds ground beef**
    12 **bacon strips**

In a bowl, combine the first eight ingredients. Add beef and mix well. Shape into two 6-in. rolls. Place six bacon strips side by side on a large sheet of waxed paper. Place one beef roll over bacon. Roll up, wrapping bacon around roll; secure with toothpicks. Repeat. Place in an ungreased 13-in. x 9-in. x 2-in. baking pan. Bake at 375° for 45-50 minutes or until meat is no longer pink and a meat thermometer reads 160°. Discard toothpicks. **Yield:** 8 servings.

------ 🍴 🍴 🍴 ------

Sticky Bones

(Pictured at far left)

I grew up in the heart of Nebraska cattle country and can't remember a time when I didn't cook with beef. I never had a recipe for short ribs that impressed me until this one. —*Berta Joy, Gering, Nebraska*

     1 **cup vinegar**
   1/2 **cup ketchup**
   1/2 **cup honey**
     2 **tablespoons Worcestershire sauce**
     1 **teaspoon salt**
     1 **teaspoon ground mustard**
     1 **teaspoon paprika**
     1 **garlic clove, minced**
   1/4 **teaspoon pepper**
     4 **pounds bone-in beef short ribs**

In a saucepan, combine vinegar, ketchup, honey, Worcestershire sauce, salt, mustard, paprika, garlic and pepper. Bring to a boil. Reduce heat; cover and simmer for 15 minutes. Set aside 1 cup for basting. Place ribs in a greased roasting pan; pour remaining marinade over ribs. Cover and refrigerate for at least 2 hours. Drain and discard marinade. Bake, uncovered, at 325° for 1 hour or until meat is tender, basting frequently with reserved marinade. **Yield:** 4 servings.

until a meat thermometer inserted into pork reads 155°. Brush with marmalade. Bake 5-10 minutes longer or until thermometer reads 160°-170°. Let stand for 5 minutes. Discard toothpicks and slice. **Yield:** 2-3 servings.

Curry Beef Stir-Fry

This hearty, fast and tasty stir-fry has been a menu mainstay in our house for years. We love the crisp vegetables and Oriental-style sauce. I appreciate great-tasting foods that are good for you. —Diana Faulds
Strathroy, Ontario

☑ Uses less fat, sugar or salt. Includes Nutritional Analysis and Diabetic Exchanges.

  1 tablespoon cornstarch
  1 tablespoon light soy sauce
  6 tablespoons cold water, *divided*
  2 tablespoons vegetable oil, *divided*
  1 pound boneless sirloin steak, cut into thin strips
  1 garlic clove, minced
1/8 teaspoon ground ginger *or* 1/2 teaspoon minced fresh gingerroot
  1 small onion, cut into 1/2-inch wedges
  1 cup sliced celery
  1 medium green pepper, cut into 1-inch pieces
  3 medium tomatoes, cut into 1/2-inch wedges
SAUCE:
  1 tablespoon cornstarch
1/2 cup cold water
  3 tablespoons ketchup
  1 tablespoon light soy sauce
  1 teaspoon curry powder
Hot cooked rice

In a large bowl, combine cornstarch, soy sauce, 2 tablespoons water and 1 tablespoon oil until smooth; add beef and toss to coat. In a large skillet or wok, stir-fry beef, garlic and ginger in remaining oil until meat reaches desired doneness. Remove meat with a slotted spoon and keep warm. Add the onion, celery, green pepper and remaining water to the skillet. Cover and cook for 2 minutes. Add tomatoes and beef. For sauce, combine the cornstarch, water, ketchup, soy sauce and curry until smooth; add to the skillet. Bring to a boil; cook and stir for 2 minutes. Serve over rice. **Yield:** 6 servings. **Nutritional Analysis:** One serving (calculated without rice) equals 205 calories, 453 mg sodium, 51 mg cholesterol, 12 gm carbohydrate, 19 gm protein, 9 gm fat, 2 gm fiber. **Diabetic Exchanges:** 2 meat, 2 vegetable.

Pear-Stuffed Tenderloin

(Pictured above)

This succulent entree is a classic you'll be proud to serve your family. There's very little fuss to making this main dish, and the meat always turns out tender.
—Aloma Hawkins, Bixby, Missouri

  1 cup chopped peeled ripe pears
1/4 cup chopped hazelnuts *or* almonds, toasted
1/4 cup soft bread crumbs
1/4 cup finely shredded carrot
  2 tablespoons chopped onion
1/8 teaspoon ground ginger *or* 1/2 teaspoon minced fresh gingerroot
1/4 teaspoon salt
1/4 teaspoon pepper
  1 pork tenderloin (3/4 to 1 pound)
Vegetable oil
  2 tablespoons orange marmalade

In a bowl, combine the first eight ingredients; set aside. Make a lengthwise cut three-quarters of the way through the tenderloin; open and flatten to 1/4-in. thickness. Spread pear mixture over tenderloin. Roll up from a long side; tuck in ends. Secure with toothpicks. Place tenderloin on a rack in a shallow roasting pan. Brush lightly with oil. Bake, uncovered, at 425° for 20-25 minutes or

Kentucky Stuffed Peppers

I learned to cook by helping my mother prepare fabulous meals in our large country kitchen after church. The things I like to make most use the fresh vegetables and fruits from our garden. —Lucille Terry
Frankfort, Kentucky

  4 large sweet red *and/or* yellow peppers
  1 can (14-1/2 ounces) diced tomatoes
  1 large onion, chopped
  2 tablespoons butter *or* margarine
  2 cups cooked rice
  1 cup diced fully cooked ham
  1 jar (4-1/2 ounces) sliced mushrooms, drained
  1 teaspoon sugar
Dash hot pepper sauce
  3/4 cup shredded cheddar cheese

Cut tops off peppers and remove seeds. Place peppers in a large kettle and cover with water. Bring to a boil; cook for 3-5 minutes. Drain and rinse in cold water; set aside. Drain tomatoes, reserving juice; set tomatoes and juice aside. In a skillet, saute onion in butter until tender. Add the rice, ham, mushrooms, sugar, hot pepper sauce and reserved tomatoes; mix well. Loosely spoon into peppers. Place in an ungreased shallow 2-qt. baking dish. Pour reserved tomato juice over peppers. Cover and bake at 350° for 35-40 minutes; sprinkle with cheese. Bake 5 minutes longer or until peppers are tender and cheese is melted. **Yield:** 4 servings.

———— 🍳 🍳 🍳 ————

Whole Wheat Veggie Pizza

(Pictured at right and on page 72)

A wonderful crust layered with herbed tomato sauce and toppings encourages my family of six to dig right in to this low-fat main course. —Denise Warner
Red Lodge, Montana

☑ Uses less fat, sugar or salt. Includes Nutritional Analysis and Diabetic Exchanges.

2-1/2 cups all-purpose flour
  1/2 cup whole wheat flour
  2 packages (1/4 ounce *each*) quick-rise yeast
  1 teaspoon garlic powder
  1/2 teaspoon salt
  1 cup water (120° to 130°)
  2 tablespoons olive *or* vegetable oil
SAUCE:
  1 can (14-1/2 ounces) diced tomatoes, undrained
  1 tablespoon minced fresh parsley
1-1/2 teaspoons sugar

1-1/2 teaspoons Italian seasoning
1-1/2 teaspoons dried basil
  1/2 teaspoon garlic powder
  1/4 teaspoon pepper
TOPPINGS:
  1 cup chopped zucchini
  1 cup sliced fresh mushrooms
  1/4 cup *each* chopped onion, sweet red and green pepper
  1 teaspoon olive *or* vegetable oil
1-1/4 cups shredded reduced-fat mozzarella cheese

In a mixing bowl, combine the first five ingredients. Add water and oil; beat until smooth. Turn onto a floured surface; knead until smooth and elastic, about 5 minutes. Place in a greased bowl, turning once to grease top. Cover and let rise in a warm place until doubled, about 30 minutes. Punch dough down. Divide in half; roll each portion into a 12-in. circle. Transfer to greased 12-in. pizza pans. Prick dough with a fork. Bake at 400° for 8-10 minutes or until lightly browned. Combine sauce ingredients in a saucepan. Bring to a boil; reduce heat. Simmer, uncovered, 15-18 minutes, stirring occasionally. In a skillet, saute vegetables in oil until tender. Spread each pizza with 1 cup sauce (refrigerate the remaining sauce for another use). Sprinkle with vegetables and cheese. Bake for 12-15 minutes or until cheese is melted. **Yield:** 2 pizzas (6 slices each). **Nutritional Analysis:** One slice equals 179 calories, 203 mg sodium, 5 mg cholesterol, 28 gm carbohydrate, 7 gm protein, 5 gm fat, 2 gm fiber. **Diabetic Exchanges:** 1-1/2 starch, 1/2 vegetable, 1/2 fat.

Bacon 'n' Egg Lasagna

(Pictured below)

My sister-in-law served this special dish for Easter breakfast one year, and our whole family loved the mix of bacon, eggs, noodles and cheese. Now I sometimes assemble it the night before and bake it in the morning for a terrific hassle-free brunch entree.
—Dianne Meyer, Graniteville, Vermont

> 1 pound sliced bacon, diced
> 1 large onion, chopped
> 1/3 cup all-purpose flour
> 1/2 to 1 teaspoon salt
> 1/4 teaspoon pepper
> 4 cups milk
> 12 lasagna noodles, cooked and drained
> 12 hard-cooked eggs, sliced
> 2 cups (8 ounces) shredded Swiss cheese
> 1/3 cup grated Parmesan cheese
> 2 tablespoons minced fresh parsley

In a skillet, cook bacon until crisp. Remove with a slotted spoon to paper towels. Drain, reserving 1/3 cup drippings. In the drippings, saute onion until tender. Stir in flour, salt and pepper until blended. Gradually stir in milk. Bring to a boil; cook and stir for 2 minutes. Remove from the heat. Spread 1/2 cup sauce in a greased 13-in. x 9-in. x 2-in. baking dish. Layer with four noodles, a third of the eggs and bacon, Swiss cheese and white sauce. Repeat layers twice. Sprinkle with Parmesan cheese. Bake, uncovered, at 350° for 35-40 minutes or until bubbly. Sprinkle with parsley. Let stand 15 minutes before cutting. **Yield:** 12 servings.

Lazy Pierogi Bake

A favorite dish in our family is pierogi—tasty pockets of dough filled with cottage cheese and onions. Making pierogi is time-consuming, so my mom created this easy casserole. —Sandy Starks, Amherst, New York

> 1 package (16 ounces) spiral pasta
> 1 pound sliced bacon, diced
> 2 medium onions, chopped
> 2 garlic cloves, minced
> 1/2 pound fresh mushrooms, sliced
> 2 cans (14 ounces *each*) sauerkraut, rinsed and well drained
> 3 cans (10-3/4 ounces *each*) condensed cream of mushroom soup, undiluted
> 1/2 cup milk
> 1/2 teaspoon celery seed
> 1/8 teaspoon pepper

Cook pasta according to package directions. Meanwhile, in a skillet, cook bacon until crisp. Remove to paper towels. Drain, reserving 2 tablespoons drippings. In the drippings, saute onions and garlic until tender. Add mushrooms; cook until tender. Stir in sauerkraut and half of the bacon. In a bowl, combine the soup, milk, celery seed and pepper. Drain pasta. Place a fourth of the pasta in two greased 13-in. x 9-in. x 2-in. baking dishes. Top each with a fourth of the sauerkraut and soup mixtures. Repeat layers. Cover and bake at 350° for 25 minutes. Uncover; sprinkle with remaining bacon. Bake 10-15 minutes longer or until heated through. **Yield:** 16 servings.

Four-Seafood Fettuccine

Here's an easy entree that tastes like you spent hours in the kitchen. —Jeri Dobrowski
Beach, North Dakota

> 12 ounces fettuccine
> 2 garlic cloves, minced
> 3 tablespoons butter *or* margarine
> 3 tablespoons all-purpose flour
> 1 cup milk
> 1 can (12 ounces) evaporated milk
> 1 cup cooked *or* canned crabmeat, drained, flaked and cartilage removed
> 1 cup cooked *or* canned lobster, drained and chopped
> 1 can (6-1/2 ounces) chopped clams, drained
> 1 can (4-1/2 ounces) tiny shrimp, drained
> 1/2 cup shredded Parmesan cheese
> 1 tablespoon minced fresh parsley
> 1/4 teaspoon pepper

Cook fettuccine according to package directions. Meanwhile, in a large saucepan, saute garlic in butter. Stir in flour until blended. Gradually add milk and evaporated milk. Bring to a boil; cook and stir for 2 minutes or thickened. Add the crab, lobster, clams, shrimp, Parmesan cheese, parsley and pepper; heat through. Drain fettuccine; top with seafood mixture. **Yield:** 6 servings.

Beef Rouladen

Until I entered kindergarten, we spoke German in our home and kept many old-world customs. We always enjoyed the food of our family's homeland. Mom usually prepared this for my birthday dinner.
—*Helga Schlape, Florham Park, New Jersey*

>   3 pounds boneless beef round steak (1/2 inch thick)
>   1/2 teaspoon salt
>   1/4 teaspoon pepper
>   6 bacon strips
>   3 whole dill pickles, halved lengthwise
>   2 tablespoons vegetable oil
>   2 cups water
>   1 medium onion, chopped
>   2 tablespoons minced fresh parsley
>   2 teaspoons beef bouillon granules, optional
>   1/4 cup all-purpose flour
>   1/2 cup cold water
>   1/2 teaspoon browning sauce, optional

Cut steak into six serving-size pieces; pound to 1/4-in. thickness. Sprinkle with salt and pepper. Place a bacon strip down the center of each piece; arrange a pickle half on one edge. Roll up and secure with a toothpick. In a skillet, heat oil over medium-high heat. Brown beef on all sides. Add water, onion, parsley and bouillon if desired. Bring to a boil. Reduce heat; cover and simmer for 1-1/2 to 2 hours or until meat is tender. Remove to a serving platter and keep warm. For gravy, skim fat from drippings. Combine flour, cold water and browning sauce; stir into drippings. Bring to a boil; cook and stir for 2 minutes or until thickened. Serve with beef. **Yield:** 6 servings.

Pork Loin with Spinach Stuffing

(Pictured above right)

I can't say whether leftovers from this eye-catching roast are good, because we never have any! I've been making this flavorful main dish for years.
—*Lois Kinneberg, Phoenix, Arizona*

>   1 package (10 ounces) frozen chopped spinach, thawed and squeezed dry
>   1/2 cup chopped onion
>   1 garlic clove, minced
>   3 tablespoons butter *or* margarine
>   1 cup soft bread crumbs
>   1/2 teaspoon salt
>   1 boneless pork loin roast (3-1/2 pounds)
>   1/4 cup orange juice
>   2 tablespoons soy sauce
>   1 tablespoon ketchup
>   1 cup (8 ounces) sour cream
>   2 tablespoons prepared horseradish
>   1 teaspoon Dijon mustard
>   1/2 teaspoon seasoned salt
>   1/4 teaspoon dill weed

Set aside 1/2 cup spinach for sauce. In a skillet, saute onion, garlic and remaining spinach in butter until tender. Remove from the heat; stir in bread crumbs and salt. Separate roast into two pieces; spoon spinach mixture onto one piece of meat. Top with the second piece; tie with kitchen string. Place in a shallow roasting pan. Combine the orange juice, soy sauce and ketchup; pour half over roast. Bake, uncovered, at 350° for 1 hour. Baste with remaining orange juice mixture. Cover and bake 1 hour or until a meat thermometer reads 160°-170°. Let stand 10 minutes before slicing. In a saucepan, combine the sour cream, horseradish, mustard, seasoned salt, dill and reserved spinach. Cook over medium heat just until heated through (do not boil). Serve warm with pork. **Yield:** 10-12 servings.

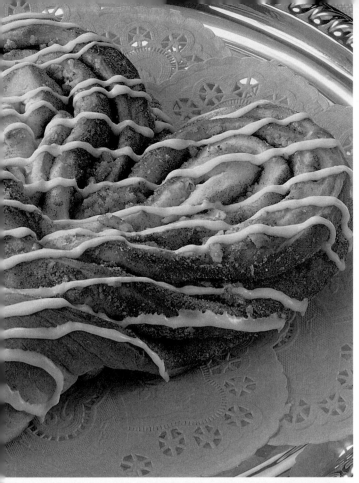

Breads & Muffins

Oven-fresh breads, rolls and muffins make a tasty snack or accompaniment to any meal.

HOME-BAKED GOODIES. Clockwise from upper left: Buttermilk Blueberry Muffins (p. 120), Heart-Shaped Coffee Cake (p. 117), Strawberry Muffin Cones (p. 111) and Cinnamon-Swirl Pear Bread (p. 114).

Tomato Rosemary Focaccia

(Pictured above)

This quick Italian flat bread is a delicious savory snack and is also good with soup or a salad.
—Dorothy Smith, El Dorado, Arkansas

    1 tube (10 ounces) refrigerated pizza crust
    2 tablespoons olive *or* vegetable oil
    2 garlic cloves, minced
 1/4 teaspoon salt
    1 tablespoon minced fresh rosemary *or*
       1 teaspoon dried rosemary, crushed, *divided*
    2 to 3 plum tomatoes, thinly sliced
    1 small red onion, thinly sliced

Unroll pizza crust onto a greased baking sheet. Combine the oil, garlic, salt and half of the rosemary; spread over crust. Top with tomatoes and onion; sprinkle with remaining rosemary. Bake at 425° for 12-15 minutes or until golden. Cut into rectangles. **Yield:** 6 servings.

Walnut Wheat Bread

My husband and I like to eat this wholesome bread warm from the oven. Walnuts give it a nice crunch.
—Rosadene Herold, Lakeville, Indiana

✓ Uses less fat, sugar or salt. Includes Nutritional Analysis and Diabetic Exchanges.

1-1/4 to 1-1/2 cups all-purpose flour
1-1/2 cups whole wheat flour
   3/4 cup chopped walnuts
     2 tablespoons brown sugar
     1 package (1/4 ounce) active dry yeast
     1 teaspoon salt
   3/4 cup water
   1/3 cup plain low-fat yogurt
     2 tablespoons margarine

In a large mixing bowl, combine 3/4 cup all-purpose flour, whole wheat flour, walnuts, brown sugar, yeast and salt. In a saucepan, heat water, yogurt and margarine to 120°-130°; stir into flour mixture. Add enough of the remaining all-purpose flour to form a soft dough. Turn onto a floured surface; knead until smooth and elastic, about 6-8 minutes. Cover and let rise in a warm place until doubled, about 1 hour. Punch dough down. Turn onto a lightly floured surface; divide into thirds. Shape each portion into a 15-in. rope. Place ropes on a greased baking sheet and braid; pinch ends to seal and tuck under. Cover and let rise until doubled, about 30 minutes. Bake at 375° for 23-28 minutes or until golden brown. Remove from pan to cool on a wire rack. **Yield:** 1 loaf (16 slices). **Nutritional Analysis:** One slice equals 133 calories, 167 mg sodium, trace cholesterol, 19 gm carbohydrate, 4 gm protein, 5 gm fat, 2 gm fiber. **Diabetic Exchanges:** 1 starch, 1 fat.

Apple Cinnamon Muffins

Late September is a great time to enjoy the harvest from local apple orchards. Our city hosts the annual Applejack Festival, which draws thousands to try various apple specialties. This is one of my favorites.
—Judi Klee, Nebraska City, Nebraska

1-1/2 cups all-purpose flour
   1/2 cup sugar
1-3/4 teaspoons baking powder
   1/2 teaspoon salt
   1/2 teaspoon ground cinnamon
   1/8 teaspoon ground nutmeg
     1 egg
   1/2 cup milk
     3 tablespoons vegetable oil
     3 tablespoons applesauce
     1 medium tart apple, peeled and grated
TOPPING:
   1/4 cup packed brown sugar
     1 tablespoon all-purpose flour
     2 tablespoons cold butter *or* margarine
   1/2 cup old-fashioned oats
   1/4 cup finely chopped nuts

In a bowl, combine the first six ingredients. In another bowl, combine the egg, milk, oil and applesauce. Stir into dry ingredients just until moistened. Fold in apple. Fill greased or paper-lined muffin cups two-thirds full. For topping, combine brown sugar and flour. Cut in butter until crumbly. Stir in oats and nuts. Sprinkle over muffins. Bake at 400° for 18-22 minutes or until a toothpick comes out clean. Cool for 5 minutes before removing from pan to a wire rack. Serve warm. **Yield:** 1 dozen.

🥣 🥣 🥣

Strawberry Muffin Cones

(Pictured on page 109)

Youngsters love the "ice cream cone" look and ease of eating these muffins. Adults who try them say snacking on these cones makes them feel like kids again!
—Barb Kietzer, Niles, Michigan

      2 cups all-purpose flour
  1/2 cup sugar
      2 teaspoons baking powder
  1/2 teaspoon baking soda
  1/2 teaspoon salt
      2 eggs
      1 carton (6 ounces) strawberry yogurt
  1/2 cup vegetable oil
      1 cup chopped fresh strawberries
    15 cake ice cream cones (about 3 inches tall)
      1 cup (6 ounces) semisweet chocolate chips
      1 tablespoon shortening
Colored sprinkles

In a large bowl, combine the first five ingredients. In another bowl, beat eggs, yogurt, oil and strawberries; stir into dry ingredients just until moistened. Place the ice cream cones in muffin cups; spoon about 3 tablespoon batter into each cone. Bake at 375° for 19-21 minutes or until a toothpick inserted near the center comes out clean. Cool completely. In a saucepan over low heat, melt chocolate chips and shortening; stir until smooth. Dip muffin tops in chocolate; decorate with sprinkles. **Yield:** 15 servings. **Editor's Note:** These muffin cones are best served the same day they're prepared. Muffins can be baked in paper liners instead of ice cream cones.

🥣 🥣 🥣

Cinnamon Love Knots

(Pictured at right)

My sister-in-law and I enjoy these flavorful yeast rolls for breakfast or brunch, served with cups of steaming coffee. —Marlene Fetter, Alpena, Michigan

      2 packages (1/4 ounce *each*) active dry yeast
  1/2 cup warm water (110° to 115°)
  1/2 cup warm milk (110° to 115°)
  1/2 cup butter *or* margarine, softened
  1/2 cup sugar
      2 eggs, beaten
      1 teaspoon salt
4-1/2 to 5 cups all-purpose flour
TOPPING:
      2 cups sugar
      2 tablespoons ground cinnamon
  3/4 cup butter *or* margarine, melted

In a large mixing bowl, dissolve yeast in water. Let stand for 5 minutes. Add milk, butter, sugar, eggs and salt. Stir in enough flour to form a stiff dough. Turn onto a floured surface; knead until smooth and elastic, about 6-8 minutes. Place in a greased bowl, turning once to grease top. Cover and let rise in a warm place until doubled, about 1-1/2 hours. Punch dough down; divide into three portions. Cover two with plastic wrap. Shape one portion into 12 balls. Roll each ball into an 8-in. rope. Combine sugar and cinnamon. Dip rope into melted butter, then coat with cinnamon-sugar. Tie into a knot. Tuck and pinch ends under and place on ungreased baking sheets. Repeat with remaining dough. Cover and let rise until doubled, about 30 minutes. Bake at 375° for 12-14 minutes or until golden brown. **Yield:** 3 dozen.

Specialty Breads for Breakfast

DO YOU have a hard time rousing the sleepyheads in your house every morning? This rise-and-shine selection of sweet and savory waffles, French toast and pancakes is sure to awaken tired taste buds!

— ☕ ☕ ☕ —

Hawaiian Waffles

(Pictured below)

I created this waffle recipe to recapture the memorable tropical tastes we enjoyed while visiting Hawaii.
—Darlene Markel, Stayton, Oregon

    1 can (20 ounces) crushed pineapple,
        undrained
    1/2 cup sugar
    1/2 cup flaked coconut
    1/2 cup light corn syrup
    1/4 cup pineapple juice
WAFFLES:
    2 cups all-purpose flour
    4 teaspoons baking powder
    1 tablespoon sugar
    1/2 teaspoon salt
    2 eggs, *separated*
    1 cup milk
    1/4 cup butter *or* margarine, melted
    1 can (8 ounces) crushed pineapple, well
        drained
    1/4 cup flaked coconut
    1/4 cup chopped macadamia nuts
Additional chopped macadamia nuts, toasted,
    optional

In a saucepan, combine the first five ingredients. Bring to a boil. Reduce heat. Simmer, uncovered, for 12-15 minutes or until sauce begins to thicken; set aside. In a bowl, combine the flour, baking powder, sugar and salt. Combine egg yolks, milk and butter; stir into dry ingredients just until combined. Stir in pineapple, coconut and nuts. Beat egg whites until stiff peaks form; fold into batter (batter will be thick). Preheat waffle iron. Fill and bake according to manufacturer's directions. Top with pineapple sauce and additional nuts if desired. **Yield:** sixteen 4-inch waffles.

— ☕ ☕ ☕ —

Strawberry-Topped Waffles

Topped with a sweet strawberry sauce, these tender from-scratch waffles will make a breakfast or brunch truly special. —Sue Mackey, Galesburg, Illinois

    2 pints fresh strawberries
    5 tablespoons sugar, *divided*
    2 cups all-purpose flour
    2 teaspoons baking powder
    1/2 teaspoon baking soda
    1/2 teaspoon salt
    2 eggs
    2 cups (16 ounces) sour cream
    1 cup milk
    3 tablespoons vegetable oil
Whipped topping *or* vanilla ice cream
Additional strawberries, optional

Place strawberries and 3 tablespoons of sugar in a food processor or blender. Cover and process until coarsely chopped; set aside. In a bowl, combine the flour, baking powder, baking soda, salt and remaining sugar. Combine the eggs, sour cream, milk and oil; stir into dry ingredients just until combined. Preheat waffle iron. Fill and bake according to manufacturer's directions. Serve with strawberry topping, whipped topping and additional strawberries if desired. **Yield:** 6-8 waffles.

— ☕ ☕ ☕ —

Low-Cholesterol Pancakes

When my husband and I developed high cholesterol, I found this great way to convert our favorite pancake recipe. —Dorothy Anne Adams, Valier, Montana

✓ Uses less fat, sugar or salt. Includes Nutritional Analysis and Diabetic Exchanges.

1 cup all-purpose flour
3 tablespoons sugar
1-1/2 teaspoons baking powder
1/2 teaspoon baking soda
1 cup buttermilk
1/4 cup vegetable oil
1 teaspoon vanilla extract
3 egg whites

In a bowl, combine the first four ingredients. In another bowl, combine buttermilk, oil and vanilla; add to dry ingredients. In a mixing bowl, beat egg whites until soft peaks form; fold into batter. Pour batter by 1/4 cupfuls onto a hot griddle coated with nonstick cooking spray. Turn when bubbles form on top of pancakes. Cook until second side is lighly browned. **Yield:** 12 pancakes. **Nutritional Analysis:** One pancake equals 104 calories, 149 mg sodium, 1 mg cholesterol, 12 gm carbohydrate, 3 gm protein, 5 gm fat, trace fiber. **Diabetic Exchanges:** 1 starch, 1 fat.

Bacon and Chive Waffles

These savory waffles are also a deliciously different light supper. —Edie DeSpain, Logan, Utah

1-1/2 cups all-purpose flour
1/2 cup whole wheat flour
1 tablespoon baking powder
1/4 teaspoon onion salt
1/4 teaspoon celery salt
3 eggs, *separated*
1-3/4 cups milk
1/4 cup vegetable oil
1 tablespoon minced fresh parsley
1 tablespoon minced chives
1 teaspoon Worcestershire sauce
1 cup (4 ounces) shredded cheddar cheese
6 bacon strips, cooked and crumbled
Thinly sliced tomato

In a bowl, combine the first five ingredients. In another bowl, combine the egg yolks, milk, oil, parsley, chives and Worcestershire sauce; stir into dry ingredients just until combined. Stir in cheese and bacon. Beat the egg whites until stiff peaks form; fold into batter. Preheat waffle iron. Fill and bake according to manufacturer's directions. Top with tomato slices. **Yield:** 6-8 waffles.

⌡*Warming Waffles*

Keep waffles warm until serving by placing them on a rack set on a baking sheet in a 350° oven.

Orange-Cinnamon French Toast

(Pictured above)

Everyone eats at the same time when you fix this tasty oven-baked French toast. —Bernice Smith
Sturgeon Lake, Minnesota

✓ Uses less fat, sugar or salt. Includes Nutritional Analysis and Diabetic Exchanges.

2 to 4 tablespoons butter *or* margarine, melted
2 tablespoons honey
1/2 teaspoon ground cinnamon
3 eggs
1/2 cup orange juice
1/8 teaspoon salt, optional
6 slices bread
Additional honey, optional

In a bowl, combine butter, honey and cinnamon. Pour into a greased 13-in. x 9-in. x 2-in. baking pan; spread to coat bottom of pan. In a shallow bowl, beat eggs, orange juice and salt if desired. Dip bread into egg mixture and place in prepared pan. Bake at 400° for 15-20 minutes or until golden brown. Invert onto a serving platter; serve with honey if desired. **Yield:** 6 slices. **Nutritional Analysis:** One slice (prepared with 2 tablespoons reduced-fat margarine, egg substitute equivalent to 3 eggs, and without salt and additional honey) equals 158 calories, 261 mg sodium, 1 mg cholesterol, 23 gm carbohydrate, 6 gm protein, 5 gm fat, 1 gm fiber. **Diabetic Exchanges:** 1-1/2 starch, 1 fat.

eggs, butter, honey, salt, extract, 4 cups flour and reserved pears and syrup. Beat until smooth. Add enough remaining flour to form a soft dough. Turn onto a floured surface; knead until smooth and elastic, about 6-8 minutes. Place in a greased bowl, turning once to grease top. Cover and let rise in a warm place until doubled, about 1-1/4 hours. Punch dough down; divide into thirds. Roll each portion into a 16-in. x 8-in. rectangle. Combine cinnamon and remaining 3/4 cup sugar; sprinkle over dough to within 1/2 in. of edges. Roll up, jelly-roll style, starting with a short side; pinch seams to seal. Place, seam side down, in three greased 9-in. x 5-in. x 3-in. loaf pans. Cover and let rise until doubled, about 45 minutes. Bake at 375° for 20 minutes. Cover loosely with foil. Bake 15-20 minutes longer or until bread tests done. Remove from pans to wire racks to cool. **Yield:** 3 loaves.

Finnish Cardamom Braids

Every Finn I know often serves Nissua, a sweet bread with cardamom. I believe my mom's recipe beats all others, hands down! Her bread is soft and fluffy while others can be dry. No matter how many Nissua braids she makes for a popular annual craft fair, they're all gone by noon! —Anne Heinonen, Howell, Michigan

>   2 packages (1/4 ounce *each*) active dry
>   yeast
> 1/4 cup warm water (110° to 115°)
>   2 cups warm milk (110° to 115°)
> 3/4 cup sugar
> 1/2 cup butter *or* margarine, softened
> 1-1/2 teaspoons salt
> 3/4 teaspoon ground cardamom
>   2 eggs
>   7 to 8 cups all-purpose flour

In a mixing bowl, dissolve yeast in warm water. Add milk, sugar, butter, salt, cardamom, eggs and 3 cups flour; beat until smooth. Stir in enough remaining flour to form a soft dough. Turn onto a floured surface; knead until smooth and elastic, about 6-8 minutes. Place in a greased bowl, turning once to grease top. Cover and let rise in a warm place until doubled, about 1 hour. Punch dough down. Turn onto a lightly floured surface; divide in half. Divide each half into thirds. Shape each piece into a 13-in. rope. Place three ropes on a greased baking sheet. Braid ropes; pinch ends to seal and tuck under. Repeat with remaining dough. Cover and let rise until doubled, about 45 minutes. Bake at 350° for 25-30 minutes or until golden brown. Remove from pans to wire racks to cool. **Yield:** 2 loaves.

Cinnamon-Swirl Pear Bread

(Pictured above and on page 108)

Pears add moisture to this delightful bread. I've been making it for over 20 years, and it's become a favorite of my family and friends. Try slices toasted to go along with Sunday brunch. —Joan Anderson
Winnipeg, Manitoba

>   3 cups chopped peeled ripe pears (about 3
>   medium)
> 1/2 cup water
> 1-1/4 cups plus 1 teaspoon sugar, *divided*
>   3 packages (1/4 ounce *each*) active dry
>   yeast
> 1/2 cup warm water (110° to 115°)
>   4 eggs, lightly beaten
> 1/2 cup butter *or* margarine, softened
> 1/2 cup honey
>   2 teaspoons salt
>   1 teaspoon almond extract
>   10 to 11 cups all-purpose flour
>   1 tablespoon ground cinnamon

In a saucepan, combine pears, water and 1/2 cup sugar. Simmer, uncovered, for 10-12 minutes or until tender. Drain well, reserving syrup. Add cold water if necessary to syrup to measure 1 cup; set aside. In a mixing bowl, dissolve yeast in warm water. Add 1 teaspoon sugar; let stand for 10 minutes. Add

Morning Glory Muffins

I enjoy preparing all sorts of foods and trying new dishes. These muffins are a hearty morning treat full of carrots, raisins, walnuts, coconut and apples.
—Richard Case, Johnstown, Pennsylvania

    1 cup whole wheat flour
  3/4 cup sugar
  1/2 cup oat bran
  1/2 cup all-purpose flour
    2 teaspoons baking soda
  1/2 teaspoon salt
    3 eggs
  3/4 cup applesauce
  1/4 cup vegetable oil
  1/4 cup molasses
    2 teaspoons vanilla extract
  1/4 teaspoon orange extract
    2 cups grated carrots
  1/2 cup raisins
  1/2 cup walnuts
  1/2 cup flaked coconut
    1 medium tart apple, peeled and finely
      chopped

In a bowl, combine the dry ingredients. In another bowl, combine eggs, applesauce, oil, molasses and extracts; mix well. Stir into the dry ingredients just until moistened. Fold in carrots, raisins, walnuts, coconut and apple. Fill greased or paper-lined muffin cups three-fourths full. Bake at 350° for 25-30 minutes or until a toothpick comes out clean. Cool for 5 minutes before removing from pans to wire racks. **Yield:** about 1-1/2 dozen.

— 🥄 🥄 🥄 —

Cranberry Orange Scones

(Pictured at right)

Moist and scrumptious, these scones come out perfect every time. I savor the chewy dried cranberries and sweet orange glaze. There's nothing better than serving these remarkable scones warm with delicate orange butter.
—Karen McBride
Indianapolis, Indiana

    2 cups all-purpose flour
   10 teaspoons sugar, *divided*
    1 tablespoon grated orange peel
    2 teaspoons baking powder
  1/2 teaspoon salt
  1/4 teaspoon baking soda
  1/3 cup cold butter *or* margarine
    1 cup dried cranberries
  1/4 cup orange juice
  1/4 cup half-and-half cream
    1 egg

    1 tablespoon milk
GLAZE (optional):
  1/2 cup confectioners' sugar
    1 tablespoon orange juice
ORANGE BUTTER:
  1/2 cup butter, softened
    2 to 3 tablespoons orange marmalade

In a bowl, combine flour, 7 teaspoons sugar, orange peel, baking powder, salt and baking soda. Cut in butter until the mixture resembles coarse crumbs; set aside. In a small bowl, combine cranberries, orange juice, cream and egg. Add to flour mixture and stir until a soft dough forms. On a floured surface, gently knead 6-8 times. Pat dough into an 8-in. circle. Cut into 10 wedges. Separate wedges and place on an ungreased baking sheet. Brush with milk; sprinkle with remaining sugar. Bake at 400° for 12-15 minutes or until lightly browned. Combine glaze ingredients if desired; drizzle over scones. Combine orange butter ingredients; serve with warm scones. **Yield:** 10 scones.

🥄 *Flour Facts*

Flour should be stored in a cool, dry place. All-purpose and whole wheat flour will keep for 1 year stored at 70° and 2 years at 40°. Flour can be frozen in airtight containers, but let it come to room temperature before using.

Crawfish Corn Bread

(Pictured below)

Moist and crusty, with tasty flecks of crawfish tail meat and zippy peppers, this is a tempting, distinctive corn bread. I like to serve it warm alongside soups and stews for a memorable lunch or supper.
—*Eloise Walker, Rayville, Louisiana*

   1 medium onion, finely chopped
1/2 cup finely chopped green pepper
1/2 cup vegetable oil, *divided*
   1 to 2 medium jalapeno peppers, minced*
   2 cups cornmeal
   3 teaspoons baking powder
   1 teaspoon salt
1/2 teaspoon baking soda
   3 eggs
   1 cup milk
   1 can (14-3/4 ounces) cream-style corn
1-1/2 cups (6 ounces) shredded cheddar cheese
3/4 cup sliced green onions
   1 cup crawfish tail meat, cooked

In a skillet, saute onion and green pepper in 1 tablespoon oil until tender. Remove from the heat. Stir in jalapenos; set aside. In a bowl, combine cornmeal, baking powder, salt and baking soda. In another bowl, beat the eggs, milk and remaining oil; stir into the dry ingredients just until blended. Stir in the corn, cheese, green onions, crawfish and reserved jalapeno mixture. Pour into a greased 13-in. x 9-in. x 2-in. baking pan. Bake at 400° for 35-40 minutes or until a toothpick inserted near the center comes out clean. Cut into squares. Serve warm. Refrigerate leftovers. **Yield:** 15 servings. ***Ed-itor's Note:** When cutting or seeding hot peppers, use rubber or plastic gloves to protect your hands. Avoid touching your face.

— 🥄 🥄 🥄 —

Sweet Potato Crescents

My family agrees our Thanksgiving feast wouldn't be complete without these light-as-air crescents. They're a nice accompaniment to any menu. Baking them always puts me in the holiday spirit.
—*Rebecca Bailey, Fairbury, Nebraska*

   2 packages (1/4 ounce *each*) active dry
      yeast
   1 cup warm water (110° to 115°)
   1 can (15 ounces) cut sweet potatoes,
      drained and mashed
1/2 cup sugar
1/2 cup shortening
   1 egg
1-1/2 teaspoons salt
   5 to 5-1/2 cups all-purpose flour
1/4 cup butter *or* margarine, melted

In a large mixing bowl, dissolve yeast in water; let stand for 5 minutes. Beat in the sweet potatoes, sugar, shortening, egg, salt and 3 cups of flour. Add enough remaining flour to form a stiff dough. Turn onto a floured surface; knead until smooth and elastic, about 6-8 minutes. Place in a greased bowl, turning once to grease top. Cover and let rise in a warm place until doubled, about 1 hour. Punch dough down; divide into thirds. Roll each portion into a 12-in. circle; cut each into 12 wedges. Brush

with butter. Roll up from the wide end and place, pointed end down, 2 in. apart on greased baking sheets. Cover and let rise until doubled, about 40 minutes. Bake at 375° for 13-15 minutes or until golden brown. Remove from pans to wire racks. **Yield:** 3 dozen.

— 🥄 🥄 🥄 —

Tomato-Basil Drop Biscuits

I grow fresh basil in my garden each summer. I use it in almost everything I cook. It really gets your taste buds going.—Shirley Glaab, Hattiesburg, Mississippi

- 1/2 cup finely chopped green onions
- 1 tablespoon olive _or_ vegetable oil
- 3/4 cup chopped fresh tomato, drained
- 1/4 cup minced fresh basil _or_ 4 teaspoons dried basil
- 2 cups all-purpose flour
- 1 tablespoon baking powder
- 1 teaspoon salt
- 1/4 teaspoon coarsely ground black pepper
- 1/3 cup shortening
- 2/3 cup milk

In a small skillet, saute onions in oil until tender. Add tomato; cook 1 minute longer. Remove from the heat; stir in basil. Cool slightly. In a bowl, combine the flour, baking powder, salt and pepper. Cut in shortening until the mixture resembles coarse crumbs. Stir in milk and tomato mixture just until combined. Drop by heaping teaspoonfuls 2 in. apart onto greased baking sheets. Bake at 425° for 10-12 minutes or until golden brown. Remove to wire racks. Serve warm. **Yield:** about 1-1/2 dozen.

— 🥄 🥄 🥄 —

Heart-Shaped Coffee Cake

(Pictured above right and on page 109)

I love to make this delicious coffee cake for anniversaries, Valentine's Day and other special occasions. I found this recipe more than 30 years ago, and I've been making it ever since. It's always a hit with family and friends.   —Norma Hammond, Leland, Iowa

- 1 package (1/4 ounce) active dry yeast
- 1/4 cup warm water (110° to 115°)
- 1 cup warm milk (110° to 115°)
- 3/4 cup butter _or_ margarine, melted, _divided_
- 2 eggs, beaten
- 1/4 cup sugar
- 1 teaspoon salt
- 3-1/2 to 4 cups all-purpose flour

FILLING:
- 1/2 cup sugar

- 1/2 cup finely chopped walnuts
- 2 teaspoons ground cinnamon

ICING:
- 2 tablespoons butter _or_ margarine, softened
- 2 cups confectioners' sugar
- 1 teaspoon vanilla extract
- 5 to 6 tablespoons milk

In a large mixing bowl, combine yeast and water. Add milk, 1/2 cup butter, eggs, sugar, salt and 2 cups flour. Add enough remaining flour to form a soft dough. Turn onto a floured surface; knead until smooth and elastic, about 6-8 minutes. Place in a greased bowl, turning once to grease top. Cover and let rise in a warm place until doubled, about 1 hour. Punch dough down; let rest for 10 minutes. Divide in half. On a floured surface, roll each portion into a 15-in. x 10-in. rectangle. Brush with remaining butter. Combine filling ingredients; sprinkle over dough. Roll up, jelly-roll style, starting with a long side; pinch seams to seal. Place, seam side up, on two greased baking sheets. Fold each roll in half lengthwise with seams touching, with one side 1-1/2 in. longer than the other. With scissors, make a lengthwise cut down the middle to within 1 in. of open ends. Open and lay flat; arrange into a heart shape. Cover and let rise until doubled, about 30 minutes. Bake at 350° for 15-20 minutes or until golden brown. Cool on wire racks. In a mixing bowl, cream butter, sugar and vanilla. Add enough milk to achieve desired consistency; drizzle over hearts. **Yield:** 2 coffee cakes.

— 🍵 🍵 🍵 —

'I Wish I Had That Recipe...'

"THE MOST WONDERFUL Peanut Butter Muffins were served with our dinner at Olde Jericho Tavern in Bainbridge, New York," says Barbara Eggleston, Frewsburg, New York.

Those memorable Peanut Butter Muffins were created by Kevin Dupe, a chef at Olde Jericho Tavern, in operation since 1793.

"This tasty muffin with a chocolate cookie base was inspired by my daughter, Kourtney, who loves peanut butter," Kevin says.

Owned by Cheryl and Jerry Jones, Olde Jericho Tavern serves buffet luncheon and dinner along with menu service. Prime rib specials and the seafood dinner are popular with patrons.

Located at 4 North Main, it is open Wednesday through Sunday, with hours varying between 11:30 a.m. and 9 p.m. 1-607/967-5893.

Peanut Butter Muffins

1-1/2 cups chocolate wafer crumbs
   2 tablespoons plus 1/2 cup sugar, *divided*
   1/2 cup butter *or* margarine, melted
   2 cups all-purpose flour
   1 tablespoon baking powder
   1/2 teaspoon salt
   1 egg
   3/4 cup milk
   1/3 cup vegetable oil
   1/2 cup peanut butter

In a bowl, combine crumbs and 2 tablespoons sugar. Stir in the butter; set aside. In another bowl, combine the flour, baking powder, salt and remaining sugar. Whisk together the egg, milk and oil; stir into dry ingredients just until moistened. Place peanut butter in a microwave-safe bowl. Cover and microwave on high for 20-30 seconds or until softened. Fold into batter. Press about 1 tablespoon reserved crumb mixture onto the bottom of 12 ungreased muffin cups. Divide the batter evenly between cups. Sprinkle with remaining crumbs. Bake at 400° for 15-18 minutes or until a toothpick comes out clean. Cool for 5 minutes before removing from pan to a wire rack to cool completely. **Yield:** 1 dozen.

— 🍵 🍵 🍵 —

Rosemary Focaccia

This herbed bread is great for dipping or serving with soup. The dough is very easy to work with.
—*Tina Repak, Johnstown, Pennsylvania*

   2 cups all-purpose flour
   1 package (1/4 ounce) quick-rise yeast
   2 teaspoons minced fresh rosemary *or* 1/2 teaspoon dried rosemary, crushed
   2 teaspoons salt
   1 teaspoon sugar
3/4 cup warm water (120° to 130°)
   1 tablespoon olive *or* vegetable oil
   1 to 2 tablespoons grated Parmesan cheese
Salt and pepper to taste

In a bowl, combine the first five ingredients; stir in water. Turn onto a floured surface; knead until smooth and elastic, about 5 minutes. Cover and let rest for 10-15 minutes. Press dough into a greased 13-in. x 9-in. x 2-in. baking pan. Cover and let rise in a warm place until doubled, about 40 minutes. With greased fingertips, make indentations 1/4 in. deep over surface of dough. Brush with oil; sprinkle with cheese, salt and pepper. Bake at 400° for 15-20 minutes or until golden brown. Cool for 5 minutes. Cut into strips or squares; serve warm. **Yield:** 6-8 servings.

— 🍵 🍵 🍵 —

Orange Crescents

The bold orange flavor of these sweet rolls satisfies at breakfast, brunch, dessert or snacktime. My family and friends love them and often request that I make a batch. We consider them a real treat! —*Dianne Brooks Augusta, Kansas*

   1 package (1/4 ounce) active dry yeast
1/4 cup warm water (110° to 115°)
3/4 cup sugar, *divided*
   1 teaspoon salt
   2 eggs
1/2 cup sour cream
   8 tablespoons butter *or* margarine, melted, *divided*
3-1/4 to 3-3/4 cups all-purpose flour
   2 tablespoons grated orange peel
GLAZE:
3/4 cup sugar
1/4 cup butter *or* margarine
   2 tablespoons orange juice
1/2 cup sour cream

In a mixing bowl, dissolve yeast in water. Add 1/4 cup sugar, salt, eggs, sour cream and 6 tablespoons butter; mix well. Beat in 2 cups flour until smooth. Add enough remaining flour to form a soft dough.

Turn onto a floured surface; knead until smooth and elastic, about 6-8 minutes. Place in a greased bowl, turning once to grease top. Cover and let rise in a warm place until doubled, about 1-1/2 hours. Punch dough down; divide in half. Roll each portion into a 12-in. circle. Brush each with 1 tablespoon butter. Combine orange peel and remaining sugar; sprinkle over dough. Cut each into 12 wedges. Roll up, starting with the wide side. Place point side down in two greased 13-in. x 9-in. x 2-in. baking pans, curving ends slightly to form a crescent. Cover and let rise in a warm place for 45 minutes or until doubled. Bake at 350° for 20-30 minutes or until golden brown. In a saucepan, combine glaze ingredients. Bring to a boil; cook and stir for 3 minutes. Pour over warm rolls. Store in the refrigerator. **Yield:** 2 dozen.

🍵 🍵 🍵

Never-Fail Yeast Rolls

This simple recipe produces sweet, tender rolls and requires no kneading. It's the perfect way for a child to make an impressive contribution to a meal. It's also nice for an adult who wants homemade rolls without the usual fuss. —Karen Gentry, Somerset, Kentucky

    1 **package (1/4 ounce) active dry yeast**
1-1/2 **cups warm water (110° to 115°)**
3-1/4 **cups all-purpose flour**
    1 **package (9 ounces) yellow *or* white cake mix**
  1/2 **teaspoon salt**
Melted butter *or* margarine

In a large mixing bowl, dissolve yeast in warm water. Beat in the flour, dry cake mix and salt (do not knead). Place in a greased bowl. Cover and let rise in a warm place until doubled, about 1 hour. Punch dough down; divide in half. Roll each portion into a 12-in. circle; cut each circle into 12 wedges. Roll up, beginning at the wide end; place point side down on greased baking sheets. Brush with butter. Cover and let rise until doubled, about 25 minutes. Bake at 350° for 12-15 minutes or until golden brown. **Yield:** 2 dozen.

🍵 🍵 🍵

Date Pecan Tea Bread

(Pictured at right)

Packed with dates and nuts, this moist, sweet bread is excellent on its own and even better topped with the chunky cream cheese spread. We enjoy it during the holidays and for after-school and late-night snacks.
—Carole Resnick, Cleveland, Ohio

2-1/2 **cups chopped dates**
1-1/2 **cups boiling water**
1-1/2 **teaspoons baking soda**
1-3/4 **cups all-purpose flour**
  1/4 **teaspoon *each* ground cloves, cinnamon, ginger and nutmeg**
    2 **tablespoons butter *or* margarine, softened**
1-1/4 **cups sugar**
    1 **egg**
    2 **teaspoons vanilla extract**
1-1/2 **cups coarsely chopped pecans**
SPREAD:
    1 **package (3 ounces) cream cheese, softened**
    2 **tablespoons chopped dates**
    2 **tablespoons coarsely chopped pecans**
    1 **tablespoon milk**

Place dates in a bowl. Combine boiling water and baking soda; pour over dates. Combine flour, cloves, cinnamon, ginger and nutmeg in another bowl; set aside. In a mixing bowl, cream butter and sugar. Beat in egg and vanilla. Add dry ingredients alternately with date mixture. Stir in pecans. Pour into a greased and floured 9-in. x 5-in. x 3-in. loaf pan. Bake at 350° for 65-75 minutes or until a toothpick inserted near the center comes out clean. Cool for 10 minutes before removing from pan to a wire rack to cool completely. In a small bowl, combine spread ingredients. Chill for 1 hour. Serve with the bread. **Yield:** 1 loaf (1/2 cup spread).

Pumpkin Pecan Loaves

(Pictured below)

Among all of my pumpkin bread recipes, this caramel-glazed creation is the pick of the crop. Often, I'll wrap up a loaf and give it as a gift to teachers or Sunday school leaders. —Brenda Jackson
Garden City, Kansas

3-1/3 cups all-purpose flour
  3 cups sugar
  2 teaspoons baking soda
1-1/2 teaspoons salt
  1 teaspoon ground cinnamon
  1 teaspoon ground nutmeg
  1 can (15 ounces) solid-pack pumpkin
  1 cup vegetable oil
  4 eggs, lightly beaten
2/3 cup water
1/2 cup chopped pecans
CARAMEL GLAZE:
  1/4 cup butter *or* margarine
  1/4 cup sugar
  1/4 cup packed brown sugar
  1/4 cup whipping cream
  2/3 cup confectioners' sugar
  1 teaspoon vanilla extract

In a bowl, combine the first six ingredients. Combine the pumpkin, oil, eggs and water; mix well. Stir into dry ingredients just until combined; fold in the pecans. Spoon into two greased 9-in. x 5-in. x 3-in. loaf pans. Bake at 350° for 60-65 minutes or until a toothpick inserted near the center comes out clean. Cool for 10 minutes before removing from pans to wire racks. For glaze, combine butter, sug-

ars and cream in a saucepan. Cook until sugar is dissolved. Cool for 20 minutes. Stir in the confectioners' sugar and vanilla until smooth. Drizzle over cooled loaves. **Yield:** 2 loaves.

— 🎺 🎺 🎺 —

Buttermilk Blueberry Muffins

(Pictured on page 108)

These pretty golden muffins are moist, flavorful and include very little fat. —Jean Howard
Hopkinton, Massachusetts

✓ Uses less fat, sugar or salt. Includes Nutritional Analysis and Diabetic Exchanges.

  2 cups all-purpose flour
1/2 cup packed brown sugar
  1 tablespoon baking powder
  1 teaspoon baking soda
1/2 teaspoon grated lemon peel
1/2 teaspoon ground nutmeg
  1 cup blueberries
  1 cup nonfat vanilla yogurt
  1 cup buttermilk

In a large bowl, combine the first six ingredients. Gently fold in blueberries. Combine yogurt and buttermilk; stir into dry ingredients just until moistened. Fill greased or paper-lined muffin cups two-thirds full. Bake at 400° for 18-20 minutes or until a toothpick comes out clean. Cool for 5 minutes before removing from pan to a wire rack. **Yield:** 1 dozen. **Nutritional Analysis:** One muffin equals 145 calories, 267 mg sodium, 1 mg cholesterol, 31 gm carbohydrate, 4 gm protein, 1 gm fat, 1 gm fiber. **Diabetic Exchange:** 2 starch.

— 🎺 🎺 🎺 —

Pepper Cheese Bread

As a mother of seven children—six of them still at home—I cook a lot. I like to get each of them to help in the kitchen because this allows me time with them that I might not have otherwise. My husband usually has a large garden, so I'm always looking for new ways to cook our garden produce. —Jan Woodall
Cadiz, Kentucky

1-1/2 cups finely diced green peppers
  3 tablespoons olive *or* vegetable oil, *divided*
  2 tablespoons active dry yeast
1/2 cup warm water (110° to 115°)
  1 teaspoon sugar
  1 cup milk
  2 tablespoons honey
1-1/2 teaspoons salt
1-1/2 cups (6 ounces) shredded cheddar cheese

3 eggs
4-1/2 cups all-purpose flour
1/2 cup wheat germ
1 tablespoon water

In a skillet, saute peppers in 1 tablespoon oil for 15 minutes or until tender; set aside. In a mixing bowl, dissolve yeast in warm water. Add sugar; let stand for 5 minutes. In a saucepan, heat the milk, honey, salt and remaining oil to 110°-115°. Remove from the heat; stir in cheese. Stir in 2 eggs and reserved peppers; add to yeast mixture. Add 2 cups flour and wheat germ; beat until smooth. Stir in enough remaining flour to form a soft dough. Do not knead. Place in a greased bowl. Cover and let rise in a warm place until doubled, about 1 hour. Punch dough down; spoon into two greased 8-in. x 4-in. x 2-in. loaf pans. Cover and let rise until doubled, about 1 hour. Beat water and remaining egg; brush over loaves. Bake at 375° for 25-30 minutes or until golden brown. **Yield:** 2 loaves.

——— ▼ ▼ ▼ ———

Idaho Spudnuts

(Pictured above)

Raising eight children on a potato farm in Idaho, Mother was creative at using an abundant crop. We especially liked her light, fluffy potato doughnuts. We encouraged Mother to let us help make them often. Now I prepare them to share with friends and neighbors.
—Sandi Jones, Windsor, California

1 pound russet potatoes, peeled and quartered
2 packages (1/4 ounce *each*) active dry yeast
1-1/2 cups warm milk (110° to 115°)
1/2 cup vegetable oil
1/2 cup sugar
2 eggs
1 teaspoon salt
7-1/2 cups all-purpose flour
Oil for deep-fat frying
4 cups confectioners' sugar
1/3 cup water
1 teaspoon vanilla extract

Place potatoes in a saucepan and cover with water. Bring to a boil; cook until tender. Drain, reserving 1/2 cup cooking liquid; cool to 110°-115°. Discard remaining cooking liquid. Mash potatoes without milk or butter. In a large mixing bowl, dissolve yeast in reserved cooking liquid. Add mashed potatoes, milk, oil, sugar, eggs and salt. Add enough flour to form a soft dough. Place in a greased bowl, turning once to grease top. Cover and let rise in a warm place until doubled, about 1 hour. Punch dough down; let rise again until doubled, about 20 minutes. Roll out on a floured surface to 1/2-in. thickness. Cut with a floured 3-in. doughnut cutter. In an electric skillet or deep-fat fryer, heat oil to 375°. Fry doughnuts, a few at a time, until golden brown. Combine glaze ingredients; dip warm doughnuts in glaze. Cool on wire racks. **Yield:** 4 dozen.

Cookies & Bars

You'll find kids and adults alike sneaking into the cookie jar or brownie pan for a taste of these sweet treats.

PIECES OF PLEASURE. Clockwise from upper left: Shortbread Lemon Bars (p. 124), Triple Chocolate Kisses (p. 131), Chocolate Mint Brownies (p. 130), Chewy Peanut Butter Bars (p. 129) and Dipped Sandwich Cookies (p. 128).

mixing bowl, combine the filling ingredients; mix well. Pour over hot crust. Bake for 14-16 minutes or until set and lightly browned. Meanwhile, in a bowl, combine topping ingredients. Spread over filling. Bake 7-9 minutes longer or until topping is set. Cool on a wire rack. Refrigerate overnight. Cut into bars just before serving. **Yield:** 3 dozen.

— 🏆 🏆 🏆 —

Honey Peanut Squares

I serve this soft, nutty candy every year at our Christmas open house. Honey roasted peanuts make this sweet treat even more special. —Norene Wright
Manilla, Indiana

> 4 **cups honey roasted peanuts, *divided***
> 1 **can (14 ounces) sweetened condensed milk**
> 1 **package (10-1/2 ounces) miniature marshmallows**
> 1 **package (10 ounces) peanut butter chips**
> 1/2 **cup butter *or* margarine**
> 1/2 **cup peanut butter**

Line a 13-in. x 9-in. x 2-in. pan with foil and coat with nonstick cooking spray. Sprinkle 2 cups peanuts in the pan. In a saucepan, combine the milk, marshmallows, peanut butter chips, butter and peanut butter. Cook and stir until smooth. Pour over peanuts; spread evenly. Sprinkle with remaining peanuts; press down. Cover and refrigerate for at least 45 minutes. Lift foil out of pan; cut into squares. Store in an airtight container. **Yield:** about 4 dozen.

— 🏆 🏆 🏆 —

Apricot-Filled Cookies

The recipe for these rich, buttery cookies originally called for dates. Apricots have long been my favorite fruit, so using them as a substitute seemed natural.
—Bonnie Waliezer, Brush Prairie, Washington

> 1/2 **cup shortening**
> 1 **cup sugar**
> 2 **eggs**
> 1 **teaspoon vanilla extract**
> 2-1/2 **cups all-purpose flour**
> 1/2 **teaspoon salt**
> 1/4 **teaspoon baking soda**
> **FILLING:**
> 2 **cups canned apricots, mashed**
> 2/3 **cup sugar**
> 2/3 **cup water**
> 1/2 **cup finely chopped almonds**
> 1 **teaspoon lemon juice**

Shortbread Lemon Bars

(Pictured above and on page 122)

I've put together two family cookbooks over the years, and this recipe ranks among my favorites. These special lemon bars have a yummy shortbread crust and a refreshing flavor. I'm never afraid to make this dessert for guests since I know it will be a hit.
—Margaret Peterson, Forest City, Iowa

> 1-1/2 **cups all-purpose flour**
> 1/2 **cup confectioners' sugar**
> 1 **teaspoon grated lemon peel**
> 1 **teaspoon grated orange peel**
> 3/4 **cup cold butter *or* margarine**
> **FILLING:**
> 4 **eggs**
> 2 **cups sugar**
> 1/3 **cup lemon juice**
> 1/4 **cup all-purpose flour**
> 2 **teaspoons grated lemon peel**
> 2 **teaspoons grated orange peel**
> 1 **teaspoon baking powder**
> **TOPPING:**
> 2 **cups (16 ounces) sour cream**
> 1/3 **cup sugar**
> 1/2 **teaspoon vanilla extract**

In a food processor, combine flour, confectioners' sugar, and lemon and orange peel. Cut in butter until crumbly; process until mixture forms a ball. Pat into a greased 13-in. x 9-in. x 2-in. baking pan. Bake at 350° for 12-14 minutes or until set and the edges are lightly browned. Meanwhile, in a

In a mixing bowl, cream shortening and sugar. Beat in eggs and vanilla. Combine flour, salt and baking soda; gradually add to the creamed mixture. Cover and refrigerate for 1 hour. Meanwhile, in a saucepan, combine filling ingredients. Cook and stir until thickened, about 15 minutes. Cool completely. Divide dough in half. On a lightly floured surface, roll out each portion to 1/8-in. thickness. Cut one portion with a 2-1/2-in. round cookie cutter. Cut second portion with a 2-1/2-in. doughnut cutter. Place 1 in. apart on ungreased baking sheets. Bake at 375° for 8-10 minutes or until edges are very lightly browned. Remove to wire racks to cool. Spread bottom of solid cookies with filling; top with cutout cookies. **Yield:** about 1-1/2 dozen.

—————— 🥢 🥢 🥢 ——————

Spiced Pumpkin Bars

These bars are moist, with bold pumpkin and spice flavors. When I want to lower the cholesterol, I use egg whites in place of the eggs. —*Richard Case*
Johnstown, Pennsylvania

 2 cups all-purpose flour
1-1/2 cups sugar
 1 tablespoon baking powder
 2 teaspoons ground cinnamon
 1 teaspoon baking soda
 1/2 teaspoon salt
 1/2 teaspoon ground ginger
 1/4 teaspoon ground nutmeg
 1/4 teaspoon ground cloves
 4 eggs
1-3/4 cups cooked *or* canned pumpkin
 1 cup unsweetened applesauce
Confectioners' sugar, optional

In a bowl, combine the dry ingredients. In another bowl, combine eggs, pumpkin and applesauce; mix well. Stir into the dry ingredients. Spread into a greased 15-in. x 10-in. x 1-in. baking pan. Bake at 350° for 20-25 minutes or until lightly browned. Do not overbake. Cool on a wire rack before cutting. Dust with confectioners' sugar if desired. **Yield:** 2-1/2 dozen.

Excellent Additions

For a tasty twist on chocolate chip cookies, chill the chocolate chip cookie dough, wrap the dough around mini Snickers candy bars, then bake.

Your favorite peanut butter cookies will stay nice and moist if you add 1/2 cup of sour cream when you're mixing the dough.

Peanut Butter Chocolate Cookies
(Pictured below)

This recipe was featured in our Sunday paper and I just had to try it. Kids really love the peanut butter surprise inside the cookie. —*June Formanek*
Belle Plaine, Iowa

 1/2 cup butter *or* margarine, softened
 1/2 cup sugar
 1/2 cup packed brown sugar
 1 cup creamy peanut butter, *divided*
 1 egg, lightly beaten
 1 teaspoon vanilla extract
1-1/2 cups all-purpose flour
 1/2 cup baking cocoa
 1/2 teaspoon baking soda
 3/4 cup confectioners' sugar

In a large mixing bowl, cream butter, sugars and 1/4 cup peanut butter. Add egg and vanilla; mix well. Combine flour, cocoa and baking soda; add to creamed mixture and mix well. Blend confectioners' sugar with remaining peanut butter until smooth. Roll into 24 balls, 1 in. each. Divide dough into 24 pieces; flatten each into a 3-in. circle. Place one peanut butter ball on each circle; bring edges over to completely cover it. (Dough may crack; reshape cookies as needed.) Place cookies with seam side down on ungreased baking sheets. Flatten each cookie slightly with the bottom of a glass dipped in sugar. Bake at 375° for 7-9 minutes or until set. **Yield:** 2 dozen.

Caramel Apple Bites

(Pictured below)

Kids will find this fun recipe appealing. They can help by dipping the baked cookies in caramel and nuts—and by eating the treats! These treats seem to disappear at my house. —Darlene Markel
Sublimity, Oregon

FILLING:
- 1/3 cup chopped unpeeled apple
- 1/3 cup evaporated milk
- 1/3 cup sugar
- 1/3 cup chopped walnuts

DOUGH:
- 1/2 cup butter *or* margarine, softened
- 1/4 cup confectioners' sugar
- 1/4 cup packed brown sugar
- 1 egg
- 1 teaspoon vanilla extract
- 1/4 teaspoon salt
- 2 cups all-purpose flour

TOPPING:
- 1 package (14 ounces) caramels
- 2/3 cup evaporated milk
- Green toothpicks
- 1 cup chopped walnuts

In a small saucepan, combine filling ingredients. Cook and stir over medium heat until thickened; set aside to cool. In a mixing bowl, cream butter and sugars. Add egg, vanilla and salt; beat well. Add flour; mix well. Shape dough into 1-in. balls. Flatten and place 1/4 teaspoon filling in center of each. Fold dough over filling and reshape into balls. Place 1 in. apart on greased baking sheets. Bake at 350° for 12-15 minutes or until lightly browned. Remove to wire racks to cool. In a saucepan over low heat, cook caramels and evaporated milk, stirring occasionally, until caramels are melted. Insert a toothpick into each cookie and dip into caramel until completely coated. Dip bottoms into nuts. Place on wire racks to set. **Yield:** about 3 dozen.

Turtle Pretzels

These pretzels are quick to make and so yummy. They make great fresh-from-the-kitchen presents. Just put in a decorated container and add a bow!
—Barbara Loudenslager, O'Fallon, Missouri

- 1 package (14 ounces) caramels
- 1 tablespoon water
- 1 package (10 ounces) pretzel rods
- 8 ounces German sweet chocolate *or* semisweet chocolate
- 2 teaspoons shortening
- 1 cup finely chopped pecans

In a double boiler, melt caramels in water. Dip half of each pretzel into the hot caramel. Place on a greased sheet of foil to cool. In a saucepan, melt chocolate and shortening over low heat. Dip caramel-coated end of pretzels into the chocolate; sprinkle with nuts. Return to foil. **Yield:** about 2-1/2 dozen.

Black Walnut Cookies

These are the first cookies I learned to bake. Grandmother and I made them for the holidays when I was a child. Hulling and shelling those nuts was a difficult and time-consuming job for Grandma. Our whole family enjoyed these yummy cookies even more knowing how much love she put into making them.
— *Mrs. Doug Black, Conover, North Carolina*

 1 **cup butter (no substitutes), softened**
 2 **cups packed brown sugar**
 2 **eggs**
 1 **teaspoon vanilla extract**
3-1/2 **cups all-purpose flour**
 1 **teaspoon baking soda**
 1/4 **teaspoon salt**
 2 **cups chopped black walnuts *or* walnuts,
     *divided***

In a mixing bowl, cream the butter and brown sugar. Beat in the eggs and vanilla. Combine the flour, baking soda and salt; gradually add to the creamed mixture. Stir in 1-1/4 cups of walnuts. Finely chop the remaining nuts. Shape dough into two 15-in. logs. Roll logs in chopped nuts, pressing gently. Wrap each in plastic wrap. Refrigerate for 2 hours or until firm. Unwrap and cut into 1/4-in. slices. Place 2 in. apart on greased baking sheets. Bake at 300° for 12 minutes. Cool on wire racks. **Yield:** 10 dozen.

Chewy Surprise Cookies

With four daughters, six grandchildren and one great-grandchild, I've baked lots of cookies. This recipe is one of my favorites. — *Lavon Timken
Cimmaron, Kansas*

1-1/2 **cups butter-flavored shortening**
1-1/2 **cups peanut butter**
 2 **cups sugar, *divided***
1-1/2 **cups packed brown sugar**
 4 **eggs**
3-3/4 **cups all-purpose flour**
 2 **teaspoons baking soda**
1-1/2 **teaspoons baking powder**
 3/4 **teaspoon salt**
 1 **package (10 ounces) Milk Duds**

In a mixing bowl, cream the shortening, peanut butter, 1-1/2 cups of sugar and brown sugar. Add eggs, one at a time, beating well after each addition. Combine dry ingredients; gradually add to the creamed mixture. Chill for at least 1 hour. Shape 4 teaspoons of dough around each Milk Dud so it is completely covered. Roll balls in remaining sugar. Place 2 in. apart on ungreased baking sheets.

Bake at 350° for 10-12 minutes or until set. Cool for 5 minutes before removing to wire racks. **Yield:** about 8 dozen.

Peppermint Meringues

(Pictured above)

These melt-in-your-mouth cookies are super as a Christmas gift or to pass around when guests drop in.
— *Dixie Terry, Marion, Illinois*

☑ Uses less fat, sugar or salt. Includes Nutritional Analysis and Diabetic Exchanges.

 2 **egg whites**
 1/8 **teaspoon salt**
 1/8 **teaspoon cream of tartar**
 1/2 **cup sugar**
 2 **peppermint candy canes, crushed**

In a mixing bowl, beat egg whites until foamy. Sprinkle with salt and cream of tartar; beat until soft peaks form. Gradually add sugar, beating until stiff peaks form, about 7 minutes. Drop by teaspoonfuls onto ungreased foil or paper-lined baking sheets; sprinkle with the crushed candy. Bake at 225° for 1-1/2 hours. Turn off heat; leave cookies in the oven with the door ajar for at least 1 hour or until cool. Store in an airtight container. **Yield:** 3 dozen. **Nutritional Analysis:** One cookie equals 21 calories, 12 mg sodium, 0 cholesterol, 5 gm carbohydrate, trace protein, 0 fat, 0 fiber. **Diabetic Exchange:** 1/2 fruit.

Almond Pie Bars

I love almonds in anything, and they really shine in this recipe. These chewy bars are easy to pick up and eat.
—*Pat Habiger, Spearville, Kansas*

      2 cups all-purpose flour
  1/2 cup confectioners' sugar
      1 cup cold butter (no substitutes)
FILLING:
      2 cups sugar
      1 cup chopped almonds
      2 tablespoons all-purpose flour
      4 eggs, beaten
  1/2 cup butter (no substitutes), melted
  1/3 light corn syrup
  1/2 teaspoon almond extract

For crust, combine flour and confectioners' sugar. Cut in butter until mixture resembles coarse crumbs. Press into a greased 13-in. x 9-in. x 2-in. baking pan. Bake at 350° for 10-15 minutes or until lightly browned. In a bowl, combine sugar, almonds and flour; stir in remaining ingredients. Pour over crust. Bake at 350° for 25-30 minutes or until center is almost set. Cool on a wire rack. Cut into bars. Store in the refrigerator. **Yield:** 6-1/2 dozen.

——— 🏆 🏆 🏆 ———

Polka-Dot Cookies

While living in Florida, I found this cookie recipe in a book on cooking with oranges. —*Mary Ann Rafalski North Huntingdon, Pennsylvania*

  1/2 cup butter (no substitutes), softened
  1/2 cup sugar
      1 egg
      2 tablespoons orange juice concentrate
      1 tablespoon grated orange peel
      2 cups all-purpose flour
1-1/4 teaspoons baking powder
  1/4 teaspoon salt
CHOCOLATE FROSTING:
  1/4 cup semisweet chocolate chips
1-1/2 teaspoons butter (no substitutes)
      1 tablespoon milk
  1/2 cup confectioners' sugar

In a mixing bowl, cream butter and sugar. Add egg, concentrate and orange peel. Combine dry ingredients; gradually add to creamed mixture. Cover and refrigerate for 2 hours. Divide dough in half. On a lightly floured surface, roll out each portion to 1/8-in. thickness. Cut with a 2-in. round cookie cutter dipped in flour. Place 2 in. apart on greased baking sheets. Bake at 350° for 6-7 minutes or until edges begin to brown. Remove to wire racks to cool. For frosting, melt chocolate chips and but-

Dipped Sandwich Cookies

(Pictured above and on page 122)

With a lemon filling and chocolate coating, these buttery sandwich cookies are often requested at my house—particularly for special occasions.
—*Jane Delahoyde, Poughkeepsie, New York*

      1 cup butter (no substitutes), softened
  1/2 cup sugar
      1 egg yolk
      1 teaspoon vanilla extract
      2 cups all-purpose flour
LEMON FILLING:
  1/2 cup butter (no substitutes), softened
      2 cups confectioners' sugar
      2 tablespoons lemon juice
DIPPING CHOCOLATE:
      4 squares (1 ounce *each*) semisweet chocolate
      2 tablespoons butter (no substitutes)
  1/2 cup finely chopped nuts

In a mixing bowl, cream butter and sugar. Beat in egg yolk and vanilla. Gradually add flour. Shape into 1-in. balls. Place 2 in. apart on ungreased baking sheets. With a glass dipped in sugar, flatten into 2-in. circles. Bake at 350° for 10-12 minutes or until firm. Remove to wire racks to cool. Combine filling ingredients. Spread on the bottom of half of the cookies; top with remaining cookies. Melt chocolate and butter; stir until smooth. Dip each cookie halfway in chocolate, then in nuts. Place on waxed paper to harden. **Yield:** 2 dozen.

ter. Stir in milk and confectioners' sugar until blended. Place in a heavy-duty resealable plastic bag; cut a small hole in corner of bag. Pipe polka dots on cookies. **Yield:** 4 dozen.

— ▼ ▼ ▼ —

Molasses Cutouts

You'll have fun decorating these spicy cutouts. They really stand out. —Deb Anderson, Joplin, Missouri

2/3 **cup shortening**
1-1/4 **cups sugar**
  2 **eggs**
  2 **tablespoons buttermilk**
  2 **tablespoons molasses**
3-1/2 **cups all-purpose flour**
  1 **teaspoon baking soda**
  1 **teaspoon baking powder**
  1 **teaspoon salt**
  1 **teaspoon ground ginger**
1/2 **teaspoon ground cloves**
Confectioners' sugar icing and miniature chocolate chips and M&Ms, optional

In a mixing bowl, cream shortening and sugar. Add eggs, one at a time, beating well after each addition. Beat in buttermilk and molasses. Combine dry ingredients; gradually add to the creamed mixture and mix well. Chill for several hours. On a lightly floured surface, roll dough to 1/8-in. thickness. Cut with 5-in. cookie cutters dipped in flour. Place 2 in. apart on greased baking sheets. Bake at 375° for 8-10 minutes or until edges just begin to brown. Remove to wire racks to cool. Decorate as desired. **Yield:** about 2 dozen.

— ▼ ▼ ▼ —

Date Drops

These cake-like cookies are nutritious, flavorful and firm enough to pack well in brown-bag lunches. —Doris Barb, El Dorado, Kansas

1/2 **cup butter (no substitutes), softened**
3/4 **cup packed brown sugar**
  2 **eggs**
1/4 **cup milk**
1/2 **teaspoon vanilla extract**
1-1/2 **cups all-purpose flour**
  1 **teaspoon baking powder**
1/4 **teaspoon salt**
  1 **cup quick-cooking oats**
  1 **cup chopped dates**
1/2 **cup chopped walnuts**

In a mixing bowl, cream the butter and brown sugar. Beat in eggs, milk and vanilla. Combine flour, baking powder and salt; gradually add to creamed mixture and mix well. Stir in oats, dates and nuts. Drop by rounded teaspoonfuls 1 in. apart onto greased baking sheets. Bake at 350° for 12-15 minutes or until edges are lightly browned and tops are firm to the touch. Cool on wire racks. **Yield:** about 6 dozen.

— ▼ ▼ ▼ —

Chewy Peanut Butter Bars

(Pictured below and on page 123)

This recipe combines three of my favorite foods— peanut butter, coconut and chocolate—into one mouthwatering dessert. It's very rich and filling, so a small piece usually satisfies even a real sweet tooth. —Mrs. Sanford Wickham, Holbrook, Nebraska

  1 **cup all-purpose flour**
1/3 **cup sugar**
1/2 **cup cold butter** *or* **margarine**
FILLING:
  2 **eggs**
1/2 **cup corn syrup**
1/2 **cup sugar**
1/4 **cup crunchy peanut butter**
1/4 **teaspoon salt**
1/2 **cup flaked coconut**
1/2 **cup semisweet chocolate chips**

In a bowl, combine flour and sugar; cut in the butter until crumbly. Press into a greased 13-in. x 9-in. x 2-in. baking pan. Bake at 350° for 14-16 minutes or until lightly browned. In a mixing bowl, mix eggs, corn syrup, sugar, peanut butter and salt until smooth. Fold in coconut and chocolate chips. Pour over crust. Return to the oven for 15-20 minutes or until golden. **Yield:** 3 dozen.

Chocolate Mint Brownies

(Pictured below and on page 123)

These brownies get more moist if you leave them in the refrigerator a day or two. The problem at our house is no one can leave them alone for that long!
—*Helen Baines, Elkton, Maryland*

    1 cup all-purpose flour
  1/2 cup butter *or* margarine, softened
  1/2 teaspoon salt
    4 eggs
    1 teaspoon vanilla extract
    1 can (16 ounces) chocolate-flavored syrup
    1 cup sugar
FILLING:
    2 cups confectioners' sugar
  1/2 cup butter *or* margarine, softened
    1 tablespoon water
  1/2 teaspoon mint extract
    3 drops green food coloring
TOPPING:
    1 package (10 ounces) mint chocolate chips
    9 tablespoons butter *or* margarine

Combine the first seven ingredients in a mixing bowl; beat on medium speed for 3 minutes. Pour batter into a greased 13-in. x 9-in. x 2-in. baking pan. Bake at 350° for 30 minutes (top of brownies will still appear wet). Cool completely on a wire rack. Combine filling ingredients in a mixing bowl; beat until creamy. Spread over cooled brownies. Refrigerate until set. For topping, melt the chocolate chips and butter over low heat in a small saucepan. Let cool for 30 minutes or until lukewarm, stirring occasionally. Spread over filling. Chill before cutting. Store in the refrigerator. **Yield:** 5-6 dozen.

— 🍳 🍳 🍳 —

Almond Sugar Cookies

We made these crisp cookies often when I worked in the lunchroom at our daughters' grade school. The almond flavor makes them unique. —*Linda Holt Wichita Falls, Texas*

    2 cups butter-flavored shortening
    1 cup sugar
    1 cup packed brown sugar
    2 eggs
    1 teaspoon vanilla extract
    1 teaspoon almond extract
    4 cups all-purpose flour
    2 teaspoons baking soda
    2 teaspoons cream of tartar
Additional sugar *or* colored sugar

In a large mixing bowl, cream the shortening and sugars. Add eggs, one at a time, beating well after each addition. Beat in extracts. Combine the flour, baking soda and cream of tartar; gradually add to creamed mixture. Drop by tablespoonfuls 2 in. apart onto ungreased baking sheets. Flatten with a glass dipped in sugar. Bake at 350° for 10-12 minutes or until lightly browned. Remove to wire racks to cool. **Yield:** 5 dozen.

— 🍳 🍳 🍳 —

Ginger Drop Cookies

My mother shared the recipe for these soft spice cookies. —*Bethel Walters, Willow River, Minnesota*

    1 cup shortening
    1 cup packed brown sugar
    1 cup molasses
    2 eggs
    4 cups all-purpose flour
    2 teaspoons baking soda
    2 teaspoons ground cinnamon
    2 teaspoons ground ginger
    1 teaspoon salt
  1/2 cup water

In a mixing bowl, cream shortening and brown sugar. Add molasses and eggs; mix well. Combine dry ingredients; add to the creamed mixture alternately with water. Refrigerate for at least 8 hours. Drop dough by tablespoonfuls 2 in. apart onto greased baking sheets. Bake at 350° for 10-12 minutes or until lightly browned. Remove to wire racks to cool. **Yield:** about 5-1/2 dozen.

Orange Slice Bars

These tasty bars are a portable way to satisfy a sweet tooth. —Elaine Norton, Sandusky, Michigan

> 1 **pound candy orange slices, cut into 1/8-inch strips**
> 6 **tablespoons hot water**
> 1/2 **cup butter *or* margarine, softened**
> 2-1/4 **cups packed brown sugar**
> 4 **eggs**
> 1 **teaspoon vanilla extract**
> 2-1/2 **cups all-purpose flour**
> 2 **teaspoons baking powder**
> 1/2 **teaspoon salt**
> 1/2 **cup chopped walnuts**
> **Confectioners' sugar**

In a bowl, combine candy and water. Cover and soak overnight; drain well and set aside. In a mixing bowl, cream butter and brown sugar. Add eggs, one at a time, beating well after each addition. Beat in vanilla. Combine flour, baking powder and salt; gradually add to creamed mixture. Fold in walnuts and reserved candy. Spread into a greased 15-in. x 10-in. x 1-in. baking pan. Bake at 350° for 25-30 minutes or until golden brown. Cool on a wire rack. Dust with confectioners' sugar. Cut into bars. **Yield:** about 4 dozen.

Apricot Pecan Tassies

The apricot filling makes these adorable little tarts extra special. They never last long when I fix them for the holidays. —Paula Magnus, Republic, Washington

> 1/2 **cup plus 1 tablespoon butter (no substitutes), softened, *divided***
> 6 **tablespoons cream cheese, softened**
> 1 **cup all-purpose flour**
> 3/4 **cup packed brown sugar**
> 1 **egg, lightly beaten**
> 1/2 **teaspoon vanilla extract**
> 1/4 **teaspoon salt**
> 2/3 **cup diced dried apricots**
> 1/3 **cup chopped pecans**

In a mixing bowl, cream 1/2 cup butter and cream cheese. Gradually add flour, beating until mixture forms a ball. Cover and refrigerate for 15 minutes. Meanwhile, in a bowl, combine brown sugar, egg, vanilla, salt and remaining butter. Stir in apricots and pecans; set aside. Roll dough into 1-in. balls. Press onto the bottom and up the sides of greased miniature muffin cups. Spoon 1 teaspoon apricot mixture into each cup. Bake at 325° for 25 minutes or until golden brown. Cool in pans on wire racks. **Yield:** 2 dozen.

Triple Chocolate Kisses

(Pictured above and on page 122)

These crisp meringue cookies with a chocolate center are easy to make but look like you spent a lot of time. When our son and daughter-in-law moved into their first home on Valentine's Day, I made them a nice dinner and gave them a batch of these treats. —Evelyn Lindburg, Shenandoah, Iowa

> 2 **egg whites**
> 1/4 **teaspoon cream of tartar**
> 1/2 **cup sugar**
> 1/4 **teaspoon almond extract**
> 1 **square (1 ounce) semisweet chocolate, grated**
> 42 **milk chocolate kisses**
> **Baking cocoa**

In a mixing bowl, beat egg whites until foamy. Add cream of tartar; beat until soft peaks form, about 6 minutes. Gradually add sugar, beating until stiff peaks form, about 6 minutes. Beat in extract. Fold in grated chocolate. Insert a medium open-star tip in a pastry or plastic bag. Fill with the meringue. On lightly greased baking sheets, pipe forty-two 1-in. circles. Press a chocolate kiss into the center of each. Pipe meringue around each kiss in continuous circles from the base to the top until kiss is completely covered. Dust with cocoa. Bake at 325° for 15-18 minutes or until the edges are lightly browned. Immediately remove to wire racks to cool. **Yield:** 3-1/2 dozen.

bined. Pour over crust. Cut pears into 1/8-in. slices; arrange in a single layer over filling. Combine sugar and cinnamon; sprinkle over pears. Bake at 375° for 28-30 minutes (center will be soft set and will become firmer upon cooling). Cool on a wire rack for 45 minutes. Cover and refrigerate for at least 2 hours before cutting. Store in the refrigerator. **Yield:** 16 bars.

Apricot-Nut Drop Cookies

Most everyone who comes to our home asks for my "famous" apricot cookies. They are really good, and I try not to eat them all myself!   —Patricia Crawford Garland, Texas

       3/4 cup butter-flavored shortening
   1-1/4 cups packed brown sugar
          1 egg
          2 tablespoons milk
          1 teaspoon vanilla extract
   1-3/4 cups all-purpose flour
          1 teaspoon baking powder
       3/4 teaspoon baking soda
       1/2 teaspoon salt
          1 cup chopped dried apricots
          1 cup chopped pecans

In a mixing bowl, cream shortening and brown sugar. Beat in egg, milk and vanilla. Combine flour, baking powder, baking soda and salt; gradually add to the creamed mixture. Stir in the apricots and pecans. Drop by rounded tablespoonfuls 3 in. apart onto ungreased baking sheets. Bake at 375° for 10-13 minutes or until light golden brown. Cool for 2 minutes before removing to wire racks. **Yield:** about 4-1/2 dozen.

Pear Custard Bars

(Pictured above)

When I take this crowd-pleasing treat to a potluck, I come home with an empty pan every time. Cooking and baking come naturally for me—as a farm girl, I helped my mother feed my 10 siblings.   —Jeannette Nord San Juan Capistrano, California

       1/2 cup butter *or* margarine, softened
       1/3 cup sugar
       3/4 cup all-purpose flour
       1/4 teaspoon vanilla extract
       2/3 cup chopped macadamia nuts
FILLING/TOPPING:
          1 package (8 ounces) cream cheese, softened
       1/2 cup sugar
          1 egg
       1/2 teaspoon vanilla extract
          1 can (15-1/4 ounces) pear halves, drained
       1/2 teaspoon sugar
       1/2 teaspoon ground cinnamon

In a mixing bowl, cream butter and sugar. Beat in the flour and vanilla until combined. Stir in the nuts. Press into a greased 8-in. square baking pan. Bake at 350° for 20 minutes or until lightly browned. Cool on a wire rack. Increase heat to 375°. In a mixing bowl, beat cream cheese until smooth. Add sugar, egg and vanilla; mix until com-

Coconut Granola Bars

These quick-to-fix bars are wholesome and delicious. I sometimes make them for bake sales.
—Maria Cade, Fort Rock, Oregon

       3/4 cup packed brown sugar
       2/3 cup peanut butter
       1/2 cup corn syrup
       1/2 cup butter *or* margarine, melted
          2 teaspoons vanilla extract
          3 cups old-fashioned oats
          1 cup (6 ounces) semisweet chocolate chips
       1/2 cup flaked coconut
       1/2 cup sunflower kernels
       1/3 cup wheat germ
          2 teaspoons sesame seeds

In a large bowl, combine brown sugar, peanut butter, corn syrup, butter and vanilla. Combine the remaining ingredients; add to peanut butter mixture and stir to coat. Press into two greased 13-in. x 9-in. x 2-in. baking pans. Bake at 350° for 25-30 minutes or until golden brown. Cool on wire racks. Cut into bars. **Yield:** 3 dozen.

Cookie a Day

These chewy cookies, packed with wholesome and delicious ingredients, don't keep the cookie jar full very long. My husband and I devour these low-fat treats. —*Holly Cicchirillo, Chino Valley, Arizona*

✓ Uses less fat, sugar or salt. Includes Nutritional Analysis and Diabetic Exchanges.

- 1 cup unsweetened applesauce
- 2 egg whites
- 1/2 cup apple jelly, melted and cooled
- 3 cups old-fashioned oats
- 1 cup whole wheat cereal flakes
- 3/4 cup packed brown sugar
- 1/2 cup all-purpose flour
- 1/3 cup whole wheat flour
- 1 teaspoon baking soda
- 1 teaspoon salt
- 1 teaspoon ground cinnamon
- 1/2 teaspoon ground allspice
- 1/2 teaspoon ground ginger
- 1/4 teaspoon ground cloves
- 1 cup raisins
- 1/2 cup chopped dates
- 1/2 cup chopped walnuts
- 2 tablespoons orange juice
- 2 tablespoons lemon juice
- 1 tablespoon vanilla extract

In large mixing bowl, combine the applesauce, egg whites and jelly. Combine dry ingredients; add to applesauce mixture. Stir in the remaining ingredients. Drop by rounded tablespoonfuls 2 in. apart onto baking sheets coated with nonstick cooking spray. Flatten slightly. Bake at 350° for 12 minutes or until set. Remove to wire racks to cool. **Yield:** 3 dozen. **Nutritional Analysis:** One cookie equals 111 calories, 109 mg sodium, 0 cholesterol, 23 gm carbohydrate, 2 gm protein, 2 gm fat, 2 gm fiber. **Diabetic Exchanges:** 1 starch, 1/2 fat.

✓ *Better Brownies*

For moist, chewy brownies, add 2 tablespoons of corn syrup to your batter before baking.

Fruit 'n' Nut Cookies

(Pictured below)

Once after making a fruitcake, I had some fruit and nuts left over. I mixed them into a basic cookie dough along with pineapple and coconut. These soft, colorful cookies are a nice addition to a Christmas dessert tray. —*Jennie Loftus, Gasport, New York*

- 3/4 cup butter *or* margarine, softened
- 3/4 cup shortening
- 1-1/4 cups packed brown sugar
- 2 eggs
- 1 teaspoon vanilla extract
- 4 cups all-purpose flour
- 2 teaspoons baking powder
- 1/2 teaspoon salt
- 1 can (8 ounces) crushed pineapple, drained
- 1/2 cup chopped dates
- 1/2 cup chopped red maraschino cherries
- 1/2 cup chopped green maraschino cherries
- 1/2 cup flaked coconut
- 1/2 cup chopped pecans *or* walnuts

In a large mixing bowl, cream the butter, shortening and brown sugar. Add eggs, one at a time, beating well after each addition. Beat in vanilla. Combine flour, baking powder and salt; gradually add to the creamed mixture. Stir in remaining ingredients. Shape into three 10-in. rolls; wrap each in plastic wrap. Refrigerate for 2 hours or until firm. Unwrap and cut into 1/4-in. slices. Place 2 in. apart on ungreased baking sheets. Bake at 375° for 8-10 minutes or until golden brown. Remove to wire racks to cool. **Yield:** 7 dozen.

Cakes & Pies

*Luscious layered cakes and palate-pleasing pies
are fantastic finishes to everyday suppers
as well as special-occasion dinners.*

— 🥤 🥤 🥤 —

TRIED-AND-TRUE TREATS. Clockwise from upper left: Black Forest Pie (p. 142), Cheddar Apple Pizza (p. 145), Upside-Down Cranberry Crunch (p. 143), Cupid's Chocolate Cake (p. 139) and Fancy Cream Cupcakes (p. 137).

Pecan Carrot Bundt Cake

(Pictured below)

The pecans and citrus flavor make this dessert special. It's a moist cake with sweet, creamy frosting.
—Joan Taylor, Adrian, Minnesota

- 1 cup butter *or* margarine, softened
- 1 cup sugar
- 1 cup packed brown sugar
- 4 eggs
- 2 tablespoons grated lemon peel
- 2 tablespoons grated orange peel
- 3 cups all-purpose flour
- 2 teaspoons baking powder
- 1 teaspoon baking soda
- 1 teaspoon ground cinnamon
- 1/2 teaspoon salt
- 2 tablespoons orange juice
- 2 tablespoons lemon juice
- 1 pound carrots, grated
- 1 cup raisins
- 1 cup chopped pecans

FROSTING:
- 1 package (3 ounces) cream cheese, softened
- 1-1/2 to 2 cups confectioners' sugar
- 1 teaspoon vanilla extract
- 1/2 cup chopped pecans

In a mixing bowl, cream butter and sugars. Add eggs, one at a time, beating well after each. Beat in lemon and orange peels. Combine dry ingredients; gradually add to creamed mixture alternately with juices. Stir in carrots, raisins and pecans. Pour into a greased and floured 10-in. fluted tube pan. Bake at 350° for 50-60 minutes or until a toothpick inserted near the center comes out clean. Cool for 10 minutes; remove from pan to a wire rack. For frosting, in a mixing bowl, beat the cream cheese, confectioners' sugar and vanilla until smooth. Frost cake; sprinkle with pecans. **Yield:** 12-16 servings.

Lemon Chiffon Cake

This fluffy cake is a real treat drizzled with the sweet-tart lemon glaze. *—Rebecca Baird*
Salt Lake City, Utah

✓ Uses less fat, sugar or salt. Includes Nutritional Analysis and Diabetic Exchanges.

- 1/2 cup evaporated skim milk
- 1/2 cup light sour cream
- 1/4 cup lemon juice
- 2 tablespoons vegetable oil
- 2 teaspoons vanilla extract
- 1 teaspoon grated lemon peel
- 1 teaspoon lemon extract
- 2 cups cake flour
- 1-1/2 cups sugar
- 1 tablespoon baking powder
- 1/2 teaspoon salt
- 1 cup egg whites (about 7)
- 1/2 teaspoon cream of tartar

LEMON GLAZE:
- 1-3/4 cups confectioners' sugar
- 3 tablespoons lemon juice

In a large mixing bowl, combine the first seven ingredients. Sift together the flour, sugar, baking powder and salt; gradually beat into lemon mixture until smooth. In a small mixing bowl, beat egg whites until foamy. Add cream of tartar; beat until stiff peaks form. Gently fold into the lemon mixture. Pour into an ungreased 10-in. tube pan with removable bottom. Bake at 325° for 45-55 minutes or until cake springs back when lightly touched. Immediately invert pan; cool completely. Remove cake to a serving platter. Combine glaze ingredients; drizzle over cake. **Yield:** 16 servings. **Nutritional Analysis:** One serving equals 228 calories, 157 mg sodium, 3 mg cholesterol, 47 gm carbohydrate, 4 gm protein, 3 gm fat, trace fiber. **Diabetic Exchanges:** 1 starch, 1 fruit, 1/2 fat.

Molasses Pumpkin Pie

When our sons come home at Thanksgiving to hunt with their dad, I make this pie recipe from Grandma Fetting. We celebrate Thanksgiving in our cabin in the northwoods, a 40-year tradition. *—Lois Fetting*
Nelson, Wisconsin

Pastry for single-crust pie (9 inches)
    2 eggs
  1/2 cup sugar
    1 teaspoon ground cinnamon
  1/2 teaspoon salt
  1/2 teaspoon ground ginger
  1/2 teaspoon ground nutmeg
1-3/4 cups canned *or* cooked pumpkin
    3 tablespoons molasses
  3/4 cup evaporated milk
Whipped topping

Line a 9-in. pie plate with the pastry. Trim to 1/2 in. beyond edge of plate; flute edges. Set aside. In a mixing bowl, beat the eggs, sugar, cinnamon, salt, ginger and nutmeg. Beat in the pumpkin and molasses; gradually add milk. Pour into the crust. Cover the edges loosely with foil. Bake at 425° for 10 minutes. Remove foil. Reduce heat to 350°; bake 28-32 minutes longer or until a knife inserted near the center comes out clean. Cool on a wire rack for 2 hours. Chill until serving. Serve with whipped topping. Refrigerate leftovers. **Yield:** 6-8 servings.

Fancy Cream Cupcakes

(Pictured at right and on page 134)

These cute, tender cupcakes are creamy and not too sweet. They look fancy but are quick to fix...and even a big platter of these timeless treats disappears in no time.
—Merrilee Chambers
Haines Junction, Yukon Territory

  1/2 cup shortening
1-1/2 cups sugar
    4 egg whites
    1 teaspoon vanilla extract
    2 cups all-purpose flour
3-1/2 teaspoons baking powder
    1 teaspoon salt
    1 cup milk
    1 cup whipping cream
    2 tablespoons confectioners' sugar
    4 to 5 drops red food coloring, optional
  1/4 teaspoon almond extract

In a mixing bowl, cream shortening and sugar. Add egg whites, one at a time, beating well after each addition. Beat in vanilla. Combine dry ingredients; add to creamed mixture alternately with milk. Fill paper- or foil-lined muffin cups two-thirds full. Bake at 350° for 15-20 minutes or until a toothpick comes out clean. Cool for 10 minutes; remove to wire racks to cool completely. For filling, in a mixing bowl, beat cream until soft peaks form. Grad-

ually beat in confectioners' sugar and food coloring if desired until stiff peaks form. Beat in almond extract. Cut a 1-in. cone shape from the center of each cupcake; set cone aside. Fill indentation with filling. Cut each cone in half from top to bottom; place two halves on filling for butterfly wings. If desired, pipe a thin strip of filling between wings for butterfly body. **Yield:** 22 cupcakes.

Coffee Mallow Pie

(Pictured on page 4)

This terrific pie holds up well in the refrigerator overnight. *—Dorothy Smith, El Dorado, Arkansas*

  1 cup water
  1 tablespoon instant coffee granules
  4 cups miniature marshmallows
  1 tablespoon butter *or* margarine
  1 cup whipping cream, whipped
  1 pastry shell (9 inches), baked
1/2 cup chopped walnuts *or* pecans, toasted
Additional whipped cream and chocolate curls, optional

In a heavy saucepan, bring water to a boil; stir in coffee until dissolved. Reduce heat; add marshmallows and butter. Cook and stir over low heat until marshmallows are melted and mixture is smooth. Set saucepan in ice and whisk mixture constantly until cooled. Fold in whipped cream; spoon into pastry shell. Sprinkle with nuts. Refrigerate for at least 3 hours before serving. Garnish with whipped cream and chocolate curls if desired. **Yield:** 6-8 servings.

Carrot Ice Cream Pie

(Pictured above)

This refreshing dessert tastes a little bit like orange sherbet. I make several pies at a time and keep them on hand in the freezer. My guests are always surprised to learn they're eating carrots! —*Bethel Anderson*
St. James, Minnesota

1-1/3 cups graham cracker crumbs (about 21 squares)
1/3 cup packed brown sugar
1/3 cup butter *or* margarine, melted
1/3 cup lemonade concentrate
2-1/4 cups chopped carrots
1/4 cup sugar
1 quart vanilla ice cream, softened

In a small bowl, combine cracker crumbs and brown sugar; stir in butter. Press onto the bottom and up the sides of an ungreased 9-in. pie plate. Refrigerate for 30 minutes. Meanwhile, place lemonade concentrate, carrots and sugar in a food processor or blender; cover and process until carrots are finely chopped and mixture is blended. Transfer to a bowl; stir in ice cream until well blended. Pour into crust. Cover and freeze for 8 hours or overnight. Remove from the freezer 15-20 minutes before serving. **Yield:** 6-8 servings.

Fruit Volcano Cake

Eating light is easy with scrumptious recipes like this pretty and fruity cake. —*Elizabeth Kinn*
Derby, New York

✓ Uses less fat, sugar or salt. Includes Nutritional Analysis and Diabetic Exchanges.

1 cup all-purpose flour
2/3 cup sugar
2 teaspoons baking powder
Pinch salt
1/2 cup nonfat peach yogurt
1 teaspoon vanilla extract
Egg substitute equivalent to 2 eggs
2 medium fresh peaches, peeled and sliced
1/4 cup fresh raspberries
1/4 cup fresh blueberries
TOPPING:
1 teaspoon sugar
1/8 teaspoon ground cinnamon

In a mixing bowl, combine flour, sugar, baking powder and salt. Combine yogurt and vanilla; add to dry ingredients just until combined. In a mixing bowl, beat egg substitute on medium speed for 2 minutes; fold into batter. Pour into a 9-in. round baking pan coated with nonstick cooking spray. Arrange peach slices around the edge of pan. Sprinkle with berries. Combine sugar and cinnamon; sprinkle over fruit. Bake at 350° for 35-40 minutes or until a toothpick inserted near the center comes out clean and peaches are tender. **Yield:** 8 servings. **Nutritional Analysis:** One serving equals 159 calories, 159 mg sodium, trace cholesterol, 34 gm carbohydrate, 4 gm protein, 1 gm fat, 1 gm fiber. **Diabetic Exchanges:** 1-1/2 starch, 1 fruit.

Sugar Plum Cake

My Southern grandmothers taught me to cook when I was a boy. As I grew older, I specialized in cakes, pies and pastries. I bake several of these cakes each Christmas to give as gifts. —*Mark Brown*
Birmingham, Alabama

2 cups self-rising flour*
2 cups sugar
1 teaspoon ground cinnamon
1 teaspoon ground cloves
3/4 cup vegetable oil
2 jars (6 ounces *each*) strained plum baby food
3 eggs, beaten
1 cup chopped pecans
GLAZE:
1 cup plus 2 tablespoons confectioners' sugar
1 jar (4 ounces) strained plum-apple baby food
2 tablespoons milk

In a large bowl, combine flour, sugar, cinnamon and cloves. Stir in oil, baby food and eggs. Fold in pecans. Pour into a greased and floured 10-in. tube pan. Bake at 350° for 50-60 minutes or until a toothpick inserted near the center comes out clean. Cool for 10 minutes before removing from pan to a wire rack to cool completely. In a small bowl, combine glaze ingredients until smooth. Drizzle over top and sides of cake. **Yield:** 16-20 servings.
*Editor's Note: As a substitute for each cup of self-rising flour, place 1-1/2 teaspoons baking powder and 1/2 teaspoon salt in a measuring cup. Add all-purpose flour to measure 1 cup.

Chocolate Cream Pie

Our teenage son, John, has done lots of baking with 4-H. His favorite is this flaky crust filled with old-fashioned creamy chocolate pudding.
—*Mary Anderson, De Valls Bluff, Arkansas*

1-1/2 cups sugar
1/3 cup all-purpose flour
3 tablespoons baking cocoa
1/2 teaspoon salt
1-1/2 cups water
1 can (12 ounces) evaporated milk
5 egg yolks, beaten
1/2 cup butter *or* margarine
1 teaspoon vanilla extract
1 pastry shell (9 inches), baked
Whipped topping

In a large saucepan, combine the first six ingredients until smooth. Cook and stir over medium-high heat until thickened and bubbly, about 2 minutes. Reduce heat; cook and stir 2 minutes longer. Remove from the heat. Stir 1 cup hot mixture into egg yolks. Return all to pan; bring to a gentle boil, stirring constantly. Remove from the heat; stir in butter and vanilla. Cool slightly. Pour warm filling into pastry shell. Cool for 1 hour. Refrigerate until set. Just before serving, garnish with whipped topping. **Yield:** 6-8 servings.

Cupid's Chocolate Cake

(Pictured at right and on page 134)

I'm pleased to share the recipe for the very best chocolate cake I have ever tasted. I prepare this treat every year on Valentine's Day. —*Shelaine Duncan
North Powder, Oregon*

1 cup butter *or* margarine, softened
2-1/2 cups sugar

4 eggs
2-1/2 teaspoons vanilla extract, *divided*
2-3/4 cups all-purpose flour
1 cup baking cocoa
2 teaspoons baking soda
1/2 teaspoon baking powder
1/2 teaspoon salt
2 cups water
1 cup whipping cream
1/4 cup confectioners' sugar
4 cups buttercream frosting of your choice

In a mixing bowl, cream butter and sugar. Add the eggs, one at a time, beating well after each addition. Beat on high speed until light and fluffy. Stir in 1-1/2 teaspoons vanilla. Combine dry ingredients; add to the creamed mixture alternately with water. Pour into three greased and floured 9-in. round baking pans. Bake at 350° for 25-30 minutes or until a toothpick inserted near the center comes out clean. Cool for 10 minutes before removing from pans to wire racks to cool completely. For filling, in a mixing bowl, beat cream until stiff peaks form. Beat in confectioners' sugar and remaining vanilla. Place bottom cake layer on a serving plate; spread with half of the filling. Repeat. Place top layer on cake; frost top and sides of cake with buttercream frosting. Store in the refrigerator. **Yield:** 12-14 servings.

Orange Loaf Cake

(Pictured below)

Our state's abundant orange juice is put to excellent use in this moist cake. The subtle citrus flavor is irresistible! —Dawn Congleton, Orlando, Florida

✓ Uses less fat, sugar or salt. Includes Nutritional Analysis and Diabetic Exchanges.

1-3/4 cups cake flour
1 cup sugar
2 teaspoons baking powder
1/4 teaspoon salt
1/2 cup vegetable oil
1/2 cup orange juice
4 egg whites
2 tablespoons confectioners' sugar

In a mixing bowl, combine the dry ingredients. Add oil and orange juice; beat until smooth. In another mixing bowl, beat egg whites until stiff peaks form. Fold into orange juice mixture. Coat a 9-in. x 5-in. x 3-in. loaf pan with nonstick cooking spray; dust with flour. Pour batter into pan. Bake at 350° for 1 hour or until a toothpick inserted near the center comes out clean. Cool for 10 minutes before removing from pan to a wire rack to cool completely. Dust with confectioners' sugar. **Yield:** 12 servings. **Nutritional Analysis:** One serving equals 152 calories, 134 mg sodium, 0 cholesterol, 35 gm carbohydrate, 3 gm protein, trace fat, trace fiber. **Diabetic Exchange:** 2 starch.

Glazed Raspberry Pie

(Pictured on front cover)

This recipe has been passed down in my family and copied for countless people over the years. There's no mistaking that raspberries give this tall pie its good looks and divine flavor. —Gillian Batchelor
Crescent Valley, British Columbia

5 cups fresh raspberries, *divided*
1 cup water, *divided*
1 cup sugar
3 tablespoons cornstarch
2 tablespoons lemon juice
1 package (3 ounces) cream cheese, softened
1 tablespoon butter *or* margarine, softened
1 tablespoon milk
1 pastry shell (9 inches), baked
Fresh mint, optional

In a saucepan, combine 2/3 cup raspberries and 2/3 cup water. Simmer, uncovered, for 3 minutes. Strain raspberries and discard seeds; set juice aside. In another saucepan, combine sugar, cornstarch and remaining water until smooth. Add raspberry juice. Bring to a boil over medium heat; cook and stir for 2 minutes or until thickened. Remove from the heat; stir in lemon juice. Cool. In a small mixing bowl, beat cream cheese, butter and milk until smooth. Spread onto the bottom and up the sides of pastry shell. Fill pastry shell with the remaining raspberries. Slowly pour glaze over berries. Refrigerate until serving. Garnish with mint if desired. **Yield:** 6-8 servings.

🍷 🍷 🍷

Creamy Apricot Pie

I keep this wonderful dessert recipe close at hand. It's easy to prepare, and it's so cool and satisfying on a warm summer day. —Charlotte Cramer
Othello, Washington

1 can (14 ounces) apricot halves
1 egg yolk
1 can (12 ounces) evaporated milk
1 package (3 ounces) cook-and-serve vanilla pudding mix
1 pastry shell (9 inches), baked
2 teaspoons cornstarch
1 can (5-1/4 ounces) apricot nectar
1/4 cup sliced almonds, toasted

Drain apricots, reserving 1/2 cup juice; set apricots aside. In a saucepan, combine egg yolk, milk and reserved apricot juice; stir in the pudding mix until smooth. Bring to a boil over medium heat;

cook and stir until thickened. Chop 1/2 cup apricots; add to pudding. Pour into pastry shell. Refrigerate. For glaze, combine cornstarch and apricot nectar in a saucepan until smooth. Bring to a boil over medium heat; cook and stir for 2 minutes or until thickened. Cut the remaining apricots into thirds; arrange over pudding layer. Spoon glaze over top. Sprinkle with almonds. Chill until serving. **Yield:** 6-8 servings.

— 🥄 🥄 🥄 —

Strawberry Pie

(Pictured above)

Starring fresh-from-the-patch berries, this ruby-red pie comes from Barbara Budlow Schneider. The recipe appears in our family cookbook. —Linda Skiles
Lyons, Wisconsin

1-1/4 **cups sugar**
  1 **tablespoon cornstarch**
  1 **cup water**
  1 **package (3 ounces) strawberry gelatin**
  3 **tablespoons lemon juice**
  1 **quart fresh strawberries, halved**
  1 **pastry shell (9 inches), baked**
Whipped topping, optional

In a saucepan, combine the sugar and cornstarch. Stir in water until smooth. Bring to a boil; cook and stir for 2 minutes. Remove from the heat. Add the gelatin and lemon juice; stir until dissolved. Allow to cool to room temperature, about 30 minutes. Add the strawberries and stir gently to coat. Spoon

into the pastry shell. Chill until set, about 3 hours. Serve with the whipped topping if desired. **Yield:** 6-8 servings.

— 🥄 🥄 🥄 —

Frozen Brownie Dough Dessert

This cool, rich-tasting treat is always a hit, and it's so easy to fix. Cookie dough ice cream was my inspiration for this creation. —Dawn Hall, Swanton, Ohio

1/2 **gallon Swiss almond frozen yogurt**
  1 **package fudge brownie mix (8-inch pan size)**
  3 **tablespoons water**
  3 **tablespoons hot fudge ice cream topping, warmed**

Remove yogurt from freezer and allow to soften while preparing crust. In a bowl, combine brownie mix and water. Press two-thirds of the brownie mixture into a greased 9-in. round springform pan; set aside. Place yogurt in a large bowl. Shape remaining brownie mixture into 1-1/2-in. balls; gently stir into yogurt. Spoon over crust. Drizzle with fudge topping. Freeze overnight. **Yield:** 12 servings.

Upside-Down Disaster

If some of the fruit topping sticks to the bottom of the pan after inverting a baked upside-down cake onto a serving plate, gently scrape it off of the pan and replace it on top of the warm cake.

Black Forest Pie

(Pictured above and on page 134)

With three active children, I don't usually fuss with fancy desserts. This one is simple but impressive—it's the one I make to show how much I care. The tempting combination of chocolate and tangy red cherries is guaranteed to make someone feel special.
—*Trudy Black, Dedham, Massachusetts*

- 3/4 cup sugar
- 1/3 cup baking cocoa
- 2 tablespoons all-purpose flour
- 1/3 cup milk
- 1/4 cup butter *or* margarine
- 2 eggs, lightly beaten
- 1 can (21 ounces) cherry pie filling, *divided*
- 1 unbaked pastry shell (9 inches)

Whipped topping, optional

In a saucepan, combine sugar, cocoa, flour and milk until smooth. Add butter. Bring to a boil; cook and stir for 2 minutes or until thickened. Remove from the heat. Stir a small amount of hot mixture into eggs. Return all to the pan. Fold in half of the pie filling. Pour into pastry shell. Bake at 350° for 35-40 minutes or until filling is almost set. Cool completely on a wire rack. Just before serving, top with remaining pie filling and whipped topping if desired. **Yield:** 6-8 servings.

Mark's Chocolate Fudge Cake

The hint of cinnamon blends nicely with the chocolate. I was proud to win a blue ribbon for this cake in a church baking contest.
—*Mark Brown*
Birmingham, Alabama

- 2 cups all-purpose flour
- 2 cups sugar
- 1 teaspoon baking soda
- 1 teaspoon ground cinnamon
- 1 cup water
- 1/2 cup butter *or* margarine
- 1/2 cup shortening
- 1/4 cup baking cocoa
- 2 eggs
- 1 cup buttermilk
- 1 teaspoon vanilla extract

ICING:
- 1/2 cup butter *or* margarine
- 1/3 cup baking cocoa
- 1/3 cup milk
- 3-1/2 cups confectioners' sugar
- 1 tablespoon vanilla extract
- 1 cup chopped pecans

In a large mixing bowl, combine flour, sugar, baking soda and cinnamon; set aside. In a small saucepan, bring water, butter, shortening and cocoa to a boil. Add to dry ingredients and mix well. In a small mixing bowl, beat eggs, buttermilk and vanilla. Stir into cocoa mixture. Pour into a greased 13-in. x 9-in. x 2-in. baking pan. Bake at 350° for 25-30 minutes or until a toothpick inserted near the center comes out clean. Meanwhile, in a saucepan, combine butter, cocoa and milk; bring to a boil, stirring constantly. Remove from the heat. Add confectioners' sugar and vanilla; mix well. Spread over hot cake; sprinkle with pecans. Cool on a wire rack. **Yield:** 12-15 servings.

Butter Pecan Cake

Especially at Thanksgiving and Christmas, this cake is one that my family's enjoyed for many years.
—*Becky Miller, Tallahassee, Florida*

- 2-2/3 cups chopped pecans
- 1-1/4 cups butter (no substitutes), softened, *divided*
- 2 cups sugar
- 4 eggs
- 3 cups all-purpose flour
- 2 teaspoons baking powder
- 1/2 teaspoon salt
- 1 cup milk
- 2 teaspoons vanilla extract

FROSTING:
1 cup butter (no substitutes), softened
8 to 8-1/2 cups confectioners' sugar
1 can (5 ounces) evaporated milk
2 teaspoons vanilla extract

Place pecans and 1/4 cup of butter in a baking pan. Bake at 350° for 20-25 minutes or until toasted, stirring frequently; set aside. In a mixing bowl, cream sugar and remaining butter. Add eggs, one at a time, beating well after each addition. Combine flour, baking powder and salt; add to the creamed mixture alternately with milk. Stir in vanilla and 1-1/3 cups of toasted pecans. Pour into three greased and floured 9-in. round cake pans. Bake at 350° for 25-30 minutes. Cool for 10 minutes; remove from pans to cool on a wire rack. For frosting, cream butter and sugar in a mixing bowl. Add milk and vanilla; beat until smooth. Stir in remaining toasted pecans. Spread frosting between layers and over top and sides of cake. **Yield:** 12-16 servings.

——— ☕ ☕ ☕ ———

Praline Pumpkin Torte

This favorite harvest cake stays moist to the very last bite. It's perfect for Thanksgiving or Christmas.
—Esther Sinn, Princeton, Illinois

3/4 cup packed brown sugar
1/3 cup butter (no substitutes)
3 tablespoons whipping cream
3/4 cup chopped pecans
CAKE:
4 eggs
1-2/3 cups sugar
1 cup vegetable oil
2 cups cooked *or* canned pumpkin
1/4 teaspoon vanilla extract
2 cups all-purpose flour
2 teaspoons baking powder
2 teaspoons pumpkin pie spice
1 teaspoon baking soda
1 teaspoon salt
TOPPING:
1-3/4 cups whipping cream
1/4 cup confectioners' sugar
1/4 teaspoon vanilla extract
Additional chopped pecans

In a heavy saucepan, combine brown sugar, butter and cream. Cook and stir over low heat until sugar is dissolved. Pour into two well-greased 9-in. round baking pans. Sprinkle with pecans; cool. In a mixing bowl, beat eggs, sugar and oil. Add pumpkin and vanilla. Combine dry ingredients; add to pumpkin mixture and beat just until blended. Care-

fully spoon over brown sugar mixture. Bake at 350° for 30-35 minutes or until a toothpick inserted near the center comes out clean. Cool for 5 minutes; remove from pans to wire racks to cool completely. Place one cake layer, praline side up, on a serving plate. In a mixing bowl, beat cream until soft peaks form. Beat in sugar and vanilla. Spread two-thirds over cake. Top with second cake layer and remaining whipped cream. Sprinkle with additional pecans if desired. Store in the refrigerator. **Yield:** 12-14 servings.

——— ☕ ☕ ☕ ———

Upside-Down Cranberry Crunch

(Pictured below and on page 134)

For special occasions, I often serve this sweet-tart dessert. I've also used raspberries, strawberries and blueberries instead of cranberries with great results.
—Carol Miller, Northumberland, New York

3 cups fresh *or* frozen cranberries, thawed
1-3/4 cups sugar, *divided*
1/2 cup chopped pecans
2 eggs
1/2 cup butter *or* margarine, melted
1 cup all-purpose flour
Whipped cream *or* vanilla ice cream, optional

Place cranberries in a greased 8-in. square baking dish. Sprinkle with 3/4 cup sugar and pecans. In a mixing bowl, beat eggs, butter, flour and remaining sugar until smooth. Spread over cranberry mixture. Bake at 325° for 1 hour or until a toothpick inserted near the center of cake comes out clean. Run knife around edges of dish; immediately invert onto a serving plate. Serve with whipped cream or ice cream if desired. **Yield:** 8 servings.

Lemon Pineapple Pie

(Pictured below)

No one will guess this creamy, refreshing pie is low in fat and sugar. You'll get asked to share the recipe.
—Eileen Crowley, Prairie du Chien, Wisconsin

✓ Uses less fat, sugar or salt. Includes Nutritional Analysis and Diabetic Exchanges.

- 1 cup reduced-fat graham cracker crumbs (about 16 squares)
- 1/4 cup margarine, melted
- 1 package (.8 ounce) sugar-free cook-and-serve vanilla pudding mix
- 2 cups water, *divided*
- 1 package (.3 ounce) sugar-free lemon gelatin
- 1 can (8-1/4 ounces) unsweetened crushed pineapple, well drained
- 1 carton (8 ounces) light frozen whipped topping, thawed

Sliced lemon and strawberries and fresh mint, optional

Combine graham cracker crumbs and margarine; press onto the bottom and up the sides of a 9-in. pie plate. Bake at 350° for 8-10 minutes or until set and lightly browned; cool on a wire rack. In a saucepan, combine pudding and 1-1/2 cups water; bring to a boil. Cook and stir for 2 minutes; cool. In another saucepan, bring remaining water to a boil. Add gelatin; stir to dissolve. Stir into pudding mixture. Add pineapple; cool completely. Fold in whipped topping; pour into crust. Refrigerate for 2 hours before serving. Garnish with lemon, strawberries and mint if desired. **Yield:** 8 servings. **Nutritional Analysis:** One serving (calculated without garnish) equals 189 calories, 139 mg sodium, trace cholesterol, 21 gm carbohydrate, 2 gm protein, 9 gm fat, 1 gm fiber. **Diabetic Exchanges:** 2 fat, 1 starch.

— 🛒 🛒 🛒 —

Triple-Layer Mocha Cake

This rich cake is tall and delicious with a special frosting. It makes a dramatic presentation. —Mark Brown Birmingham, Alabama

- 1 cup shortening
- 2-1/2 cups sugar
- 5 eggs, *separated*
- 5 tablespoons strong brewed coffee
- 2 teaspoons vanilla extract
- 3 cups cake flour
- 4 teaspoons baking cocoa
- 1 teaspoon baking soda
- 1/2 teaspoon salt
- 1 cup buttermilk

FROSTING:
- 5-1/2 to 6 cups confectioners' sugar
- 1 tablespoon baking cocoa
- 1-1/2 cups butter *or* margarine, softened
- 3 tablespoons plus 1-1/2 teaspoons strong brewed coffee
- 1-1/2 teaspoons vanilla extract

In a mixing bowl, cream shortening and sugar. Add egg yolks, one at a time, beating well after each addition. Beat in coffee and vanilla. Combine dry ingredients; add to the creamed mixture alternately with buttermilk. In another bowl, beat egg whites until stiff peaks form; fold into batter. Pour into three greased and floured 9-in. round baking pans. Bake at 350° for 25-30 minutes or until a toothpick inserted near the center comes out clean. Cool for 10 minutes before removing from pans to wire racks to cool completely. For frosting, combine confectioners' sugar and cocoa. In a mixing bowl, cream butter and sugar mixture. Beat in coffee and vanilla. Spread between layers and over top and sides of cake. **Yield:** 12-14 servings.

— 🛒 🛒 🛒 —

Pecan Apple Pie

My husband loves this crumb-topped pie and begs me to bake it often. The caramel topping makes each bite absolutely delectable.
—Anne Betts Kalamazoo, Michigan

Pastry for double-crust pie (9 inches)
- 1 cup sugar
- 1/3 cup all-purpose flour
- 2 teaspoons ground cinnamon

1/4 teaspoon salt
12 cups tart thinly sliced peeled apples
(about 10 apples)
TOPPING:
1 cup packed brown sugar
1/2 cup all-purpose flour
1/2 cup quick-cooking oats
1/2 cup cold butter *or* margarine
1/2 to 1 cup chopped pecans
1/2 cup caramel ice cream topping

Line two 9-in. pie plates with pastry. Trim and flute edges; set aside. In a large bowl, combine sugar, flour, cinnamon and salt; add apples and toss to coat. Pour into pastry shells. For topping, combine brown sugar, flour and oats; cut in butter until crumbly. Sprinkle over the apples. Cover edges loosely with foil. Bake at 375° for 25 minutes. Remove foil; bake 25-30 minutes longer or until filling is bubbly. Sprinkle with pecans; drizzle with caramel topping. Cool on wire racks. **Yield:** 2 pies (6-8 servings each).

Angel Food Cake

Looking for a little lighter dessert? Turn to this angel food cake. Each heavenly slice is moist and tasty.
—Sharon Voth, Alexander, Manitoba

✓ Uses less fat, sugar or salt. Includes Nutritional Analysis and Diabetic Exchanges.

1 cup cake flour
1-1/2 cups sugar, *divided*
2 cups egg whites (about 5 large eggs)
1-1/4 teaspoons cream of tartar
1 teaspoon vanilla extract
1/4 teaspoon almond extract
1/4 teaspoon salt

Sift flour and 1/2 cup sugar together four times; set aside. In a mixing bowl, combine egg whites, cream of tartar, extracts and salt; beat on high until soft peaks form but mixture is still moist and glossy. Add remaining sugar, 1/4 cup at a time, beating well after each addition. Sift flour mixture, a fourth at a time, over the egg white mixture; fold in gently, using about 15 strokes for each addition. Spoon batter into an ungreased 10-in. tube pan (pan will be very full). Bake at 375° for 35-40 minutes or until top crust is golden brown and cracks feel dry. Immediately invert cake in pan to cool completely. Loosen sides of cake from pan and remove. **Yield:** 16 servings. **Nutritional Analysis:** One serving equals 101 calories, 106 mg sodium, 0 cholesterol, 24 gm carbohydrate, 2 gm protein, trace fat. **Diabetic Exchanges:** 1-1/2 starch.

Cheddar Apple Pizza

(Pictured above and on page 134)

Apples, cheese and nuts are a great combination. At harvesttime, this popular sweet pizza can be prepared with fruit right from the tree. —Anna Beckley
Windsor, Pennsylvania

Pastry for a single-crust pie
4 large tart apples, peeled and cut into
1/4-inch slices (about 5 cups)
1/2 cup shredded cheddar, mozzarella *or* Swiss cheese
1/2 cup packed brown sugar
1/2 cup chopped walnuts
1/2 teaspoon ground cinnamon
1/2 teaspoon ground nutmeg
2 tablespoons cold butter *or* margarine

Roll pastry to fit a greased 12-in. pizza pan; flute edges. Bake at 400° for 10 minutes. Arrange apples in a single layer in a circular pattern to completely cover pastry. Sprinkle with cheese. Combine the brown sugar, walnuts, cinnamon and nutmeg; sprinkle over cheese. Cut butter into small pieces and dot top of pizza. Bake for 20 minutes or until apples are tender. Cut into wedges; serve warm. **Yield:** 12 servings.

Sweet on Sugar

Try adding a bit of confectioners' sugar to the pastry dough. Folks who normally would leave the edge of the crust can't help but gobble it up!

batter. Divide in half; gradually fold chocolate mixture into one portion. Alternately spoon the plain and chocolate batters into an ungreased 10-in. tube pan. Swirl with a knife. Bake at 325° for 55 minutes. Increase temperature to 350°; bake 10-15 minutes longer or until top springs back when lightly touched. Immediately invert cake; cool completely. For frosting, melt semisweet chocolate and butter in a small saucepan over low heat. Stir in cream and vanilla. Remove from the heat; whisk in confectioners' sugar until smooth. Immediately spoon over cake. Cool. **Yield:** 12-16 servings.

— 🥤 🥤 🥤 —

Cherry Crumb Pie

I keep a file of simple recipes and a variety of ingredients on hand so my grandkids can choose what they'd like to make when they stop by. Granddaughter Andrea is proud to serve this impressive dessert.
—*Flo Burtnett, Gage, Oklahoma*

- 1 tablespoon cornstarch
- 1 tablespoon cold water
- 1 can (21 ounces) cherry pie filling
- 1 graham cracker crust (9 inches)

TOPPING:
- 1/3 cup all-purpose flour
- 1/3 cup quick-cooking oats
- 2 tablespoons sugar
- 2 tablespoons brown sugar
- 3 tablespoons cold butter *or* margarine

In a bowl, combine cornstarch and water until smooth. Stir in pie filling. Pour into crust. For topping, combine flour, oats and sugars in a small bowl; cut in the butter until crumbly. Sprinkle over filling. Bake at 375° for 35-40 minutes or until crust is golden brown and filling is bubbly. Cool on a wire rack; refrigerate until chilled. **Yield:** 6-8 servings.

— 🥤 🥤 🥤 —

Walnut Torte

A hint of citrus complements the rich walnut taste of this fabulous three-layer cake. Toasted chopped walnuts make a great garnish on top of the smooth buttercream frosting.
—*Kathryn Anderson Wallkill, New York*

- 9 eggs, *separated*
- 1 cup sugar
- 1/2 cup water
- 1 tablespoon grated orange peel
- 2 teaspoons grated lemon peel
- 1 teaspoon vanilla extract

Marble Chiffon Cake

(Pictured above)

This confection's a proven winner—it earned a blue ribbon and was named Division Champion at the county fair some years back! —*LuAnn Heikkila Floodwood, Minnesota*

- 2 squares (1 ounce *each*) unsweetened chocolate
- 1-3/4 cups sugar, *divided*
- 1/4 cup hot water
- 1/4 teaspoon baking soda
- 2 cups all-purpose flour
- 1 tablespoon baking powder
- 1 teaspoon salt
- 7 eggs, *separated*
- 3/4 cup water
- 1/2 cup vegetable oil
- 2 teaspoons vanilla extract
- 1/2 teaspoon cream of tartar

FROSTING:
- 4 squares (1 ounce *each*) semisweet chocolate
- 1 tablespoon butter *or* margarine
- 7 tablespoons whipping cream
- 1 teaspoon vanilla extract
- 1-1/2 cups confectioners' sugar

In a small saucepan, melt unsweetened chocolate over low heat. Add 1/4 cup sugar, hot water and baking soda; mix well and set aside. In a mixing bowl, combine flour, baking powder, salt and remaining sugar. Form a well in the center; add yolks, water, oil and vanilla; blend until moistened. Beat 3 minutes on medium speed; set aside. In another mixing bowl, beat egg whites and cream of tartar on high until stiff peaks form. Gradually fold into

3 cups finely ground walnuts
1/2 cup dry bread crumbs
2 teaspoons baking powder
1 teaspoon ground cinnamon
1 teaspoon ground cloves
1/2 teaspoon salt
1/4 teaspoon cream of tartar
BUTTERCREAM FROSTING:
1/2 cup shortening
1/2 cup butter *or* margarine, softened
1 teaspoon vanilla extract
4 cups confectioners' sugar
3 tablespoons milk
Additional walnuts, chopped and toasted

Line three 9-in. round cake pans with waxed paper; grease the paper and set aside. In a mixing bowl, beat egg yolks until slightly thickened. Gradually add sugar, beating until thick and lemon-colored. Beat in the water, peels and vanilla. Combine the walnuts, bread crumbs, baking powder, cinnamon, cloves and salt; add to batter. Beat until smooth. In another mixing bowl, beat egg whites and cream of tartar until stiff peaks form. Fold half into the batter; fold in remaining whites. Pour into prepared pans. Bake at 350° for 20-25 minutes or until a toothpick inserted near the center comes out clean. Cool for 10 minutes before removing from pans to wire racks. Carefully remove waxed paper. For frosting, in a mixing bowl, cream shortening and butter. Beat in vanilla. Gradually beat in sugar. Add milk; beat until light and fluffy. Spread frosting between layers and over top and sides of cake. Garnish with toasted walnuts. **Yield:** 12-15 servings. **Editor's Note:** This recipe does not contain flour.

— 🏆 🏆 🏆 —

Blushing Peach Pie

Red-hot candies give the filling in this pie its rosy "blushing" color. My husband, Roy (publisher of Taste of Home), ranks this beautiful fruit pie as one of his all-time favorites. —Bobbi Reiman, Greendale, Wisconsin

Pastry for double-crust pie (9 inches)
6 cups sliced peeled fresh peaches
2 tablespoons lemon juice
2/3 cup sugar
1/3 cup all-purpose flour
1/4 teaspoon salt
Dash ground nutmeg
3 tablespoons red-hot candies
2 tablespoons butter *or* margarine

Line a 9-in. pie plate with bottom pastry; trim even with edge of plate. Set aside. In a bowl, toss the peaches with lemon juice. Combine the sugar, flour, salt and nutmeg; add to peaches and toss to combine. Pour into crust. Sprinkle with red-hots; dot with butter. Roll out remaining pastry to fit top of pie. Place over filling. Trim, seal and flute edges. Cut slits in top. Cover edges loosely with foil. Bake at 425° for 25 minutes. Reduce heat to 350°; remove foil and bake 20 minutes longer or until crust is golden brown and filling is bubbly. Cool on a wire rack. **Yield:** 6-8 servings.

— 🏆 🏆 🏆 —

Cranberry Cherry Pie

(Pictured below)

Guests won't believe how quickly you made this sweet-tart pie. It starts with convenient canned pie filling. —Marilyn Williams, Matthews, North Carolina

3/4 cup sugar
2 tablespoons cornstarch
1 can (21 ounces) cherry pie filling
2 cups cranberries
Pastry for double-crust pie (9 inches)
Milk and additional sugar

In a bowl, combine sugar and cornstarch. Stir in pie filling and cranberries. Line a 9-in. pie plate with bottom pastry; trim to 1 in. beyond edge of plate. Pour filling into crust. Roll out remaining pastry to fit top of pie. Cut slits in pastry or cut out stars with a star-shaped cookie cutter. Place pastry over filling; trim, seal and flute edges. Arrange star cutouts on pastry. Brush with milk and sprinkle with sugar. Cover edges loosely with foil. Bake at 375° for 55-60 minutes or until crust is golden brown and filling is bubbly. Cool on a wire rack. **Yield:** 6-8 servings.

Mocha Chip Bundt Cake

My mom gave me the recipe for this easy-to-make moist cake. It always goes over big at all our FFA banquets. —Debbie Jeznach, Haines City, Florida

    2 tablespoons instant coffee granules
  1/2 cup hot water
    1 package (18-1/4 ounces) chocolate cake
      mix
    1 package (3.9 ounces) instant chocolate
      pudding mix
  3/4 cup sour cream
  1/2 cup vegetable oil
    3 eggs
1-1/2 cups semisweet chocolate chips
GLAZE:
  3/4 cup whipping cream
1-1/2 cups semisweet chocolate chips

In a mixing bowl, dissolve coffee granules in hot water. Beat in the cake mix, pudding mix, sour cream, oil and eggs. Stir in the chocolate chips. Pour into a greased and floured 10-in. fluted tube pan. Bake at 350° for 1 hour or until a toothpick inserted near the center comes out clean. Cool for 10 minutes before inverting onto a wire rack to cool completely. In a saucepan, heat cream to simmering. Remove from the heat; whisk in chocolate chips until smooth. Drizzle over cake. **Yield:** 12-16 servings.

——— 🥤 🥤 🥤 ———

Apple Snack Cake

(Pictured below)

The apple provides natural sweetness and helps make this cake moist and delicious. I'm a former home economics teacher who loves to delight family and friends with homemade goodies. —Julia Helvey Columbia, Missouri

1-1/2 cups all-purpose flour
  1/4 cup baking cocoa
    1 teaspoon baking soda
  1/2 teaspoon salt
    1 cup water
  1/4 cup vegetable oil
    1 teaspoon lemon juice
    1 teaspoon vanilla extract
    1 cup chopped peeled tart apples
  2/3 cup sugar
  1/4 teaspoon ground cinnamon

In a medium bowl, combine flour, cocoa, baking soda and salt. Combine water, oil, lemon juice and vanilla; add to the dry ingredients and stir just until combined. Toss apples with sugar and cinnamon; fold into batter. Pour into a greased 8-in. square baking pan. Bake at 350° for 30-35 minutes or until cake tests done. **Yield:** 9 servings.

——— 🥤 🥤 🥤 ———

Blueberry Pie

My pie has a wonderful fresh blueberry flavor and a bit of tang from lemon peel. —Richard Case Johnstown, Pennsylvania

    4 cups fresh *or* frozen blueberries
    1 tablespoon lemon juice
1-1/4 to 1-1/2 cups sugar
  1/4 cup quick-cooking tapioca
    1 tablespoon cornstarch
  1/2 teaspoon grated lemon peel
  1/2 teaspoon ground cinnamon
Pastry for a double-crust pie (9 inches)
    1 tablespoon butter *or* margarine

In a bowl, combine berries and lemon juice. Add sugar, tapioca, cornstarch, lemon peel and cinnamon; toss gently. Let stand for 15 minutes. Line a 9-in. pie plate with bottom pastry; trim to 1 in. beyond edge of plate. Add filling; dot with butter. Place remaining pastry over filling. Cut slits in top. Trim, seal and flute edges. Cover edges loosely with foil. Bake at 350° for 30 minutes. Remove foil; bake 20-30 minutes longer or until crust is golden brown. Cool on a wire rack. **Yield:** 6-8 servings.

——— 🥤 🥤 🥤 ———

Banana Chiffon Cake

Simple yet delicious desserts were my Aunt Allie's specialty. This cake was one of her best. —Nancy Horsburgh, Everett, Ontario

2-1/4 cups cake flour
1-1/2 cups sugar
    1 tablespoon baking powder

1 teaspoon salt
1 cup mashed ripe bananas (about 2 medium)
1/3 cup vegetable oil
1/3 cup water
5 eggs, *separated*
1 teaspoon vanilla extract
Chocolate frosting *or* frosting of your choice

In a large bowl, combine flour, sugar, baking powder and salt. Make a well in the center; add bananas, oil, water, egg yolks and vanilla. Beat until smooth. In a small mixing bowl, beat egg whites until stiff peaks form. Fold into batter. Pour into an ungreased 10-in. tube pan. Bake at 325° for 60-65 minutes or until cake springs back when lightly touched. Immediately invert pan; cool completely. Remove cake from pan; frost top and sides. **Yield:** 12 servings.

Pistachio Dream Cake

This moist delightful cake is good for you and yummy, too. The quick frosting is cool and creamy.
—Audrey Grimm, Mesa, Arizona

☑ Uses less fat, sugar or salt. Includes Nutritional Analysis and Diabetic Exchanges.

1 package (18-1/4 ounces) light yellow cake mix
1 package (1 ounce) instant sugar-free pistachio pudding mix
1 carton (8 ounces) nonfat plain yogurt
3 egg whites
1 teaspoon vanilla extract
1 cup diet lemon-lime soda
FROSTING:
1-1/2 cups cold skim milk
1 package (1 ounce) instant sugar-free pistachio pudding mix
2 cups light whipped topping

In a mixing bowl, combine dry cake and pudding mixes, yogurt, egg whites and vanilla; beat on low speed for 1 minute. Gradually beat in soda. Pour into a 13-in. x 9-in. x 2-in. baking pan coated with nonstick cooking spray. Bake at 350° for 20-25 minutes or until a toothpick inserted near the center comes out clean. Cool. For frosting, combine milk and dry pudding mix in a mixing bowl; beat on low for 2 minutes. Fold in whipped topping. Spread over cake. Store in the refrigerator. **Yield:** 20 servings. **Nutritional Analysis:** One serving equals 148 calories, 300 mg sodium, 1 mg cholesterol, 28 gm carbohydrate, 3 gm protein, 2 gm fat, 0 fiber. **Diabetic Exchange:** 2 starch.

Caramel Pear Pie
(Pictured above)

A dear friend shared the recipe for this attractive pie. The caramel drizzle and streusel topping make it almost too pretty to eat. Knowing this dessert is waiting is great motivation for our children to eat all their vegetables. —*Mary Kaehler, Lodi, California*

6 cups sliced peeled ripe pears (about 6 medium)
1 tablespoon lemon juice
1/2 cup plus 3 tablespoons sugar, *divided*
2 tablespoons quick-cooking tapioca
3/4 teaspoon ground cinnamon
1/4 teaspoon salt
1/4 teaspoon ground nutmeg
1 unbaked pastry shell (9 inches)
3/4 cup old-fashioned oats
1 tablespoon all-purpose flour
1/4 cup cold butter *or* margarine
18 caramels
5 tablespoons milk
1/4 cup chopped pecans

In a large bowl, combine pears and lemon juice. In another bowl, combine 1/2 cup sugar, tapioca, cinnamon, salt and nutmeg. Add to pears; stir gently. Let stand for 15 minutes. Pour into pastry shell. In a bowl, combine the oats, flour and remaining sugar. Cut in butter until crumbly. Sprinkle over pears. Bake at 400° for 45 minutes. Meanwhile, in a saucepan over low heat, melt caramels with milk. Stir until smooth; add pecans. Drizzle over pie. Bake 8-10 minutes longer or until crust is golden brown and filling is bubbly. Cool on a wire rack. **Yield:** 6-8 servings.

Just Desserts

For some folks, dessert is the main part of the meal! From crisps, cobblers and candies to cheesecakes, puddings, ice cream and more, no sweet tooth will ever have to do without.

EYE-CATCHING ASSORTMENT. Clockwise from upper left: Banana Crepes (p. 174), Apple-of-Your Eye Cheesecake (p. 172), Pretzel Fruit Pizza (p. 166), Chocolate Peanut Sweeties (p. 153), Valentine Berries and Cream (p. 163) and Pear Sundae French Toast (p. 159).

Cool Lime Cheesecake

(Pictured above)

I started baking this treat several years ago, and it immediately won raves. The mixture of tart lime and sweet creamy cheesecake is absolutely scrumptious. At any get-together, it's a showstopping dessert that's always enjoyed.
—Karen Donhauser
Frazer, Pennsylvania

2-1/4 cups graham cracker crumbs (about 36
    squares)
  1/3 cup sugar
  1/2 cup butter *or* margarine, melted
FILLING:
  20 ounces cream cheese, softened
  3/4 cup sugar
    1 cup (8 ounces) sour cream
    3 tablespoons all-purpose flour
    3 eggs
  2/3 cup lime juice
    1 teaspoon vanilla extract
    1 drop green food coloring, optional
Whipped cream and lime slices

In a bowl, combine crumbs and sugar; stir in butter. Press onto the bottom and 1 in. up the side of a greased 10-in. springform pan. Bake at 375° for 8 minutes. Cool. In a mixing bowl, beat cream cheese and sugar until smooth. Add sour cream and flour; beat well. Beat in eggs on low speed just until combined. Stir in lime juice, vanilla and food coloring if desired just until mixed. Pour into crust. Bake at 325° for 50-55 minutes or until

center is almost set. Cool on a wire rack for 1 hour. Refrigerate overnight. Remove sides of pan. Garnish with whipped cream and lime. **Yield:** 12-14 servings.

Caramel Banana Sundaes

When I don't have time to bake, I often rely on this quick dessert.
—Jeanne Mays
North Richland Hills, Texas

    3 tablespoons brown sugar
    2 tablespoons butter *or* margarine
    2 tablespoons whipping cream
  1/2 teaspoon rum extract
  1/2 teaspoon vanilla extract
  1/4 teaspoon ground cinnamon
    2 medium firm bananas, cut into 1/2-inch
      slices
Vanilla ice cream

In a skillet, combine brown sugar, butter, cream, extracts and cinnamon. Bring to a boil over medium heat, stirring constantly. Cook for 2 minutes. Remove from the heat; add bananas and stir until coated. Return to heat; cook 2 minutes longer, stirring occasionally. Serve warm over ice cream. **Yield:** 4 servings.

Apple Bread Pudding

My young grandson loves to help me make his favorite dessert. When Frankie eats this comforting pudding, he declares, "Yum yum in my tummy."
—Dorothy Popotnik, Willoughby, Ohio

  10 slices Italian *or* French bread, cubed,
    divided
    1 jar (25 ounces) chunky applesauce
  1/8 teaspoon ground nutmeg
    2 eggs
    2 cups milk
  1/2 cup sugar
  1/2 teaspoon vanilla extract
  1/8 teaspoon ground cinnamon
Whipped topping, optional

Place half of the bread cubes in a greased 11-in. x 7-in. x 2-in. baking dish. Spoon applesauce over bread; sprinkle with nutmeg. Top with remaining bread. In a bowl, whisk the eggs, milk, sugar and vanilla. Pour over bread. Sprinkle with cinnamon. Bake, uncovered, at 325° for 50-60 minutes or until a knife inserted near the center comes out clean. Serve with whipped topping if desired. **Yield:** 8-10 servings.

Raspberry Tapioca Pudding

This ruby-red pudding was a favorite dessert when I was a child growing up in a German family.
—Helga Schlape, Florham Park, New Jersey

    1 package (10 ounces) frozen sweetened
      raspberries, thawed
    1 cup red grape juice
  1/3 cup sugar
    1 lemon peel strip (1 inch)
  1/4 cup quick-cooking tapioca
  1/2 cup whipping cream
    2 tablespoons confectioners' sugar

Mash and strain raspberries, reserving juice. Discard seeds. Add enough water to juice to measure 2 cups; pour into a large saucepan. Add grape juice, sugar and lemon peel. Bring to a boil; reduce heat. Simmer, uncovered, for 10 minutes. Remove lemon peel. Add tapioca. Cook and stir for 10 minutes. Pour into bowls. Cover and chill for 4 hours or until set. In a mixing bowl, beat cream and confectioners' sugar until soft peaks form. Serve with pudding. **Yield:** 6 servings.

Oatmeal Ice Cream Sandwiches

I'm known for my desserts. These sandwiches combine the cookies I like best with ice cream. —Gary Maly
West Chester, Ohio

    1 cup butter-flavored shortening
    1 cup packed brown sugar
  1/2 cup sugar
    2 eggs
    1 teaspoon vanilla extract
    2 cups quick-cooking oats
1-1/2 cups all-purpose flour
    1 teaspoon baking soda
    1 teaspoon salt
  1/2 teaspoon ground cinnamon
    1 cup vanilla *or* white chips
    1 cup chopped pecans
  1/2 gallon vanilla ice cream

In a mixing bowl, cream shortening and sugars. Beat in eggs and vanilla. Combine dry ingredients; gradually add to the creamed mixture. Stir in the chips and pecans. Drop by heaping teaspoonfuls 3 in. apart onto lightly greased baking sheets. Bake at 375° for 10-12 minutes or until golden brown. Remove to wire racks to cool. To make ice cream sandwiches, place a scoop of ice cream on the bottom of half of the cookies. Top with remaining cookies; wrap in plastic wrap. Place on a baking sheet; freeze. **Yield:** about 2 dozen sandwiches.

Chocolate Peanut Sweeties

(Pictured below and on page 150)

Inspired by my passion for peanut butter and chocolate, I combined a trusted recipe for peanut butter eggs with the salty crunch of pretzels. Now our kids have fun helping me make and eat these heavenly treats.
—Gina Kintigh, Connellsville, Pennsylvania

    1 cup peanut butter*
  1/2 cup butter (no substitutes), softened
    3 cups confectioners' sugar
    5 dozen miniature pretzel twists (about 3
      cups)
1-1/2 cups milk chocolate chips
    1 tablespoon vegetable oil

In a mixing bowl, beat peanut butter and butter until smooth. Beat in confectioners' sugar until combined. Shape into 1-in. balls; press one on each pretzel. Place on waxed paper-lined baking sheets. Refrigerate until peanut butter mixture is firm, about 1 hour. In a microwave-safe bowl or heavy saucepan, melt chocolate chips and oil. Dip the peanut butter ball into chocolate. Return to baking sheet, pretzel side down. Refrigerate for at least 30 minutes before serving. Store in the refrigerator. **Yield:** 5 dozen. ***Editor's Note:** Reduced-fat or generic-brand peanut butter is not recommended for use in this recipe.

Rhubarb-Topped Cheesecake

(Pictured below)

No one will believe that this creamy dessert, topped with tangy rhubarb, is actually a light treat.
—*Ruth Eisenreich, Catonsville, Maryland*

☑ Uses less fat, sugar or salt. Includes Nutritional Analysis and Diabetic Exchanges.

   3/4 cup graham cracker crumbs (about 10 squares)
   1/2 teaspoon ground cinnamon
   3 tablespoons reduced-fat margarine, melted
   2 packages (8 ounces *each*) light cream cheese, softened
   3/4 cup sugar
Egg substitute equivalent to 4 eggs
   1 cup (8 ounces) nonfat vanilla yogurt
   1/4 cup lemon juice
   1 teaspoon grated lemon peel
TOPPING:
   3 cups diced fresh *or* frozen rhubarb
   1 cup sugar
   2 tablespoons plus 1/2 cup cold water, *divided*
   1 tablespoon cornstarch
Red food coloring, optional

In a small bowl, combine cracker crumbs and cinnamon; stir in margarine. Press onto the bottom of a 9-in. springform pan; set aside. In a mixing bowl, beat cream cheese and sugar until smooth. Slowly add egg substitute; beat on low just until combined. Beat in the yogurt, lemon juice and peel just until combined. Pour over crust. Bake at 350° for 35-40 minutes or until center is almost set. Cool on a wire rack for 10 minutes. Carefully run a knife around edge of pan to loosen; cool 1 hour longer. Refrigerate overnight. In a saucepan, combine rhubarb, sugar and 2 tablespoons water. Bring to a boil. Reduce heat; simmer until rhubarb is tender, about 10 minutes. Combine cornstarch and remaining water until smooth; stir into rhubarb mixture. Bring to a boil; cook and stir for 2 minutes or until thickened. Add food coloring if desired. Cover and refrigerate until cool. Spoon over slices of cheesecake. **Yield:** 12 servings. **Nutritional Analysis:** One serving with 2 tablespoons topping equals 259 calories, 272 mg sodium, 14 mg cholesterol, 42 gm carbohydrate, 8 gm protein, 7 gm fat, 1 gm fiber. **Diabetic Exchanges:** 2 starch, 1-1/2 fat, 1 fruit.

— 🥄 🥄 🥄 —

Pecan Cream Cheese Squares

This rich, easy dessert is perfect after a light meal. It's a quick way to dress up a boxed cake mix.
—*Dorothy Pritchett, Wills Point, Texas*

   1 package (18-1/4 ounces) yellow cake mix
   3 eggs
   1/2 cup butter *or* margarine, softened
   2 cups chopped pecans
   1 package (8 ounces) cream cheese, softened
3-2/3 cups confectioners' sugar

In a mixing bowl, combine cake mix, 1 egg and butter. Stir in pecans; mix well. Press into a greased 13-in. x 9-in. x 2-in. baking pan. In a mixing bowl, beat the cream cheese, sugar and remaining eggs until smooth. Pour over pecan mixture. Bake at 350° for 45-55 minutes or until golden brown. Cool on a wire rack; cut into squares. Store in the refrigerator. **Yield:** 3 dozen.

— 🥄 🥄 🥄 —

Chocolate Truffles

You may be tempted to save this recipe for a special occasion since these smooth, creamy chocolates are divine. They're easy to make anytime.
—*Darlene Wiese-Appleby, Creston, Ohio*

   3 cups (18 ounces) semisweet chocolate chips
   1 can (14 ounces) sweetened condensed milk
   1 tablespoon vanilla extract
Chopped flaked coconut, chocolate sprinkles, colored sprinkles, baking cocoa *and/or* finely chopped nuts, optional

In a microwave-safe bowl, heat chocolate chips and milk at 50% power until chocolate is melted. Stir in vanilla. Chill for 2 hours or until mixture is easy to handle. Shape into 1-in. balls. Roll in coconut, sprinkles, cocoa or nuts if desired. **Yield:** about 4 dozen.

——— 🍵 🍵 🍵 ———

Sherbet Angel Torte

For a cool, light and dramatic dessert, you can't miss with this lovely torte. —Amy Nichols
Brownville, Maine

✓ Uses less fat, sugar or salt. Includes Nutritional Analysis and Diabetic Exchanges.

1 prepared angel food cake (16 ounces)
1 quart raspberry sherbet
1 carton (8 ounces) light frozen whipped topping, thawed
1/2 cup reduced-sugar raspberry preserves, warmed
Fresh raspberries, optional

Freeze the cake for at least 2 hours or overnight. Split cake horizontally into three layers. Place bottom layer on a freezer-safe serving plate; spread with about 1 cup sherbet. Repeat layers. Add top cake layer. Fill center with remaining sherbet. Frost top and sides with whipped topping. Gently spread preserves over top of cake. Loosely cover and store in freezer. Thaw in the refrigerator for 30 minutes before slicing with a serrated knife. Garnish with raspberries if desired. **Yield:** 12 servings. **Nutritional Analysis:** One serving (calculated without garnish) equals 249 calories, 224 mg sodium, 3 mg cholesterol, 50 gm carbohydrate, 3 gm protein, 4 gm fat, trace fiber. **Diabetic Exchanges:** 2 starch, 1 fruit.

——— 🍵 🍵 🍵 ———

Sweetheart Walnut Torte

(Pictured above right)

I always donate one of these lightly sweet tortes for our church bake sale. But the ladies in charge quickly put it aside for one of them to buy! —Gladys Jenik
Orland Park, Illinois

1/2 cup butter *or* margarine, softened
1/2 cup sugar
4 egg yolks
1/3 cup milk
1/2 teaspoon vanilla extract
1 cup all-purpose flour
2 teaspoons baking powder
1/8 teaspoon salt

MERINGUE:
4 egg whites
1/8 teaspoon cream of tartar
3/4 cup sugar
1 cup chopped walnuts
Walnut halves
FILLING:
1 cup cold milk
1 package (3.9 ounces) instant chocolate pudding
1 cup whipping cream, whipped

Grease two 9-in. heart-shaped pans. Line with waxed paper and grease the paper; set aside. In a mixing bowl, cream butter and sugar. Add egg yolks, milk and vanilla; mix well. Combine flour, baking powder and salt; gradually add to creamed mixture. Pour into prepared pans. In a mixing bowl, beat egg whites and cream of tartar until soft peaks form. Gradually add sugar; beat until stiff and glossy. Fold in chopped nuts. Spread evenly over batter, sealing edges to sides of pan. Arrange walnut halves over meringue in one pan. Bake at 300° for 55 minutes or until golden brown. Cool for 10 minutes; remove to wire racks. Invert so meringue side is up; cool completely. In a mixing bowl, beat milk and pudding mix until thickened. Fold in whipped cream. Place plain cake, meringue side up, on serving plate. Spread with half of the filling; top with remaining cake. Frost sides with remaining filling. **Yield:** 12-16 servings.

Blueberry Cream Nut Roll

For a special occasion or family treat during blueberry season, try this wonderful dessert.
—*Schelby Thompson, Winter Haven, Florida*

> 6 eggs, *separated*
> 3/4 cup sugar, *divided*
> 1-1/3 cups ground walnuts
> 1 teaspoon baking powder
> 1/2 teaspoon ground cinnamon
> 1/8 teaspoon salt

FILLING:

> 1 cup whipping cream
> 1/4 cup confectioners' sugar
> 1/2 teaspoon vanilla extract
> 1-1/2 cups fresh blueberries

Additional confectioners' sugar and blueberries

In a mixing bowl, beat egg yolks for 1 minute. Add 1/2 cup sugar; beat until thick and lemon-colored. In a small bowl, combine walnuts, baking powder and cinnamon; fold into yolk mixture. In another mixing bowl, beat egg whites and salt until soft peaks form; gradually beat in remaining sugar until stiff peaks form. Fold a small amount of egg white mixture into nut mixture; gradually fold in remaining egg whites. Line a greased 15-in. x 10-in. x 1-in. baking pan with waxed paper; grease and flour the paper. Spread batter evenly into pan. Bake at 350° for 20-25 minutes or until lightly browned. Cool in pan for 5 minutes. Turn onto a kitchen towel dusted with confectioners' sugar. Gently peel off waxed paper. Roll up in towel, jelly-roll style, starting with a long side. Cool on a wire rack. For filling, whip the cream, sugar and vanilla; set aside 1/2 cup for garnish. Unroll cake; spread with remaining filling. Sprinkle with blueberries. Roll up; cover and refrigerate until serving. Dust with confectioners' sugar; garnish with blueberries and reserved whipped topping. **Yield:** 10-12 servings. **Editor's Note:** This recipe does not contain flour.

— 🍶 🍶 🍶 —

Chocolate Peanut Butter Pizza

(Pictured above)

This is probably the most unusual "pizza" you'll ever see! It's great for kids, although adults snap it up, too. Everyone loves the chewy crust and the flavor. Chocolate and peanut butter are a nice combination.
—*Bernice Arnett, Marshfield, Missouri*

> 1/2 cup shortening
> 1/2 cup peanut butter
> 1/2 cup packed brown sugar
> 1/2 cup sugar
> 2 eggs, lightly beaten
> 1/2 teaspoon vanilla extract
> 1-1/2 cups all-purpose flour
> 2 cups miniature marshmallows
> 1 cup (6 ounces) semisweet chocolate chips

In a mixing bowl, cream shortening, peanut butter and sugars. Beat in eggs and vanilla. Stir in flour and mix well. Pat into a greased 12-in. pizza pan. Bake at 375° for 12 minutes. Sprinkle with the marshmallows and chocolate chips. Return to the oven for 4-6 minutes or until lightly browned. **Yield:** 16-20 servings.

Autumn Apple Tart

There are so many apple orchards in our state. This tasty tart is one of my favorite ways to use this fall fruit.
—*Grace Howaniec, Waukesha, Wisconsin*

CRUST:

> 1-1/4 cups all-purpose flour
> 1 teaspoon baking powder
> 1/2 teaspoon salt
> 1 tablespoon sugar
> 1/2 cup butter *or* margarine
> 1 egg, beaten
> 2 tablespoons milk

6 medium baking apples, peeled, cored and sliced 1/4 inch thick
TOPPING:
1/3 to 1/2 cup sugar
2 tablespoons butter *or* margarine
4-1/2 teaspoons all-purpose flour
1/2 teaspoon ground cinnamon
1/2 teaspoon ground nutmeg

Combine flour, baking powder, salt and sugar in a medium bowl. Cut in butter with pastry blender until crumbly. Combine egg and milk; add to flour/butter mixture. Stir to blend. With lightly floured hands, press dough into a 12-in.-diameter tart pan (with removable bottom). Press dough up sides to form a 1-in. rim. (May use a 13-in. x 9-in. x 2-in. baking pan instead of tart pan.) Fill tart shell with overlapping apple slices, beginning at outer edge. Combine topping ingredients; sprinkle evenly over apples. Bake at 350° for 50-60 minutes or until apples are tender. Cut into wedges. Serve warm or at room temperature. **Yield:** 12 servings.

Chocolate Dessert Waffles

The mild chocolate flavor and cake-like texture make these waffles a delightful dessert. —*Phalice Ayers Spokane, Washington*

1/4 cup butter *or* margarine, softened
1 cup sugar
2 eggs
2 squares (1 ounce *each*) unsweetened chocolate, melted and cooled
1 teaspoon vanilla extract
1-1/2 cups all-purpose flour
2 teaspoons baking powder
1/4 teaspoon salt
1/2 cup milk
Whipped cream, fresh fruit *or* ice cream

In a mixing bowl, cream butter and sugar. Add eggs, one at a time, beating well after each addition. Stir in chocolate and vanilla. Combine flour, baking powder and salt; add to the creamed mixture alternately with milk. Preheat waffle iron. Fill and bake according to manufacturer's directions. Serve with whipped cream, fruit or ice cream. **Yield:** 4-6 waffles.

Classic Combination
The next time you make cook-and-serve chocolate pudding, stir in some creamy peanut butter after removing the pudding from the heat.

Cheesecake Squares
(Pictured below)

I lived on a dairy farm when I was young, and my mom always had a lot of sour cream to use. She never wasted any, and this cheesecake was one of my family's favorites. It's great topped with blackberry sauce. —*Shirley Forest, Eau Claire, Wisconsin*

2 packages (8 ounces *each*) cream cheese, softened
1 cup ricotta cheese
1-1/2 cups sugar
4 eggs
1/4 cup butter *or* margarine, melted and cooled
3 tablespoons cornstarch
3 tablespoons all-purpose flour
1 tablespoon vanilla extract
2 cups (16 ounces) sour cream
Seasonal fresh fruit, optional

In a mixing bowl, beat cream cheese, ricotta and sugar until smooth. Add the eggs, one at a time, mixing well after each addition. Add butter, cornstarch, flour and vanilla; beat until smooth. Fold in sour cream. Pour into a greased 13-in. x 9-in. x 2-in. baking pan. Bake, uncovered, at 325° for 1 hour. Do not open oven door. Turn oven off. Let cheesecake stand in closed oven for 2 hours. Cool completely on a wire rack. Chill several hours or overnight. Top each square with fruit if desired. **Yield:** 20 servings.

Yogurt Ice Pops

(Pictured below)

Fresh-tasting and fun, these strawberry ice pops get smooth, creamy goodness from yogurt.
—*Pat Manchur, Sanford, Manitoba*

✓ Uses less fat, sugar or salt. Includes Nutritional Analysis and Diabetic Exchanges.

Artificial sweetener equivalent to 1/3 cup sugar
    1 cup cold water, *divided*
    1 envelope unflavored gelatin
    3 cups frozen unsweetened strawberries, thawed and drained
    2 cartons (8 ounces *each***) nonfat strawberry** *or* **vanilla yogurt**
  16 Popsicle molds *or* **paper cups (3 ounces** *each***) and Popsicle sticks**

In a bowl, combine sweetener and 3/4 cup cold water. Combine gelatin and remaining water in a saucepan; let stand for 2 minutes. Heat until gelatin is dissolved; remove from the heat. In batches, place the strawberries, sweetened water, gelatin mixture and yogurt in a blender or food processor; cover and process until smooth. Fill molds or cups with about 1/4 cup strawberry mixture; top with holders or insert sticks into cups. Freeze. **Yield:** 16 servings. **Nutritional Analysis:** One serving equals 28 calories, 16 mg sodium, trace cholesterol, 6 gm carbohydrate, 2 gm protein, trace fat, 1 gm fiber. **Diabetic Exchange:** 1/2 fruit.

Banana Ice Cream

I remember this citrus ice cream from my birthdays and summer holidays at my grandparents' lake cottage.
—*Tammy Mikesell, Columbia City, Indiana*

  3 eggs, beaten
  3 cups sugar
  6 cups cold milk, *divided*
  1 package (3.4 ounces) instant vanilla pudding mix
  1 cup orange juice
  1 cup lemon juice
  1 cup mashed ripe bananas (2 to 3 medium)
  4 cups half-and-half cream

In a saucepan, combine the eggs, sugar and 4 cups of the milk. Cook and stir over medium heat until the mixture reaches 160° and is thick enough to coat a metal spoon. Cool. Meanwhile, in a mixing bowl, combine the pudding mix and remaining milk. Beat on low speed for 2 minutes. Stir juices, bananas, cream and pudding into the cooled egg mixture. Freeze in batches in an ice cream freezer according to manufacturer's instructions. Refrigerate extra mixture until it can be frozen. **Yield:** about 3-1/2 quarts.

— 🍴 🍴 🍴 —

Pumpkin Chiffon Torte

After a sumptuous holiday meal, this light and tasty dessert is perfect. Gingersnaps make up the tasty crust.
—*Lynn Kumm, Osmond, Nebraska*

✓ Uses less fat, sugar or salt. Includes Nutritional Analysis and Diabetic Exchanges.

  1 cup finely crushed gingersnaps (about 24)
  3 tablespoons butter *or* **margarine, melted**
  2 envelopes unflavored gelatin
1/2 cup milk
1/2 cup sugar
  1 can (15 ounces) solid-pack pumpkin
1/2 teaspoon salt
1/2 teaspoon ground cinnamon
1/4 teaspoon ground ginger
1/4 teaspoon ground cloves
  1 carton (8 ounces) frozen whipped topping, thawed
Additional whipped topping, optional

In a small bowl, combine cookie crumbs and butter. Press onto the bottom of a greased 9-in. springform pan; set aside. In a saucepan, combine gelatin and milk; let stand for 5 minutes. Heat milk mixture to just below boiling; remove from the heat. Stir in sugar until dissolved. Add the pumpkin, salt, cinnamon, ginger and cloves; mix well. Fold in whipped topping. Pour over crust. Refrigerate until set, about 3 hours. Remove sides of pan just before serving. Garnish with additional whipped topping if desired. **Yield:** 16 servings. **Nutritional Analysis:** One serving (prepared with skim milk and light whipped topping) equals 138 calories, 168 mg sodium, trace cholesterol, 21 gm carbohydrate, 2 gm protein, 5 gm fat, 1 gm fiber. **Diabetic Exchanges:** 1 starch, 1 fat, 1/2 fruit.

Strawberry Cheesecake

Whenever one of my three sons or eight grandchildren has a birthday, I make this pretty, creamy cheesecake. They all love it...and I do, too!
—Luverene Dove, Appleton, Minnesota

1-1/4 cups graham cracker crumbs (about 20 crackers)
  1/4 cup sugar
  1/3 butter *or* margarine, melted
    2 packages (10 ounces *each*) frozen sweetened strawberries, thawed
    1 tablespoon cornstarch
    3 packages (8 ounces *each*) cream cheese, softened
    1 can (14 ounces) sweetened condensed milk
  1/4 cup lemon juice
    3 eggs
    1 tablespoon water, optional

Combine graham cracker crumbs, sugar and butter. Press onto the bottom of an ungreased 9-in. springform pan. Refrigerate for 30 minutes. In a blender or food processor, combine strawberries and cornstarch; cover and process until smooth. Pour into a saucepan; bring to a boil. Boil and stir for 2 minutes. Set aside 1/3 cup strawberry sauce; cool. Cover and refrigerate remaining sauce for serving. In a mixing bowl, beat cream cheese until light and fluffy. Gradually beat in milk. Add lemon juice; mix well. Add eggs; beat on low just until combined. Pour half of the cream cheese mixture over crust. Drop half of the reserved strawberry mixture by 1/2 teaspoonfuls onto cream cheese layer. Carefully spoon remaining cream cheese mixture over sauce. Drop remaining strawberry sauce by 1/2 teaspoonfuls on top. With a knife, cut through top layer only to swirl strawberry sauce. Bake at 300° for 45-50 minutes or until center is almost set. Cool on a wire rack for 10 minutes. Carefully run a knife around edge of pan to loosen; cool 1 hour longer. Refrigerate overnight. Remove side of pan. Thin chilled strawberry sauce with water if desired; serve with cheesecake. Store in the refrigerator. **Yield:** 12-16 servings.

Pear Sundae French Toast

(Pictured above and on page 150)

Coming upon this creation in a potluck line, I left with a full plate and the recipe. Now my family "oohs" and "aahs" as soon as I bring out this fruit-topped favorite. It's great as a fanciful finish to a meal.
—Carol Schumacher, Menoken, North Dakota

  1/4 cup plus 3 tablespoons packed brown sugar, *divided*
    6 tablespoons butter *or* margarine, *divided*
1-1/4 teaspoons ground cinnamon, *divided*
    3 medium ripe pears, peeled and sliced (about 2-1/2 cups)
    3 eggs, lightly beaten
  3/4 cup milk
    1 teaspoon vanilla extract
  1/4 teaspoon ground nutmeg
    6 slices French bread (1 inch thick)
Ice cream

In a skillet, combine 1/4 cup brown sugar, 2 tablespoons butter and 1/4 teaspoon cinnamon; cook and stir until sugar is dissolved. Add pears; cook until tender. In a bowl, combine the eggs, milk, vanilla, nutmeg, and remaining brown sugar and cinnamon. Dip bread in egg mixture to coat each side. Melt remaining butter in a skillet. Fry bread over medium heat for 2 minutes on each side or until golden brown. Top with ice cream and pear mixture. **Yield:** 6 servings.

4 cups soft bread cubes, lightly toasted
(about 5 slices)
1 cup flaked coconut, *divided*

Combine sugar and water in a saucepan; bring to a boil. Remove from the heat; add butter and rhubarb. Cover and let stand 15 minutes. Drain, reserving liquid. Blend liquid with egg and vanilla. Combine bread cubes, rhubarb mixture, egg mixture and 3/4 cup coconut. Place in a greased 1-qt. baking dish. Sprinkle with the remaining coconut. Bake at 325° for 45 minutes or until a knife inserted near the center comes out clean. **Yield:** 6 servings.

Banana Split Brownie Pizza

Our daughter entered this dessert in a bake-off at our county fair one year and was named overall champion in the youth division. —Lisa Hughes, Angleton, Texas

    3/4 cup shortening, melted
    1/4 cup butter *or* margarine, melted
    3/4 cup baking cocoa
      2 cups sugar
      4 eggs, beaten
      1 teaspoon vanilla extract
  1-1/2 cups all-purpose flour
      1 teaspoon baking powder
    1/2 teaspoon salt
  TOPPING:
      2 packages (8 ounces *each*) cream cheese,
        softened
    2/3 cup sugar
      1 can (8 ounces) pineapple tidbits
      1 ripe banana, sliced
      1 to 2 cups fresh strawberries, halved
    1/4 cup chopped pecans, toasted
      1 square (1 ounce) semisweet chocolate
      1 tablespoon butter (no substitutes)

In a large bowl, combine shortening, butter and cocoa. Stir in sugar, eggs and vanilla. Combine flour, baking powder and salt; stir into the egg mixture. Spread evenly over a well-greased 12-in. to 14-in. pizza pan. Bake at 350° for 20-25 minutes. Cool. In a mixing bowl, beat cream cheese and sugar until smooth; spread over brownie crust. Drain the pineapple, reserving juice; dip banana slices in juice (then discard the juice). Arrange bananas, pineapple and strawberries over cream cheese layer; sprinkle with pecans. In a small saucepan over low heat, melt chocolate and butter; drizzle over top of pizza. Chill for 1 hour. Refrigerate any leftovers. **Yield:** 12 servings. **Editor's Note:** Purchased caramel or strawberry sauce may be substituted for the chocolate topping.

Maine Potato Candy

(Pictured above)

Years ago, folks in Maine ate potatoes daily and used leftovers in bread, doughnuts and candy.
—Barbara Allen, Chelmsford, Massachusetts

      4 cups confectioners' sugar
      4 cups flaked coconut
    3/4 cup cold mashed potatoes (without added
        milk or butter)
  1-1/2 teaspoons vanilla extract
    1/2 teaspoon salt
      1 pound dark candy coating

In a large bowl, combine sugar, coconut, potatoes, vanilla and salt; mix well. Line a 9-in. square pan with foil; butter foil. Spread coconut mixture into pan. Cover and refrigerate overnight. Cut into 2-in. x 1-in. rectangles. Cover and freeze. In a microwave or double boiler, melt candy coating. Dip bars in coating; place on waxed paper to harden. Store in an airtight container. **Yield:** 2 pounds.

Rhubarb Coconut Bread Pudding

The combination of rhubarb and coconut in this recipe is surprisingly good. —*Bonnie Alsatt*
Elberfeld, Indiana

      1 cup sugar
    3/4 cup water
      2 tablespoons butter *or* margarine
      3 cups sliced fresh *or* frozen rhubarb
        (1/2-inch pieces)
      1 egg, beaten
    1/2 teaspoon vanilla extract

Sour Cream Cheesecake

This smooth cheesecake is not overly sweet, and the pound cake makes a convenient crust. It's a tradition at holiday time. —*Nick Mescia, Surprise, Arizona*

    1 **loaf (10-3/4 ounces) frozen pound cake, thawed and cut into 1/8-inch slices**
    3 **packages (8 ounces *each*) cream cheese, softened**
1-3/4 **cups sugar**
    4 **eggs**
    4 **cups (32 ounces) sour cream**
    2 **teaspoons vanilla extract**
TOPPING:
    1 **cup (8 ounces) sour cream**
Cherry pie filling

Arrange cake slices in two overlapping layers on the bottom and around the sides of a 10-in. spring-form pan; set aside. In a mixing bowl, beat cream cheese and sugar until smooth. Add eggs; beat on low just until combined. Add sour cream and vanilla; beat just until combined. Pour over cake slices. Bake at 350° for 60-70 minutes or until center is almost set. Cool on a wire rack for 10 minutes. Carefully run a knife around edge of pan to loosen; cool 1 hour longer. Refrigerate overnight. Remove sides of pan. Just before serving, spread sour cream over cheesecake; top with cherry pie filling. **Yield:** 12-14 servings.

— 🍷 🍷 🍷 —

Raspberry Crisp

I grow raspberries, so I'm always thrilled to find new ways to use the fruit. But one "old" way that my family loves is this crisp, which is my mom's recipe.
    —*Donna Craik, Ladysmith, British Columbia*

    4 **cups fresh raspberries, *divided***
3/4 **cup sugar**
    2 **tablespoons cornstarch**
1-3/4 **cups quick-cooking oats**
    1 **cup all-purpose flour**
    1 **cup packed brown sugar**
1/2 **teaspoon baking soda**
1/2 **cup cold butter *or* margarine**
Whipped cream

Crush 1 cup raspberries; add enough water to measure 1 cup. In a saucepan, combine sugar and cornstarch; stir in raspberry mixture. Bring to a boil; cook and stir for 2 minutes or until thickened. Remove from the heat; stir in remaining raspberries. Cool. In a bowl, combine oats, flour, brown sugar and baking soda. Cut in butter until mixture resembles coarse crumbs. Press half of the crumbs into a greased 9-in. square baking dish. Spread with cooled berry mixture. Sprinkle with remaining crumbs. Bake at 350° for 25-30 minutes or until top is lightly browned. Serve warm with whipped cream. **Yield:** 8 servings.

— 🍷 🍷 🍷 —

Mocha Ice Cream

(Pictured below)

I've enjoyed this recipe for chocolate ice cream for over 40 years. Coffee really enhances the flavor.
    —*Dick McCarty, Lake Havasu City, Arizona*

2-1/4 **cups sugar**
 3/4 **cup baking cocoa**
 1/3 **cup all-purpose flour**
    1 **tablespoon instant coffee granules**
Dash salt
    3 **cups milk**
    4 **eggs, beaten**
    4 **cups half-and-half cream**
    2 **cups whipping cream**
    3 **tablespoons vanilla extract**

In a large heavy saucepan, combine the sugar, cocoa, flour, coffee and salt. Gradually add milk and eggs; stir until smooth. Cook and stir over medium-low heat until mixture is thick enough to coat a metal spoon and reaches 160°, about 15 minutes. Refrigerate until chilled. Stir in the remaining ingredients. Fill ice cream freezer cylinder two-thirds full; freeze according to manufacturer's instructions. Refrigerate remaining mixture until ready to freeze. Remove from the freezer 10 minutes before serving. **Yield:** about 2-1/2 quarts.

Love Is a Many-Splendored Treat

LOVE is often a main ingredient in homemade sweet treats. Those dear to you are sure to be pleased when you prepare a luscious dessert just for them.

It doesn't have to be Valentine's Day, Sweetest Day or even your anniversary. A strawberry-topped chocolate heart, melt-in-your-mouth truffles or fluffy mousse can make just about any day special for your sweetheart.

These desserts are beautiful and delicious, and best of all, they have love written all over them.

Raspberry White Chocolate Mousse
(Pictured below)

This treasured treat is surprisingly easy and a delightful change of pace from heavier cakes and pies. Raspberry sauce is an appealing base for the fluffy white chocolate mousse.
—Mary Lou Wayman
Salt Lake City, Utah

1 package (10 ounces) sweetened frozen raspberries, thawed

FESTIVE TREATS. Valentine Berries and Cream, Raspberry White Chocolate Mouse and True Love Truffles (shown above, clockwise from top) will be savored by sweethearts.

2 **tablespoons sugar**
1 **tablespoon orange juice concentrate**
2 **cups whipping cream**
6 **ounces white baking chocolate**
1 **teaspoon vanilla extract**
1/4 **cup milk chocolate chips**
1 **teaspoon vegetable oil**

In a blender, combine the raspberries, sugar and orange juice concentrate; cover and process until smooth. Press through a sieve; discard seeds. Refrigerate sauce. In a saucepan over low heat, cook and stir cream and white chocolate until chocolate is melted. Stir in vanilla. Transfer to a mixing bowl. Cover and refrigerate for 6 hours or until thickened, stirring occasionally. Beat cream mixture on high speed until light and fluffy, about 1-1/2 minutes (do not overbeat). Just before serving, melt chocolate chips and oil in a microwave or saucepan. Spoon 2 tablespoons of raspberry sauce on each plate. Pipe or spoon 1/2 cup chocolate mousse over sauce; drizzle with melted chocolate. Store leftovers in the refrigerator. **Yield:** 8 servings.

— 🍵 🍵 🍵 —

Valentine Berries and Cream

(Pictured at left and on page 150)

Everyone was so impressed with this scrumptious filled chocolate heart served at a banquet held by our adult Sunday school class. I got the recipe, and now I enjoy rave reviews from family and friends when I serve it.
—Tamera O'Sullivan, Apple Valley, Minnesota

8 **squares (1 ounce** *each*) **semisweet chocolate**
1 **tablespoon shortening**
2 **packages (3 ounces** *each*) **cream cheese, softened**
1/4 **cup butter** *or* **margarine, softened**
1-1/2 **cups confectioners' sugar**
1/3 **cup baking cocoa**
2 **tablespoons milk**
1 **teaspoon vanilla extract**
2-1/2 **cups whipping cream, whipped,** *divided*
1-1/2 **cups fresh strawberries, halved**

Line a 9-in. heart-shaped or square baking pan with foil; set aside. In a heavy saucepan over low heat, melt chocolate and shortening; stir until smooth. Pour into prepared pan, swirling to coat the bottom and 1-1/2 in. up the sides, Refrigerate for 1 minute, then swirl the chocolate to reinforce sides of heart or box. Refrigerate for 30 minutes or until firm. Using foil, lift from pan; remove foil and place chocolate heart on a serving plate. In a mixing bowl, beat the cream cheese and butter until smooth. Com-

bine confectioners' sugar and cocoa; add to creamed mixture with milk and vanilla. Beat until smooth. Gently fold two-thirds of the whipped cream into cream cheese mixture. Spoon into heart. Insert star tip #32 into a pastry or plastic bag; fill with the remaining whipped cream. Pipe around the edge of heart. Garnish with strawberries. **Yield:** 8-10 servings.

— 🍵 🍵 🍵 —

True Love Truffles

(Pictured at far left)

Years ago, I began giving these minty truffles in tins as Christmas gifts. Now I can't go a year without sharing them. They also make a perfect Valentine's treat.
—Kim Weiesnbach, Claremore, Oklahoma

1-1/2 **cups sugar**
3/4 **cup butter (no substitutes)**
1 **can (5 ounces) evaporated milk**
2 **packages (4.67 ounces** *each*) **mint Andes candies (56 pieces total)**
1 **jar (7 ounces) marshmallow creme**
1 **teaspoon vanilla extract**
22 **ounces white baking chocolate,** *divided*
1/2 **cup semisweet chocolate chips**
Green food coloring, optional

In a heavy saucepan, combine sugar, butter and milk. Bring to a boil over medium heat, stirring constantly. Reduce heat; cook and stir until a candy thermometer reads 236° (soft-ball stage). Remove from the heat. Stir in candies until melted and mixture is well blended. Stir in marshmallow creme and vanilla until smooth. Spread into a buttered 15-in. x 10-in. x 1-in. pan; cover and refrigerate for 1 hour. Cut into 96 pieces; roll each into a ball (mixture will be soft). Place on a waxed paper-lined baking sheet. In a heavy saucepan or microwave-safe bowl, melt 18 oz. of white chocolate and chocolate chips. Dip balls in melted chocolate; place on waxed paper to harden. Melt the remaining white chocolate; add food coloring if desired. Drizzle over truffles. Store in an airtight container. **Yield:** 8 dozen.

Decorating Candies

To easily drizzle melted chocolate over candies, pour the melted chocolate into a heavy-duty resealable plastic bag. Cut off a very small corner and drizzle in an "s" shape or circular pattern. If you're not happy with the results, drizzle in the opposite direction for a pretty design.

Orange Pineapple Dessert

This fruity dessert goes over well at church dinners and potlucks. I've shared the recipe many times.
—Shirley Radtka, Massillon, Ohio

✓ Uses less fat, sugar or salt. Includes Nutritional Analysis and Diabetic Exchanges.

    2 packages (.3 ounce *each*) sugar-free orange gelatin
    2 cups boiling water
   16 ice cubes (about 3 cups)
    1 can (20 ounces) unsweetened crushed pineapple, drained
    1 can (11 ounces) mandarin oranges, drained and cut into pieces
    1 cup (8 ounces) nonfat sour cream
    1 carton (12 ounces) light frozen whipped topping, thawed
    1 prepared angel food cake (10 inches), cut into 1-inch cubes

In a bowl, dissolve gelatin in boiling water. Add ice cubes and stir until slightly thickened. Remove any unmelted ice. Stir in pineapple and oranges. Stir in sour cream until blended. Fold in whipped topping and cake cubes until well coated. Spoon into an ungreased 13-in. x 9-in. x 2-in. dish; cover and refrigerate until serving. **Yield:** 18 servings. **Nutritional Analysis:** One serving equals 170 calories, 200 mg sodium, 1 mg cholesterol, 32 gm carbohydrate, 4 gm protein, 3 gm fat, trace fiber. **Diabetic Exchanges:** 1 starch, 1 fruit, 1/2 fat.

Almond Pear Tartlets

(Pictured above)

Although they're quick to fix, you'll want to savor these pretty pastries slowly. Delicately spiced pears are complemented by an almond sauce and a crispy crust. Be prepared to share the recipe. —Marie Rizzio
Traverse City, Michigan

    1 egg, lightly beaten
  1/2 cup plus 6 tablespoons sugar, *divided*
  3/4 cup whipping cream
    2 tablespoons butter *or* margarine, melted
  1/2 teaspoon almond extract
    1 package (10 ounces) frozen puff pastry shells, thawed
    2 small ripe pears, peeled and thinly sliced
  1/2 teaspoon ground cinnamon
  1/8 teaspoon ground ginger
  1/2 cup slivered almonds, toasted, optional

In a saucepan, combine the egg, 1/2 cup sugar, cream and butter. Cook and stir until the sauce is thickened and a thermometer reads 160°. Remove from the heat; stir in extract. Cover and refrigerate. On an unfloured surface, roll each pastry into a 4-in. circle. Place in an ungreased 15-in. x 10-in. x 1-in. baking pan. Top each with pear slices. Combine cinnamon, ginger and remaining sugar; sprinkle over pears. Bake at 400° for 20 minutes or until pastry is golden brown. Sprinkle with almonds if desired. Serve warm with the chilled cream sauce. **Yield:** 6 servings.

Strudel Sticks

I like to prepare these pretty fruit- and coconut-filled pastries ahead and freeze them until needed.
—Louise Holmes, Winchester, Tennessee

    1 cup cold butter (no substitutes)
    2 cups all-purpose flour
  1/2 cup sour cream
    1 egg, *separated*
    1 cup peach *or* apricot preserves, *divided*
   30 vanilla wafers, crushed
  1/2 cup flaked coconut
   20 pecan halves
GLAZE:
  1/2 cup confectioners' sugar
    2 to 3 teaspoons milk
  1/8 teaspoon vanilla extract

In a bowl, cut the butter into the flour until mixture resembles coarse crumbs. Combine the sour cream and egg yolk; add to the flour mixture, stirring with a fork to form a soft dough. Divide in half; wrap in plastic wrap. Refrigerate several hours or overnight. On a floured surface, roll each portion of dough into a 12-in. square. Spread with preserves. Combine crushed wafers and coconut; sprinkle over preserves. Roll up jelly-roll style; seal seam. Place seam side down on a greased baking sheet. Cut widthwise with a sharp knife three-fourths of the way through dough every 1 in. Beat the egg white until foamy; brush over pastry. Place a pecan half on each slice. Bake at 350° for 25-30 minutes or until golden. Combine glaze ingredients; drizzle over pastries. **Yield:** 2 pastries (10 servings each).

Custard Bread Pudding

This is an economical dessert that has real down-home appeal. I sometimes drizzle it with confectioners' sugar icing for added sweetness. —*Barbara Little*
Bedford, Indiana

- **2 eggs**
- **2 cups milk**
- **1 cup sugar**
- **1 tablespoon butter *or* margarine, melted**
- **1 teaspoon ground cinnamon**
- **10 slices day-old bread (crusts removed), cut into 1/2-inch cubes**
- **1 cup raisins**

SAUCE:
- **2/3 cup sugar**
- **2 tablespoons all-purpose flour**
- **1 cup water**
- **7 tablespoons butter *or* margarine**
- **1 teaspoon vanilla extract**

In a large bowl, combine eggs, milk, sugar, butter and cinnamon. Add bread cubes and raisins; mix well. Pour into a greased 11-in. x 7-in. x 2-in. baking dish. Bake at 350° for 50-60 minutes or until a knife inserted near the center comes out clean. Meanwhile, in a saucepan, combine sugar, flour and water until smooth. Add butter. Bring to a boil over medium heat; cook and stir for 2 minutes. Remove from the heat; stir in vanilla. Serve warm over the warm pudding. Refrigerate leftovers. **Yield:** 8 servings.

Marbled Cheesecake

(Pictured at right)

No one will believe this smooth, delectable cheesecake is prepared with lighter ingredients. It's a special dessert that always prompts compliments.
—*Phyllis Carr, Luttrell, Tennessee*

☑ Uses less fat, sugar or salt. Includes Nutritional Analysis and Diabetic Exchanges.

- **1 cup reduced-fat chocolate wafer crumbs (about 35 wafers)**
- **2 tablespoons margarine, melted**
- **3 packages (8 ounces *each*) light cream cheese, softened**
- **1-1/4 cups sugar**
- **1 tablespoon all-purpose flour**
- **Egg substitute equivalent to 2 eggs**
- **1 cup (8 ounces) light sour cream**
- **2 teaspoons vanilla extract**
- **2 squares (1 ounce *each*) semisweet chocolate, melted and cooled**
- **Fresh raspberries and chocolate curls, optional**

Combine wafer crumbs and margarine. Press onto the bottom of a greased 9-in. springform pan; set aside. In a mixing bowl, beat cream cheese and sugar until smooth. Add flour and beat well. Beat in egg substitute, sour cream and vanilla just until blended. Remove 1-1/2 cups batter to a small bowl; stir in chocolate until well blended. Pour half of remaining plain batter over crust. Top with half of chocolate batter; repeat layers. Cut through batter with a knife to swirl the chocolate. Bake at 325° for 55-60 minutes or until center is almost set. Cool on a wire rack for 1 hour. Cover and refrigerate for 4 hours or overnight. (Top of cheesecake will crack.) Remove sides of pan. Garnish with raspberries and chocolate curls if desired. **Yield:** 12 servings. **Nutritional Analysis:** One serving (calculated without garnish) equals 321 calories, 404 mg sodium, 28 mg cholesterol, 42 gm carbohydrate, 10 gm protein, 12 gm fat, 1 gm fiber. **Diabetic Exchanges:** 3 starch, 2 fat.

Pretzel Fruit Pizza

(Pictured on page 150)

I created this recipe while working as an independent kitchen consultant for a national company. My husband and children love every bite.
—*Bethany Perry, South Hamilton, Massachusetts*

    3 cups finely crushed pretzels
    2/3 cup sugar
1-1/4 cups cold butter *or* margarine
    1 can (14 ounces) sweetened condensed
       milk
    1/4 cup lime juice
    1 tablespoon grated lime peel
1-1/2 cups whipped topping
    7 to 8 cups assorted fresh fruit

In a bowl, combine pretzels and sugar; mix well. Cut in butter until mixture resembles coarse crumbs. Press into a 14-in. pizza pan. Bake at 375° for 8-10 minutes or until set. Cool on a wire rack; refrigerate for 30 minutes. Meanwhile, in a bowl, combine milk, lime juice and peel. Fold in whipped topping; spread over crust. Cover and chill. Top with fruit just before serving. **Yield:** 8 servings.

—❦ ❦ ❦—

Candy Bar Fudge

(Pictured below)

I created this recipe to duplicate a delightful rich fudge I tried in a shop while visiting our daughter.
—*Mary Lou Bridge, Taylor Ridge, Illinois*

    6 Snickers candy bars (2.07 ounces *each*)
    3 cups sugar
    3/4 cup butter (no substitutes)
    2/3 cup evaporated milk
    2 cups (12 ounces) semisweet chocolate
       chips

    1 jar (7 ounces) marshmallow creme
    1 teaspoon vanilla extract

Line a 9-in. square pan with foil. Butter the foil and set pan aside. Cut candy bars into 1/2-in. slices; set aside. In a heavy saucepan, bring sugar, butter and milk to a boil over medium heat. Cook and stir until a candy thermometer reads 234° (soft-ball stage), about 3 minutes. Remove from the heat. Stir in chocolate chips, marshmallow creme and vanilla until smooth. Pour half into prepared pan. Sprinkle with candy bar slices. Top with remaining chocolate mixture and spread evenly. Let stand at room temperature to cool. Lift out of pan and remove foil. Cut into squares. **Yield:** 4 pounds (about 7 dozen).

—❦ ❦ ❦—

Marmalade Turnovers

A church friend prepares these delicate pastries for gatherings, but they're usually gone before she gets the platter to the serving table. —*Anna Jean Allen West Liberty, Kentucky*

    1/2 cup butter (no substitutes), softened
    1 jar (5 ounces) sharp American cheese
       spread
    1 cup all-purpose flour
    1/3 cup orange marmalade

In a bowl, combine butter and cheese. Add flour; stir until mixture forms a ball. Cover and refrigerate for 1 hour. On a lightly floured surface, roll dough to 1/8-in. thickness; cut into 2-3/4-in. circles. Place 1/2 teaspoon marmalade on each circle. Fold pastry over and seal edges with a fork. Cut slits in top of pastry. Place 2 in. apart on ungreased baking sheets. Bake at 350° for 5-9 minutes or until lightly browned. Remove to wire racks to cool. **Yield:** 2-1/2 dozen.

—❦ ❦ ❦—

Cherry Angel Trifle

Who can resist a light fluffy dessert with lots of tart cherry flavor? It's lovely on the table and a nice make-ahead dessert when entertaining.
—*Barbara Sherman, Homosassa, Florida*

✓ Uses less fat, sugar or salt. Includes Nutritional Analysis and Diabetic Exchanges.

    1 package (.3 ounce) sugar-free cherry
       gelatin
    1 cup boiling water
    1 prepared angel food cake (10 inches), cut
       into 1-inch cubes

1 can (20 ounces) light cherry pie filling
1 carton (8 ounces) frozen nonfat whipped topping, thawed

Dissolve gelatin in water; refrigerate for 15 minutes. Place half of the cake cubes in a 3-qt. trifle or serving bowl; top with half of the gelatin and pie filling. Repeat layers. Top with whipped topping. Refrigerate for at least 1 hour. **Yield:** 16 servings. **Nutritional Analysis:** One serving equals 150 calories, 219 mg sodium, 0 cholesterol, 33 gm carbohydrate, 3 gm protein, trace fat, trace fiber. **Diabetic Exchanges:** 1-1/2 starch, 1 fruit.

— ♥ ♥ ♥ —

Blueberry-Topped Custard

(Pictured at right)

A silky smooth texture, rich vanilla flavor and fruit topping make this dessert extra special. It's pretty, too.
— *DeEtta Rasmussen, Fort Madison, Iowa*

1/2 cup sugar
2 tablespoons all-purpose flour
1/8 teaspoon salt
1-1/2 cups half-and-half cream
1 teaspoon grated lemon peel
3 egg yolks, lightly beaten
2 tablespoons butter *or* margarine
1 tablespoon vanilla extract
1 can (15 ounces) blueberries
1 tablespoon cornstarch

In a saucepan, combine sugar, flour and salt. Gradually add cream and lemon peel until blended. Bring to a boil; cook and stir for 2 minutes or until thickened and bubbly. Remove from the heat. Stir a small amount of hot mixture into egg yolks. Return all to pan; bring to a gentle boil, stirring constantly. Remove from the heat; stir in butter and vanilla. Pour into parfait glasses or dessert dishes. Cool. Drain blueberries, reserving juice. Spoon blueberries over custard. In a saucepan, combine cornstarch and blueberry juice until smooth. Bring to a boil over medium heat; cook and stir for 1-2 minutes or until thickened. Spoon over berries. **Yield:** 4 servings.

— ♥ ♥ ♥ —

Pineapple Rice Pudding

(Pictured above right)

An aunt who lived in Hawaii shared the recipe for this distinctive tropical-tasting pudding. It's now my family's favorite comfort food. — *Joan Hallford*
North Richland Hills, Texas

DELICIOUS DESSERTS include Pineapple Rice Pudding and Blueberry-Topped Custard (shown above).

4 cups milk, *divided*
3 cups cooked long grain rice
2/3 cup sugar
1/2 teaspoon salt
1 package (3 ounces) cream cheese, softened
2 eggs
1 teaspoon vanilla extract
PINEAPPLE SAUCE:
1 can (20 ounces) pineapple chunks
1/4 cup packed brown sugar
1 tablespoon cornstarch
1 tablespoon butter *or* margarine
1/8 teaspoon salt
1/2 teaspoon vanilla extract

In a saucepan, combine 3-1/2 cups milk, rice, sugar and salt; bring to a boil over medium heat. Cook for 15 minutes or until thick and creamy, stirring occasionally. In a mixing bowl, beat cream cheese. Beat in eggs and remaining milk. Stir into rice mixture. Cook and stir for 2 minutes over medium heat until mixture reaches 160°. Add vanilla. Spoon into six dessert dishes. Drain pineapple, reserving juice; set pineapple aside. In a saucepan, combine brown sugar, cornstarch, butter, salt and pineapple juice. Bring to boil; cook and stir for 2 minutes or until thickened. Stir in vanilla and pineapple. Spoon over pudding. **Yield:** 6 servings.

STUNNING SWEETS like Blackberry Custard Torte, White Chocolate Parfaits and Maple Cream Bonbons (shown above, clockwise from upper left) are "berry" good!

White Chocolate Parfaits

(Pictured above)

This elegant dessert is great served on a warm summer night or at a dinner party. You can substitute other berries until you find your favorite combination.
—*Jennifer Eilts, Central City, Nebraska*

    3/4 cup whipping cream
    1/4 cup sugar
      2 teaspoons cornstarch
      2 egg yolks
      4 squares (1 ounce *each*) white baking
        chocolate

      1 teaspoon vanilla extract
      3 cups whipped topping
    1-1/2 cups fresh blueberries
    1-1/2 cups fresh raspberries
    Sliced strawberries and additional whipped
      topping, optional

In a saucepan, heat the cream just to a boil. In a bowl, combine sugar and cornstarch; stir in yolks until combined. Stir a small amount of hot cream into yolk mixture; return all to pan. Cook and stir for 2 minutes or until mixture reaches 160° and is thickened. Stir in chocolate until melted; add vanilla. Cool to room temperature, about 15 minutes.

Fold in whipped topping. Place 1/4 cup each in four parfait glasses. Combine blueberries and raspberries; place 1/4 cup in each glass. Repeat layers of chocolate mixture and berries twice. Cover and refrigerate for at least 1 hour. Garnish with strawberries and whipped topping if desired. **Yield:** 4 servings.

— ♦ ♦ ♦ —

Maple Cream Bonbons
(Pictured at left)

My family always smiles when I fix these chocolates. They recall the winter when I put trays of the candy centers on top of my van in the garage to freeze before dipping. Later, I drove off and was horrified to see the little balls rolling on the highway!
—*Ginny Truwe, Mankato, Minnesota*

    1 cup butter (no substitutes), softened
3-1/2 cups confectioners' sugar
    3 tablespoons maple flavoring
    2 cups chopped walnuts
    2 cups semisweet chocolate chips
    1 cup butterscotch chips

In a mixing bowl, cream the butter, sugar and maple flavoring until smooth. Stir in walnuts. Shape into 1-in. balls; place on waxed paper-lined baking sheets. Freeze until firm. In a microwave or heavy saucepan, melt the chips; dip balls and place on waxed paper-lined baking sheets. Refrigerate until hardened. Store in the refrigerator. **Yield:** 5 dozen.

— ♦ ♦ ♦ —

Blackberry Custard Torte
(Pictured at left)

Blackberries are my husband's favorite fruit, so I make this outstanding dessert especially for him. It's worth the effort. I love seeing a smile appear on his face.
—*Ann Fox, Austin, Texas*

    1 cup all-purpose flour
1/2 cup sugar
1-1/2 teaspoons baking powder
1/2 cup cold butter *or* margarine
    1 egg
FILLING:
    3 egg yolks
    2 cups (16 ounces) sour cream
1/2 cup sugar
1/4 teaspoon vanilla extract
    4 cups fresh *or* frozen blackberries, drained, *divided*
Whipped cream

In a bowl, combine the flour, sugar and baking powder. Cut in butter until mixture resembles coarse crumbs. Stir in egg until dough forms a ball. Press onto the bottom and 2 in. up the sides of an ungreased 9-in. springform pan. For filling, in a bowl, beat the egg yolks, sour cream, sugar and vanilla just until combined. Sprinkle 2 cups blackberries over crust. Carefully pour sour cream mixture over berries. Bake at 325° for 1-1/2 hours or until center is almost set. Cool on a wire rack (center will fall). Remove sides of pan. Top with whipped cream and remaining blackberries. This dessert is best eaten the same day it's prepared. Refrigerate any leftovers. **Yield:** 12-14 servings. **Editor's Note:** Even a tight-fitting springform pan may leak. To prevent drips, place the pan on a shallow baking pan in the oven.

— ♦ ♦ ♦ —

Lemon Crackle

This unique dessert is a cross between lemon pie and fruit crisp. It's refreshingly tart with a pleasant contrast of textures.
—*Ruth "Sunny" Tiedeman Bartlesville, Oklahoma*

1/4 cup butter *or* margarine, softened
    1 cup packed brown sugar
    1 cup all-purpose flour
1/2 teaspoon baking soda
    1 cup flaked coconut
1/3 cup finely crushed saltines (about 10 crackers)
FILLING:
    1 cup sugar
    2 tablespoons cornstarch
1/4 teaspoon salt
    1 cup water
    6 tablespoons lemon juice
1/2 cup butter *or* margarine
    2 egg yolks, beaten
Whipped topping, optional

In a mixing bowl, cream butter and brown sugar. Combine flour and baking soda; add to creamed mixture with coconut and cracker crumbs. Toss with a fork until crumbly. Press half into a greased 11-in. x 7-in. x 2-in. baking dish. In a saucepan, combine sugar, cornstarch and salt. Stir in water and lemon juice until smooth. Add butter and egg yolks. Bring to a boil over medium-low heat, stirring constantly. Cook and stir for 2 minutes or until thickened. Remove from the heat; pour over crust. Top with reserved crumb mixture. Bake at 325° for 20 minutes. Cool. Cut into squares. Serve with whipped topping if desired. Store in the refrigerator. **Yield:** 12-16 servings.

Baked Apples

Simple baked apples like this can be a wonderful way to end a hearty meal. We especially enjoy this dessert when the weather turns a little cooler.
—Marcia Weber, Elkhorn, Nebraska

✓ Uses less fat, sugar or salt. Includes Nutritional Analysis and Diabetic Exchanges.

    4 medium baking apples, cored
    4 teaspoons sugar-free strawberry jam
1/2 teaspoon ground cinnamon
1-1/2 cups orange juice

Place apples in a foil-lined 8-in. square baking pan. Spoon 1 teaspoon jam into the center of each apple; sprinkle with cinnamon. Pour orange juice into pan. Bake, uncovered, at 400° for 20-25 minutes or until apples are tender. Serve immediately. **Yield:** 4 servings. **Nutritional Analysis:** One serving equals 126 calories, 1 mg sodium, 0 cholesterol, 36 gm carbohydrate, 1 gm protein, trace fat. **Diabetic Exchange:** 2 fruit.

— ▼ ▼ ▼ —

Blackberry Cobbler

(Pictured below)

It's fun to pick blackberries, especially when we know this dessert will be the result.
—Tina Hankins, Laconia, New Hampshire

1/4 cup butter *or* margarine, softened
1/2 cup sugar
    1 cup all-purpose flour
    2 teaspoons baking powder
1/2 cup milk
    2 cups fresh *or* frozen blackberries
3/4 cup raspberry *or* apple juice
Ice cream *or* whipped cream, optional

In a mixing bowl, cream butter and sugar. Combine flour and baking powder; add to creamed mixture alternately with milk. Stir just until moistened. Pour into a greased 1-1/2-qt. baking pan. Sprinkle with blackberries. Pour juice over all. Bake at 350° for 45-50 minutes or until golden brown. Serve warm; top with ice cream or whipped cream if desired. **Yield:** 6-8 servings.

— ▼ ▼ ▼ —

Spring Rhubarb Torte

Our 40-year-old rhubarb plants provide the filling for this treat, and they're always ready first thing in spring. It's a family tradition to bake it.
—Audrey Groe, Lake Mills, Iowa

    2 cups all-purpose flour
    2 tablespoons sugar
    1 cup butter *or* margarine
FILLING:
    6 egg yolks
    2 cups sugar
1/4 cup all-purpose flour
1/8 teaspoon salt
    5 cups finely chopped fresh *or* frozen rhubarb
    1 cup half-and-half cream
MERINGUE:
    6 egg whites, room temperature
1/8 teaspoon cream of tartar
3/4 cup sugar

Combine flour and sugar; cut in the butter until crumbly. Press into a greased 13-in. x 9-in. x 2-in. baking pan. Bake at 350° for 10-15 minutes or until lightly browned. Cool. In a bowl, beat egg yolks; add sugar, flour and salt. Stir in rhubarb and cream; pour over crust. Bake at 350° for 50-60 minutes or until a knife inserted near the center comes out clean. In a mixing bowl, beat egg whites and cream of tartar on medium speed until soft peaks form. Gradually beat in the sugar, 1 tablespoon at a time, until stiff peaks form. Immediately spread over hot filling, sealing edges. Return to the oven for 12-15 minutes or until lightly browned. Cool at least 1 hour before serving. Refrigerate leftovers. **Yield:** 12-16 servings.

Chocolate Bread Pudding

Nothing was wasted on the farm where I grew up in southwest Nebraska—this pudding was made from stale bread. My father loved chocolate, so if we weren't having this dessert, we'd have homemade chocolate ice cream or chocolate cake! —Jackie Atwood
Lincoln, Nebraska

        1/4 cup butter *or* margarine
          2 cups milk
          3 tablespoons baking cocoa
    4-1/2 cups cubed day-old bread (about 9 slices)
          1 cup flaked coconut, *divided*
        3/4 cup sugar
          2 eggs, beaten
          1 teaspoon vanilla extract
        1/4 teaspoon salt
    Whipped cream and grated chocolate, optional

In a large saucepan, heat butter and milk until butter is melted; stir in cocoa. Remove from the heat and set aside. Toss bread and 3/4 cup coconut; place in a greased 1-1/2-qt. shallow baking dish. Add sugar, eggs, vanilla and salt to milk mixture; mix well. Pour over the bread. Sprinkle with the remaining coconut. Place baking dish in a 13-in. x 9-in. x 2-in. pan in oven; add 1 in. of water to pan. Bake at 350° for 50-55 minutes or until a knife inserted near the center comes out clean. Serve warm or cold; if desired, garnish with whipped cream and grated chocolate. **Yield:** 6-8 servings.

— 🥄 🥄 🥄 —

Watermelon Sherbet

Our church group serves this at the local watermelon festival, using melons from my family's fields.
—Lisa McAdoo, Rush Springs, Oklahoma

          8 cups diced seeded watermelon
    1-1/2 cups sugar
        1/2 cup lemon juice
          2 envelopes unflavored gelatin
        1/2 cup cold water
          2 cups milk

In a large bowl, combine watermelon, sugar and lemon juice. Chill for 30 minutes; place half in a blender. Blend until smooth; pour into a large bowl. Repeat with the other half; set aside. In a saucepan, cook and stir gelatin and water over low heat until gelatin dissolves. Add to watermelon mixture; mix well. Stir in the milk until well blended. Freeze in an ice cream freezer according to the manufacturer's directions. Serve immediately or freeze and allow to thaw about 20 minutes before serving. **Yield:** 1/2 gallon.

Rhubarb Raspberry Crisp

(Pictured above)

Every time I've entered our Boone County Bake-Off, I've won a blue ribbon. One summer, when the category was rhubarb, this recipe was the grand champion! See if your family thinks it's a winner, too. The orange juice and peel give it zest. —Mabeth Shaw
Lebanon, Indiana

          4 cups chopped fresh rhubarb (1-inch
              pieces)
        2/3 cup sugar
    Juice and peel of 1 orange
          1 cup all-purpose flour
        1/2 cup packed brown sugar
        1/2 teaspoon ground cinnamon
        1/2 cup cold butter *or* margarine, cut into
              small pieces
        1/2 cup rolled oats
        1/4 cup chopped pecans
        1/2 pint fresh raspberries

In a large bowl, combine rhubarb, sugar, orange juice and peel. In another bowl, combine flour, brown sugar and cinnamon. Cut in butter until crumbly. Add oats and pecans; mix well. Turn rhubarb mixture into an 8-in. square baking pan. Sprinkle evenly with raspberries and cover with crumb topping. Bake at 350° for 45 minutes or until topping is browned. **Yield:** 9 servings.

Add eggs; beat on low just until combined. Stir in vanilla. Pour over crust. Toss apples with lemon juice, sugar and cinnamon; spoon over filling. Bake at 350° for 55-60 minutes or until center is almost set. Cool on a wire rack for 10 minutes. Carefully run a knife around edge of pan to loosen. Drizzle with 4 tablespoons caramel topping. Cool for 1 hour. Chill overnight. Remove sides of pan. Just before serving, garnish with whipped cream. Drizzle with remaining caramel; sprinkle with pecans. Store in refrigerator. **Yield:** 12 servings.

Peanut Butter Chocolate Cups

Our children love these candies. They're a quick holiday treat. —Aljene Wendling, Seattle, Washington

> 1 milk chocolate candy bar (7 ounces)
> 1/4 cup butter (no substitutes)
> 1 tablespoon shortening
> 1/4 cup creamy peanut butter

In a microwave or heavy saucepan, melt chocolate, butter and shortening; stir until smooth. Place foil or paper miniature baking cups in a miniature muffin tin. Place 1 tablespoon of chocolate mixture in each cup. In a microwave or saucepan, heat peanut butter until melted. Spoon into cups. Top with remaining chocolate mixture. Refrigerate for 30 minutes or until firm. **Yield:** 1 dozen.

Raspberry Cheesecake Trifle

This is a rich, lovely dessert for a crowd. Plus, there's no last-minute fuss since you make it ahead of time. —Wendy Block Abbotsford, British Columbia

> 1 package (9 ounces) white cake mix
> 1 package (8 ounces) cream cheese, softened
> 1/4 cup confectioners' sugar
> 1-1/2 cups whipping cream, whipped
> 3 cups fresh raspberries
> 2 squares (1 ounce *each*) semisweet chocolate, coarsely grated *or* shaved

Prepare and bake cake mix according to package directions. Cool; cut into 1-in. cubes. In a small mixing bowl, beat cream cheese and sugar until smooth. Fold in whipped cream. In a trifle bowl, layer half of the cake cubes, 1 cup of raspberries, half of the cream cheese mixture and half of the chocolate. Repeat layers. Top with the remaining raspberries. Refrigerate for 4 hours or overnight. **Yield:** 12-14 servings.

Apple-of-Your-Eye Cheesecake

(Pictured above and on page 150)

My most-often-requested dessert, this exquisite cheesecake with apples, caramel and pecans wins me more compliments than anything else I make. My husband's co-workers say it's too pretty to cut...but agree it's well worth it to do so. —Debbie Wilson Sellersburg, Indiana

> 1 cup graham cracker crumbs
> 3 tablespoons sugar
> 1/2 teaspoon ground cinnamon
> 1/4 cup butter *or* margarine, melted
> 2 tablespoons finely chopped pecans

FILLING:
> 3 packages (8 ounces *each*) cream cheese, softened
> 3/4 cup sugar
> 3 eggs
> 3/4 teaspoon vanilla extract

TOPPING:
> 2-1/2 cups chopped peeled apples
> 1 tablespoon lemon juice
> 1/4 cup sugar
> 1/2 teaspoon ground cinnamon
> 6 tablespoons caramel ice cream topping, *divided*

Sweetened whipped cream
> 2 tablespoons chopped pecans

Combine the first five ingredients; press onto the bottom of a lightly greased 9-in. springform pan. Bake at 350° for 10 minutes; cool. In a mixing bowl, beat cream cheese and sugar until smooth.

Pears with Raspberry Sauce

Two seasonal favorites—pears and raspberries—are showcased in this simple recipe. —Florence Palmer
Marshall, Illinois

✓ Uses less fat, sugar or salt. Includes Nutritional Analysis and Diabetic Exchanges.

  6 medium ripe pears
  2 tablespoons honey
  2 tablespoons lemon juice
1/4 cup reduced-sugar raspberry fruit spread
  2 tablespoons vinegar
  2 cups fresh *or* frozen unsweetened
    raspberries

Core and peel pears; set upright in a 9-in. square baking dish. Combine honey and lemon juice; pour over pears. Cover and bake at 350° for 1-1/2 hours or until tender, basting occasionally. Meanwhile, in a saucepan, combine the fruit spread and vinegar; stir in raspberries. Cook over medium-low heat until heated through; spoon over pears. Serve warm. **Yield:** 6 servings. **Nutritional Analysis:** One serving equals 166 calories, 4 mg sodium, 0 cholesterol, 42 gm carbohydrate, 1 gm protein, 1 gm fat, 7 gm fiber. **Diabetic Exchange:** 2-1/2 fruit.

— ▧ ▧ ▧ —

Chocolate Cobbler

It's impossible to resist the flavorful chocolate sauce that appears when this delightful cake bakes. Chocolate lovers will be delighted with this dessert.
—Margaret McNeil, Memphis, Tennessee

    1 cup self-rising flour*
  1/2 cup sugar
    2 tablespoons plus 1/4 cup baking cocoa,
      divided
  1/2 cup milk
    3 tablespoons vegetable oil
    1 cup packed brown sugar
1-3/4 cups hot water
Vanilla ice cream, optional

In a bowl, combine the flour, sugar and 2 tablespoons cocoa. Stir in milk and oil until smooth. Pour into a greased 8-in. square baking pan. Combine the brown sugar and remaining cocoa; sprinkle over batter. Pour hot water over top (do not stir). Bake at 350° for 40-45 minutes or until top of cake springs back when lightly touched. Serve warm with ice cream if desired. **Yield:** 6-8 servings.
*Editor's Note: As a substitute for self-rising flour, place 1-1/2 teaspoons baking powder and 1/2 teaspoon salt in a measuring cup. Add all-purpose flour to measure 1 cup.

▧ ▧ ▧

'I Wish I Had That Recipe...'

"WHILE living in Pennsylvania, my husband and I discovered The Washington House in Sellersville, which serves the best bread pudding," says Melanie McKay, Mukwonago, Wisconsin.

Washington House owners Elayne Brick and William Quigley credit pastry chef Deb Mathie for Almond Bread Pudding.

Deb recalls, "I played with a recipe from my mom, and the result has been popular."

Located at 136 N. Main Street, The Washington House serves lunch Monday through Saturday, 11:30 a.m. to 2:30 p.m., brunch Sunday 10 a.m. to 2 p.m. Dinner starts at 5 p.m. (4 p.m. on Sunday). Phone: 1-215/257-3000.

Almond Bread Pudding

    6 croissants
    8 eggs
    3 cups milk
    2 cups sugar
    2 teaspoons vanilla extract
    1 teaspoon almond extract
  1/4 cup almond paste, cut into small cubes
  1/2 cup chopped almonds
STRAWBERRY CARAMEL SAUCE:
    2 cups sugar
    2 cups whipping cream
  1/2 cup frozen sweetened sliced
      strawberries, thawed

Cut croissants into 1/2-in. pieces; place in a greased 13-in. x 9-in. x 2-in. baking dish. In a bowl, beat eggs, milk, sugar and extracts. Pour over croissants; let stand for 10 minutes. Dot with almond paste; sprinkle with almonds (dish will be full). Bake at 350° for 35-40 minutes or until a knife inserted near the center comes out clean. Meanwhile, in a heavy saucepan over medium heat, cook and stir sugar with a wooden spoon until sugar has melted and turned a deep amber color, about 20 minutes. Add 1 cup cream (mixture will bubble). Stir in remaining cream; cook 10-15 minutes longer or until caramelized sugar is completely dissolved. Remove from the heat; stir in strawberries. Serve over bread pudding. **Yield:** 12-15 servings.

— ▧ ▧ ▧ —

Baked Custard

Mother made this comforting custard when I was growing up on the farm. It was wonderful after a chilly evening of doing chores. Now I fix it for my husband and four sons.
—Mary Kay Morris
Cokato, Minnesota

        2 eggs
        2 cups milk
    1/3 cup sugar
    1/4 teaspoon salt
Dash ground cinnamon
Dash ground nutmeg

In a bowl, whisk the eggs, milk, sugar and salt. Pour into four ungreased 8-oz. custard cups; sprinkle with cinnamon and nutmeg. Place in a 13-in. x 9-in. x 2-in. baking pan; pour hot water in pan to a depth of 1/2 in. Bake, uncovered, at 350° for 50-55 minutes or until a knife inserted near the center comes out clean. Remove cups to a wire rack to cool. Serve warm or chilled. Store in the refrigerator. **Yield:** 4 servings.

— 🍷 🍷 🍷 —

Banana Crepes

(Pictured below and on page 150)

I like to serve this impressive treat at parties. Pleasant banana-orange flavor makes it great for dinner or brunch. —Freda Becker, Garrettsville, Ohio

        2 eggs
    3/4 cup milk
        1 tablespoon butter *or* margarine, melted
        1 tablespoon sugar
    1/8 teaspoon salt
    1/2 cup all-purpose flour
Additional butter *or* margarine

ORANGE SAUCE:
    1/2 cup butter *or* margarine
    2/3 cup sugar
    2/3 cup orange juice
        4 teaspoons grated orange peel
        6 medium firm bananas

In a bowl, whisk eggs, milk, melted butter, sugar and salt. Beat in flour until smooth; let stand 20 minutes. Melt 1 teaspoon butter in an 8-in. nonstick skillet. Pour 2 tablespoons batter into the center of skillet; lift and turn pan to cover bottom. Cook until lightly browned; turn and brown the other side. Remove to a wire rack. Repeat with remaining batter, adding butter to skillet as needed. When cool, stack crepes with waxed paper or paper towels in between. For sauce, combine butter, sugar, orange juice and peel in a skillet. Bring to a boil; remove from the heat. Peel bananas; cut in half lengthwise. Add to orange sauce; cook over medium heat until heated through, about 1 minute. Place one banana half in the center of each crepe; roll up jelly-roll style. Place folded side down on a plate; drizzle with orange sauce. **Yield:** 12 crepes.

— 🍷 🍷 🍷 —

Orange Chocolate Cheesecake

White chocolate and oranges are perfect together in this pretty dessert.
—Tangee Bradley
Columbia, South Carolina

        2 cups vanilla wafer crumbs
        6 tablespoons butter *or* margarine, melted
    1/4 cup sugar
FILLING:
        4 packages (8 ounces *each*) cream cheese, softened
        1 cup sugar

4 **eggs**
1 **cup (8 ounces) sour cream**
10 **squares (1 ounce *each*) white baking
  chocolate, melted**
TOPPING:
1 **cup (8 ounces) sour cream**
3 **tablespoons sugar**
1/2 **to 1 teaspoon orange extract**
2 **cans (11 ounces *each*) mandarin oranges,
  well drained**

Combine the first three ingredients; press onto the bottom and 1-1/2 in. up the sides of a greased 10-in. springform pan. Bake at 350° for 10 minutes; cool completely. In a mixing bowl, beat cream cheese and sugar until fluffy. Add eggs and sour cream, beating just until blended. Add chocolate; mix well. Pour into crust. Bake at 350° for 1 to 1-1/4 hours or until center is nearly set. Cool to room temperature, about 1-1/2 to 2 hours. In a small bowl, combine sour cream, sugar and extract; spread over filling. Bake at 450° for 5-7 minutes or until set. Refrigerate, uncovered, for 1 hour. Arrange the oranges in a spiral design on the cheesecake. Cover and chill for at least 4 hours. **Yield:** 12-16 servings.

— ☕ ☕ ☕ —

Lemon Schaum Torte

(Pictured on page 4)

Our family has enjoyed this delicious dessert for over 75 years.   —Cindy Steffen, Cedarburg, Wisconsin

6 **egg whites**
1 **teaspoon vanilla extract**
1/8 **teaspoon cream of tartar**
2 **cups sugar, *divided***
9 **egg yolks**
1/2 **cup lemon juice**
1 **tablespoon grated lemon peel**
4 **cups whipping cream**
2/3 **cup confectioners' sugar**
Ground cinnamon

In a mixing bowl, beat egg whites, vanilla and cream of tartar until soft peaks form. Gradually beat in 1 cup sugar, 1 tablespoon at a time, on high speed until stiff glossy peaks form and sugar is dissolved. Spread meringue on the bottom and up the sides of a greased 13-in. x 9-in. x 2-in. baking dish. Bake at 275° for 1 hour. Turn oven off and let stand in oven for 1 hour. Do not open door. Remove from the oven; cool on a wire rack. In the top of a double boiler, combine egg yolks and remaining sugar. Gradually stir in lemon juice and peel. Cook and stir over simmering water for 15 minutes or until mixture is thickened and reaches 160°. Cover and refrigerate until cool. In a mixing bowl, beat cream and confectioners' sugar until stiff peaks form. Spread half over meringue; cover with lemon mixture. Top with remaining cream mixture. Sprinkle with cinnamon. Refrigerate overnight. **Yield:** 12-15 servings.

Refreshing Lime Sherbet

(Pictured above)

*One spoonful of this fresh-tasting and delicious treat and you'll never eat store-bought lime sherbet again!
—Lorraine Searing, Colorado Springs, Colorado*

4-1/4 **cups sugar**
1-1/2 **cups lime juice**
3 **tablespoons lemon juice**
2 **tablespoons grated lime peel**
7-1/2 **cups milk**
1/2 **cup buttermilk**
1 **drop green food coloring, optional**

In a bowl, combine sugar, lime juice, lemon juice and lime peel until well blended. Gradually stir in milk, buttermilk and food coloring if desired; mix well. Pour into the cylinder of an ice cream freezer and freeze according to manufacturer's directions. Remove from the freezer 10 minutes before serving. **Yield:** about 2-1/2 quarts. **Editor's Note:** Recipe may need to be frozen in two batches.

bine confectioners' sugar, water, almond extract and the remaining vanilla until smooth. Spread over top. Melt chocolate chips and shortening; pipe in diagonal lines in one direction over frosting. Beginning 1 in. from side of heart, use a sharp knife to draw right angles across the piped lines. Refrigerate until set. **Yield:** 10-12 servings.

— 🥄 🥄 🥄 —

Pink Lemonade Dessert

This refreshing treat is light and cool and goes very well after a big meal. Plus, you can make it ahead.
—Nancy McDonald, Burns, Wyoming

> 2 cups crushed butter-flavored crackers (about 50)
> 1/4 cup confectioners' sugar
> 1/2 cup butter *or* margarine, melted
> 1 can (14 ounces) sweetened condensed milk
> 3/4 cup pink lemonade concentrate
> 1 carton (12 ounces) frozen whipped topping, thawed
> 2 to 3 teaspoons red food coloring, optional

In a bowl, combine cracker crumbs and sugar. Stir in butter. Press into a greased 13-in. x 9-in. x 2-in. dish; set aside. In a blender or food processor, combine milk and lemonade concentrate; cover and process until well blended. Fold in the whipped topping and food coloring if desired. Spread evenly over crust. Cover and refrigerate for 2 hours or until firm. **Yield:** 12 servings.

— 🥄 🥄 🥄 —

Banana Cream Cheesecake

This lovely company dessert can be made a day or two in advance. —Margie Snodgrass, Wilmore, Kentucky

> 1-3/4 cups graham cracker crumbs (about 28 squares)
> 1/4 cup sugar
> 1/2 cup butter *or* margarine, melted
> 1 package (8 ounces) cream cheese, softened
> 1/2 cup sugar
> 1 carton (8 ounces) frozen whipped topping, thawed, *divided*
> 3 to 4 medium firm bananas, sliced
> 1-3/4 cups cold milk
> 1 package (3.4 ounces) instant banana cream pudding mix

In a small bowl, combine cracker crumbs and sugar; stir in butter. Set aside 1/2 cup for topping. Press remaining crumb mixture onto the bottom

Heart's Delight Eclair

(Pictured above)

This lovely and luscious treat is rumored to have been the favorite dessert of European royalty long ago. I know that it's won the hearts of everyone I've ever made it for. Enjoy!
—Lorene Milligan
Chemainus, British Columbia

> 1 package (17-1/4 ounces) frozen puff pastry, thawed
> 3 cups cold milk
> 1 package (5.1 ounces) instant vanilla pudding mix
> 2 cups whipping cream
> 1 teaspoon vanilla extract, *divided*
> 1 cup confectioners' sugar
> 1 tablespoon water
> 1/4 teaspoon almond extract
> 1/2 cup semisweet chocolate chips
> 1 teaspoon shortening

On a lightly floured surface, roll each puff pastry sheet into a 12-in. square. Using an 11-in. heart pattern, cut each pastry into a heart shape. Place on greased baking sheets. Bake at 400° for 12-15 minutes or until golden brown. Remove to wire racks to cool. Meanwhile, combine milk and pudding mix until thickened. In a mixing bowl, beat cream and 1/2 teaspoon of vanilla until stiff peaks form. Carefully fold into pudding. Split puff pastry hearts in half. Place one layer on a serving plate. Top with a third of the pudding mixture. Repeat twice. Top with remaining pastry. In a bowl, com-

and up the sides of a greased 9-in. springform pan or 9-in. square baking pan. Bake at 350° for 5-7 minutes. Cool on a wire rack. In a mixing bowl, beat cream cheese and sugar until smooth. Fold in 2 cups of whipped topping. Arrange half of the banana slices in crust; top with half of the cream cheese mixture. Repeat layers. In a bowl, beat milk and pudding mix until smooth; fold in remaining whipped topping. Pour over cream cheese layer. Sprinkle with reserved crumb mixture. Refrigerate for 1-2 hours or until set. **Yield:** 10 servings.

— 🥄 🥄 🥄 —

Almond Rhubarb Cobbler

In spring, I often make this tangy biscuit-topped treat for family. —*Pat Habiger, Spearville, Kansas*

　　1　cup sugar, *divided*
　1/2　cup water
　　6　cups cut fresh *or* frozen rhubarb (1/2-inch pieces)
　　2　tablespoons all-purpose flour
　　2　tablespoons butter *or* margarine
　1/2　cup slivered almonds, toasted
TOPPING:
　　1　cup all-purpose flour
　　2　tablespoons sugar
1-1/2　teaspoons baking powder
　1/4　teaspoon salt
　1/4　cup cold butter *or* margarine
　　1　egg
　1/4　cup milk

In a large saucepan, bring 1/2 cup sugar and water to a boil. Add rhubarb. Reduce heat; cover and simmer until tender, about 5 minutes. Combine flour and remaining sugar; stir into rhubarb mixture. Return to a boil; cook and stir for 2 minutes or until thickened and bubbly. Stir in butter and almonds. Reduce heat to low; stir occasionally. In a bowl, combine flour, sugar, baking powder and salt; cut in butter until crumbly. Whisk egg and milk; stir into crumb mixture just until moistened. Pour hot rhubarb mixture into a 2-qt. shallow baking dish. Drop topping into six mounds over rhubarb mixture. Bake, uncovered, at 400° for 20-25 minutes or until golden brown. Serve warm. **Yield:** 6 servings.

— 🥄 🥄 🥄 —

Poached Pear Surprise
(Pictured at right)

Pears are my husband's favorite fruit, so he immediately declared this dessert "a keeper". It's elegant but easy, satisfying yet light. Plus, it's fun to watch the looks on the faces of our grandkids and great-grandkids when they discover the surprise filling.
　　　　　—*Barbara Smith, Cannon Falls, Minnesota*

　　4　medium ripe pears
　　1　cup water
　1/2　cup sugar
　　1　teaspoon vanilla extract
　1/3　cup finely chopped walnuts
　　2　tablespoons confectioners' sugar
　　1　teaspoon milk
CHOCOLATE SAUCE:
　1/3　cup water
　1/3　cup sugar
　1/4　cup butter *or* margarine
1-1/3　cups semisweet chocolate chips
Fresh mint, optional

Core pears from bottom, leaving stems intact. Peel pears. Cut 1/4 in. from bottom to level if necessary. In a saucepan, bring water and sugar to a boil. Add pears; reduce heat. Cover and simmer for 10-15 minutes or until tender. Remove from the heat; stir vanilla into sugar syrup. Spoon over pears. Cover and refrigerate until chilled. Meanwhile, combine walnuts, confectioners' sugar and milk; set aside. For chocolate sauce, combine water, sugar and butter in a small saucepan; bring to a boil. Remove from the heat; stir in chocolate chips until melted. To serve, drain pears well; spoon nut mixture into cavities. Place on dessert plates; top with some of the chocolate sauce. Insert a mint leaf near stem if desired. Serve with the remaining chocolate sauce. **Yield:** 4 servings.

Potluck Pleasers

***There's no need to panic when you have to feed
a crowd. These large-quantity recipes come from
experienced cooks, so they're sure to satisfy.***

SUPER FOR GROUPS. Clockwise from upper left: Pineapple Pepper Chicken (p. 194), Marinated Cucumbers (p. 191), Lemon Pudding Dessert (p. 181), Layered Picnic Loaves (p. 185) and Baked Rice with Sausage (p. 186).

Beans 'n' Greens

(Pictured below)

Tasty and a snap to make, this side dish is a guaranteed salad bar star. The tangy marinade dresses up the green beans, lettuce and spinach nicely. I keep the recipe at the front of my easy-to-make file.
—Dorothy Pritchett, Wills Point, Texas

    1 cup olive *or* vegetable oil
1/4 cup vinegar
1-1/2 teaspoons salt
1-1/2 teaspoons sugar
1/2 teaspoon celery seed
1/2 teaspoon paprika
    2 cans (14-1/2 ounces *each*) cut green beans, drained *or* 4 cups cooked cut fresh green beans (2-inch pieces)
    8 cups torn lettuce
    4 cups torn fresh spinach
    2 cups (8 ounces) shredded Swiss cheese

In a jar with a tight-fitting lid, combine the first six ingredients; shake well. Pour over green beans; let stand for 15 minutes. Just before serving, drain beans, reserving marinade. In a salad bowl, combine the beans, lettuce, spinach and Swiss cheese. Drizzle with reserved marinade; toss to coat. **Yield:** 14-18 servings.

Mini Cheesecake Cups

Since there's no crust, these mini cheesecakes are extra easy to fix. Plus, there's no cutting required and they travel well to various gatherings.
—Jeannette Mack, Rushville, New York

    3 packages (8 ounces *each*) cream cheese, softened
    1 cup sugar
    1 teaspoon vanilla extract
1/4 teaspoon salt
    5 eggs
1/4 cup confectioners' sugar
    1 cup (8 ounces) sour cream
Mandarin oranges, pineapple tidbits, halved maraschino cherries *and/or* chopped nuts

In a large mixing bowl, beat the cream cheese until smooth. Gradually add sugar, vanilla and salt; mix well. Add eggs, one at a time, beating well after each addition. Spoon into paper-lined miniature muffin cups, 2 tablespoons in each. Bake at 325° for 20-25 minutes or until set. Cool completely. Combine confectioners' sugar and sour cream; spread over cheesecakes. Decorate with fruit and/or nuts. Chill for at least 1 hour. Store in the refrigerator. **Yield:** 4 dozen. **Editor's Note:** Cooled cheesecakes can be frozen for up to 4 weeks in an airtight container. Before serving, thaw at room temperature and top with sour cream mixture, fruit and/or nuts.

Raisin-Chip Oatmeal Cookies

The texture of these cookies is just right with plump raisins, sweet chocolate chips, crunchy nuts and yummy coconut. Any leftover cookies freeze nicely.
—Iris Diachuk, Drayton Valley, Alberta

    2 cups butter *or* margarine, softened
1-2/3 cups sugar
1-2/3 cups packed brown sugar
    4 eggs
    1 tablespoon vanilla extract
    4 cups all-purpose flour
2-1/2 cups quick-cooking oats
2-1/2 cups old-fashioned oats
    2 teaspoons baking powder
    2 teaspoons baking soda
    1 teaspoon salt
    1 teaspoon ground cinnamon
    4 cups (24 ounces) semisweet chocolate chips
    3 cups coarsely chopped nuts
    2 cups raisins
    1 cup flaked coconut

In a large mixing bowl, cream butter and sugars. Add eggs, one at a time, beating well after each addition. Beat in vanilla. Combine dry ingredients; gradually add to the creamed mixture. Stir in the chocolate chips, nuts, raisins and coconut. Drop by heaping tablespoonsful 2 in. apart onto ungreased baking sheets. Bake at 350° for 12-14 minutes or until golden brown. Remove to wire racks to cool. **Yield:** 12 dozen. **Editor's Note:** Cookie dough will fit in a large mixing bowl if the recipe is made in two batches.

— 🥄 🥄 🥄 —

Refrigerator Cucumber Slices

My family can never get enough of these sweet cucumber slices in the summer. They're crunchy, delicious and simple to make. At picnics or potlucks, I bring a big batch—folks tend to come back for more.
—Denise Baumert, Jameson, Missouri

> 4 **pounds cucumbers (about 6 large), cut into 1/4-inch slices**
> 3 **medium onions, cut into 1/8-inch slices**
> 3 **cups sugar**
> 3 **cups cider vinegar**
> 4 **teaspoons canning/pickling salt**
> 1-1/2 **teaspoons mustard seed**
> 1/2 **teaspoon alum**

In a large container, combine cucumbers and onions. In a large bowl, combine the remaining ingredients, stirring until sugar is dissolved. Pour over cucumber mixture; mix well. Cover and chill overnight. May be refrigerated for up to 2 weeks. **Yield:** about 2-1/2 quarts.

— 🥄 🥄 🥄 —

Baked Macaroni 'n' Cheese

Everyone loves the golden color and cheesy goodness so much that I'm asked to bring this dish to all our get-togethers. —Karen Ochs, Erie, Pennsylvania

> 1 **package (16 ounces) elbow macaroni**
> 2 **pounds process American cheese, cubed**
> 8 **ounces Swiss cheese, cubed**
> 1 **medium green pepper, chopped**
> 1 **medium onion, chopped**
> 1 **jar (2 ounces) diced pimientos, drained**
> 4 **eggs**
> 4 **cups milk**
> 1 **teaspoon salt**
> 1/2 **teaspoon pepper**
> 1/4 **teaspoon paprika**

Cook macaroni according to package directions. Drain and rinse in cold water. Add cheeses, green pepper, onion and pimientos. Combine eggs, milk, salt and pepper; pour over macaroni mixture and mix well. Pour into two greased 13-in. x 9-in. x 2-in. baking dishes. Sprinkle with paprika. Bake, uncovered, at 350° for 30-35 minutes or until bubbly and browned. **Yield:** 18 (3/4-cup) servings.

Lemon Pudding Dessert
(Pictured above and on page 178)

After a big meal, folks really go for this light lemon treat. The shortbread crust is the perfect base for the fluffy top layers. I've prepared this sunny dessert for church suppers for years and always get recipe requests. —Muriel Dewitt, Maynard, Massachusetts

> 1 **cup cold butter *or* margarine**
> 2 **cups all-purpose flour**
> 1 **package (8 ounces) cream cheese, softened**
> 1 **cup confectioners' sugar**
> 1 **carton (8 ounces) frozen whipped topping, thawed, *divided***
> 3 **cups cold milk**
> 2 **packages (3.4 ounces *each*) instant lemon pudding mix**

In a bowl, cut butter into the flour until crumbly. Press into an ungreased 13-in. x 9-in. x 2-in. baking pan. Bake at 350° for 18-22 minutes or until set. Cool on a wire rack. In a mixing bowl, beat cream cheese and sugar until smooth. Fold in 1 cup whipped topping. Spread over crust. In a mixing bowl, beat milk and pudding mix on low speed for 2 minutes. Carefully spread over the cream cheese layer. Top with the remaining whipped topping. Refrigerate for at least 1 hour. **Yield:** 12-16 servings.

Shredded Beef Sandwiches

Whatever group you're cooking for, they'll love these flavor-packed sandwiches. The beef is slow-cooked until tender, and the light, tangy barbecue sauce is mouth-watering. —JoLynn Hill, Roosevelt, Utah

- 1 boneless chuck roast (about 4 pounds)
- 1 large onion, thinly sliced
- 1 cup ketchup
- 1/4 cup lemon juice
- 3 tablespoons Worcestershire sauce
- 2 tablespoons vinegar
- 2 tablespoons brown sugar
- 1 teaspoon salt
- 1/4 teaspoon pepper
- 1/2 teaspoon liquid smoke
- 24 hamburger buns, split

Cut roast in half; place in a slow cooker. Top with onion. Combine the next eight ingredients; pour over roast. Cover and cook on low for 8-9 hours or until the meat is tender. Remove roast and cool slightly; shred meat with two forks. Skim fat from cooking liquid. Return meat to slow cooker; heat through. Using a slotted spoon, place 1/3 cup meat mixture on each bun. **Yield:** 24 servings.

— 🏳 🏳 🏳 —

Coconut Chocolate Cake

I hope other families enjoy this cake as much as my family does. I've given almost 100 copies of this recipe to others who have tried the cake and liked it.
—Dorothy West, Nacogdoches, Texas

- 2 cups all-purpose flour
- 2 cups sugar
- 1 teaspoon baking soda
- 1/2 teaspoon salt
- 1 cup butter *or* margarine
- 1 cup water
- 1/4 cup baking cocoa
- 2 eggs
- 1/2 cup buttermilk
- 1 teaspoon vanilla extract

TOPPING:
- 1 can (12 ounces) evaporated milk, *divided*
- 1-1/4 cups sugar, *divided*
- 20 large marshmallows
- 1 package (14 ounces) flaked coconut
- 2 cups slivered almonds, toasted, *divided*
- 1/2 cup butter *or* margarine
- 1 cup (6 ounces) semisweet chocolate chips

In a mixing bowl, combine flour, sugar, baking soda and salt. In a saucepan, combine butter, water and cocoa. Cook and stir until butter is melted; add to dry ingredients. Combine eggs, buttermilk and

Slow-Cooked Short Ribs

(Pictured above)

Smothered in a mouth-watering barbecue sauce, these meaty ribs are a popular entree wherever I serve them. The recipe is great for a busy cook—after everything is combined, the slow cooker does all the work.
—Pam Halfhill, Medina, Ohio

- 2/3 cup all-purpose flour
- 2 teaspoons salt
- 1/2 teaspoon pepper
- 4 to 4-1/2 pounds boneless beef short ribs
- 1/4 to 1/3 cup butter *or* margarine
- 1 large onion, chopped
- 1-1/2 cups beef broth
- 3/4 cup cider *or* red wine vinegar
- 3/4 cup packed brown sugar
- 1/2 cup chili sauce
- 1/3 cup ketchup
- 1/3 cup Worcestershire sauce
- 5 garlic cloves, minced
- 1-1/2 teaspoons chili powder

In a large resealable plastic bag, combine the flour, salt and pepper. Add ribs in batches and shake to coat. In a large skillet, brown ribs in butter. Transfer to a 5-qt. slow cooker. In the same skillet, combine the remaining ingredients. Cook and stir until mixture comes to a boil; pour over ribs (slow cooker will be full). Cover and cook on low for 9-10 hours or until meat is tender. **Yield:** 12-15 servings.

vanilla; add to chocolate mixture and mix well. Pour into a greased 15-in. x 10-in. x 1-in. baking pan. Bake at 350° for 20-25 minutes or until a toothpick comes out clean. Meanwhile, in a saucepan, combine 1 cup evaporated milk, 3/4 cup sugar and marshmallows; cook and stir until marshmallows are melted. Remove from heat; stir in coconut. Immediately sprinkle 1 cup almonds over cake. Spread coconut mixture over top. Sprinkle with remaining almonds (pan will be full). In a saucepan, combine butter with remaining milk and sugar. Cook and stir until butter is melted. Remove from heat; stir in chocolate chips until melted. Drizzle over almonds. Cool completely. **Yield:** 35 servings.

Boston Cream Pie

This impressive dessert can be made without much fuss. It's pretty, tasty and very popular.
—*Clara Honeyager, Mukwonago, Wisconsin*

- **4 packages (18-1/4 ounces *each*) yellow cake mix**
- **11 cups cold milk**
- **4 packages (5.1 ounces *each*) instant vanilla pudding mix**
- **4 jars (16 ounces *each*) hot fudge topping, warmed**
- **96 maraschino cherries, optional**

Prepare cake mixes according to package directions. Bake in four greased 13-in. x 9-in. x 2-in. baking pans; cool. In a mixing bowl, beat milk and pudding mixes on low for 2-3 minutes. Cover and chill for at least 30 minutes. Cut each cake into 24 pieces; split each piece horizontally. Place about 1 heaping tablespoon of pudding between layers. Top with 1 tablespoon fudge topping. Garnish with a cherry if desired. **Yield:** 96 servings.

Sweet 'n' Sour Beans

(Pictured at right)

This recipe is popular on both sides of the border. It came from a friend in Alaska, then traveled with me to old Mexico, where I lived for 5 years, and is now a potluck favorite in my Arkansas community. It's easy to keep the beans warm and serve from a slow cooker.
—*Barbara Short, Mena, Arkansas*

- **8 bacon strips, diced**
- **2 medium onions, halved and thinly sliced**
- **1 cup packed brown sugar**
- **1/2 cup cider vinegar**
- **1 teaspoon salt**
- **1 teaspoon ground mustard**
- **1/2 teaspoon garlic powder**
- **1 can (28 ounces) baked beans, undrained**
- **1 can (16 ounces) kidney beans, rinsed and drained**
- **1 can (15-1/2 ounces) pinto beans, rinsed and drained**
- **1 can (15 ounces) lima beans, rinsed and drained**
- **1 can (15-1/2 ounces) black-eyed peas, rinsed and drained**

In a large skillet, cook bacon until crisp. Remove to paper towels. Drain, reserving 2 tablespoons drippings. In the drippings, saute onions until tender. Add brown sugar, vinegar, salt, mustard and garlic powder. Bring to a boil. In a slow cooker, combine beans and peas. Add onion mixture and bacon; mix well. Cover and cook on high for 3-4 hours or until heated through. **Yield:** 15-20 servings.

Temperature Control
When heading out to a picnic, pack hot dishes with hot dishes and cold dishes with cold dishes. Wrapping your hot dishes in aluminum foil and then in newspaper keeps them insulated. Pack cold dishes last to keep them cooler longer.

Creamy Fruit Salad

(Pictured below)

With crowd-pleasing fruits like apples, bananas and grapes plus crunchy pecans, this wonderful salad doesn't last long on potluck buffets. I never bring home leftovers—just an empty bowl. —Bernice Morris
Marshfield, Missouri

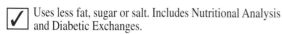 Uses less fat, sugar or salt. Includes Nutritional Analysis and Diabetic Exchanges.

- 1/3 cup orange juice
- 1/3 cup unsweetened pineapple juice
- 1/4 cup sugar
- 1 egg, beaten
- 1 tablespoon plus 1/4 cup lemon juice, divided
- 1 cup whipping cream, whipped *or* 2 cups whipped topping
- 6 medium red apples, diced
- 6 medium firm bananas, sliced
- 3 cups halved green grapes
- 1/4 cup chopped pecans

In a heavy saucepan, combine orange and pineapple juices, sugar, egg and 1 tablespoon of lemon juice. Bring to a boil over medium-high heat, stirring constantly. Remove from the heat. When cool, fold in the whipped cream. In a large serving bowl, toss apples with remaining lemon juice. Add bananas and grapes. Add the dressing; stir to coat. Refrigerate. Fold in pecans just before serving. **Yield:** 20 servings. **Nutritional Analysis:** One serving (prepared with egg substitute equivalent to 1 egg and light whipped topping) equals 111 calories, 7 mg sodium, trace cholesterol, 23 gm carbohydrate, 1 gm protein, 2 gm fat, 2 gm fiber. **Diabetic Exchanges:** 1-1/2 fruit, 1/2 fat.

— ▽ ▽ ▽ —

Curry Chicken Casserole

When I've invited a crowd over for the holidays, this is the recipe I reach for. It's a rich, meaty dish that makes plenty and satisfies one and all.
—Julia Garnett, Virginia Beach, Virginia

- 13 large onions, diced
- 4 medium bunches celery, sliced
- 6 cans (8 ounces *each*) mushroom stems and pieces, drained
- 2 cups butter or margarine
- 9 packages (4 ounces *each*) long grain and wild rice mix
- 13-1/2 cups water
- 12 cans (10-3/4 ounces *each*) condensed golden mushroom soup, undiluted
- 13 cups sour cream
- 1/4 cup curry powder
- 72 cups cubed cooked chicken (36 pounds boneless skinless chicken breasts)
- 1 can (8 ounces) grated Parmesan cheese

In several large saucepans or Dutch ovens over medium heat, saute the onions, celery and mushrooms in butter until tender. Stir in rice with contents of seasoning packets and water; bring to a boil. Reduce heat; cover and simmer until rice is tender, about 25 minutes. Add the soup, sour cream and curry powder; mix well. Fold in chicken. Spoon into nine greased 13-in. x 9-in. x 2-in. baking dishes. Sprinkle with cheese. Bake, uncovered, at 350° for 45-60 minutes or until bubbly. **Yield:** 100 servings.

— ▽ ▽ ▽ —

Double-Chip Cookies

These buttery cookies are packed with vanilla and peanut butter chips plus walnuts. I'm never left with any to take home after a potluck dinner.
—Diana Dube, Rockland, Maine

- 2 cups butter *or* margarine, softened
- 1-1/2 cups sugar
- 1-1/2 cups packed brown sugar
- 4 eggs

3 teaspoons vanilla extract
5 cups all-purpose flour
3 teaspoons baking soda
1 teaspoon salt
3 cups chopped walnuts
1 package (12 ounces) vanilla *or* white chips
1 package (10 ounces) peanut butter chips

In a large mixing bowl, cream butter and sugars. Add eggs, one at a time, beating well after each addition. Beat in vanilla. Combine the flour, baking soda and salt; gradually add to the creamed mixture. Stir in walnuts and chips. Drop by rounded tablespoonfuls 2 in. apart onto ungreased baking sheets. Bake at 350° for 10-12 minutes or until golden brown. Remove to wire racks to cool. **Yield:** about 10 dozen. **Editor's Note:** Cookie dough will fit in a large mixing bowl if the recipe is made in two batches.

Layered Picnic Loaves

(Pictured at right and on page 178)

This big sandwich, inspired by one I tried at a New York deli, is a favorite with our football-watching crowd. Made ahead, it's easily carted to any gathering. Kids and adults alike say it's super.
— *Marion Lowery, Medford, Oregon*

2 unsliced loaves (1 pound *each*) Italian bread
1/4 cup olive *or* vegetable oil
3 garlic cloves, minced
2 teaspoons Italian seasoning, *divided*
1/2 pound deli roast beef
3/4 pound sliced mozzarella cheese
16 fresh basil leaves
3 medium tomatoes, thinly sliced
1/4 pound thinly sliced salami
1 jar (6-1/2 ounces) marinated artichoke hearts, drained and sliced
1 package (10 ounces) ready-to-serve salad greens
1/2 pound deli chicken
1 medium onion, thinly sliced
1/4 teaspoon salt
1/8 teaspoon pepper

Cut loaves in half horizontally; hollow out tops and bottoms, leaving 1/2-in. shells (discard removed bread or save for another use). Combine oil and garlic; brush inside bread shells. Sprinkle with 1 teaspoon Italian seasoning. Layer bottom of each loaf with a fourth of the roast beef, mozzarella, basil, tomatoes, salami, artichokes, salad greens, chicken and onion. Repeat layers. Season with salt,

pepper and remaining Italian seasoning. Drizzle with remaining oil mixture if desired. Replace bread tops; wrap tightly in plastic wrap. Refrigerate for at least 1 hour before slicing. **Yield:** 2 loaves (12 servings each).

Roundup-Day Beans

The hearty noon meal at our spring cattle roundup always features these sweet, smoky beans. Neighbors gather to help for a day of work and socialization.
— *Jenny Hughson, Mitchell, Nebraska*

2 pounds ground beef
1 cup chopped onion
1-1/2 cups chopped green pepper
3 cans (53 ounces *each*) pork and beans
1 cup ketchup
6 tablespoons brown sugar
1/4 cup molasses
2 tablespoons liquid smoke, optional
1-1/2 teaspoons salt
1 teaspoon pepper

In large Dutch ovens, cook beef, onion and green pepper over medium heat until meat is no longer pink and vegetables are tender. Drain. Add the remaining ingredients; bring to a boil. Reduce heat; cover and simmer for 30 minutes. **Yield:** 45-50 servings.

TAKE-ALONG TREATS like Creamy Orange Salad, Italian Vegetable Salad, Baked Rice with Sausage and Butterscotch Pecan Slices (shown above, clockwise from top) are guaranteed crowd-pleasers.

Baked Rice with Sausage

(Pictured above and on page 178)

This recipe is perfect for potlucks or church suppers since it produces a big batch and has flavors with broad appeal. Most folks can't guess that the secret ingredient is chicken noodle soup mix. —Naomi Flood
Emporia, Kansas

2 pounds bulk Italian sausage
4 celery ribs, thinly sliced
1 large onion, chopped
1 large green pepper, chopped

4-1/2 cups water
3/4 cup dry chicken noodle soup mix (1-1/2 envelopes)
1 can (10-3/4 ounces) condensed cream of chicken soup, undiluted
1 cup uncooked long grain rice
1/4 cup dry bread crumbs
2 tablespoons butter *or* margarine, melted

In a large skillet, cook sausage, celery, onion and green pepper over medium heat until meat is no longer pink and vegetables are tender; drain. In a large saucepan, bring water to a boil; add dry soup mix. Reduce heat; simmer, uncovered, for 5 minutes or until the noodles are tender. Stir in canned soup, rice and sausage mixture; mix well. Transfer to a greased 13-in. x 9-in. x 2-in. baking dish. Cover and bake at 350° for 40 minutes. Toss bread crumbs and butter; sprinkle over rice mixture. Bake, uncovered, for 10-15 minutes or until rice is tender. Let stand 10 minutes before serving. **Yield:** 12-14 servings.

Italian Vegetable Salad

(Pictured at left)

Even our two small children eat their vegetables when I serve this colorful and nutritious combination. To make it a main dish, I'll stir pepperoni slices and cooked cooled pasta into the crunchy, creamy blend. —Debbie Laubach, La Prairie, Minnesota

✓ Uses less fat, sugar or salt. Includes Nutritional Analysis and Diabetic Exchanges.

    5 cups broccoli florets (1 large bunch)
    5 cups cauliflowerets (1 small head)
    4 plum tomatoes, chopped
    1 medium cucumber, peeled and sliced
    1 medium sweet onion, thinly sliced
    1 cup sliced carrots
    2 cans (2-1/4 ounces *each*) sliced ripe olives, drained
1/2 cup sliced stuffed olives
    1 bottle (8 ounces) Italian salad dressing
    1 bottle (8 ounces) creamy Italian salad dressing
    2 cups (8 ounces) shredded mozzarella cheese

In a large salad bowl, combine the first eight ingredients. Combine salad dressings; pour over vegetable mixture and toss to coat. Cover and refrigerate for at least 4 hours. Stir in cheese just before serving. **Yield:** 14 servings. **Nutritional Analysis:** One serving (prepared with fat-free salad dressings and part-skim mozzarella cheese) equals 121 calories, 531 mg sodium, 10 mg cholesterol, 11 gm carbohydrate, 6 gm protein, 6 gm fat, 2 gm fiber. **Diabetic Exchanges:** 2 vegetable, 1-1/2 fat.

> ### Salad Solution
>
> When hosting a potluck, ask guests to bring 1 or 2 cups of their favorite salad ingredient. You provide the lettuce and an assortment of salad dressings, and everyone can enjoy a great tossed salad with very little work.

Creamy Orange Salad

(Pictured at far left)

This cool, light and pretty salad has a refreshing orange taste that complements any big meal. With just five ingredients, it's very simple to prepare. I've served it for my family and shared it at potlucks.
—Priscilla Weaver, Hagerstown, Maryland

    1 package (6 ounces) orange gelatin
    2 cups boiling water
    2 packages (3 ounces *each*) cream cheese, softened
    1 can (14 ounces) sweetened condensed milk
    1 carton (8 ounces) frozen whipped topping, thawed
Maraschino cherry, fresh mint stem and mandarin oranges, optional

In a bowl, dissolve gelatin in water. In a mixing bowl, beat cream cheese until fluffy. Gradually blend in the hot gelatin mixture, beating on low speed until smooth. Stir in the milk; fold in whipped topping. Transfer to a 2-1/2-qt. serving bowl. Refrigerate for 4 hours or until firm. If desired, garnish with a flower made of cherry, mint and oranges. **Yield:** 10-12 servings.

Butterscotch Pecan Slices

(Pictured at far left)

I love the rich, buttery flavor these crisp cookies get from pecans and brown sugar. Once the dough is in the refrigerator, I can have freshly baked cookies in just minutes. When company drops in, I'm prepared with a tasty treat. —Esther Thys, Belle Plaine, Iowa

    6 tablespoons butter *or* margarine, softened
2/3 cup packed brown sugar
    1 egg
1/2 teaspoon vanilla extract
1-1/4 cups all-purpose flour
1/2 teaspoon baking powder
1/4 teaspoon salt
3/4 cup finely chopped pecans, *divided*

In a mixing bowl, cream the butter and brown sugar. Beat in egg and vanilla. Combine flour, baking powder and salt; gradually add to the creamed mixture. Stir in 1/2 cup pecans. Shape into two 7-in. rolls; wrap each in plastic wrap. Refrigerate for 2 hours or until firm. Unwrap and cut into 1/4-in. slices. Place 2 in. apart on ungreased baking sheets. Sprinkle with remaining nuts; press gently. Bake at 350° for 10-12 minutes or until edges begin to brown. **Yield:** 4 dozen.

Greek Pasta and Beef

(Pictured below)

This delightfully different casserole gives everyday macaroni and cheese an international flavor. A co-worker who's a pro at Greek cooking shared the recipe years ago. It brings raves whenever I serve it.
—Dorothy Bateman, Carver, Massachusetts

    1 pound ground beef
    1 large onion, chopped
    1 garlic clove, minced
    1 can (8 ounces) tomato sauce
 1/2 cup water
    1 teaspoon salt
 1/2 teaspoon ground cinnamon
 1/4 teaspoon ground nutmeg
 1/4 teaspoon pepper
    1 pound elbow macaroni, cooked and
      drained
    1 egg, lightly beaten
 1/2 cup grated Parmesan cheese
SAUCE:
 1/4 cup butter *or* margarine
 1/4 cup all-purpose flour
 1/4 teaspoon ground cinnamon
    3 cups milk
    2 eggs, lightly beaten
 1/3 cup grated Parmesan cheese

In a skillet, cook beef, onion and garlic over medium heat until meat is no longer pink; drain. Stir in tomato sauce, water and seasonings. Cover and simmer for 10 minutes, stirring occasionally. Meanwhile, in a bowl, combine the macaroni, egg and Parmesan cheese; set aside. In a large saucepan, melt the butter; stir in flour and cinnamon until smooth. Gradually add milk. Bring to a boil over medium heat; cook and stir for 2 minutes or until slightly thickened. Remove from the heat; cool slightly. Stir a small amount of hot mixture into eggs; return all to pan. Cook and stir for 2 minutes. Remove from the heat; stir in cheese. In a greased 3-qt. baking dish, spread half of the macaroni mixture. Top with beef mixture and remaining macaroni mixture. Pour sauce over the top. Bake, uncovered, at 350° for 45-50 minutes or until bubbly and heated through. Let stand 5 minutes before serving. **Yield:** 12 servings.

— 🍵 🍵 🍵 —

Spinach Parmesan

This easy dish is a satisfying solution to breakfast or brunch. It's a great addition to any buffet, plus it's guaranteed to serve a big bunch. —Dixie Terry
Marion, Illinois

    8 packages (10 ounces *each*) frozen
      chopped spinach, thawed
    1 medium onion, finely chopped
 1/2 cup butter *or* margarine
    6 eggs, lightly beaten
1-1/2 cups dry bread crumbs
1-1/3 cups grated Parmesan cheese, ***divided***
    1 tablespoon Worcestershire sauce
    1 teaspoon salt
 1/4 teaspoon pepper

Drain spinach, reserving 1 cup liquid. Saute onion in butter until tender. In a bowl, combine spinach, eggs, bread crumbs, 1 cup Parmesan cheese, Worcestershire sauce, salt, pepper, onion mixture and reserved liquid. Spread in two greased 13-in. x 9-in. x 2-in. baking dishes. Sprinkle with remaining Parmesan cheese. Bake, uncovered, at 350° for 25-30 minutes or until set. **Yield:** 40-48 servings.

— 🍵 🍵 🍵 —

Ice Cream Sundae Cake

If you're looking for a cool, make-ahead dessert that will delight a crowd, this is it! —Luanna Martin
Denver, Pennsylvania

    6 eggs, ***separated***
    2 cups sugar, ***divided***

1-1/3 cups all-purpose flour
  1/2 cup baking cocoa
1-1/2 teaspoons baking powder
  2/3 cup water
    1 teaspoon vanilla extract
    1 gallon vanilla ice cream, softened
    2 jars (11-3/4 ounces *each*) hot fudge
      topping, warmed
1-1/2 cups chopped salted peanuts
    2 cartons (8 ounces *each*) frozen whipped
      topping, thawed
    2 cups crushed cream-filled sandwich
      cookies

In a mixing bowl, beat egg whites until foamy. Gradually beat in 1 cup sugar until stiff peaks form; set aside. In another mixing bowl, beat egg yolks until thick and lemon-colored, about 2 minutes. Gradually beat in remaining sugar; beat 2 minutes longer. Combine flour, cocoa and baking powder; add to egg yolk mixture alternately with water. Beat in vanilla. Gently fold in egg whites. Transfer to two greased 13-in. x 9-in. x 2-in. baking pans. Bake at 350° for 16-20 minutes or until a toothpick comes out clean. Cool on a wire rack. Spread each cake with ice cream. Drizzle with fudge topping; sprinkle with peanuts. Spread with whipped topping; sprinkle with cookies. Cover and freeze until firm. Remove from the freezer 15 minutes before serving. **Yield:** 2 desserts (15 servings each).

— ▛ ▛ ▛ —

Holiday Hash Brown Bake

With the chopped red and green peppers, this dish is perfect for Christmastime. And you don't have to worry about leftovers—there never seem to be any!
—Russell Moffett, Irvine, California

    2 packages (2 pounds *each*) frozen cubed
      hash brown potatoes, thawed
    5 cups (20 ounces) shredded cheddar
      cheese
    2 cans (10-3/4 ounces *each*) condensed
      cream of chicken soup, undiluted
    4 cups (32 ounces) sour cream
    2 small green peppers, chopped
    2 small sweet red peppers, chopped
    1 medium onion, chopped

In a large bowl, combine all ingredients; mix well. Transfer to two greased 13-in. x 9-in. x 2-in. baking dishes. Cover and bake at 350° for 40 minutes. Uncover; bake 25-30 minutes longer or until heated through. **Yield:** 24 servings. **Editor's Note:** Recipe can be prepared ahead and refrigerated. Remove from the refrigerator 30 minutes before baking.

Frosted Banana Bars

(Pictured above)

I make these moist bars whenever I have ripe bananas on hand, then store them in the freezer to share later at a potluck. With creamy frosting and big banana flavor, this treat is a real crowd-pleaser.
—Debbie Knight, Marion, Iowa

    1/2 cup butter *or* margarine, softened
1-1/2 cups sugar
    2 eggs
    1 cup (8 ounces) sour cream
    1 teaspoon vanilla extract
    2 cups all-purpose flour
    1 teaspoon baking soda
  1/4 teaspoon salt
    2 medium ripe bananas, mashed (about 1
      cup)
FROSTING:
    1 package (8 ounces) cream cheese,
      softened
  1/2 cup butter *or* margarine, softened
    2 teaspoons vanilla extract
3-3/4 to 4 cups confectioners' sugar

In a mixing bowl, cream butter and sugar. Add eggs, sour cream and vanilla. Combine flour, baking soda and salt; gradually add to the creamed mixture. Stir in bananas. Spread into a greased 15-in. x 10-in. x 1-in. baking pan. Bake at 350° for 20-25 minutes or until a toothpick inserted near the center comes out clean. Cool. For frosting, in a mixing bowl, beat cream cheese, butter and vanilla. Gradually beat in enough confectioners' sugar to achieve desired consistency. Frost bars. Store in the refrigerator. **Yield:** 3-4 dozen.

low heat until chocolate is melted. Remove from the heat; stir in walnuts and remaining vanilla. Spread over crust. Sprinkle with remaining oat mixture. Bake at 350° for 25 minutes or until golden brown. Cool. Cut into squares. **Yield:** 4 dozen.

— 🍴 🍴 🍴 —

Cajun Meat Loaf

A jambalaya of flavors greets guests who sample my zippy meat loaf. I received the recipe years ago from a friend who lived in Jamaica. —Anna Free
Cleveland, Ohio

40 **bay leaves**
1/2 **cup salt**
1/4 **cup *each* pepper, white pepper, cayenne, pepper, ground cumin and nutmeg**
40 **green onions, thinly sliced**
15 **medium onions, chopped**
10 **medium green peppers, chopped**
40 **garlic cloves, minced**
4 **cups butter *or* margarine**
1 **cup Worcestershire sauce**
2/3 **cup hot pepper sauce**
6 **cans (12 ounces *each*) evaporated milk**
1 **bottle (64 ounces) ketchup**
8 **packages (8 ounces *each*) dry bread crumbs (20 cups)**
3 **dozen eggs, beaten**
30 **pounds lean ground beef**
10 **pounds ground pork**

Combine seasonings; set aside. In a Dutch oven, saute the onions, green peppers and garlic in butter until tender. Add Worcestershire sauce, hot pepper sauce and reserved seasonings. Cook and stir for 8-10 minutes. Discard bay leaves. Remove from the heat; stir in milk and ketchup. Cool. Add bread crumbs and eggs; mix well. In several large bowls, combine the beef, pork and vegetable mixture; mix well. Pat into 11 greased 13-in. x 9-in. x 2-in. baking pans. Bake at 350° for 65-75 minutes or until a meat thermometer reads 160°-170°; drain. Let stand 10 minutes before cutting. **Yield:** 175-200 servings.

— 🍴 🍴 🍴 —

Family Gathering Potatoes

This delicious Amish side dish always wins raves. Almost everyone comes back for seconds—or thirds! —Sara Yoder, Mt. Hope, Ohio

2 **pounds process American cheese, cubed**
4 **cans (10-3/4 ounces *each*) condensed cream of celery soup, undiluted**

Chocolate Oat Squares

(Pictured above)

When you bring these treats to a group meal, guests will be tempted to start at the dessert table. Chock-full of chocolate and walnuts, they'll satisfy any sweet tooth. I often make a batch just for my family. —Jennifer Eilts, Central City, Nebraska

1 **cup plus 2 tablespoons butter *or* margarine, softened, *divided***
2 **cups packed brown sugar**
2 **eggs**
4 **teaspoons vanilla extract, *divided***
3 **cups quick-cooking oats**
2-1/2 **cups all-purpose flour**
1-1/2 **teaspoons salt, *divided***
1 **teaspoon baking soda**
1 **can (14 ounces) sweetened condensed milk**
2 **cups (12 ounces) semisweet chocolate chips**
1 **cup chopped walnuts**

In a mixing bowl, cream 1 cup butter and brown sugar. Beat in eggs and 2 teaspoons vanilla. Combine the oats, flour, 1 teaspoon salt and baking soda; stir into creamed mixture. Press two-thirds of oat mixture into a greased 15-in. x 10-in. x 1-in. baking pan. In a saucepan, combine milk, chocolate chips and remaining butter and salt. Cook and stir over

4 cans (10-3/4 ounces *each*) condensed
   cream of chicken soup, undiluted
4 cups (32 ounces) sour cream
1-1/3 cups butter *or* margarine, *divided*
4 teaspoons seasoned salt
2 teaspoons garlic powder
2 teaspoons pepper
20 pounds potatoes, peeled, cubed and
   cooked
2 cups crushed Club crackers (about 40)

In four Dutch ovens or soup kettles, combine cheese, soups, sour cream, 1 cup butter, seasoned salt, garlic powder and pepper. Cook and stir until cheese is melted and mixture is smooth. Add potatoes; mix well. Transfer to four greased 13-in. x 9-in. x 2-in. baking dishes (dishes will be full). Bake, uncovered, at 350° for 45-60 minutes or until bubbly. Melt remaining butter; toss with cracker crumbs. Sprinkle over potatoes. Bake 10-15 minutes longer or until topping is lightly browned. Let stand for 5 minutes before serving. **Yield:** 60-65 servings.

— ❦ ❦ ❦ —

Harvest Vegetable Casserole

This is a great way to use fresh garden vegetables on a large scale with only minimal preparation. It's colorful, flavorful and good for you. —Edna Hoffman
Hebron, Indiana

2 large green peppers
1 large sweet red pepper
4 large carrots
4 large tomatoes
3 medium zucchini
1-1/2 pounds green beans
4 large onions, thinly sliced
1/4 cup vegetable oil
1 medium head cauliflower, cut into florets
1 package (10 ounces) frozen peas
1 to 2 tablespoons salt
1 tablespoon chicken bouillon granules
3 cups boiling water
1 cup medium pearl barley
3 garlic cloves, minced
1/4 cup lemon juice
2 teaspoons paprika
Minced fresh parsley

Cut peppers, carrots and tomatoes into chunks; cut zucchini and beans into 1-in. pieces. In large skillets, saute onions in oil until tender. Add peppers; cook and stir for 1 minute. Stir in carrots, tomatoes, zucchini, beans, cauliflower and peas. Add salt; stir. In a bowl, dissolve bouillon in water; stir in the barley and garlic. Transfer to three greased 13-in.

x 9-in. x 2-in. baking dishes. Top with vegetable mixture. Drizzle with lemon juice; sprinkle with paprika. Cover and bake at 350° for 1-1/2 hours or until barley and vegetables are tender. Sprinkle with parsley. **Yield:** about 28 (3/4-cup) servings.

— ❦ ❦ ❦ —

Marinated Cucumbers

(Pictured below and on page 178)

These cucumber slices make a cool summer side dish dressed in a light, tangy vinegar and oil mixture seasoned with herbs. The refreshing salad is always a hit when served with cold sandwiches or grilled meat.
—Mary Helen Hinson, Lumberton, North Carolina

6 medium cucumbers, thinly sliced
1 medium onion, sliced
1 cup vinegar
1/4 to 1/3 cup sugar
1/4 cup olive *or* vegetable oil
1 teaspoon salt
1 teaspoon dried oregano
1/2 teaspoon garlic powder
1/2 teaspoon dried marjoram
1/2 teaspoon lemon-pepper seasoning
1/2 teaspoon ground mustard

In a bowl, combine the cucumbers and onion. In a jar with a tight-fitting lid, combine the remaining ingredients; shake well. Pour over cucumber mixture. Cover and refrigerate for at least 4 hours. Serve with a slotted spoon. **Yield:** 12 servings.

Fudgy Toffee Bars

(Pictured at far right)

Sweet treats always go over well in my family, especially during the holidays. We think these rich bars—dotted with walnuts, toffee bits, chocolate chips and coconut—are better than candy! They're nice to share with a group. —Diane Bradley, Sparta, Michigan

1-3/4 cups all-purpose flour
  3/4 cup confectioners' sugar
  1/4 cup baking cocoa
  3/4 cup cold butter *or* margarine
    1 can (14 ounces) sweetened condensed milk
    1 teaspoon vanilla extract
    2 cups (12 ounces) semisweet chocolate chips, *divided*
    1 cup coarsely chopped walnuts
  1/2 cup flaked coconut
  1/2 cup English toffee bits *or* almond brickle chips

In a bowl, combine flour, sugar and cocoa. Cut in butter until mixture resembles coarse crumbs. Press firmly into a greased 13-in. x 9-in. x 2-in. baking pan. Bake at 350° for 10 minutes. Meanwhile, in a saucepan, heat milk, vanilla and 1 cup of chocolate chips, stirring until smooth. Pour over the crust. Sprinkle with nuts, coconut, toffee bits and remaining chocolate chips; press down firmly. Bake for 18-20 minutes. **Yield:** 3 dozen.

Topknot Rolls

(Pictured at far right)

These golden dinner rolls have a fine texture and a delightful buttery flavor. They brighten any meal. Even though they look special, they're not difficult to make. —Bernadine Stine, Roanoke, Indiana

    2 packages (1/4 ounce *each*) active dry yeast
    2 teaspoons plus 1/2 cup sugar, *divided*
1-1/4 cups warm water (110° to 115°)
    3 eggs, beaten
  3/4 cup butter *or* margarine, melted, cooled, *divided*
5-1/2 cups all-purpose flour
    2 teaspoons salt
Softened butter *or* margarine

In a mixing bowl, dissolve yeast and 2 teaspoons of sugar in water. Let stand for 5 minutes. Add eggs, 1/2 cup melted butter, 2 cups flour, salt and remaining sugar. Beat until smooth. Add enough remaining flour to form a soft dough. Turn onto a floured surface; knead until smooth and elastic, about 6-8 minutes. Place in a greased bowl, turning once to grease top. Cover and let rise in a warm place for 1-1/2 to 2 hours or until doubled. Punch dough down; divide in half. On a floured surface, roll each portion into a 15-in. x 8-in. rectangle. Spread generously with softened butter. Roll up, jelly-roll style, starting with a long side. Using a sharp knife, cut into 1-in. slices. Place cut side up in greased muffin cups. Cover and let rise until doubled, about 45 minutes. Bake at 375° for 8-10 minutes or until golden brown. Brush with remaining melted butter. **Yield:** 2-1/2 dozen.

Lettuce Salad with Warm Dressing

(Pictured at right)

It's fun to share a different kind of tossed salad. The warm, tangy dressing wilts the greens in the most delicious way. Almonds provide a bit of crunch to round out this colorful side dish. —Diane Hixon
Niceville, Florida

☑ Uses less fat, sugar or salt. Includes Nutritional Analysis and Diabetic Exchanges.

    1 large bunch green leaf lettuce, torn (about 12 cups)
    1 large bunch red leaf lettuce, torn (about 12 cups)
  1/2 pound fresh mushrooms, sliced
    3 green onions, sliced
    4 bacon strips, cooked and crumbled, optional
DRESSING:
  1/2 cup cider *or* red wine vinegar
  1/2 cup olive *or* vegetable oil
  1/4 cup water
    1 tablespoon sugar
    2 teaspoons lemon juice
    1 teaspoon Dijon mustard
    1 teaspoon Worcestershire sauce
  3/4 teaspoon garlic salt *or* 1/8 teaspoon garlic powder
  1/4 teaspoon pepper

In a large salad bowl, toss lettuce, mushrooms, onions and bacon if desired. In a small saucepan, combine the dressing ingredients. Cook and stir over medium heat until heated through. Just before serving, drizzle warm dressing over the salad; toss to coat. **Yield:** 18 servings. **Nutritional Analysis:** One serving with 1 tablespoon dressing (prepared with garlic powder and without bacon) equals 68 calories, 14 mg sodium, 0 cholesterol, 3 gm carbohydrate, 1 gm protein, 6 gm fat, 1 gm fiber. **Diabetic Exchanges:** 1 vegetable, 1 fat.

'TIS THE SEASON. When you need a host of holiday helpings, reach for Topknot Rolls, Confetti Spaghetti, Fudgy Toffee Bars and Lettuce Salad with Warm Dressing (shown above, clockwise from top).

Confetti Spaghetti

(Pictured above)

Folks will go back for seconds of this hearty main dish.
—*Katherine Moss, Gaffney, South Carolina*

- 1 package (12 ounces) spaghetti
- 1-1/2 pounds ground beef
- 1 medium green pepper, chopped
- 1 medium onion, chopped
- 1 can (14-1/2 ounces) diced tomatoes, undrained
- 1 can (8 ounces) tomato sauce
- 1 tablespoon brown sugar
- 1 teaspoon salt
- 1 teaspoon chili powder
- 1/2 teaspoon pepper
- 1/4 teaspoon garlic powder
- 1/8 teaspoon cayenne pepper
- 3/4 cup shredded cheddar cheese

Cook spaghetti according to package directions. Meanwhile, in a large skillet, cook beef, green pepper and onion over medium heat until meat is no longer pink; drain. Stir in the tomatoes, tomato sauce, brown sugar, salt, chili powder, pepper, garlic powder and cayenne. Drain spaghetti; add to the beef mixture. Transfer to a greased 13-in. x 9-in. x 2-in. baking dish. Cover and bake at 350° for 30 minutes. Uncover; sprinkle with cheese. Bake 5 minutes longer or until the cheese is melted. **Yield:** 12 servings.

minutes or until thickened. Set aside. Heat oil in a large skillet over medium-high heat. Add the chicken; brown on all sides. Place in two greased 13-in. x 9-in. x 2-in. baking dishes. Pour reserved sauce over chicken. Bake, uncovered, at 350° for 45 minutes. Add pineapple and green pepper. Bake 15 minutes longer or until heated through. **Yield:** 12 servings.

— 🍴 🍴 🍴 —

Cheesy Corn Squares

My family loves corn, and I love to come up with new ways to fix it. I created this recipe a couple of years ago. It's great with soups, stews and chili.
—*Peggy Paul, Florence, South Carolina*

    1-1/4 cups all-purpose flour
        2 tablespoons minced fresh parsley
        1 teaspoon baking soda
        1 teaspoon seasoned salt
      1/2 teaspoon dried basil
      1/2 teaspoon dried oregano
      1/2 teaspoon pepper
        4 eggs, beaten
        1 can (15-1/4 ounces) whole kernel corn, drained
        1 cup ricotta cheese
      1/3 cup finely chopped onion
      1/4 cup grated Parmesan cheese
      1/4 cup vegetable oil
        2 cups (8 ounces) shredded mozzarella cheese, *divided*
        1 teaspoon paprika

In a large bowl, combine the first seven ingredients. Stir in eggs, corn, ricotta, onion, Parmesan, oil and 1-1/2 cups of mozzarella; mix well. Pour into a greased 13-in. x 9-in. x 2-in. baking pan. Sprinkle with paprika and remaining mozzarella. Bake, uncovered, at 350° for 30-35 minutes or until golden brown. Cut into small squares. **Yield:** 5 dozen.

— 🍴 🍴 🍴 —

Classic Red Beans and Rice

This regional favorite has broad appeal because it is hearty and tasty but not too hot. It's a good way to add variety to the menu.
—*Shirley Johnson*
Kenner, Louisiana

        6 pounds dry red kidney beans, sorted and rinsed
        9 quarts water
       18 garlic cloves, minced
        6 bay leaves
    1-1/2 teaspoons browning sauce, optional

Pineapple Pepper Chicken

(Pictured above and on page 178)

I came up with this recipe years ago by combining a couple of family favorites. Easy and versatile, it's great for potlucks. I can make the sauce ahead and use all wings or leg quarters when they're on sale. This is a welcome entree at senior citizen fellowship dinners.
—*Phyllis Minter, Wakefield, Kansas*

        4 cups unsweetened pineapple juice
    2-1/2 cups sugar
        2 cups vinegar
    1-1/2 cups water
        1 cup packed brown sugar
      2/3 cup cornstarch
      1/2 cup ketchup
        6 tablespoons soy sauce
        2 teaspoons chicken bouillon granules
      3/4 teaspoon ground ginger
        3 tablespoons vegetable oil
        2 broiler/fryer chickens (3 to 3-1/2 pounds *each*), cut up
        1 can (8 ounces) pineapple chunks, drained
        1 medium green pepper, julienned

In a saucepan, combine the first 10 ingredients; stir until smooth. Bring to a boil; cook and stir for 2

2 pounds sliced bacon, diced
3 pounds fully cooked smoked sausage, halved and cut into 1/4-inch slices
1-1/2 pounds cubed fully cooked ham
1 cup vegetable oil
2 cups all-purpose flour
6 medium onions, chopped
6 green onions, chopped
6 celery ribs, chopped
3 medium green peppers, chopped
1/2 cup minced fresh parsley
1/3 cup salt
2 tablespoons pepper
22 cups hot cooked rice
Hot pepper sauce, optional

Place beans in large kettles; add water to cover by 2 in. Bring to a boil; boil for 2 minutes. Remove from heat. Cover and let stand for 1 hour. Drain and discard liquid. To beans, add 9 qts. water, garlic, bay leaves and browning sauce if desired. Bring to a boil. Reduce heat; cover and simmer 1-1/2 to 2 hours or until beans are tender. Meanwhile, in large skillets, cook bacon until crisp. Remove with a slotted spoon to paper towels. In the drippings, cook sausage and ham until lightly browned. Remove and set aside. Add oil to drippings in skillets. Stir in flour until smooth; cook and stir over medium heat until reddish brown, about 12-14 minutes. Add onions, celery and green peppers; cook and stir until tender. Stir into bean mixture. Add bacon, sausage, ham, parsley, salt and pepper. Bring to a boil. Reduce heat; cover and simmer for 30 minutes. Remove bay leaves. Serve over rice with hot sauce if desired. **Yield:** 65 servings (about 1 cup beans and 1/3 cup rice).

—— 🍴 🍴 🍴 ——

Cream Cake Dessert

(Pictured at right)

Folks really go for this light cake with fluffy cream filling. My son first tried this treat while in high school and asked me to get the recipe. I've used it countless times since for all sorts of occasions. It's easy to transport to a potluck because the cream is on the inside. —Peggy Stott, Burlington, Iowa

1 package (18-1/4 ounces) yellow cake mix
1 package (3.4 ounces) instant vanilla pudding mix
1/2 cup shortening
1 cup water
4 eggs
FILLING:
5 tablespoons all-purpose flour
1 cup milk

1/2 cup butter *or* margarine, softened
1/2 cup shortening
1 cup sugar
1 teaspoon vanilla extract
1/2 teaspoon salt
Fresh raspberries, optional

In a mixing bowl, beat cake mix, pudding mix and shortening on low speed until crumbly. Add the water and eggs; beat on medium for 2 minutes. Pour into a greased and floured 13-in. x 9-in. x 2-in. baking pan. Bake at 350° for 30-35 minutes or until a toothpick inserted near the center comes out clean. Cool for 10 minutes; invert onto a wire rack to cool completely. Meanwhile, in a saucepan, combine flour and milk until smooth. Bring to a boil; cook and stir for 2 minutes or until thickened. Cool completely. In a mixing bowl, cream the butter, shortening, sugar, vanilla and salt; beat in milk mixture until sugar is dissolved, about 5 minutes. Split cake into two horizontal layers. Spread filling over the bottom layer; replace top layer. Cut into serving-size pieces. Garnish with raspberries if desired. **Yield:** 16-20 servings.

🥄 *Make Molds Easier*

Instead of making a molded gelatin salad in one large serving bowl to take to a potluck, put the mixture in foil cupcake liners. The individual servings are easy to handle and keep the gelatin separated from other food on the plate.

Apricot Glazed Chicken

The tender chicken with garlic-apricot glaze prompts sincere compliments. This is an attractive main dish for a group. —Ruby Williams, Bogalusa, Louisiana

9 broiler/fryer chickens (3-1/2 to 4 pounds *each*), quartered
2 tablespoons dried minced garlic
2 tablespoons salt
1-1/2 teaspoons pepper
1 can (49-1/2 ounces) chicken broth, *divided*
4 jars (12 ounces *each*) apricot preserves

Place chicken in six greased 13-in. x 9-in. x 2-in. baking dishes. Sprinkle with garlic, salt and pepper. Pour about 1 cup broth in each dish. Cover and bake at 350° for 30 minutes; drain. Bake, uncovered, for 30-40 minutes. Combine preserves and remaining broth; spoon over chicken. Bake 9-12 minutes longer or until chicken is golden brown and juices run clear. **Yield:** 36 servings.

Potluck Rice Pilaf

(Pictured below)

A fun and tasty alternative to potatoes, this savory rice is a popular side dish at gatherings. I especially like its mild soy sauce flavor and flecks of green onion and toasted slivered almonds. —Annette Rodgers Rosston, Arkansas

1/2 cup butter *or* margarine
4 cups uncooked long grain rice
2 quarts water
2 tablespoons chicken bouillon granules
10 green onions, thinly sliced
2/3 cup soy sauce
1 cup slivered almonds, toasted

In a Dutch oven, melt butter. Add rice; cook and stir for 3-5 minutes or until lightly browned. Add water and bouillon; bring to a boil. Reduce heat; cover and simmer for 15-20 minutes or until rice is tender and liquid is absorbed. Remove from the heat; stir in the onions and soy sauce. Cover and let stand for 5 minutes. Stir in the almonds. **Yield:** 20-22 servings.

Buttermilk Pan Rolls

I've made these rolls for family and at the Eskimo village school where I cook. I've had many compliments, and people always ask me when I'm going to serve them again. —Elaine Kellum Anaktuvuk Pass, Alaska

18 to 23 cups all-purpose flour
1 cup buttermilk blend powder
1/2 cup sugar
2 tablespoons salt
4-1/2 teaspoons active dry yeast
1 teaspoon baking soda
7 cups warm water (120° to 130°)
1 cup vegetable oil

Combine 15 cups flour, buttermilk powder, sugar, salt, yeast and baking soda. Add water and oil. Beat until smooth. Stir in enough remaining flour to form a soft dough. Turn onto a floured surface; knead until smooth and elastic, about 10 minutes. Place in a greased bowl, turning once to grease top. Cover and let rise in a warm place until doubled, about 1-1/4 hours. Punch dough down. Divide into 80 pieces. With lightly floured hands, shape each into a ball. Place in two greased 15-in. x 10-in. x 1-in. baking pans. Cover and let rise until doubled, about 30 minutes. Bake at 375° for 20-30 minutes or until lightly browned. Remove from pans to wire racks. **Yield:** 80 rolls.

Chicken Gumbo

This fresh-tasting, flavorful main dish is well-received when I cook it for church suppers. It's a colorful mixture of traditional ingredients. —Willa Govoro, St. Clair, Missouri

6 **celery ribs, chopped**
3 **medium green peppers, chopped**
3 **medium onions, chopped**
3/4 **cup butter** *or* **margarine**
10 **quarts chicken broth**
7 **cans (14-1/2 ounces** *each***) diced tomatoes, undrained**
3 **bay leaves**
2 **tablespoons minced fresh parsley**
1 **tablespoon pepper**
2 to 3 **tablespoons garlic powder**
2 **teaspoons salt**
2 **cups uncooked long grain rice**
10 **cups cubed cooked chicken**
6 **cups cubed fully cooked ham**
1 **package (16 ounces) frozen chopped okra**
2 **pounds cooked small shrimp, peeled and deveined, optional**

In a large soup kettle or kettles, saute celery, green peppers and onions in butter until tender. Add the next seven ingredients; bring to a boil. Stir in rice. Reduce heat; cover and simmer for 15-20 minutes or until rice is tender. Stir in chicken, ham, okra and shrimp. Simmer for 8-10 minutes or until shrimp turn pink and okra is tender. Discard bay leaves. **Yield:** 48 (1-cup) servings.

— ▼ ▼ ▼ —

Rave-Review Potato Salad

My husband really flipped over this deliciously different potato salad the first time he tasted it. An oil and vinegar marinade gives the potatoes a wonderful flavor boost. This recipe is one of my most-requested.
—*Dorothy Bateman, Carver, Massachusetts*

✓ Uses less fat, sugar or salt. Includes Nutritional Analysis and Diabetic Exchanges.

10 **medium red potatoes, peeled**
1/3 **cup chopped chives**
1/4 **cup vegetable oil**
1/4 **cup vinegar**
2 **tablespoons grated onion**
1-1/2 **teaspoons salt, optional**
1/4 **teaspoon pepper**
1/2 **cup mayonnaise**
1/2 **cup plain yogurt**
1/2 **cup thinly sliced celery**
1/2 **cup chopped green pepper** *or* **cucumber**

Place potatoes in a Dutch oven and cover with water. Bring to a boil; cook until tender, 20-30 minutes. Meanwhile, in a large bowl, combine chives, oil, vinegar, onion, salt if desired and pepper; mix well. Drain potatoes; cool slightly. Cut into cubes; add to oil mixture and toss to coat. Cover and re-frigerate for at least 2 hours. In a small bowl, combine mayonnaise and yogurt; chill. Just before serving, fold the mayonnaise mixture, celery and green pepper into potato salad. **Yield:** 12 servings.
Nutritional Analysis: One 2/3-cup serving (prepared with fat-free mayonnaise and nonfat yogurt and without salt) equals 152 calories, 88 mg sodium, trace cholesterol, 25 gm carbohydrate, 3 gm protein, 5 gm fat, 2 gm fiber. **Diabetic Exchanges:** 1-1/2 starch, 1 fat.

Lemon-Curry Deviled Eggs

(Pictured above)

I enjoy prettying up a potluck or brunch buffet with a platter of these zippy eggs. You might also consider adding this dish to a salad plate or a soup-and-salad lunch. —*Judith Miller, Walnut, California*

16 **hard-cooked eggs**
1/3 to 1/2 **cup sour cream**
2 **tablespoons lemon juice**
1/2 **teaspoon salt**
1/2 **teaspoon paprika**
1/2 **teaspoon ground mustard**
1/2 **teaspoon curry powder**
Dash Worcestershire sauce

Cut eggs in half lengthwise. Remove yolks; set whites aside. In a bowl, mash yolks. Add the remaining ingredients; mix well. Spoon into egg whites. Refrigerate until serving. **Yield:** 16 servings.

Cooking for One or Two

These small-serving dishes are full of flavor.

PERFECT PORTIONS. Clockwise from upper left: Chocolate Pudding for One, Turkey-Stuffed Peppers, Tomatoes with Vinaigrette (pp. 208 and 209); Peach Strawberry Smoothie, Moist Bran Muffins, Cottage Cheese Crab Salad (pp. 202 and 203); Glazed Baby Carrots, Tarragon Flounder (pp. 210 and 211); Vanilla Custard Cups, Taco Plate for Two, Avocado Orange Salad (p. 200).

Autumn Squash

I make this pretty dish with squash from my garden. It has a delicious, crunchy topping. —*Joanne Linde*
Williams Lake, British Columbia

- 1 **cup mashed cooked acorn *or* butternut squash**
- 1/2 **cup crushed butter-flavored crackers, *divided***
- 4 **tablespoons butter *or* margarine, melted, *divided***
- 1 **egg, lightly beaten**
- 2 **tablespoons brown sugar**
- 1 **to 2 teaspoons prepared mustard**
- 1/8 **teaspoon salt**
- 1/8 **teaspoon pepper**

In a bowl, combine the squash, 1/4 cup cracker crumbs, 2 tablespoons butter, egg, brown sugar, mustard, salt and pepper; mix well. Pour into a greased 2-1/2-cup baking dish. Combine remaining crumbs and butter; sprinkle over top. Bake, uncovered, at 350° for 20 minutes or until a knife comes out clean. **Yield:** 2 servings.

Barley Burger Stew

I found this hearty recipe in an old cookbook I bought at a flea market. The beef and barley blend hits the spot on cool days. —*Judy McCarthy, Derby, Kansas*

- 1/2 **pound ground beef**
- 1 **small onion, chopped**
- 1/4 **cup chopped celery**
- 2-1/4 **cups tomato juice**
- 1/2 **cup water**
- 1/4 **cup medium pearl barley**
- 1 **to 1-1/2 teaspoons chili powder**
- 1/2 **teaspoon salt**
- 1/4 **teaspoon pepper**

In a saucepan, cook beef, onion and celery until meat is no longer pink; drain. Stir in tomato juice, water, barley, chili powder, salt and pepper. Bring to a boil. Reduce heat; cover and simmer for 50-60 minutes or until barley is tender. **Yield:** 2 servings.

Seeding and Peeling Avocados

Cut a firm-ripe avocado lengthwise all the way around; gently twist the halves in opposite directions to separate. Pierce the seed with the blade of a knife, twist the knife and lift out the seed. To peel, cut lengthwise down the middle of the skin; pull the skin down and off the fruit.

Taco Plate for Two

(Pictured below right and on page 198)

Green chilies give a warm zip to this quick entree. My husband, Paul, and I enjoy splitting this delicious meaty dish. —*Sue Ross, Casa Grande, Arizona*

- 1/2 **pound ground beef**
- 1/2 **cup chopped onion**
- 1/3 **cup taco sauce**
- 1/4 **cup chopped green chilies**
- 1/4 **teaspoon salt**
- 1 **cup broken tortilla chips**
- 1/2 **cup shredded cheddar cheese**

In a skillet, cook beef and onion over medium heat until meat is no longer pink; drain. Stir in the taco sauce, chilies and salt. Cover and cook over medium-low heat for 6-8 minutes or until heated through. Spoon over chips; sprinkle with cheese. **Yield:** 2 servings.

Avocado Orange Salad

(Pictured at right and on page 198)

My mom passed this recipe on to me. It's a longtime family favorite. The tangy oranges, crisp lettuce and mellow flavor of the avocado are terrific together.
—*Catherine Shelton, Las Vegas, Nevada*

- 2 **cups torn salad greens**
- 1 **navel orange, peeled and sectioned**
- 1 **large ripe avocado, peeled and sliced**
- 1 **small onion, chopped**

CITRUS DRESSING:
- 1/4 **cup vegetable oil**
- 2 **tablespoons orange juice**
- 1 **tablespoon lemon juice**
- 1 **tablespoon sugar**
- 1/2 **teaspoon grated orange peel**
- 1/8 **teaspoon salt**
- 1/8 **teaspoon celery seed**

On two salad plates, arrange greens, orange, avocado and onion. In a jar with a tight-fitting lid, combine dressing ingredients; shake well. Drizzle over salads. Serve immediately. **Yield:** 2 servings.

Vanilla Custard Cups

(Pictured at right and on page 198)

When I was living with my mother, she loved custard, so I'd make this comforting dessert each week. Without leftovers, there's no chance of getting tired of this treat! —*Billie Bohannan, Imperial, California*

☑ Uses less fat, sugar or salt. Includes Nutritional Analysis and Diabetic Exchanges.

1 egg
1 cup milk
3 tablespoons brown sugar
3/4 teaspoon vanilla extract
1/8 teaspoon salt, optional
1/8 teaspoon ground nutmeg

In a bowl, beat egg, milk, brown sugar, vanilla and salt if desired until blended. Pour into two ungreased 6-oz. custard cups. Sprinkle with nutmeg. Place cups in a 9-in. square baking pan. Fill pan with hot water to a depth of 1 in. Bake, uncovered, at 350° for 30-35 minutes or until a knife inserted near the center comes out clean. **Yield:** 2 servings. **Nutritional Analysis:** One serving (prepared with egg substitute equivalent to one egg, skim milk and without salt) equals 149 calories, 121 mg sodium, 3 mg cholesterol, 26 gm carbohydrate, 8 gm protein, 1 gm fat, 0 fiber. **Diabetic Exchanges:** 1/2 milk, 1 starch.

MEXICAN FIESTA. Taco Plate for Two, Orange Avocado Salad and Vanilla Custard Cups (shown above) have south-of-the-border appeal.

Simple Spanish Rice

Green peppers and tomato give lovely color to this nicely seasoned side dish. It's just right for two people.
—Vivian Wolfram, Mountain Home, Arkansas

✓ Uses less fat, sugar or salt. Includes Nutritional Analysis and Diabetic Exchanges.

1/2 cup chopped green pepper
1 medium tomato, peeled, seeded and diced
1/4 cup finely chopped onion
1 tablespoon vegetable oil
1/2 cup uncooked long grain rice
1 cup chicken broth
1/2 teaspoon salt, optional
1/4 teaspoon pepper

In a saucepan, saute green pepper, tomato and onion in oil until tender. Add rice; cook and stir for 2 minutes. Stir in broth, salt if desired and pepper; bring to a boil. Reduce heat; cover and simmer 25 minutes or until rice is tender. **Yield:** 2 servings. **Nutritional Analysis:** One serving (prepared with low-sodium broth and without salt) equals 292 calories, 62 mg sodium, 2 mg cholesterol, 48 gm carbohydrate, 6 gm protein, 8 gm fat, 2 gm fiber. **Diabetic Exchanges:** 3 starch, 1-1/2 fat.

Swiss Cheese Souffle

This Parmesan-topped souffle is nicely sized for one. You can eat this savory sensation right from the baking dish. —Angela Sansom, New York, New York

1/2 teaspoon plus 1 tablespoon butter *or* margarine, *divided*
2 tablespoons grated Parmesan cheese, *divided*
1 tablespoon all-purpose flour
1/4 cup milk
1/4 teaspoon chopped chives
1/8 teaspoon Worcestershire sauce
1 egg, *separated*
1/3 cup shredded Swiss cheese

Butter the bottom and sides of a 1-cup round baking dish with 1/2 teaspoon butter. Sprinkle buttered surface with 1 tablespoon Parmesan cheese; set aside. In a small saucepan, melt remaining butter; stir in flour until smooth. Gradually stir in milk. Add chives and Worcestershire sauce. Bring to a boil; cook and stir for 1 minute or until thickened. Remove from the heat. Stir a small amount into egg yolk; return all to pan, stirring constantly. Transfer to a bowl; set aside. In a mixing bowl, beat egg white until stiff peaks form; fold half into yolk mixture. Fold in Swiss cheese, then remaining egg white. Pour into prepared baking dish. Sprinkle with remaining Parmesan cheese. Bake at 375° for 30-35 minutes or until lightly browned and a knife inserted near the center comes out clean. **Yield:** 1 serving.

Cottage Cheese Crab Salad

(Pictured at right and on page 199)

This is a great summer main dish. Dijon mustards adds a touch of zing to the dressing. My husband, David, and I especially enjoy this salad on warm days.
—Elisa Lochridge, Aloha, Oregon

1/2 cup small-curd cottage cheese
1/4 cup sour cream
1 teaspoon Dijon mustard
1/8 teaspoon garlic powder
1/8 teaspoon pepper
1 package (8 ounces) imitation crabmeat, chopped
1/4 cup chopped celery
1/4 cup chopped green onions
Lettuce leaves
1 medium tomato, cut into wedges

In a bowl, combine the cottage cheese, sour cream, mustard, garlic powder and pepper. Stir in the crab, celery and onions. Serve on lettuce-lined plates with tomato wedges. **Yield:** 2 servings.

Moist Bran Muffins

(Pictured at right and on page 199)

These tender, slightly sweet muffins are a tasty way to round out any meal. The recipe makes a small quantity perfect for a couple or a single person.
—Mildred Ross, Badin, North Carolina

1/2 cup All-Bran
1/2 cup milk
2 tablespoons vegetable oil
1/2 cup all-purpose flour
2 tablespoons sugar
1 teaspoon baking powder
1/4 teaspoon salt

In a bowl, combine the bran and milk; let stand for 5 minutes. Stir in the oil. Combine the remaining ingredients; stir into bran mixture just until moistened. Fill greased or paper-lined muffin cups half full. Bake at 400° for 18-22 minutes or until a toothpick comes out clean. Cool for 5 minutes before removing from pan to a wire rack. **Yield:** 4 muffins.

PREPARE A PICNIC for just the two of you with Cottage Cheese Crab Salad, Moist Bran Muffins and Peach Strawberry Smoothie (shown above).

Peach Strawberry Smoothie

(Pictured above and on page 199)

This creamy delight is easy to make. For a mixed-berry version, try using a half cup of strawberries and a half cup of raspberries. —*Harriet Cummings Lancaster, Pennsylvania*

✓ Uses less fat, sugar or salt. Includes Nutritional Analysis and Diabetic Exchanges.

1 cup sliced fresh strawberries
1 cup fresh *or* frozen unsweetened sliced peaches
1 cup plain *or* vanilla yogurt
1 to 2 tablespoons sugar
Dash ground cinnamon

If desired, set aside a few strawberry slices for garnish. Place the remaining berries in a blender; add peaches, yogurt and sugar. Cover and process until smooth. Pour into chilled glasses; sprinkle with cinnamon. Garnish with the reserved berries. **Yield:** 2 servings. **Nutritional Analysis:** One serving (prepared with nonfat yogurt and artificial sweetener equivalent to 1 tablespoon sugar) equals 152 calories, 97 mg sodium, 2 mg cholesterol, 30 gm carbohydrate, 9 gm protein, trace fat, 4 gm fiber. **Diabetic Exchanges:** 1 skim milk, 1 fruit.

A DOWN-HOME DINNER of Apricot Chicken, Baked Rice and Garlic Brussels Sprouts (shown above) makes a festive feast for one.

Apricot Chicken

(Pictured above)

I have fixed this tender glazed chicken for myself on many special occasions. With the pretty golden-orange sauce, it looks as good as it tastes.
—*Winifred Brown, Jamesburg, New Jersey*

✓ Uses less fat, sugar or salt. Includes Nutritional Analysis and Diabetic Exchanges.

- **1 tablespoon apricot preserves**
- **1 tablespoon Russian *or* French salad dressing**
- **Pinch ginger, optional**
- **1 bone-in chicken breast half**
- **Salt and pepper to taste**

In a small bowl, combine preserves, salad dressing and ginger if desired; set aside. Place chicken in a greased 8-in. square baking pan; sprinkle with salt and pepper. Top with apricot mixture. Bake, uncovered, at 350° for 50-55 minutes or until chicken juices run clear. **Yield:** 1 serving. **Nutritional Analysis:** One serving (prepared with low-fat French dressing and a skinless chicken breast and without salt) equals 212 calories, 200 mg sodium, 73 mg cholesterol, 16 gm carbohydrate, 27 gm protein, 4 gm fat, trace fiber. **Diabetic Exchanges:** 3-1/2 very lean meat, 1 fruit.

Baked Rice

(Pictured above)

This rice has a mild, pleasant flavor. For color and extra nutrition, I sometimes add a bit of carrot, celery, tomato, peas or corn—whatever I have handy.
—*Mary Jo Massnick, Stuart, Florida*

- **1/2 cup chicken broth**
- **1/4 cup uncooked long grain rice**
- **1 teaspoon minced fresh parsley**
- **Salt and pepper to taste**
- **1/4 cup shredded cheddar *or* Swiss cheese**

In a greased 12-oz. baking dish, combine broth, rice, parsley, salt and pepper. Cover and bake at 350° for 30-35 minutes or until rice is tender. Sprinkle with cheese; bake 4 minutes longer or until cheese is melted. **Yield:** 1 serving.

Garlic Brussels Sprouts

(Pictured at left)

If you want a simple way to dress up a basic vegetable, this is it! These brussels sprouts are easy and delicious.
—Chris Tucker, Portland, Oregon

5 brussels sprouts, halved
1 garlic clove, minced
1 teaspoon butter *or* margarine, melted
1 tablespoon shredded Parmesan cheese, optional

Place the brussels sprouts and garlic in a small saucepan; add 1 in. of water. Bring to a boil; reduce heat. Cover and simmer for 6-8 minutes or until the sprouts are crisp-tender; drain. Drizzle with butter. Sprinkle with Parmesan cheese if desired. **Yield:** 1 serving.

—— ☕ ☕ ☕ ——

Tex-Mex Ham 'n' Eggs

For a satisfying combo, you can't beat ham, eggs, potatoes and cheese. Plus the salsa adds zip.
—Page Alexander, Baldwin City, Kansas

1 cup chopped fully cooked ham
1/2 cup chopped onion
2 tablespoons olive *or* vegetable oil, *divided*
2 cups frozen shredded hash brown potatoes
2 eggs
2 tablespoons milk
Salt and pepper to taste
1/2 cup shredded cheddar cheese
2 to 3 tablespoons salsa *or* picante sauce

In a skillet, saute ham and onion in 1 tablespoon of oil until ham is lightly browned and onion is tender; remove and keep warm. Add remaining oil to skillet; cook potatoes over medium heat until tender, turning to brown. In a small bowl, beat eggs, milk, salt and pepper; add to skillet. As eggs set, lift edges, letting uncooked portion flow underneath. When eggs are set, spoon ham mixture over top; heat through. Sprinkle with cheese; top with salsa. Cut into wedges. **Yield:** 2 servings.

—— ☕ ☕ ☕ ——

Sesame Chicken Stir-Fry

(Pictured at right)

When our children were little, my husband frequently worked late. This eye-catching stir-fry was a satisfying alternative for me and the kids.
—Michelle McWilliams, Fort Lupton, Colorado

1 boneless skinless chicken breast half, cut into thin strips
2 teaspoons vegetable oil
7 snow peas
1 cup broccoli florets
1/3 cup julienned sweet red pepper
3 medium fresh mushrooms, sliced
3/4 cup chopped onion
1 tablespoon cornstarch
1 teaspoon sugar
1/2 cup cold water
3 to 4 tablespoons soy sauce
Hot cooked rice
1 teaspoon sesame seeds, toasted

In a skillet or wok, stir-fry chicken in oil for 6-8 minutes or until juices run clear. Remove chicken and set aside. In the same skillet, stir-fry peas, broccoli and red pepper for 2-3 minutes. Add mushrooms and onion; stir-fry for 3-4 minutes. Combine cornstarch and sugar; stir in water and soy sauce until smooth. Add to the pan. Bring to a boil; cook and stir for 1-2 minutes or until thickened. Return chicken to the pan; cook until mixture is heated through and vegetables are tender. Serve over rice. Sprinkle with sesame seeds. **Yield:** 1 serving.

Tangy Glazed Chicken
(Pictured below)

A tangy sauce with a hint of orange and sweet apple jelly is perfect over chicken. It's delicious served with potatoes or rice and a green salad. —Barbara Haney St. Louis, Missouri

✓ Uses less fat, sugar or salt. Includes Nutritional Analysis and Diabetic Exchanges.

> 2 bone-in chicken breast halves
> 1/4 teaspoon salt, optional
> 4-1/2 teaspoons butter *or* margarine
> 1 small onion, thinly sliced
> 1 celery rib, thinly sliced
> 1/2 cup chicken broth
> 1/2 cup apple jelly *or* spreadable fruit
> 3 tablespoons orange juice
> 1 tablespoon minced fresh parsley
> 1/4 to 1/2 teaspoon dried thyme

Sprinkle chicken with salt if desired. In a large skillet, melt butter over medium heat; brown chicken on all sides. Remove and keep warm. In the pan drippings, saute onion and celery until tender. Add the remaining ingredients; cook and stir until jelly

YOU AND A LOVED ONE are sure to fall for Tangy Glazed Chicken, Creamy Twice-Baked Potatoes and Mocha Cream Puffs (shown above).

is melted. Return chicken to pan. Cook, uncovered, for 30-35 minutes or until meat juices run clear. Remove skin if desired. Top chicken with onion mixture. **Yield:** 2 servings. **Nutritional Analysis:** One serving (prepared with chicken skin removed, margarine, spreadable fruit and low-sodium broth and without salt) equals 408 calories, 230 mg sodium, 75 mg cholesterol, 45 gm carbohydrate, 30 gm protein, 13 gm fat, 4 gm fiber. **Diabetic Exchanges:** 4 lean meat, 3 fruit.

--- 🍶 🍶 🍶 ---

Creamy Twice-Baked Potatoes

(Pictured at left)

These potatoes are oh-so-good with a yummy cream cheese filling. They look fancy but are very easy to make. Try doubling the recipe for a larger group.
—Linda Wheeler, Harrisburg, Pennsylvania

  2 **medium baking potatoes**
  2 **tablespoons butter *or* margarine, softened**
  1 **tablespoon milk**
1/4 **teaspoon salt**
  1 **package (3 ounces) cream cheese, cubed**
  2 **tablespoons sour cream**
Paprika

Pierce potatoes and bake at 375° for 1 hour or until tender. Cool. Cut a thin slice off the top of each potato. Scoop out the pulp and place in a mixing bowl. Add butter, milk and salt; beat until fluffy. Beat in cream cheese and sour cream. Spoon into potato shells. Sprinkle with paprika. Place on a baking sheet. Bake, uncovered, at 350° for 20-25 minutes or until heated through and tops are golden brown. **Yield:** 2 servings.

--- 🍶 🍶 🍶 ---

Mocha Cream Puffs

(Pictured at left)

If you're looking for a special-occasion dessert that doesn't take long to prepare, these chocolate-filled puffs fill the bill. These were a favored treat when it was just the two of us. —Aimee Kirk
Jacksonville, Alabama

1/4 **cup water**
  2 **tablespoons butter *or* margarine**
1/4 **cup all-purpose flour**
1/8 **teaspoon salt**
  1 **egg**
FILLING:
2/3 **cup whipping cream, *divided***
  3 **tablespoons semisweet chocolate chips**

  2 **teaspoons sugar**
Dash salt
1/2 **teaspoon vanilla extract**
1/2 **teaspoon instant coffee granules**
Confectioners' sugar

In a small saucepan over medium heat, bring water and butter to a boil. Add flour and salt all at once; stir until a smooth ball forms. Remove from the heat; let stand for 5 minutes. Add egg; beat until smooth. Drop batter into four mounds 3 in. apart on a greased baking sheet. Bake at 425° for 20-25 minutes or until golden brown. Remove puffs to a wire rack. Immediately cut a slit in each for steam to escape; cool. For filling, combine 3 tablespoons cream, chocolate chips, sugar and salt in a small saucepan. Cook on low heat until chips are melted; stir until blended. Remove from the heat; gradually stir in vanilla, coffee and remaining cream. Transfer to a small mixing bowl. Refrigerate until chilled. Just before serving, split puffs and remove soft dough. Beat filling until stiff. Fill cream puffs; replace tops. Dust with confectioners' sugar. **Yield:** 4 cream puffs.

--- 🍶 🍶 🍶 ---

Microwave Potato Wedges

These wedges taste like baked potatoes but are faster to make because they cook in the microwave. The simple seasoning makes them crispy and golden.
—Dorothy Umberger, Ceres, Virginia

✓ Uses less fat, sugar or salt. Includes Nutritional Analysis and Diabetic Exchanges.

  1 **teaspoon vegetable oil**
1/4 **teaspoon Italian seasoning**
1/4 **teaspoon paprika**
1/8 **teaspoon salt *or* salt-free seasoning blend**
  1 **unpeeled medium baking potato**
  1 **teaspoon grated Parmesan cheese**

Combine the first four ingredients on a microwave-safe plate. Cut potato lengthwise into eight wedges. Coat wedges in the seasoning mixture; arrange on the same plate. Cover and cook on high for 6-8 minutes or until tender, turning wedges once. Sprinkle with Parmesan cheese. **Yield:** 1 serving. **Nutritional Analysis:** One serving (prepared with salt-free seasoning blend and nonfat Parmesan cheese topping) equals 181 calories, 42 mg sodium, trace cholesterol, 32 gm carbohydrate, 4 gm protein, 5 gm fat, 3 gm fiber. **Diabetic Exchanges:** 2 starch, 1 fat. **Editor's Note:** This recipe was tested in an 850-watt microwave. Potatoes may be prepared in a conventional oven. Bake, uncovered, at 425° for 25 minutes or until tender.

Peach Crisp Cups

There may be only two servings in this comforting, old-fashioned dessert, but they're bursting with big peach flavor.
—Aida Von Babbel
Coquitlam, British Columbia

2 medium fresh peaches, peeled and sliced
2 teaspoons sugar
2 tablespoons quick-cooking oats
2 tablespoons all-purpose flour
1 tablespoon brown sugar
2 teaspoons chopped almonds
5 teaspoons cold butter *or* margarine
1/4 teaspoon almond extract

In a bowl, combine peaches and sugar. Pour into two greased 6-oz. baking dishes. Combine the oats, flour, brown sugar and almonds. Cut in butter until mixture resembles coarse crumbs. Sprinkle with almond extract; toss. Sprinkle over peaches. Bake, uncovered, at 375° for 30 minutes or until bubbly and golden brown. **Yield:** 2 servings.

— 🏆 🏆 🏆 —

Pound Cake S'mores

This dessert requires almost no effort and there are no leftovers. These s'mores taste as good as the camp-fire version of childhood. —Grace Yaskovic
Branchville, New Jersey

2 slices pound cake
1 tablespoon miniature marshmallows
1 tablespoon miniature semisweet chocolate chips
Caramel ice cream topping and chopped nuts, optional

Place cake slices on a baking sheet. Sprinkle with marshmallows and chocolate chips. Broil 4-6 in. from the heat for 1-2 minutes or until marshmallows are lightly browned. Transfer to a plate. If desired, drizzle with caramel topping and sprinkle with nuts. **Yield:** 1 serving.

— 🏆 🏆 🏆 —

Melon Grape Salad

After 40 years of cooking for our family, making meals for two was a big adjustment. This salad is a refreshing treat that I can prepare without a lot of fuss.
—Clara Honeyager, Mukwonago, Wisconsin

2 tablespoons orange juice
1 tablespoon honey
4-1/2 teaspoons vegetable oil
1/8 teaspoon ground ginger
Pinch paprika

Lettuce leaves
1 cup cubed cantaloupe *or* watermelon
1/2 cup seedless green and red grapes

In a bowl, combine the first five ingredients. Refrigerate. Just before serving, arrange lettuce, melon and grapes on salad plates. Drizzle with dressing. **Yield:** 2 servings.

— 🏆 🏆 🏆 —

Turkey-Stuffed Peppers

(Pictured below right and on page 198)

Most people think of stuffed peppers as having ground beef and tomato sauce. This combination, with ground turkey and a white sauce, is a welcome, tasty variation.
—Julie Grose, Lompoc, California

2 large green peppers, tops and seeds removed
1/2 pound ground turkey
1 small onion, chopped
1 garlic clove, minced
2 tablespoons butter *or* margarine
1 tablespoon all-purpose flour
1/2 teaspoon salt
1/8 teaspoon pepper
1/2 cup milk
1/2 cup chopped tomato
4 tablespoons shredded cheddar cheese, *divided*

In a large saucepan, cook peppers in boiling water for 3 minutes. Drain and rinse with cold water; set aside. In a skillet, cook the turkey, onion and garlic over medium heat until meat is no longer pink; drain and set aside. In the same skillet, melt butter. Stir in flour, salt and pepper until smooth. Gradually add milk. Bring to a boil; cook and stir for 1-2 minutes or until thickened. Return turkey mixture to skillet. Stir in tomato and 2 tablespoons cheese; heat through. Spoon into peppers; sprinkle with the remaining cheese. Place in a greased 1-qt. baking dish. Cover and bake at 350° for 25-30 minutes or until peppers are tender and filling is hot. **Yield:** 2 servings.

— 🏆 🏆 🏆 —

Tomatoes with Vinaigrette

(Pictured at right and on page 198)

This easy dressing is a tasty way to top tomatoes. This recipes has been in my family for years. My mother passed it on to me.
—Joanne Shewchuk
St. Benedict, Saskatchewan

3 tablespoons vinegar

3 tablespoons vegetable oil
2 tablespoons sugar
1 teaspoon seasoned salt
Pepper to taste
2 medium tomatoes, cut into wedges
Lettuce leaves

In a jar with a tight-fitting lid, combine the vinegar, oil, sugar, seasoned salt and pepper; shake well. Serve over tomatoes and lettuce. **Yield:** 2 servings.

— 🍷 🍷 🍷 —

Chocolate Pudding for One

(Pictured below and on page 198)

Any time I get a craving for a chocolaty treat, I whip up a dish of this rich pudding in the microwave. For a

change of pace, you can use milk chocolate chips. Both are delicious. —*Anne Boesiger, Meridian, Idaho*

1-1/2 teaspoons cornstarch
Pinch salt
1/2 cup milk
1/4 cup semisweet chocolate chips
Whipped cream and baking cocoa, optional

In a 2-cup glass measuring cup, combine the cornstarch, salt and milk until smooth; add chocolate chips. Microwave, uncovered, on high for 1 minute or until hot but not boiling; stir. Cook 30-45 seconds longer or until mixture just begins to boil; stir. Cool. Pour into a small bowl. If desired, top with whipped cream and sprinkle with baking cocoa. **Yield:** 1 serving. **Editor's Note:** This recipe was tested in an 850-watt microwave.

SIMPLY DELICIOUS. Turkey-Stuffed Peppers, Tomatoes with Vinaigrette and Chocolate Pudding for One (shown above) are especially suited for singles and empty-nesters.

Sweet Potato Pork Chops

This hearty all-in-one meal will cut down on time in the kitchen—both cooking and doing after-dinner dishes. With tender pork chops, sliced onion and sweet potato, it's simply satisfying. —Suzanne McKinley
Lyons, Georgia

  2 boneless pork chops (1/2 inch thick)
  1 teaspoon vegetable oil
  2 slices onion (1/2 inch thick)
  2 slices *each* tart apple and peeled sweet potato (1/2 inch thick)
  2 tablespoons brown sugar
  2 tablespoons water
  2 tablespoons raisins
  1 tablespoon soy sauce
  1 tablespoon Worcestershire sauce

In a skillet, brown pork chops in oil; place in a 1-qt. baking dish. Top with onion, apple and sweet potato. Combine the remaining ingredients; spoon over top. Cover and bake at 350° for 35-40 minutes. **Yield:** 2 servings.

— 🥤 🥤 🥤 —

Mandarin Sherbet Dessert

This tangy sundae is a cool, refreshing end to a festive feast or simple supper. —Nila Moran
Sunnyvale, California

  1 can (11 ounces) mandarin oranges
  3/4 cup sherbet flavor of your choice
  1 tablespoon sliced almonds, toasted
Maraschino cherry, optional

Drain oranges, reserving 2 teaspoons juice; set four oranges aside (refrigerate remaining juice and oranges for another use). Pour 1 teaspoon of juice into a small bowl; top with sherbet and reserved oranges. Drizzle with remaining juice and sprinkle with almonds. Top with a cherry if desired. **Yield:** 1 serving.

— 🥤 🥤 🥤 —

Grilled Chicken Dinner

This complete meal grilled in a foil packet is a palate-pleasing and mess-free dinner for one.
—Floyd Hulet, Apache Junction, Arizona

  1 bone-in chicken breast half
  1 medium potato, peeled and quartered
  1 large carrot, cut into 2-inch pieces
1/2 cup fresh vegetables (broccoli florets, peas *and/or* green beans)
  1 tablespoon onion soup mix

2/3 cup condensed cream of chicken soup, undiluted

Place chicken in the center of a piece of double-layered heavy-duty foil (about 18 in. square). Place vegetables around chicken. Sprinkle with soup mix. Top with soup. Fold foil around vegetables and chicken and seal tightly. Grill, uncovered, over medium-low heat for 50-60 minutes or until chicken juices run clear and potato is tender. Open foil carefully to allow steam to escape. **Yield:** 1 serving.

— 🥤 🥤 🥤 —

Giant Pineapple Turnover

Tart apple, crushed pineapple and plump raisins combine in this easy-to-make turnover.
—Carolyn Kyzer, Alexander, Arkansas

  1 sheet refrigerated pie pastry
  1 medium tart apple, peeled and coarsely chopped
  1 can (8 ounces) crushed pineapple, well drained
3/4 cup sugar
1/3 cup finely chopped celery
1/3 cup raisins
1/3 cup chopped walnuts
1/4 cup all-purpose flour
Ice cream, optional

Unfold pastry and place on a baking sheet. In a bowl, combine the apple, pineapple, sugar, celery, raisins, walnuts and flour; toss gently. Spoon filling onto half of crust, leaving 1 in. around edge. Fold pastry over filling and seal edge well. Cut slits in top. Bake at 400° for 30-35 minutes or until crust is golden brown and filling is bubbly. Cool on a wire rack. Cut into wedges. Serve with ice cream if desired. **Yield:** 4 servings.

— 🥤 🥤 🥤 —

Tarragon Flounder

(Pictured above right and on page 199)

This moist fish dish has a delicate herb flavor I enjoy. Plus, this easy recipe calls for only five ingredients.
—Donna Smith, Victor, New York

☑ Uses less fat, sugar or salt. Includes Nutritional Analysis and Diabetic Exchanges.

1/4 pound flounder fillets
1/4 cup chicken broth
  1 tablespoon butter *or* margarine, melted
1-1/2 teaspoons minced fresh tarragon *or* 1/2 teaspoon dried tarragon
1/2 teaspoon ground mustard

FROM THE SEA. Tarragon Flounder and Glazed Baby Carrots (shown above) are great when you're fishing for single-serving recipes.

Place fillets in a greased 11-in. x 7-in. x 2-in. baking dish. Combine remaining ingredients; pour over fish. Bake, uncovered, at 350° for 20-25 minutes or until fish flakes easily with a fork. Remove to a serving plate with a slotted spatula. Serve immediately. **Yield:** 1 serving. **Nutritional Analysis:** One serving (prepared with low-sodium broth and reduced-fat margarine) equals 192 calories, 250 mg sodium, 61 mg cholesterol, 1 gm carbohydrate, 25 gm protein, 10 gm fat, trace fiber. **Diabetic Exchange:** 3-1/2 lean meat.

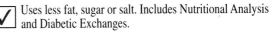

Glazed Baby Carrots

(Pictured above and on page 199)

There's no need to eat plain old boiled carrots when this recipe is so easy to fix. The slightly sweet orange glaze makes the carrots taste much better.
—*Mina Dyck, Boisevain, Manitoba*

☑ Uses less fat, sugar or salt. Includes Nutritional Analysis and Diabetic Exchanges.

- **1 cup baby carrots**
- **1 tablespoon butter *or* margarine**
- **2 teaspoons orange juice**
- **1 teaspoon sugar**
- **1/4 teaspoon ground mustard**
Pepper to taste

Place carrots in a saucepan; add 1 in. of water. Bring to a boil. Reduce heat. Cover and simmer for 5 minutes or until crisp-tender. Meanwhile, in a small saucepan, melt butter. Add orange juice, sugar, mustard and pepper; cook and stir until thickened. Drain carrots; drizzle with butter mixture. **Yield:** 1 serving. **Nutritional Analysis:** One serving (prepared with reduced-fat margarine and artificial sweetener equivalent to 1 teaspoon sugar) equals 129 calories, 175 mg sodium, 0 cholesterol, 14 gm carbohydrate, 3 gm protein, 8 gm fat, 4 gm fiber. **Diabetic Exchanges:** 1-1/2 fat, 1 starch.

My Mom's Best Meal

Six cooks savor the fond memories stirred up when they make the same tasty meals their moms lovingly served.

SCRUMPTIOUS SELECTIONS. Clockwise from upper left: Down-Home Cooking (p. 234), Chill-Chasing Comfort Food (p. 218), Saucy Spaghetti Supper (p. 226) and Special Fare for Everyday Dinners (p. 222).

Mom's favorite Sunday meal brings 'em back for more—both at home and at family's successful restaurants.

By Sandra Pichon, Slidell, Louisiana

WHEN my brother and I were growing up, Mom (Maxine Haynes, above) and Dad both loved to cook. Even though there were only four of us, they cooked like they were feeding an army.

We regularly enjoyed full-course meals with lots of vegetables, homemade biscuits, bread or corn bread and dessert. Even breakfast was not a simple meal. It commonly consisted of pork chops, milk gravy, sliced tomatoes, biscuits and eggs!

Over the years, Mom and Dad owned and operated three restaurants. One meal was on the menu every time since it's Mom's favorite: Sunday Pork Roast, Mom's Sweet Potato Bake, Country Turnip Greens and Dixie Pie.

Flavorful Sunday Pork Roast was often Sunday dinner at our house. Mom made it countless times for our family and guests, not to mention all of those restaurant customers. I think the drippings make the best gravy.

Even our small family could polish off a pan of Mom's Sweet Potato Bake. It's so rich and creamy, you'd almost think it was a dessert!

Country Turnip Greens are a Southern staple that round out any meal.

The recipe for Dixie Pie actually came from my brother, also a good cook. Mom quickly adopted it as one of her signature desserts. When she baked this old-fashioned sugar pie, family members would clamor for second servings.

After I married and moved away, I often called Mom long-distance for step-by-step instructions on the delicious foods I enjoyed while growing up.

Now Mom lives with me and my husband, Stanley. Together we continue her long tradition of good down-home food.

— ▼ ▼ ▼ —

PICTURED AT LEFT: Sunday Pork Roast, Mom's Sweet Potato Bake, Country Turnip Greens and Dixie Pie (recipes are on the next page).

Sunday Pork Roast

Mom has prepared this delectable main dish numerous times over the years for our family, friends and customers at the restaurants she and Dad owned. A simple herb rub and roasting with vegetables give this lovely golden roast remarkable flavor.

> 4 tablespoons all-purpose flour, ***divided***
> 1 teaspoon salt
> 1 teaspoon pepper
> 1 bay leaf, finely crushed
> 1/2 teaspoon dried thyme
> 1 bone-in pork loin roast (4 to 5 pounds)
> 2 medium onions, chopped
> 2 medium carrots, chopped
> 1 celery rib, chopped
> 2-1/3 cups cold water, ***divided***
> 1/3 cup packed brown sugar

Combine 2 tablespoons flour, salt, pepper, bay leaf and thyme; rub over entire roast. Place roast with fat side up in a shallow roasting pan. Arrange vegetables around the roast. Pour 2 cups cold water into pan. Bake, uncovered, at 325° for 1-1/2 hours, basting with pan juices every 30 minutes. Sprinkle with brown sugar. Bake 30 minutes longer or until a meat thermometer reads 160°. Remove roast to a serving platter; keep warm. Strain pan drippings, reserving the broth; discard vegetables. Add water to the broth to measure 1-2/3 cups. Return to pan. Combine remaining flour and cold wa-

ter until smooth; stir into pan. Bring to a boil; cook and stir for 2 minutes. Serve with the roast. **Yield:** 10-12 servings.

— ▼ ▼ ▼ —

Mom's Sweet Potato Bake

Mom loves sweet potatoes and fixed them often in this creamy, comforting casserole. With its nutty topping, it's a yummy treat!

> 3 cups cold mashed sweet potatoes (prepared without milk or butter)
> 1 cup sugar
> 1/2 cup milk
> 1/4 cup butter *or* margarine, softened
> 3 eggs
> 1 teaspoon salt
> 1 teaspoon vanilla extract
> TOPPING:
> 1/2 cup packed brown sugar
> 1/2 cup chopped pecans
> 1/4 cup all-purpose flour
> 2 tablespoons cold butter *or* margarine

In a mixing bowl, beat sweet potatoes, sugar, milk, butter, eggs, salt and vanilla until smooth. Transfer to a greased 2-qt. baking dish. In a small bowl, combine brown sugar, pecans and flour; cut in butter until crumbly. Sprinkle over potato mixture. Bake, uncovered, at 325° for 45-50 minutes or until golden brown. **Yield:** 8-10 servings.

variety. Thanksgiving and Christmas dinner were not complete without this memorable dessert.

Pastry for two single-crust pies (9 inches)
1-1/2 cups raisins
    1 cup butter *or* margarine, softened
    1 cup sugar
    1 cup packed brown sugar
    6 eggs
    2 teaspoons vanilla extract
    2 to 4 teaspoons ground cinnamon
    1 cup chopped nuts
    1 cup flaked coconut
Whipped topping and additional chopped nuts, optional

Line two 9-in. pie plates with pastry. Trim pastry to 1/2 in. beyond edge of plate; flute edges. Line crusts with a double thickness of heavy-duty foil. Bake at 450° for 10 minutes. Discard foil. Cool on wire racks. Place raisins in a saucepan and cover with water; bring to a boil. Remove from the heat; set aside. In a mixing bowl, cream butter and sugars. Beat in eggs, vanilla and cinnamon until smooth. Drain raisins. Stir raisins, nuts and coconut into creamed mixture (mixture will appear curdled). Pour into the crusts. Bake at 350° for 30-35 minutes or until set. Cool on wire racks. Garnish with whipped topping and nuts if desired. **Yield:** 2 pies (6-8 servings each).

Country Turnip Greens

This easy recipe results in a delicious dish of cooked greens sure to please any palate. The key is the rich flavor of pork and onion simmered with the fresh greens.

   3/4 pound lean salt pork *or* bacon, diced
4-1/2 pounds fresh turnip greens,* trimmed
1-1/2 cups water
    1 large onion, chopped
    1 teaspoon sugar
   1/4 to 1/2 teaspoon pepper

In a Dutch oven or soup kettle, fry salt pork just until cooked. Drain, reserving 2 tablespoons of drippings. Stir in the remaining ingredients. Bring to a boil. Reduce heat; cover and simmer for 45 minutes or until greens are tender. **Yield:** 8-10 servings. ***Editor's Note:** Fresh spinach can be substituted for the turnip greens. Reduce the cooking time to 10 minutes or until spinach is tender.

— 🝙 🝙 🝙 —

Dixie Pie

Everybody in our family loves the combination of cinnamon, coconut, nuts and raisins in this pie. Sometimes Mom would toss in a few chocolate chips for

***With her own
baker's dozen
of children,
this mother had
to "think big"
when dinnertime
rolled around.***

By Lucile Proctor, Panguitch, Utah

MOTHER had a special knack for making delicious, satisfying meals on a budget—a very important skill with 13 hungry children to feed!

Mom (Augusta Wilcox Hunt, above) used lots of venison since our family had some avid hunters. Beef and homegrown vegetables and fruits were other favorite ingredients.

Mom's Beef Stew (often made with venison) was a favorite main dish on bread-baking day. Mom would simmer her mouth-watering stew on the back of the woodstove all day while preparing four loaves of bread and two pans of crusty Yeast Biscuits.

We kids rode the school bus for 15 miles. In winter, it was dark and we were chilled by the time we arrived home in the evening. Nothing tasted better or warmed us up faster than a steaming bowl of Mom's stew on a cold day.

Mom's oven-fresh biscuits were great for sandwiches, but they were especially yummy with the stew. They were perfect for sopping up the beefy gravy!

Using cabbage and apples from our root cellar, Mom would whip up a big batch of flavorful, crunchy Apple Cabbage Slaw. Since the ingredients were always on hand, she fixed this often to feed our big family.

Even after all that stew and slaw, we kids could always find room for Mom's Marshmallow Graham Dessert. It made a sweet, light and refreshing end to a great family meal.

Mom, who especially enjoyed fishing and quilting, passed away a few years ago at age 93. Her family, which now includes 82 grandchildren, 205 great-grandchildren and five great-great-grandkids, will long remember and carry on her legacy. She taught us that good eating starts with good cooking.

— 🥄 🥄 🥄 —

PICTURED AT LEFT: Mom's Beef Stew, Apple Cabbage Slaw, Yeast Biscuits and Marshmallow Graham Dessert (recipes are on the next page).

Mom's Beef Stew

This warming, stick-to-your-ribs main dish was one Mom relied on often to feed us 13 kids. Mildly seasoned with lots of satisfying ingredients like barley, potatoes and carrots in a tomato-beef broth, it still hits the spot on cold winter days.

    2 pounds meaty beef soup bones, beef
      shanks *or* short ribs
    6 cups water
    5 medium potatoes, peeled and cubed
    5 medium carrots, chopped
    1 medium onion, chopped
  1/2 cup medium pearl barley
    1 can (28 ounces) plum tomatoes,
      undrained
    1 to 1-1/2 teaspoons salt
  1/2 teaspoon pepper
    2 garlic cloves, minced, optional
    1 bay leaf, optional
    3 tablespoons cornstarch
  1/2 cup cold water

Place soup bones and water in a soup kettle or Dutch oven. Slowly bring to a boil. Reduce heat; cover and simmer for 2 hours. Set beef bones aside until cool enough to handle. Remove meat from bones; discard bones and return meat to broth. Add the potatoes, carrots, onion, barley, tomatoes, salt, pepper, garlic and bay leaf if desired. Cover and simmer for 50-60 minutes or until vegetables and barley are tender. Discard bay leaf. Combine cornstarch and cold water until smooth; stir into stew. Bring to a boil; cook and stir for 2 minutes or until thickened. **Yield:** 10 servings.

Apple Cabbage Slaw

Chopped apple adds fruity sweetness, crunch and color to the tangy cabbage in this flavorful slaw. It's a refreshing side dish any time of the year.

☑ Uses less fat, sugar or salt. Includes Nutritional Analysis and Diabetic Exchanges.

    6 cups shredded cabbage
    3 medium red apples, chopped
    1 can (5 ounces) evaporated milk
  1/4 cup lemon juice
    2 tablespoons sugar
    2 teaspoons grated onion
    1 teaspoon celery seed
  1/2 teaspoon salt, optional
Dash pepper

In a large bowl, toss the cabbage and apples. In a small bowl, combine the remaining ingredients. Pour over cabbage mixture and toss to coat. Refrigerate until serving. **Yield:** 10 servings. **Nutritional Analysis:** One 3/4-cup serving (prepared with evaporated skim milk and sugar substitute equivalent to 2 tablespoons sugar and without salt) equals 53 calories, 26 mg sodium, 1 mg cholesterol, 12 gm carbohydrate, 2 gm protein, trace fat, 2 gm fiber. **Diabetic Exchanges:** 1 vegetable, 1/2 fruit.

Yeast Biscuits

Wonderful from-scratch yeast biscuits—golden and crusty outside and moist inside—were a staple Mom prepared regularly when I was growing up. They are just right for scooping up the gravy from bowls of beef stew and are also great for sandwiches.

3-1/4 teaspoons active dry yeast
  1/2 cup warm water (110° to 115°)
  1/2 cup sugar
  1/2 cup butter *or* margarine, softened
    1 can (5 ounces) evaporated milk
    2 eggs, lightly beaten
1-1/2 teaspoons salt
    2 cups whole wheat flour
    2 cups all-purpose flour

In a large mixing bowl, dissolve yeast in water. Add sugar, butter, milk, eggs, salt and whole wheat flour; beat until smooth. Add enough all-purpose flour to form a soft dough. Turn onto a floured surface; knead until smooth and elastic, about 10 minutes. Place in a greased bowl, turning once to grease top. Cover and let rise in a warm place until doubled, about 1-1/2 hours. Punch dough down; divide into thirds. Let rest for 5 minutes. On a floured surface, roll out each portion to 1/2-in. thickness. Cut with a 2-1/2-in. biscuit cutter. Place on lightly greased baking sheets. Cover and let rise until doubled, about 30 minutes. Bake at 375° for 10-12 minutes or until golden brown. Remove from pans and cool on wire racks. **Yield:** about 2-1/2 dozen.

Marshmallow Graham Dessert

For a light, fluffy treat, this sweet and creamy dessert with bits of pineapple mixed in just can't be beat!

    1 package (16 ounces) large marshmallows
    2 cups milk
1-1/2 teaspoons lemon extract
    1 can (20 ounces) crushed pineapple, drained
    2 cups whipping cream, whipped
    2 cups graham cracker crumbs (about 32 squares)
  1/2 cup butter *or* margarine, melted

In a heavy saucepan over low heat, melt marshmallows and milk. Remove from the heat. Cool, stirring occasionally. Stir in extract. Fold in pineapple and whipped cream. Combine cracker crumbs and butter. Press 1-1/2 cups into a greased 13-in. x 9-in. x 2-in. pan. Spread with the pineapple mixture. Sprinkle with the remaining crumb mixture. Refrigerate for 2-3 hours before serving. **Yield:** 12-16 servings.

Shear Pleasure

Use kitchen shears to make quick work of many projects. They are great for cubing raw stew meat, cutting bread cubes for bread pudding or chopping up canned whole tomatoes. They also easily make bite-size pieces out of canned fruit and cooked meat for young children.

*If you've got
an itch for
Sunday-style
home cooking,
try my mother's
from-scratch meal.*

By Debra Falkiner, St. Charles, Missouri

MY MOM is an excellent from-scratch cook who takes pride in every meal. Her everyday menus include dishes other cooks might reserve for Sundays or holidays.

Mom (Norma Falkiner of Bevier, Missouri, above) uses lots of fruits and vegetables, even in winter. She and Dad can the bounty from their immense garden, berry bushes and mini orchard.

When my brothers, sisters and I were young, our friends frequently asked to stay for dinner. Mom never said no. She would always make extra in case there was an additional person or two around the table.

These days, folks still stop by Mom's house just to see what's cooking (and to taste-test a dish or two, of course). They're never disappointed.

It's almost impossible to single out one of Mom's meals as my favorite. She always finds ways to make good foods taste even more special. Ham with Pineapple Sauce is a wonderful main dish, especially at Easter.

Her Creamy Spinach Bake was a sure way of getting us kids to eat our spinach. And everyone knows that kids and spinach don't usually mix well! This recipe has become a family tradition.

We're always thrilled to see a big basket of Mom's tasty golden Crescent Dinner Rolls. They're a delightful way to round out any meal.

The strawberries in her Upside-Down Strawberry Shortcake often come from her berry patch. It's a delightful spring treat.

Many of the recipes Mom cherishes have been passed down in her family over the years. In her honor, I compiled a five-generation cookbook. We're both very proud of it.

We hope you and your family enjoy the meal we've shared.

— 🥄 🥄 🥄 —

PICTURED AT LEFT: Ham with Pineapple Sauce, Creamy Spinach Bake, Crescent Dinner Rolls and Upside-Down Strawberry Shortcake (recipes are on the next page).

(Also pictured on front cover)

Satisfying Sandwiches

Mix ground leftover baked ham with chopped olives, green pepper, shredded cheddar cheese, Dijon mustard and mayonnaise. Stuff into hard rolls, wrap in foil and bake at 375° for 30 minutes.

Creamy Spinach Bake

This casserole has a rich, creamy sauce, french-fried onions and a cracker crumb topping. Even as children, we couldn't resist it.

> 2 packages (8 ounces *each*) cream cheese, softened
> 2 cans (10-3/4 ounces *each*) condensed cream of mushroom soup, undiluted
> 4 packages (10 ounces *each*) frozen chopped spinach, thawed and well drained
> 2 cans (2.8 ounces *each*) french-fried onions
> 2/3 cup crushed saltines (about 16 crackers)
> 1/4 cup butter *or* margarine, melted

In a bowl, beat the cream cheese until smooth. Add soup; mix well. Stir in spinach and onions. Transfer to a greased 2-1/2-qt. baking dish. Combine cracker crumbs and butter; sprinkle over spinach mixture. Bake, uncovered, at 325° for 30-35 minutes or until heated through. **Yield:** 10 servings.

Ham with Pineapple Sauce

(Also pictured on front cover)

This ham is served with a sweet pineapple sauce. A simple mixture of basic ingredients results in a mouth-watering main dish.

> 1 boneless fully cooked ham (4 to 6 pounds)
> 3/4 cup water, *divided*
> 1 cup packed brown sugar
> 4-1/2 teaspoons soy sauce
> 4-1/2 teaspoons ketchup
> 1-1/2 teaspoons ground mustard
> 1-1/2 cups undrained crushed pineapple
> 2 tablespoons plus 1 teaspoon cornstarch

Place ham on a rack in a shallow roasting pan. Bake at 325° for 1-1/4 to 2 hours or until a meat thermometer reads 140° and ham is heated through. Meanwhile, in a saucepan, combine 1/4 cup water, brown sugar, soy sauce, ketchup, mustard and pineapple. Bring to a boil. Reduce heat; cover and simmer for 10 minutes. Combine cornstarch and remaining water until smooth; stir into pineapple sauce. Bring to a boil; cook and stir for 2 minutes or until thickened. Serve with the ham. **Yield:** 16-24 servings (3 cups sauce).

Crescent Dinner Rolls

These light, golden rolls have a heavenly homemade flavor and aroma. Mom never hesitates to whip up a batch of these from-scratch rolls, since they're a delightful way to round out a meal.

    1 package (1/4 ounce) active dry yeast
  1/4 cup warm water (110° to 115°)
    1 tablespoon plus 1/2 cup sugar, *divided*
  3/4 cup warm milk (110° to 115°)
    3 eggs, lightly beaten
  1/2 cup butter *or* margarine, softened
    1 teaspoon salt
    5 to 5-1/2 cups all-purpose flour
Melted butter *or* margarine

In a large mixing bowl, dissolve yeast in warm water. Add 1 tablespoon sugar; let stand for 5 minutes. Add the milk, eggs, butter, salt and remaining sugar. Stir in enough flour to form a stiff dough. Turn onto a floured surface; knead until smooth and elastic, about 6-8 minutes. Place in a greased bowl, turning once to grease top. Cover and let rise in a warm place until doubled, about 1-1/2 hours. Punch dough down. Divide into thirds. Roll each into a 12-in. circle; cut each circle into eight wedges. Brush with melted butter; roll up wedges from the wide end and place, pointed end down, 2 in. apart on greased baking sheets. Cover and let rise in a warm place until doubled, about 30 minutes. Bake at 375° for 10-12 minutes or until golden brown. Remove from pans to wire racks. **Yield:** 2 dozen.

Upside-Down Strawberry Shortcake

For a tasty twist at dessert time, this special spring shortcake has a bountiful berry layer on the bottom. The moist and tempting cake is a treat our family has savored for many years.

    1 cup miniature marshmallows
    1 package (16 ounces) frozen sweetened sliced strawberries, thawed
    1 package (3 ounces) strawberry gelatin
  1/2 cup shortening
1-1/2 cups sugar
    3 eggs
    1 teaspoon vanilla extract
2-1/4 cups all-purpose flour
    3 teaspoons baking powder
  1/2 teaspoon salt
    1 cup milk
Fresh strawberries and whipped cream

Sprinkle marshmallows evenly into a greased 13-in. x 9-in. x 2-in. baking dish; set aside. In a bowl, combine strawberries and gelatin powder; set aside. In a mixing bowl, cream shortening and sugar. Add the eggs, one at a time, beating well after each addition. Beat in vanilla. Combine flour, baking powder and salt; add to creamed mixture alternately with milk. Pour batter over the marshmallows. Spoon strawberry mixture evenly over batter. Bake at 350° for 45-50 minutes or until a toothpick inserted near the center comes out clean. Cool on a wire rack. Cut into squares. Garnish with fresh strawberries and whipped cream. **Yield:** 12-16 servings.

Memories of Mom's special Sunday spaghetti dinner are so close, this cook can almost taste them.

By Grace Yaskovic, Branchville, New Jersey

BORN during the Depression, Mom learned early how to cook and bake. She became an expert at making a little taste like a lot.

Mom (Joan Mulholland Schweer, above) married young and raised five kids. Those kitchen skills served her well.

When we were growing up, Mom got involved in all our activities. Still, she managed to provide terrific meals and treats. She frequently hosted big Sunday dinners for the family and was famous for her Christmas cookies.

My brother, three sisters and I agree that of all the good foods she served, Mom's Hearty Spaghetti was definitely her best meal. It was also the most requested—by family and guests.

Her special spaghetti sauce features both Italian sausage and big ground beef meatballs. As it simmered, the bubbling sauce filled the house with a mouth-watering aroma.

It tasted even better than it smelled. It was hard to wait for dinner!

Alongside her steaming spaghetti, Mom served crusty Garlic Bread. She made it with freshly minced garlic that produced a robust flavor.

Her Salad with Creamy Dressing was a cool accompaniment to the savory main dish.

All five kids remembered to save room for dessert whenever Mom made buttery Pecan Crescent Cookies. With their white powdered-sugar coating, the cookies looked like brightly lit moons in a dark winter sky. These old-fashioned treats would melt in our mouths.

I cherish the memory of all of Mom's great meals. It's a pleasure to share these recipes as a special tribute to her.

— 🍴 🍴 🍴 —

PICTURED AT LEFT: Mom's Hearty Spaghetti, Garlic Bread, Salad with Creamy Dressing and Pecan Crescent Cookies (recipes are on the next page).

Mom's Hearty Spaghetti

Flavored with Italian sausage and dotted with juicy meatballs, the savory from-scratch sauce made this dish one of my mom's most-requested. We five kids were always thrilled when it was on the menu.

- 1 egg
- 1/4 cup milk
- 1 cup soft bread crumbs
- 1/2 teaspoon salt
- 1/2 teaspoon garlic powder
- 1/2 teaspoon minced fresh parsley
- 1 pound ground beef

SAUCE:
- 1 pound Italian sausage links, cut into 2-inch pieces
- 1 large onion, chopped
- 1 medium green pepper, chopped
- 2 cans (28 ounces *each*) plum *or* whole tomatoes, drained and diced
- 2 cans (8 ounces *each*) tomato sauce
- 1 can (14-1/2 ounces) beef broth
- 1 can (6 ounces) tomato paste
- 2 garlic cloves, minced
- 2 teaspoons *each* dried basil, oregano and parsley flakes
- 2 teaspoons sugar

Salt and pepper to taste
Hot cooked spaghetti
Grated Parmesan cheese

In a bowl, combine the first six ingredients. Add beef and mix well. Shape into eight meatballs. Brown in a Dutch oven over medium heat; drain and set meatballs aside. In the same pan, cook sausage, onion and green pepper until vegetables are tender; drain. Add the tomatoes, tomato sauce, broth, tomato paste, garlic and seasonings. Add meatballs; stir gently. Bring to a boil. Reduce heat; cover and simmer for 2-3 hours. Serve over spaghetti; sprinkle with Parmesan cheese. **Yield:** 8 servings.

Garlic Bread

This wonderful accompaniment could not be tastier or simpler to make. Minced fresh garlic is key to these flavor-packed crusty slices, which our big family would snatch up before they even had a chance to cool.

- 1/2 cup butter *or* margarine, melted
- 3 to 4 garlic cloves, minced
- 1 loaf (1 pound) French bread, halved lengthwise
- 2 tablespoons minced fresh parsley

In a small bowl, combine butter and garlic. Brush over cut sides of bread; sprinkle with parsley. Place, cut side up, on a baking sheet. Bake at 350° for 8 minutes. Broil 4-6 in. from the heat for 2 minutes or until golden brown. Cut into 2-in. slices. Serve warm. **Yield:** 8 servings.

Lowdown on Leftovers

For an interesting side dish, stir-fry leftover spaghetti noodles until golden, then add uncooked scrambled eggs. Cook until eggs are firm.

Leftover sausage and vegetables make a quick and tasty meal when stirred into prepared macaroni and cheese.

Mix leftover crushed pineapple with applesauce for a quick, refreshing salad.

Salad with Creamy Dressing

Mom had a magic way of combining ordinary ingredients into something extraordinary. In this refreshing salad, lettuce and vegetables are deliciously topped with a thick, hearty dressing.

    12 cups mixed salad greens
     2 large tomatoes, chopped
     1 large cucumber, chopped
     1 cup mayonnaise _or_ salad dressing
     1 cup Thousand Island salad dressing
     2 tablespoons milk
     2 hard-cooked eggs, chopped, optional

In a large bowl, toss salad greens, tomatoes and cucumber; set aside. In a small bowl, combine may-

onnaise, Thousand Island dressing and milk; mix well. If desired, gently stir in eggs. Serve over salad. Store any leftover dressing in the refrigerator. **Yield:** 8 servings (2 cups dressing).

Pecan Crescent Cookies

Rich, buttery and absolutely irresistible, these old-fashioned nut cookies were one of Mom's specialties. Any meal was a memorable event when she served this scrumptious treat.

     1 cup butter (no substitutes), softened
   1/2 cup sugar
     1 teaspoon vanilla extract
     2 cups all-purpose flour
     1 cup finely chopped pecans
Confectioners' sugar

In a mixing bowl, cream butter, sugar and vanilla. Gradually add flour. Stir in pecans. Shape rounded teaspoonfuls of dough into 2-1/2-in. logs and shape into crescents. Place 1 in. apart on ungreased baking sheets. Bake at 325° for 20-22 minutes or until set and bottoms are lightly browned. Let stand for 2-3 minutes before removing to wire racks to cool. Dust with confectioners' sugar before serving. **Yield:** 6 dozen.

Mom showers friends and family with precious presents—creative dishes she cooked up herself.

By Judi Messina, Coeur d'Alene, Idaho

THROUGH the years, my mother (Lois Rafferty of Palm Desert, California, above) has varied her cooking style.

When my older siblings were young, Mom prepared lots of traditional meals. By the time I came along, years later, Mom and Dad preferred more formal gourmet dinners.

Now she prepares an eclectic mix of favorite foods. The one common thread is Mom's flair for the creative—she has always been terrific at inventing delicious dishes.

Mom is one of the most cheerful, generous people I know. Although she's cooking for only two now, she still fixes big batches and shares food with neighbors and friends. When they see her coming with her arms full, they know they're in for a tasty treat.

One of her best main dishes is her Sirloin Sandwiches. They're so tasty, you'd never guess how easy they are to prepare.

And it's hard to resist a cheesy slice of her rich Swiss-Onion Bread Ring. We've tried it with many different kinds of meat—and it goes well with all of them.

When I was growing up, Mom loved to dress up vegetables with creamy sauces. Her Almond Celery Bake is a classic example.

In addition, Mom prepares delicious cookies and pies. Summer Berry Pie, which blends three luscious fruits, is both beautiful and refreshing.

I've learned a lot working with Mom in the kitchen, and I still call her periodically for favorite recipes or help making special dishes for my husband, Tom, and our young son.

Mom and I both hope her recipes here inspire some creativity in your kitchen.

PICTURED AT LEFT: Sirloin Sandwiches, Almond Celery Bake, Swiss-Onion Bread Ring and Summer Berry Pie (recipes are on the next page).

according to package directions. Thinly slice roast; add to the gravy and heat through. Serve on rolls. **Yield:** 12 servings.

Almond Celery Bake

It takes a creative cook like Mom to find a way to make celery star in a satisfying side dish. She combines celery slices with a creamy sauce, cheddar cheese and crunchy almonds. It's deliciously different!

　1 **bunch celery, sliced (about 6 cups)**
3/4 **cup shredded cheddar cheese**
1/2 **teaspoon paprika**
1/8 **teaspoon pepper**
　1 **can (10-3/4 ounces) condensed cream of celery soup, undiluted**
　1 **cup soft bread crumbs**
1/2 **cup slivered almonds**

Place the celery in a greased 2-qt. baking dish. Sprinkle with cheese, paprika and pepper. Top with the soup. Sprinkle with bread crumbs. Cover and bake at 375° for 45 minutes. Uncover; sprinkle with the almonds. Bake 10-15 minutes longer or until golden brown. **Yield:** 10-12 servings.

Sirloin Sandwiches

Mom is always happy to share her cooking, and these tender, tasty beef sandwiches are a real crowd-pleaser. A simple three-ingredient marinade flavors the grilled beef wonderfully.

　1 **cup soy sauce**
1/2 **cup vegetable oil**
1/2 **cup cranberry *or* apple juice**
　1 **boneless sirloin tip roast (3 to 4 pounds)**
　1 **envelope beef au jus gravy mix**
　1 **dozen French rolls, split**

In a large resealable plastic bag or shallow glass container, combine the soy sauce, oil and juice; mix well. Remove 1/2 cup for basting; cover and refrigerate. Add the roast to remaining marinade; turn to coat. Seal or cover and refrigerate for 8 hours or overnight, turning occasionally. Drain and discard the marinade. Grill roast, covered, over indirect heat, basting and turning every 15 minutes, for 1 hour or until meat reaches desired doneness (for rare, a meat thermometer should read 140°; medium, 160°; well-done, 170°). Remove from the grill; let stand for 1 hour. Cover and refrigerate overnight. Just before serving, prepare gravy mix

1-1/2 cups sugar
   6 tablespoons cornstarch
   3 cups cold water
   1 package (6 ounces) raspberry *or* strawberry gelatin
   2 cups fresh blueberries
   2 cups sliced fresh strawberries
   2 cups fresh raspberries
   2 graham cracker crusts (9 inches)
   4 cups whipped topping
Fresh mint and additional sliced strawberries

In a saucepan, combine sugar, cornstarch and water until smooth. Bring to a boil; cook and stir for 2 minutes or until thickened. Remove from the heat. Stir in gelatin until dissolved. Refrigerate for 15-20 minutes or until mixture begins to thicken. Stir in the berries. Pour into crusts and chill until set. Garnish with whipped topping, mint and strawberries. **Yield:** 2 pies (6-8 servings each).

Swiss-Onion Bread Ring

With the ease of prepared bread dough, this tempting cheesy bread has delicious down-home goodness. Its pleasant onion flavor goes great with any entree. You'll find it crisp and golden on the outside, rich and buttery on the inside.

2-1/2 teaspoons poppy seeds, *divided*
   1 tube (17.4 ounces) refrigerated white bread dough
   1 cup (4 ounces) shredded Swiss cheese
3/4 cup sliced green onions
1/4 cup butter *or* margarine, melted

Sprinkle 1/2 teaspoon poppy seeds in a greased 10-in. fluted tube pan. Cut the dough into twenty 1-in. pieces; place half in prepared pan. Sprinkle with half of the cheese and onions. Top with 1 teaspoon poppy seeds; drizzle with half of the butter. Repeat layers. Bake at 375° for 25 minutes or until golden brown. Immediately invert onto a wire rack. Serve warm. **Yield:** 1 loaf.

— 🏆 🏆 🏆 —

Summer Berry Pie

Mom puts luscious fresh blueberries, strawberries and raspberries to great use in this cool, refreshing pie. A super dessert on a hot day, it provides a nice light ending to a hearty meal.

Caring for Berries

Heaping berries in a bowl will quickly crush the delicate fruit. It's best to refrigerate them, loosely covered, in a single layer and use them within a day or two. Also, don't wash berries until you're ready to use them.

Voila! Kitchen magic puts two kids under Mom's spell and produces scrumptious surprises.

By Gina Mueller, Converse, Texas

AS CHILDREN, my brothers and I loved watching Mom (Kathy Lehman, above, of San Antonio, Texas) work magic in the kitchen.

We'd spend hours by her side, mesmerized by the sweet and savory aromas escaping from stovetop pots. But it wasn't just the lure of simmering foods that drew us near. We lingered because we sensed Mom's pleasure in caring for her family and preparing delectable dishes for us to enjoy.

Our only difficulty during those long afternoons with Mom was waiting until dinner was served. Our taste buds would tingle and our stomachs growl in happy anticipation.

Mom never disappointed us. One meal we especially enjoyed included her Squash and Pepper Skillet. She'd stir-fry zucchini and summer squash with onion, bell pepper and garlic for a marvelous blend.

The only way to distract us from this bounty of flavor was to serve something equally delicious. Mom accomplished this by dishing up plates of her Breaded Steaks. The golden coating was so good that we'd relish every bite.

Lightly seasoned, the steaks were perfectly matched with Mom's Olive Lover's Salad. It was such a family favorite that the bowl was always scraped clean!

Finally, just as we thought our stomachs might burst, Mom would bring out a luscious dessert like her tender Prune Bundt Cake. What else could we do but smile and dig in?

Mom and Dad are retired now, and I like to return to them all the wonderful gifts they shared with me— love, support and many, many fabulous meals. One day, I even hope to compile a cookbook containing all of my mother's recipes. Mom's Best Meal will be included, of course!

— ▼ ▼ ▼ —

PICTURED AT LEFT: Breaded Steaks, Squash and Pepper Skillet, Olive Lover's Salad and Prune Bundt Cake (recipes are on the next page).

Breaded Steaks

This homespun, stick-to-your-ribs steak supper was always a favorite with us kids. Mom coated tender steaks with lightly seasoned bread crumbs and fried them in oil until golden brown.

- **2 pounds sirloin tip steaks**
- **1/2 cup all-purpose flour**
- **2 eggs**
- **1 cup milk**
- **1/4 teaspoon salt**
- **1/8 teaspoon pepper**
- **1 package (15 ounces) seasoned bread crumbs**
- **1/4 cup vegetable oil**

Flatten steaks to 1/2-in. thickness. Cut into serving-size pieces; set aside. Place flour in a large resealable plastic bag. In a shallow bowl, combine the eggs, milk, salt and pepper. Place bread crumbs in another shallow bowl. Coat steaks with flour, then dip into egg mixture and coat with crumbs. In a large skillet over medium-high heat, cook steaks in oil for 2-3 minutes on each side or until golden brown and cooked to desired doneness. **Yield:** 8 servings.

Squash and Pepper Skillet

Mom knew how to get us to eat our vegetables—she'd serve this colorful blend of fresh zucchini, summer squash and bell pepper! It's tasty enough to please the whole family, and it makes a wonderful addition to any potluck.

☑ Uses less fat, sugar or salt. Includes Nutritional Analysis and Diabetic Exchanges.

- **1 medium onion, thinly sliced**
- **1 tablespoon olive *or* vegetable oil**
- **5 medium zucchini, sliced**
- **3 medium yellow summer squash, sliced**
- **1 small sweet red *or* green pepper, julienned**
- **1 garlic clove, minced**

Salt and pepper to taste

In a skillet, saute onion in oil until tender. Add squash, red pepper and garlic; stir-fry for 12-15 minutes or until vegetables are crisp-tender. Season with salt and pepper. **Yield:** 8 servings. **Nutritional Analysis:** One serving (prepared without salt) equals 53 calories, 7 mg sodium, 0 cholesterol, 8 gm carbohydrate, 3 gm protein, 2 gm fat, 3 gm fiber. **Diabetic Exchanges:** 1 vegetable, 1/2 fat.

Zucchini Secrets

Because of its tender skin, it's almost impossible to find zucchini without any blemishes. But look for small ones that are firm and free of cuts.

Refrigerate zucchini in a plastic bag for about a week. Make sure there is no moisture on the zucchini or in the plastic bag.

Olive Lover's Salad

Mom concocted this creative salad with only a handful of ingredients. Chopped olives, celery and garlic are tossed with oil and chilled for a cool refreshing side dish that's perfect with any warm meal.

> 1 can (6 ounces) pitted ripe olives, drained and chopped
> 1 jar (5-3/4 ounces) stuffed olives, drained and chopped
> 2 celery ribs, chopped
> 2 garlic cloves, minced
> 2 tablespoons olive *or* vegetable oil

In a bowl, combine olives, celery and garlic. Drizzle with oil; toss to coat. Cover and refrigerate for 4 hours or overnight. **Yield:** 3-1/2 cups.

Prune Bundt Cake

Moist and flavorful, this old-fashioned fruity cake was one of Mom's best desserts. Top with confectioners' sugar or frosting for a sweet treat that rounds out any menu.

> 1/2 cup butter-flavored shortening
> 1 cup sugar
> 2 eggs
> 2 cups all-purpose flour
> 1 teaspoon baking soda
> 1 teaspoon ground cinnamon
> 3/4 teaspoon salt
> 1/4 teaspoon *each* ground allspice, cloves and nutmeg
> 1 cup prune juice
> 1 cup finely chopped prunes, drained
> Confectioners' sugar, optional

In a mixing bowl, cream shortening and sugar until light and fluffy. Add eggs, one at a time, beating well after each addition. Combine the dry ingredients; add to the creamed mixture alternately with prune juice. Stir in the prunes. Pour into a greased 10-in. fluted tube pan. Bake at 350° for 40-45 minutes or until a toothpick inserted near the center comes out clean. Cool for 10 minutes before removing to a wire rack to cool completely. Dust with confectioners' sugar if desired. **Yield:** 12 servings.

Editors' Meals

Taste of Home magazine is edited by 1,000 cooks across North America. On the following pages, you'll "meet" six of those editors who share a family-pleasing meal.

SCRUMPTIOUS SELECTIONS. Clockwise from upper left: Holiday Make-Ahead Meal (p. 260), Memorable Brunch Buffet (p. 244), Portable Picnic Menu (p. 252) and Birthday Dinner Favorite (p. 248).

She welcomes family with a holiday feast of traditional favorites—some from recipes over 100 years old!

By Dorothy Smith, El Dorado, Arkansas

"WE'RE COMING for Christmas!" proclaimed one of our great-grandchildren—long before the holiday. "Of course you are," I confirmed heartily.

For my husband, Hershel, and me, Christmas is a wonderful time to get together with family—30 of us in all, including our three children and 10 grandchildren with their mates, plus eight great-grandchildren!

My Christmas menu reflects the way I like to cook, using recipes that have been passed down in the family or shared by friends.

We start out with rosy Cranberry Quencher. I got the recipe while visiting Hawaii, so it's no surprise pineapple juice is a main ingredient.

With the punch, we munch on Crisp Caraway Twists. These flaky appetizer sticks always go quickly, so I'm sure to have plenty on hand. Hershel's mother sent me the recipe the year we were married.

Turkey with Corn Bread Stuffing has a delicious, rich gravy that my mama taught me to make.

The flavorful corn bread stuffing recipe—Mama's version of a Southern favorite—is more than a century old. Our two daughters and son still request it for Christmas dinner.

Hershel says Sweet Potato Apple Salad from my Grandmother Dumas is also a "must" for the occasion. The poppy seed dressing has a citrus tang and really brings out the flavor.

Another of her treasures is Apple Cream Pie. A fancy and festive treat, it has sauteed apples arranged atop a creamy, delicious custard. Guests tell me they've never tasted anything quite like it.

It's a joy to share my Christmas dinner recipes, all tried and tested. I hope you'll enjoy them, too.

———— 🍽 🍽 🍽 ————

PICTURED AT LEFT: Turkey with Corn Bread Stuffing, Sweet Potato Apple Salad, Cranberry Quencher, Crisp Caraway Twists and Apple Cream Pie (recipes are on the next page).

dissolve bouillon in water; set aside. Transfer turkey to a warm platter. Remove stuffing. Pour 1/4 cup pan drippings into a saucepan; whisk in flour until smooth. Gradually add bouillon mixture. Bring to a boil; cook and stir for 2 minutes or until thickened and bubbly. Serve with turkey and stuffing. **Yield:** 6-8 servings.

Sweet Potato Apple Salad

Pairing a seasonal fruit and vegetable makes for a pretty and tasty salad to accompany a turkey dinner.

    6 medium sweet potatoes (about 2-1/2
        pounds)
  1/2 cup olive or vegetable oil
  1/4 cup orange juice
    1 tablespoon sugar
    1 tablespoon cider or white wine vinegar
    1 tablespoon Dijon mustard
    1 tablespoon finely chopped onion
1-1/2 teaspoons poppy seeds
    1 teaspoon grated orange peel
  1/2 teaspoon grated lemon peel
    2 medium tart apples (about 3/4 pound),
        chopped
    2 green onions, thinly sliced

In a large saucepan, cook sweet potatoes in boiling salted water until just tender, about 20 minutes. Cool completely. Meanwhile, in a jar with a tight-fitting lid, combine the next nine ingredients; shake well. Peel potatoes; cut each in half lengthwise, then into 1/2-in. slices. In a 4-qt. bowl, layer a fourth of the sweet potatoes, apples and onions; drizzle with a fourth of the salad dressing. Repeat layers three times. Refrigerate for 1-2 hours. Toss before serving. **Yield:** 8-10 servings.

Turkey with Corn Bread Stuffing

For Christmas dinner, we carve a succulent turkey and savor the stuffing, which gets its color and zip from olives and chilies.

    1 can (14-3/4 ounces) cream-style corn
    2 cans (4 ounces each) chopped green
        chilies
    1 can (4-1/2 ounces) sliced ripe olives,
        finely chopped
  1/2 cup shredded Co-Jack cheese
  1/2 cup finely chopped onion
  1/2 cup chopped green or sweet red pepper
    1 tablespoon minced fresh parsley
    1 egg, lightly beaten
    1 package (16 ounces) crushed corn bread
        stuffing or 6 cups crumbled corn bread
    1 turkey (8 to 10 pounds)
Melted butter or margarine
    2 chicken bouillon cubes
    2 cups boiling water
  1/4 to 1/3 cup all-purpose flour

In a large bowl, combine the first eight ingredients. Add stuffing and toss lightly. Just before baking, loosely stuff the turkey. Place remaining stuffing in a greased 1-1/2-qt. baking dish; refrigerate. Skewer openings of turkey; tie drumsticks together. Place on a rack in a roasting pan. Brush with melted butter. Bake, uncovered, at 325° for 2-3/4 to 3 hours or until a meat thermometer reads 180° for turkey and 165° for stuffing. Bake additional stuffing, covered, for 40-50 minutes or until heated through. When the turkey begins to brown, baste if needed; cover lightly with foil. For gravy,

Crisp Caraway Twists

When our big family gets together, I make two batches of these flaky cheese-filled twists (made with convenient puff pastry).

1 egg
1 tablespoon water
1 teaspoon country-style Dijon mustard
3/4 cup shredded Swiss cheese
1/4 cup finely chopped onion
2 teaspoons minced fresh parsley
1-1/2 teaspoons caraway seeds
1/4 teaspoon garlic salt
1 sheet frozen puff pastry, thawed

In a small bowl, beat egg, water and mustard; set aside. In another bowl, combine the cheese, onion, parsley, caraway seeds and garlic salt. Unfold pastry sheet; brush with egg mixture. Sprinkle cheese mixture lengthwise over half of the pastry. Fold pastry over filling; press edges to seal. Brush top with remaining egg mixture. Cut widthwise into 1/2-in. strips; twist each strip several times. Place 1 in. apart on greased baking sheets, pressing ends down. Bake at 350° for 15-20 minutes or until golden brown. Serve warm. **Yield:** about 1-1/2 dozen.

— 🥄 🥄 🥄 —

Cranberry Quencher

(Pictured on page 241)

Fruity and tart, this refreshing beverage brings the color of Christmas to your table.

1 bottle (1 gallon) cranberry-apple juice, chilled
1 can (46 ounces) pineapple juice, chilled

3/4 cup (6 ounces) lemonade *or* orange juice concentrate
Pineapple rings *or* tidbits, fresh cranberries *and/or* mint, optional

Combine cranberry-apple and pineapple juices in a large container or punch bowl. Stir in lemonade concentrate. Garnish glasses with pineapple, cranberries and/ or mint if desired. **Yield:** 6 quarts.

— 🥄 🥄 🥄 —

Apple Cream Pie

Arranging apple slices in a pretty design gives this pie the appearance of a fancy tart. Its rich custard-like filling has an elegant flavor but is easy to prepare.

4 cups thinly sliced peeled tart apples
2 tablespoons sugar
2 tablespoons lemon juice
1/4 cup butter *or* margarine
1 package (8 ounces) cream cheese, softened
1-1/2 cups cold milk, *divided*
1 package (3.4 ounces) instant vanilla pudding mix
1 teaspoon grated lemon peel
1 pastry shell (9 inches), baked
1/4 cup apricot preserves *or* strawberry jelly, melted

In a large skillet, saute apples, sugar and lemon juice in butter until apples are tender. Cool. In a mixing bowl, beat the cream cheese until smooth; gradually beat in 1 cup milk, dry pudding mix and lemon peel. Add remaining milk; beat until thickened. Spread into pastry shell. Arrange apples over filling. Brush with preserves. Refrigerate for 1 hour before serving. Brush with additional preserves if desired. **Yield:** 6-8 servings.

When she's invited a bunch for brunch, these tried-and-true dishes often make up the appetizing buffet.

By Gail Sykora, Menomonee Falls, Wisconsin

I ENJOY making almost any kind of meal, but for a holiday or family celebration, brunch is my favorite.

To me, a brunch is perfect for entertaining—I can do much of the food preparation ahead of time, then relax and visit with guests.

So, when friends or family gather in the remodeled kitchen of our 120-year-old farmhouse, I often rely on a favorite menu that began as a Christmas brunch. The meal proved to be such a success that I've repeated it on other special occasions throughout the year.

Brunch Enchiladas—rolled tortillas brimming with ham, eggs and cheddar cheese—is a flavorful, hearty dish. The casserole can be put together the day before, refrigerated overnight and baked before guests arrive. No matter what the season, it tastes great!

Another family favorite, Sausage Pinwheels, look very special. But you'll be surprised at how easy it is to make these crisp, golden-brown spirals using refrigerated crescent roll dough.

For a refreshing side dish, Frozen Cherry Salad is a wonderful choice. It can be prepared well in advance and cuts into pretty slices. (Some guests have remarked that each slice looks like a mosaic.) This cool, fruity salad is not overly sweet.

When I baked my first batch of Touch of Spring Muffins a few years ago, I knew it would not be the last! These lovely muffins blend sweet strawberry flavor and the tart goodness of rhubarb for a winning combination.

A regular breadstick becomes special wrapped with a strip of bacon and baked. Yummy eaten out of hand, Bacon Breadsticks couldn't be simpler to prepare.

Cooking and entertaining have long been an avocation of mine. It's a privilege to share my brunch recipes. I hope you'll be as pleased with them as we've been.

———— 🍴 🍴 🍴 ————

PICTURED AT LEFT: Brunch Enchiladas, Sausage Pinwheels, Bacon Breadsticks, Touch of Spring Muffins and Frozen Cherry Salad (recipes are on the next page).

Brunch Enchiladas

When I'm expecting company for brunch, the menu often features this tried-and-true casserole. With ham, eggs and plenty of cheese, the enchiladas are flavorful, hearty and fun. Plus, they can be easily assembled the day before.

✓ Uses less fat, sugar or salt. Includes Nutritional Analysis and Diabetic Exchanges.

    2 cups cubed fully cooked ham
1/2 cup chopped green onions
  10 flour tortillas (8 inches)
    2 cups (8 ounces) shredded cheddar cheese, *divided*
    1 tablespoon all-purpose flour
    2 cups half-and-half cream *or* milk
    6 eggs, beaten
1/4 teaspoon salt, optional

Combine ham and onions; place about 1/3 cup down the center of each tortilla. Top with 2 tablespoons cheese. Roll up and place seam side down in a greased 13-in. x 9-in. x 2-in. baking dish. In a bowl, combine flour, cream, eggs and salt if desired until smooth. Pour over tortillas. Cover and refrigerate for 8 hours or overnight. Remove from the refrigerator 30 minutes before baking. Cover and bake at 350° for 25 minutes. Uncover; bake for 10 minutes. Sprinkle with remaining cheese; bake 3 minutes longer or until the cheese is melted. Let stand for 10 minutes before serving. **Yield:** 10 enchiladas. **Nutritional Analysis:** One enchilada (prepared with low-fat ham, fat-free flour tortillas, reduced-fat cheddar cheese, skim milk and egg substitute equivalent to 6 eggs) equals 236 calories,

791 mg sodium, 18 mg cholesterol, 28 gm carbohydrate, 20 gm protein, 4 gm fat, 1 gm fiber. **Diabetic Exchanges:** 2 starch, 2 lean meat.

Sausage Pinwheels

These savory spirals are very simple to fix but look special on a buffet. Our guests eagerly help themselves— sometimes the eye-catching pinwheels never make it to their plates!

    1 tube (8 ounces) refrigerated crescent rolls
1/2 pound uncooked bulk pork sausage
    2 tablespoons minced chives

Unroll crescent roll dough on a lightly floured surface; press seams and perforations together. Roll into a 14-in. x 10-in. rectangle. Spread sausage to within 1/2 in. of edges. Sprinkle with chives. Carefully roll up from a long side; cut into 12 slices. Place 1 in. apart in an ungreased 15-in. x 10-in. x 1-in. baking pan. Bake at 375° for 12-16 minutes or until golden brown. **Yield:** 1 dozen.

— 🍴 🍴 🍴 —

Bacon Breadsticks

(Pictured on page 244)

When I add a plate of these breadsticks to my brunch buffet, they are guaranteed to disappear!

    6 bacon strips, halved lengthwise
  12 crisp breadsticks (about 5 inches long)

Wrap a piece of bacon around each breadstick. Place on a rack in an ungreased 15-in. x 10-in. x 1-in. baking pan. Bake at 375° for 20-25 minutes or until bacon is crisp. **Yield:** 1 dozen.

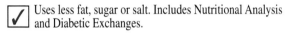

Frozen Cherry Salad

Pretty slices of this refreshing salad are dotted with colorful cherries for a festive look. The flavor is pleasant and not overly sweet. Prepared in advance and frozen, it's a treat that fits into many different menus. I serve it throughout the year.

☑ Uses less fat, sugar or salt. Includes Nutritional Analysis and Diabetic Exchanges.

- 1 package (8 ounces) cream cheese, softened
- 1 carton (8 ounces) frozen whipped topping, thawed
- 1 can (21 ounces) cherry pie filling
- 2 cans (11 ounces *each*) mandarin oranges, drained
- Maraschino cherries and orange wedges, optional

In a mixing bowl, combine the cream cheese and whipped topping. Stir in pie filling. Set aside 1/4 cup oranges for garnish. Fold remaining oranges into cream cheese mixture. Transfer to a 9-in. x 5-in. x 3-in. loaf pan. Cover and freeze overnight. Remove from the freezer 15 minutes before cutting. Garnish with reserved mandarin oranges, and cherries and oranges if desired. **Yield:** 12 servings. **Nutritional Analysis:** One serving (prepared with fat-free cream cheese, light whipped topping and re-duced-sugar pie filling and without maraschino cherries and orange wedges) equals 137 calories, 111 mg sodium, 2 mg cholesterol, 24 gm carbohydrate, 3 gm protein, 3 gm fat, 1 gm fiber. **Diabetic Exchanges:** 1 starch, 1/2 fruit, 1/2 fat.

Touch of Spring Muffins

Strawberries and rhubarb are a winning combination, and their sweet-tart pairing makes these lovely muffins delightful as part of a meal or as a snack. Remember this recipe when your backyard rhubarb is ready to cut or you see fresh stalks at the store.

- 2 cups all-purpose flour
- 1/2 cup sugar
- 1 tablespoon baking powder
- 1/2 teaspoon salt
- 1 egg
- 3/4 cup milk
- 1/3 cup vegetable oil
- 1/2 cup sliced fresh strawberries
- 1/2 cup sliced fresh rhubarb
- TOPPING:
- 6 small fresh strawberries, halved
- 2 teaspoons sugar

In a large bowl, combine flour, sugar, baking powder and salt. In another bowl, beat egg, milk and oil until smooth. Stir into the dry ingredients just until moistened. Fold in strawberries and rhubarb. Fill greased or paper-lined muffin cups three-fourths full. Place a strawberry half, cut side down, on each. Sprinkle with sugar. Bake at 375° for 22-25 minutes or until muffins test done. Cool for 5 minutes before removing from pan to a wire rack. Serve warm. **Yield:** 1 dozen.

This mouth-watering menu is applauded at family gatherings and dinner parties. The simple recipes are down-home good!

By Launa Shoemaker, Midland City, Alabama

EVERY TIME I serve my family's favorite meal, our taste buds have a party!

I've had the recipes for years and recall using them frequently back in the early 1980s for my husband, Russ, and our seven children. Breaded Ranch Chicken is a mainstay main dish I can always count on.

Daughter Lynnette always requests it for her birthday dinner. I often serve this easy entree to guests, too. Their compliments almost make me ashamed for not having spent hours preparing it!

A tangy dressing makes Sweet-Sour Pasta Salad different from others we've tried. Russ especially likes this side dish and says it fits into almost any menu. I have to agree.

This crunchy and attractive salad is excellent at potlucks, special events and summer picnics. Tricolored pasta and a blend of fresh vegetables give it plenty of eye appeal.

The recipe came from a friend in Indiana. Russ and I are both Hoosiers by birth and Southerners by choice—we moved to Alabama years ago and love it.

No matter where you live, homemade bread is always popular, and one loaf is never enough. My Home-Style Yeast Bread recipe makes enough for dinner and more. I like to give loaves as gifts and often take them to church potlucks. The bread makes yummy French toast the next morning. The dough also makes lovely rolls.

I can't honestly remember when I first made Peach Mousse. Light and delicious, it makes a nice change of pace from a dessert of cake or pie.

Preparing food for a dinner party or cooking for other special occasions is something I've always enjoyed. I know my family enjoys my style of country cooking, and I hope your family does, too!

— 🍴 🍴 🍴 —

PICTURED AT LEFT: Breaded Ranch Chicken, Sweet-Sour Pasta Salad, Home-Style Yeast Bread and Peach Mousse (recipes are on the next page).

1 package (16 ounces) tricolor spiral pasta
1 medium red onion, chopped
1 medium tomato, chopped
1 medium cucumber, peeled, seeded and chopped
1 medium green pepper, chopped
2 tablespoons minced fresh parsley
DRESSING:
1-1/2 cups sugar
1/2 cup vinegar
1 tablespoon ground mustard
1 teaspoon salt, optional
1 teaspoon garlic powder

Cook pasta according to package directions; drain and rinse with cold water. Place in a large serving bowl. Add the onion, tomato, cucumber, green pepper and parsley; set aside. In a saucepan, combine the dressing ingredients. Cook over medium-low heat for 10 minutes or until sugar is dissolved. Pour over salad and toss to coat. Cover and refrigerate for 2 hours. Serve with a slotted spoon. **Yield:** 16 servings. **Nutritional Analysis:** One serving (prepared with artificial sweetener equivalent to 1-1/2 cups sugar and without salt) equals 137 calories, 5 mg sodium, 0 cholesterol, 21 gm carbohydrate, 11 gm protein, 1 gm fat, 1 gm fiber. **Diabetic Exchanges:** 1-1/2 starch, 1 vegetable.

Breaded Ranch Chicken

A coating containing cornflakes, Parmesan cheese and ranch dressing mix adds delectable flavor to the chicken breasts in this recipe. Each piece bakes to a pretty golden color.

3/4 cup crushed cornflakes
3/4 cup grated Parmesan cheese
1 envelope ranch salad dressing mix
8 boneless skinless chicken breast halves (2 pounds)
1/2 cup butter *or* margarine, melted

In a shallow bowl, combine the cornflakes, Parmesan cheese and salad dressing mix. Dip chicken in butter, then roll in cornflake mixture to coat. Place in a greased 13-in. x 9-in. x 2-in. baking dish. Bake, uncovered, at 350° for 45 minutes or until chicken juices run clear. **Yield:** 8 servings.

— 🍵 🍵 🍵 —

Sweet-Sour Pasta Salad

Fresh garden vegetables add color and crunch to this attractive salad. Its pleasant vinaigrette-type dressing is sparked with ground mustard and garlic. I like the look of the tricolor spirals, but you can substitute other pasta shapes or use what you have on hand.

✓ Uses less fat, sugar or salt. Includes Nutritional Analysis and Diabetic Exchanges.

Peach Mousse

This smooth, creamy dessert is a light and refreshing finish for a special meal. Our children and grandchildren think it's yummy! A garnish of peach slices or other fresh fruit and mint leaves really dresses up the individual servings.

✓ Uses less fat, sugar or salt. Includes Nutritional Analysis and Diabetic Exchanges.

> 1 package (3 ounces) peach *or* orange gelatin
> 1 cup boiling water
> 3 medium ripe peaches, sliced
> 2 tablespoons honey
> 1/4 teaspoon almond extract
> 1/2 cup whipping cream, whipped *or* 1 cup whipped topping

Fresh mint and additional peach slices, optional

In a large mixing bowl, dissolve gelatin in water. In a blender, combine peaches, honey and extract; cover and process until smooth. Stir into gelatin mixture. Cover and refrigerate until syrupy, about 1-1/2 hours. Beat on high speed until doubled in volume, about 5 minutes. Fold in the whipped cream. Spoon into dessert dishes. Refrigerate until firm, about 1 hour. Garnish with mint and additional peaches if desired. **Yield:** 8 servings. **Nutritional Analysis:** One serving (prepared with sugar-free orange gelatin and light whipped topping and without garnish) equals 46 calories, 23 mg sodium, 1 mg cholesterol, 10 gm carbohydrate, 1 gm protein, 1 gm fat, 1 gm fiber. **Diabetic Exchange:** 1/2 starch.

Home-Style Yeast Bread

Everyone likes the tender texture and slightly sweet taste of this homemade bread. When I'm in the mood to bake, I usually double the recipe and share loaves with friends. The dough also makes heavenly rolls.

> 1 package (1/4 ounce) active dry yeast
> 2 cups warm water (110° to 115°)
> 1 cup sugar
> 1/2 cup butter *or* margarine, melted
> 1-1/2 teaspoons salt
> 2 eggs, beaten
> 7 to 8 cups bread flour

In a mixing bowl, dissolve yeast in warm water. Add the sugar, butter, salt, eggs and 4 cups flour. Beat until smooth. Stir in enough remaining flour to form a soft dough. Turn onto a floured surface; knead until smooth and elastic, about 6-8 minutes. Place in a greased bowl, turning once to grease top. Cover and let rise in a warm place until doubled, about 1 hour. Punch dough down. Turn onto a floured surface. Divide into thirds. Shape into loaves and place in three greased 9-in. x 5-in. x 3-in. loaf pans. Cover and let rise until doubled, about 1 hour. Bake at 350° for 25-30 minutes or until golden brown. Remove from pans to wire racks to cool. **Yield:** 3 loaves.

Pack up her great-tasting portable foods and head for your favorite picnic spot...even if it's as close as your own backyard!

By Marion Lowery, Medford, Oregon

A PICNIC is such fun for all, especially when you take along delicious foods that are easy to prepare!

I've come up with a portable menu that family and friends say is perfect for summertime outings. For us, that might be a trip to the mountains, fishing in the nearby Rogue River or a day at the coast...but I've also served this favorite meal as a patio picnic on the Fourth of July.

An herb-citrus marinade gives my Grilled Orange Chicken Strips a deliciously different taste. I thread the strips on skewers at home and pack them in an ice chest for the picnic.

We usually take along a portable, disposable grill. When the coals are hot, I call everyone together and pop on the chicken. The seasoned strips cook quickly and are so tender and tasty.

At the same time, we grill hot dogs and sausages to serve with a smorgasbord of toppings prepared earlier at home. I use a small food processor to chop or shred onions, tomatoes, green peppers, carrots, lettuce and cheddar cheese a few hours before our picnic.

Salami Pasta Salad has a nice mix of ingredients with enough salami to make it hearty. It should be made a day ahead so the flavors have time to blend.

The recipe for Golden Raisin Oatmeal Cookies has been in my file so long I'm not sure where I got it. You'll detect a hint of orange, and the golden raisins are a nice change from most oatmeal cookies.

Picnic-goers work up a thirst, so I have plenty of Picnic Fruit Punch ready. It's quick to mix up and can be stored in a gallon container half-filled with ice cubes.

Ginger ale adds fizz, and cranberry juice is responsible for the pretty color and refreshing tartness.

With a bit of planning and preparation, you can enjoy this picnic meal almost anytime. I hope you'll try some of my recipes soon.

———— 🍸 🍸 🍸 ————

PICTURED AT LEFT: Grilled Orange Chicken Strips (shown with hot dogs and sausages), Salami Pasta Salad, Golden Raisin Oatmeal Cookies and Picnic Fruit Punch (recipes are on the next page).

Grilled Orange Chicken Strips

These savory marinated chicken strips are great for a picnic or backyard barbecue. I grill them right along with a variety of sausages and hot dogs. Skewering the chicken makes it easy to handle, but you can put the strips directly on the grill or broil them in the oven if you prefer.

 Uses less fat, sugar or salt. Includes Nutritional Analysis and Diabetic Exchanges.

> 2 **tablespoons chopped fresh orange segments**
> 1/4 **cup orange juice**
> 1/4 **cup olive *or* vegetable oil**
> 2 **teaspoons lime juice**
> 3 **garlic cloves, minced**
> 1 **teaspoon dried thyme**
> 1 **teaspoon dried oregano**
> 1 **teaspoon ground cumin**
> 1/2 **teaspoon salt, optional**
> 1 **pound boneless skinless chicken breasts, cut into 1/4-inch strips**

Combine the first nine ingredients in a resealable plastic bag or shallow glass container; add chicken and turn to coat. Seal or cover and refrigerate for 1 hour. Drain and discard marinade. Thread meat on metal or soaked wooden skewers. Grill, uncovered, over medium-hot heat for 6-8 minutes or until juices run clear, turning often. **Yield:** 4 servings. **Nutritional Analysis:** One serving (prepared without salt) equals 192 calories, 56 mg sodium, 63 mg cholesterol, 2 gm carbohydrate, 23 gm protein, 9 gm fat, trace fiber. **Diabetic Exchange:** 3-1/2 meat.

Salami Pasta Salad

Popular any time of the year, this crowd-pleasing pasta salad is perfect for summer picnics. Made the day before, it has a pleasant vinaigrette dressing sparked with herbs. I set aside the Parmesan cheese and add it just before the salad is served.

> 3 **cups uncooked medium tube pasta *or* elbow macaroni**
> 1/2 **pound bulk hard salami *or* summer sausage, cubed**
> 1/2 **cup minced fresh parsley**
> 4 **green onions, sliced**
> 1/2 **cup olive *or* vegetable oil**
> 1/4 **cup cider *or* red wine vinegar**
> 4 **teaspoons minced fresh oregano *or* 1 teaspoon dried oregano**
> 4 **teaspoons minced fresh basil *or* 1 teaspoon dried basil**
> 2 **garlic cloves, minced**
> 1 **teaspoon salt**
> 1/4 **teaspoon pepper**
> 1/2 **cup shredded Parmesan cheese**

In a saucepan, cook pasta according to package directions; rinse in cold water and drain. Place in a large bowl; add salami, parsley and onions. In a small bowl, whisk together oil, vinegar and seasonings. Drizzle over pasta mixture and toss to coat. Cover and refrigerate overnight. Just before serving, stir in Parmesan cheese. **Yield:** 8 servings.

Golden Raisin Oatmeal Cookies

Here's a slightly different twist on a traditional favorite. These crisp, chewy oatmeal cookies feature golden raisins and have a mild orange tang. They're a staple in my picnic basket!

- 3/4 cup butter _or_ margarine, softened
- 1 cup packed brown sugar
- 1/2 cup sugar
- 1 egg
- 2 tablespoons water
- 1 teaspoon vanilla extract
- 3 cups quick-cooking oats
- 2/3 cup all-purpose flour
- 2 tablespoons grated orange peel
- 1 teaspoon ground cinnamon
- 1/2 teaspoon baking soda
- 2/3 cup golden raisins

In a mixing bowl, cream butter and sugars. Beat in egg, water and vanilla. Combine the oats, flour, orange peel, cinnamon and baking soda; gradually add to the creamed mixture. Stir in the raisins (dough will be stiff). Drop by level tablespoonfuls 2 in. apart onto ungreased baking sheets. Bake at 350° for 12-15 minutes or until the edges are lightly browned. Remove to wire racks to cool. **Yield:** 4 dozen.

Picnic Fruit Punch

This pink cooler is deliciously thirst-quenching on a warm day. Seeing its color, folks guess it might be pink lemonade. They're pleasantly surprised to discover the bubbly blend includes cranberry, pineapple, orange and lemon juices.

- 2 quarts cranberry juice
- 3 cups pineapple juice
- 3 cups orange juice
- 1/4 cup lemon juice
- 1 liter ginger ale, chilled
- 1 medium navel orange, sliced

Combine the juices in a large container. Refrigerate. Just before serving, stir in ginger ale and orange slices. **Yield:** 5 quarts.

A Crumb About Cookies

If you know you're going to be in a hurry when it comes time to bake cookies, try this tip: Instead of scooping up the dough one spoonful at a time, pat it into a rectangle on a baking sheet and freeze until almost solid. Slice the rectangle horizontally and vertically in even intervals, forming a grid. Pick up and roll individual pieces for baking.

Enthusiastic 49th State cook looks to local waters and her "midnight sun" garden for a satisfying supper.

By Evy Gebhardt, Kasilof, Alaska

MY HUSBAND, Paul, and I are outdoor enthusiasts living near the shores of Cook's Inlet on the Kenai Peninsula of Alaska. Our favorite menu will give you a taste of the bountiful foods from this region.

I first tried the recipe for Alaskan Halibut Lasagna when I was cooking for a commercial fishing crew. Introducing this non-traditional white lasagna to a real "meat and potatoes" group, I soon had many requests to put it on the menu again!

Thyme and garlic complement the mild halibut. Swiss cheese is a tasty alternative to mozzarella, which is more commonly used in lasagna. We catch our own halibut, but it is sold in many stores.

I used to work as the cook at a remote Alaskan fishing lodge where bakery bread was an airplane ride away. It was there I started making Sourdough Bread. This simple recipe requires no kneading and can be mastered by even the most inexperienced cook.

Gardening is a hobby of mine, and Tossed Italian Salad is one of the delicious rewards. It has a light vinaigrette dressing that's so good sprinkled over garden greens. I mix in spinach and young beet tops.

I need a greenhouse for tomatoes, green beans and cucumbers because of the cool temperatures and brief growing season. Members of the cabbage family thrive outdoors, however, in summer's long hours of daylight.

Rhubarb Custard Cake came to be after I attempted to duplicate my mother-in-law's Rhubarb Upside-Down Cake. Coming from a dairy farm in Minnesota, I try to use dairy products whenever possible. The addition of fresh cream to the cake seemed logical. The result was this elegant dessert, which is now our favorite use of rhubarb.

I hope you and your family will try it and my other recipes from the Land of the Midnight Sun soon!

— ▼ ▼ ▼ —

PICTURED AT LEFT: Alaskan Halibut Lasagna, Sourdough Bread, Tossed Italian Salad and Rhubarb Custard Cake (recipes are on the next page).

halibut, white sauce and cheese. Repeat layers. Cover and bake at 350° for 20 minutes. Uncover; bake 20 minutes longer or until bubbly. Let stand 15 minutes before serving. Sprinkle with parsley if desired. **Yield:** 8 servings.

— 🍴 🍴 🍴 —

Sourdough Bread

This no-knead bread is no fuss to make and delicious, too. It has a crisp crust and distinctive sourdough flavor from the "starter" yeast mixture you stir up in advance. I was surprised at how easy it is!

> 1 package (1/4 ounce) active dry yeast
> 3-1/2 cups warm water (110° to 115°), *divided*
> 7 cups all-purpose flour, *divided*
> 1/4 cup nonfat dry milk powder
> 2 tablespoons butter *or* margarine, melted
> 2 tablespoons sugar
> 2 teaspoons salt

Cornmeal

In a 4-qt. non-metallic bowl, dissolve yeast in 2 cups warm water; let stand for 5 minutes. Stir in 2 cups of flour until smooth. Cover loosely with a clean towel. Let stand in a warm place (80°-90°) to ferment for 48 hours; stir several times daily. (The mixture will become bubbly and rise, have a "yeasty" sour aroma and a transparent yellow liquid will form on the top.) Stir in milk powder, butter, sugar, salt, remaining water and enough remaining flour to form a soft dough. (Do not knead.) Cover and let rise in a warm place until doubled, about 1-1/2 hours. Turn onto a floured surface; punch dough down. (Do not knead.) Divide in half.

Alaskan Halibut Lasagna

I use tender, mild halibut that we catch in Cook's Inlet near our home for this delectable white lasagna. Even "meat and potatoes lovers" compliment its great taste. You can substitute cod or chicken for the halibut if you like.

> 6 tablespoons butter *or* margarine, *divided*
> 1-1/2 pounds halibut steaks, bones removed and cut into 1-inch cubes
> 2 garlic cloves, minced
> 3/4 teaspoon dried thyme
> 1/3 cup all-purpose flour
> 1/2 teaspoon salt
> 1-1/2 cups chicken broth
> 1 cup whipping cream
> 8 ounces lasagna noodles, cooked and drained
> 2 cups (8 ounces) shredded Swiss cheese

Minced fresh parsley, optional

In a large skillet over medium heat, melt 2 tablespoons butter. Add halibut, garlic and thyme. Cook until fish flakes easily with a fork, about 10 minutes. Remove and set aside. Add the remaining butter to the skillet. Stir in flour and salt until smooth; cook and stir until golden brown. Gradually add broth and cream. Bring to a boil; cook and stir for 2 minutes or until thickened. In a greased 13-in. x 9-in. x 2-in. baking dish, layer half of the noodles,

Shape each into a round loaf. Heavily grease baking sheets and sprinkle with cornmeal. Place dough on prepared pans. Cover and let rise until doubled, about 30 minutes. With a sharp knife, make three diagonal slashes across tops of loaves. Bake at 350° for 10 minutes. Brush loaves with cold water; bake 35-40 minutes longer or until golden brown. **Yield:** 2 loaves. **Editor's Note:** Dough may also be shaped into 24 rolls instead of loaves. Bake for 10 minutes, then 20-25 minutes after brushing with water.

Tossed Italian Salad

A fresh garden salad with homemade Italian-style dressing is the perfect accompaniment to my special lasagna. Nicely seasoned with garlic, herbs and a hint of lemon, the dressing is our family's favorite. As soon as the jar is empty, I make more.

    6 tablespoons olive *or* vegetable oil
    2 tablespoons vinegar
    2 tablespoons lemon juice
    1 garlic clove, minced
  1/2 teaspoon salt
  1/2 teaspoon sugar
  1/4 teaspoon onion salt
  1/4 teaspoon dried oregano
  1/4 teaspoon ground mustard
  1/4 teaspoon paprika
Dash dried thyme
    8 cups torn salad greens
Sliced cucumbers, quartered cherry tomatoes
  and shredded carrots

In a jar with a tight-fitting lid, combine the first 11 ingredients; shake well. Refrigerate for 2 hours. Just before serving, combine the greens, cucumbers, tomatoes and carrots in a salad bowl. Drizzle with dressing; toss to coat. **Yield:** 8-10 servings.

Rhubarb Custard Cake

Rhubarb thrives in my northern garden and is one of the few crops the pesky moose don't bother! Of all the rhubarb desserts I've tried, this pudding cake is my No. 1 choice. It has old-fashioned appeal but is so simple to prepare.

    1 package (18-1/4 ounces) yellow cake mix
    4 cups chopped fresh *or* frozen rhubarb
    1 cup sugar
    1 cup whipping cream
Whipped cream and fresh mint, optional

Prepare cake batter according to package directions. Pour into a greased 13-in. x 9-in. x 2-in. baking dish. Sprinkle with rhubarb and sugar. Slowly pour cream over top. Bake at 350° for 40-45 minutes or until golden brown. Cool for 15 minutes before serving. Garnish with the whipped cream and mint if desired. Refrigerate leftovers. **Yield:** 12-15 servings.

Make-ahead recipes assure a delicious Thanksgiving dinner this veteran cook serves with ease. She shares her savory secrets!

By Ruby Williams, Bogalusa, Louisiana

FOR ME, the perfect "recipe" for enjoying Thanksgiving Day is to serve a mouth-watering meal without a lot of last-minute fuss. The secret is planning.

My children, grandchildren and great-grandchildren gather at my home for holidays—it's such fun to be together. Each family brings a dish for the buffet, but I cook much of the food. I prepare all of the recipes at least partially the day before or earlier.

I make the Whole Wheat Dinner Rolls a week ahead. They bake to a pretty golden color, have a pleasant texture and slightly sweet taste. I freeze them, thaw the rolls the day of the party and pop them into the oven to warm before serving.

Family members often comment that no holiday meal would be complete without my Mushroom Corn Bread Dressing. They praise its good flavor and the crunch from the almonds, mushrooms, green onions and celery.

I also prepare the corn bread for the dressing in advance. When it cools, I crumble the bread and freeze it until the day before Thanksgiving, when I thaw and combine it with the other ingredients.

I bake the Holiday Pound Cake 2 days early. My family always asks for this tender, delicate-tasting cake. I dress it up with strawberry topping.

Even the Herbed Turkey Breast can be cooked the day before! Since our family prefers white meat, I roast a turkey breast rather than a whole bird, reserving the remaining herb-butter sauce to reheat with the meat the next day.

Seasoned with sage, thyme, marjoram and a little soy sauce, the mixture keeps the turkey moist and tasty.

Overnight Vegetable Salad is a convenient, colorful medley with a tangy marinade. It's always a hit.

PICTURED AT LEFT: Herbed Turkey Breast, Overnight Vegetable Salad, Whole Wheat Dinner Rolls and Holiday Pound Cake (recipes are on the next page).

Herbed Turkey Breast

If I cook the turkey the day before, I can spend the actual holiday visiting with my family.

- 1/2 cup butter *or* margarine
- 1/4 cup lemon juice
- 2 tablespoons soy sauce
- 2 tablespoons finely chopped green onions
- 1 tablespoon rubbed sage
- 1 teaspoon dried thyme
- 1 teaspoon dried marjoram
- 1/4 teaspoon pepper
- 1 bone-in whole turkey breast (5-1/2 to 6 pounds)

In a small saucepan, combine the first eight ingredients; bring to a boil. Remove from the heat. Place turkey in a shallow roasting pan; baste with butter mixture. Bake, uncovered, at 325° for 1-1/2 to 2 hours or until a meat thermometer reads 170°, basting every 30 minutes. **Yield:** 10-12 servings.

Overnight Vegetable Salad

This side dish goes well with almost any meal, and we never seem to tire of it.

✓ Uses less fat, sugar or salt. Includes Nutritional Analysis and Diabetic Exchanges.

- 2-1/2 cups cauliflowerets
- 2 cups sliced fresh mushrooms
- 1-1/2 cups *each* broccoli florets, sliced carrots and yellow summer squash
- 1/2 to 3/4 cup vegetable oil
- 1/2 cup cider vinegar
- 2 teaspoons sugar
- 1 teaspoon dill weed

- 3/4 teaspoon salt, optional
- 1/2 teaspoon garlic salt *or* garlic powder
- 1/2 teaspoon pepper

In a bowl, combine the vegetables; set aside. In a jar with a tight-fitting lid, combine the remaining ingredients; shake well. Pour over vegetables; toss gently. Cover and refrigerate for 8 hours or overnight. **Yield:** 12 servings. **Nutritional Analysis:** One serving (prepared with garlic powder and 1/2 cup oil and without salt) equals 105 calories, 15 mg sodium, 0 cholesterol, 6 gm carbohydrate, 1 gm protein, 9 gm fat, 2 gm fiber. **Diabetic Exchanges:** 2 fat, 1 vegetable.

Mushroom Corn Bread Dressing

This family-pleasing dressing is moist and flavorful, and it makes enough for a large gathering.

- 2 cups cornmeal
- 3 teaspoons sugar
- 3 teaspoons baking powder
- 1 teaspoon salt
- 5 eggs
- 1 can (12 ounces) evaporated milk
- 1/4 cup vegetable oil
- 2 cups chopped fresh mushrooms
- 1 cup chopped celery
- 1/2 cup chopped green onions
- 3 tablespoons butter *or* margarine
- 2 cans (14-1/2 ounces *each*) chicken broth
- 1 can (10-3/4 ounces) condensed cream of chicken soup, undiluted
- 1/4 cup sliced almonds, toasted
- 1 teaspoon poultry seasoning
- 1/4 teaspoon pepper

For corn bread, combine the first four ingredients in a bowl. Combine 2 eggs, milk and oil; stir into dry ingredients just until moistened. Pour into a greased 9-in. square baking pan. Bake at 400° for 18-20 minutes or until a toothpick comes out clean. Cool on a wire rack. In a skillet, saute mushrooms, celery and onions in butter until tender. In a large bowl, beat remaining eggs; add broth, soup, almonds, poultry seasoning, pepper and vegetables. Crumble corn bread over mixture; stir well. Pour into a greased 13-in. x 9-in. x 2-in. baking dish. Bake, uncovered, at 350° for 45-50 minutes or until a knife inserted near the center comes out clean. **Yield:** 10-12 servings.

— 🏆 🏆 🏆 —

Whole Wheat Dinner Rolls

Even from the freezer, these rolls taste fresh and good.

> 2 **packages (1/4 ounce *each*) active dry yeast**
> 2-1/4 **cups warm water (110° to 115°)**
> 1/4 **cup shortening**
> 2 **eggs**
> 1/2 **cup plus 1 tablespoon sugar**
> 2 **teaspoons salt**
> 3 **cups whole wheat flour**
> 3-1/2 **to 4 cups all-purpose flour**
> 1/4 **cup butter *or* margarine, melted**

In a large mixing bowl, dissolve yeast in warm water; let stand for 5 minutes. Add the shortening, eggs, sugar, salt and whole wheat flour; beat until smooth. Add enough all-purpose flour to form a soft dough. Turn onto a floured surface; knead until smooth and elastic, about 6-8 minutes. Place in a greased bowl, turning once to grease top. Cover and let rise in a warm place until doubled, about 1 hour. Punch dough down. Divide into four portions; shape each into 12 balls. Place 1 in. apart on greased baking sheets. Cover and let rise until dou-

bled, about 25 minutes. Bake at 375° for 11-15 minutes or until browned. Brush with butter. **Yield:** 4 dozen.

Holiday Pound Cake

I bake this moist cake 2 days before our family dinner. Ideal for serving quite a few people, its flavor mellows with a little time.

> 1 **cup butter (no substitutes), softened**
> 1/2 **cup shortening**
> 1 **package (3 ounces) cream cheese, softened**
> 2-1/2 **cups sugar**
> 5 **eggs**
> 3 **cups cake flour**
> 1 **teaspoon baking powder**
> 1/2 **teaspoon salt**
> 1 **cup buttermilk**
> 1 **teaspoon lemon extract**
> 1 **teaspoon vanilla extract**
> **Strawberry ice cream topping**
> **Sliced fresh strawberries, optional**

In a large mixing bowl, cream butter, shortening and cream cheese. Gradually add sugar, beating until light and fluffy. Add the eggs, one at a time, beating well after each addition. Combine the dry ingredients; add to creamed mixture alternately with buttermilk. Stir in extracts. Pour into a greased and floured 10-in. fluted tube pan. Bake at 325° for 1 hour and 20 minutes or until a toothpick inserted near the center comes out clean. Cool for 10 minutes; remove from pan to a wire rack. Serve with strawberry topping and fresh strawberries if desired. **Yield:** 12-16 servings.

Meals in Minutes

Mix and match these recipes to make dozens of meals that go from start to finish in 30 minutes or less.

FAST TO FIX. Clockwise from upper left: Chicken and Asparagus Dinner in a Snap (p. 270), Scrumptious Stroganoff Is a Festive Feast (p. 266), Reel in Raves with a Fast Fish Dinner (p. 276) and Toss Together a Tasty Plate of Pasta! (p. 272).

Scrumptious Stroganoff Is a Festive Feast

DURING THE SEASON of shopping for the perfect present, wouldn't it be great to give yourself the gift of time?

Consider it done. This warm and satisfying meal will please your family without taking much time away from your holiday to-do list.

Your family will love the way it tastes, and you'll love the fact that it's quick and easy to prepare. From start to finish, it takes only 30 minutes.

The menu is made up of favorite recipes shared by three accomplished cooks and combined in our test kitchen.

Mushroom Beef Stroganoff is a tried-and-true dish that is nice enough for company, says Robin De La Gardelle of Concord, California.

"I've had this recipe for more than 25 years and have used it countless times," she says. "You can serve it over noodles or rice."

Herbed Tossed Salad is a fresh-tasting side dish from Margery Bryan of Royal City, Washington. The sweet red pepper gives it crunch, spark and a festive appearance.

Candy Bar Croissants taste as good as they look. This rich, buttery treat combines convenient refrigerated crescent rolls and chocolate bars. The recipe comes from Beverly Sterling of Gasport, New York.

— 🥄 🥄 🥄 —

Mushroom Beef Stroganoff

> 2 **tablespoons butter** *or* **margarine**
> 1 **tablespoon vegetable oil**
> 1-1/2 **pounds sirloin steak, thinly sliced**
> 1 **pound fresh mushrooms, sliced**
> 1 **can (10-3/4 ounces) condensed cream of mushroom soup, undiluted**
> 2 **cups (16 ounces) sour cream**
> 1 **cup chopped green onions**
> 1/2 **teaspoon dried thyme**
> 1/2 **teaspoon dried marjoram**
> **Hot cooked noodles** *or* **rice**

In a large skillet, heat butter and oil over medium-high heat. Brown steak; remove with a slotted spoon and keep warm. Add mushrooms; saute until tender. Return steak to pan. Add soup, sour cream, onions, thyme and marjoram; heat gently (do not boil). Serve over noodles or rice. **Yield:** 6 servings.

Herbed Tossed Salad

> 1 **cup vegetable oil**
> 1/3 **cup tarragon** *or* **cider vinegar**
> 1 **garlic clove, minced**
> 2 **teaspoons minced fresh oregano** *or* **1/2 teaspoon dried oregano**
> 1 **teaspoon salt**
> 3/4 **to 1 teaspoon minced fresh basil** *or* **1/4 teaspoon dried basil**
> 1/2 **teaspoon minced fresh parsley**
> **Mixed salad greens**
> **Sliced cucumber and sweet red pepper**

In a jar with a tight-fitting lid, combine the first seven ingredients; shake well. In a large salad bowl, combine greens, cucumber and red pepper. Drizzle with dressing; toss to coat. **Yield:** about 1-1/3 cups dressing.

— 🥄 🥄 🥄 —

Candy Bar Croissants

> 1 **tube (8 ounces) refrigerated crescent rolls**
> 1 **tablespoon butter** *or* **margarine, softened**
> 2 **plain milk chocolate candy bars (1.55 ounces** *each***), broken into small pieces**
> 1 **egg, beaten**
> 2 **tablespoons sliced almonds**

Unroll crescent roll dough; separate into triangles. Brush with butter. Arrange candy bar pieces evenly over triangles; roll up from the wide end. Place point side down on a greased baking sheet; curve ends slightly. Brush with egg and sprinkle with almonds. Bake at 375° for 11-13 minutes or until golden brown. Cool on a wire rack. **Yield:** 8 servings.

A Sure Thyme-Saver

Dry thyme by hanging bunches of stems secured with a rubber band in a warm dark area. Strip the dried leaves off by running your forefinger and thumb down each stem over a piece of paper. Slide the leaves into an air-tight container. Fresh thyme, which also freezes very well, is great on vegetables as well as poultry and all meats, game and fish.

This Fish Tale Has a Sweet Ending

SPENDING time in the kitchen preparing an elaborate meal is a pleasure for those who love to cook. But some days, speed is the key ingredient.

Herb-Coated Cod is a quick and easy recipe for crisp, tasty, golden fish fillets. "My husband and sons enjoy fishing, and this recipe is one of our favorite ways to prepare it," says Harriet Stichter of Milford, Indiana.

"Monterey Green Beans is a delicious way to dress up green beans," says Sandy McKenzie of Braham, Minnesota.

Microwave Oatmeal Cake has a yummy topping. "I keep my eye out for good microwave recipes like this," says Ruby Williams of Bogalusa, Louisiana.

— 🥄 🥄 🥄 —

Herb-Coated Cod

1/4 cup butter _or_ margarine, melted
2/3 cup butter-flavored cracker crumbs
2 tablespoons grated Parmesan cheese
1/2 teaspoon dried oregano
1/2 teaspoon dried basil
1/4 teaspoon garlic powder
1 pound cod fillets

Place butter in a shallow bowl. In another bowl, combine the next five ingredients. Dip fillets in butter, then coat with crumbs. Place in a greased 13-in. x 9-in. x 2-in. baking dish. Bake, uncovered, at 400° for 15-20 minutes or until fish flakes easily with a fork. **Yield:** 4 servings.

— 🥄 🥄 🥄 —

Monterey Green Beans

1/2 cup chopped green onions
3 tablespoons butter _or_ margarine
1 package (9 ounces) frozen cut green beans
1 can (4 ounces) mushroom stems and pieces, drained
1/2 teaspoon lemon-pepper seasoning
1/4 teaspoon salt
1/2 cup shredded Monterey Jack cheese

In a saucepan, saute onions in butter until tender. Add beans, mushrooms, lemon-pepper and salt. Cover and cook over medium heat for 5 minutes or until beans are tender. Sprinkle with cheese; cover and let stand for 1 minute or until cheese is melted. **Yield:** 6 servings.

— 🥄 🥄 🥄 —

Microwave Oatmeal Cake

1 cup quick-cooking oats
1-1/2 cups water
1/2 cup butter _or_ margarine, softened
1 cup packed brown sugar
1/2 cup sugar
2 eggs
1-1/2 teaspoons vanilla extract
1-1/3 cups all-purpose flour
1 teaspoon baking soda
1 teaspoon ground cinnamon
1/2 teaspoon salt
1/4 teaspoon ground nutmeg
TOPPING:
1 cup flaked coconut
1/2 cup chopped nuts
1/2 cup packed brown sugar
1/2 cup milk
1/4 cup butter _or_ margarine
Dash salt

In a microwave-safe bowl, combine oats and water. Microwave, uncovered, on high for 2-3 minutes or until thickened, stirring once; set aside. In a mixing bowl, cream butter and sugars. Add eggs; beat well. Beat in vanilla and oat mixture. Combine dry ingredients; gradually add to oat mixture and mix well. Pour into a greased 11-in. x 7-in. x 2-in. microwave-safe dish. Shield corners with small triangles of foil.* Microwave, uncovered, at 50% power for 8 minutes. Cook on high for 6 minutes or until when center is touched, cake clings to finger while area underneath is almost dry. Place on a wire rack. Combine topping ingredients in a microwave-safe dish; heat, uncovered, on high for 6-7 minutes or until thick and bubbly, stirring every 2 minutes. Spread over warm cake. **Yield:** 8 servings. ***Editor's Note:** Shielding with small pieces of foil prevents overcooking of food in the corners of a square or rectangular dish. Secure foil firmly to dish and do not allow it to touch insides of microwave. This recipe was tested in an 850-watt microwave.

Chicken and Asparagus Dinner in a Snap

IT WOULD BE so wonderful if every family meal could be an elaborate spread. But when reality comes knocking at your door and you need to get a meal on the table in minutes instead of hours, here's a menu to reach for.

This complete meal is made up of family favorites shared by three great cooks and combined in our test kitchen. You can have everything on your table in only 30 minutes.

Crispy Chicken Cutlets are moist and tender with a golden nutty coating. They go especially well with egg noodles.

"This is an easy entree I proudly serve to company," says Debra Smith of Brookfield, Missouri. "Try it for your next spur-of-the-moment dinner party or family dinner. Even your most finicky eater will be singing its praises—and yours!"

Stir-Fried Asparagus is a fresh-tasting, nicely seasoned vegetable side dish that's a cinch to prepare. The recipe, from Jeanette Lawrence of Vacaville, California, puts to good use those tender, garden-fresh asparagus of springtime.

Honey Peach Freeze makes a cool, refreshing end to any meal. The tang of orange and lemon juice blends nicely with the honey. It's great for anyone who is on a restricted diet, and those who aren't won't know the difference.

"This lightly sweet treat has big peach flavor," says Dorothy Smith of El Dorado, Arkansas.

— 🍵 🍵 🍵 —

Crispy Chicken Cutlets

  4 boneless skinless chicken breast halves
  1 egg white
3/4 cup finely chopped pecans
  3 tablespoons all-purpose flour
1/4 teaspoon salt
1/4 teaspoon pepper
  1 tablespoon butter *or* **margarine**
  1 tablespoon vegetable oil

Flatten chicken to 1/4-in. thickness. In a shallow bowl, lightly beat the egg white. In another shallow bowl, combine the pecans, flour, salt and pepper. Dip chicken in egg white, then coat with the pecan mixture. In a large skillet, brown chicken in butter and oil over medium heat for 4-6 minutes on each side or until juices run clear. **Yield:** 4 servings.

Stir-Fried Asparagus

  3 tablespoons butter *or* **margarine**
  1 teaspoon chicken bouillon granules
1/8 teaspoon celery salt
1/8 teaspoon pepper
1-1/2 pounds fresh asparagus, trimmed and cut into 2-inch slices (about 4 cups)
  1 teaspoon soy sauce

In a large skillet, melt butter. Add bouillon, celery salt and pepper; mix well. Add asparagus and toss to coat. Cover and cook for 2 minutes over medium-high heat, stirring occasionally. Stir in soy sauce and serve immediately. **Yield:** 4 servings.

— 🍵 🍵 🍵 —

Honey Peach Freeze

✓ Uses less fat, sugar or salt. Includes Nutritional Analysis and Diabetic Exchanges.

  1 package (20 ounces) frozen sliced peaches, partially thawed
1/4 cup honey
  2 tablespoons orange juice
  1 tablespoon lemon juice

Set aside a few peach slices for garnish if desired. Place remaining peaches in a blender or food processor; add honey and juices. Cover and process until smooth. Pour into four freezer-proof dishes. Freeze. Remove from the freezer 5 minutes before serving. Garnish with reserved peaches. **Yield:** 4 servings. **Nutritional Analysis:** One serving equals 202 calories, 9 mg sodium, 0 cholesterol, 53 gm carbohydrate, 1 gm protein, trace fat, 3 gm fiber. **Diabetic Exchange:** 3-1/2 fruit.

Juicy Tidbits

Need to quickly prepare juice from a can of frozen concentrate? Slide the frozen concentrate into a pitcher, then mash it with a potato masher. It will dissolve in water a lot faster.

Use orange juice for the liquid in homemade waffle batter. It gives the waffles a sweet citrus flavor your breakfast bunch is sure to love.

Toss Together a Tasty Plate of Pasta!

WARM, SUNNY days can convince even the most dedicated cook to spend less time in the kitchen and more time outdoors.

Since fresh air builds appetites, a fast-to-fix, nutritious meal is especially appropriate. And if by chance it isn't warm and sunny outside, this colorful, light meal will help make you feel like it is.

It's not only simple, it's simply delicious.

The menu is made up of family favorites from three experienced cooks. You can have everything ready to serve in just half an hour!

Walnut Ham Linguine is a pleasing combination of textures and flavors. The recipe comes from Mike Pickerel of Columbia, Missouri. "The garlic seasons this dish wonderfully," he says.

French Vinaigrette Salad has been made and served by Gay Nell Nicholas as long as she can remember. "The oil and vinegar dressing is a light, tangy topping for the lettuce," says Gay, of Henderson, Texas.

Cocoa Mousse Pie is shared by Patti Beatty of Hamilton, Ohio.

"This is my husband's favorite dessert," says Patti. "It's cool, creamy, chocolaty and a snap to fix."

Walnut Ham Linguine

- 1 package (16 ounces) linguine *or* thin spaghetti
- 2 to 4 garlic cloves, minced
- 1/4 cup olive *or* vegetable oil
- 1/2 cup coarsely chopped walnuts
- 1/2 pound fully cooked ham slices, cut into 1/2-inch strips
- 1/3 cup grated Parmesan cheese
- 1/4 cup minced fresh parsley

Cook pasta according to package directions. Meanwhile, in a large skillet, saute garlic in oil for 1 minute. Add walnuts; saute for 2 minutes. Stir in ham; cook until heated through, about 2 minutes. Drain pasta; toss with ham mixture. Sprinkle with Parmesan and parsley. **Yield:** 4-6 servings.

French Vinaigrette Salad

- 1-1/2 cups vegetable oil
- 3/4 cup cider vinegar
- 4 teaspoons sugar
- 1 teaspoon salt
- 1 teaspoon paprika
- 1/2 teaspoon ground mustard
- 1/4 teaspoon pepper
- Torn salad greens and vegetables of your choice

In a jar with a tight-fitting lid, combine the first seven ingredients; shake well. In a large salad bowl, combine the greens and vegetables. Drizzle with dressing. Serve immediately. **Yield:** 2-1/3 cups dressing.

Cocoa Mousse Pie

✓ Uses less fat, sugar or salt. Includes Nutritional Analysis and Diabetic Exchanges.

- 1 package (3 ounces) cream cheese, softened
- 2/3 cup sugar
- 1/3 cup baking cocoa
- 1/4 cup milk
- 1 teaspoon vanilla extract
- 1 carton (8 ounces) frozen whipped topping, thawed
- 1 graham cracker crust (9 inches)
- Additional whipped topping and baking cocoa, optional

In a mixing bowl, beat cream cheese, sugar and cocoa. Beat in the milk and vanilla until smooth. Fold in the whipped topping. Spoon into the crust. Cover and freeze for 20 minutes. Garnish with additional whipped topping and cocoa if desired. **Yield:** 8 servings. **Nutritional Analysis:** One serving (prepared with light cream cheese, skim milk, light frozen whipped topping and a reduced-fat graham cracker crust) equals 262 calories, 121 mg sodium, 6 mg cholesterol, 41 gm carbohydrate, 3 gm protein, 9 gm fat, 1 gm fiber. **Diabetic Exchanges:** 2 starch, 2 fat, 1/2 fruit.

Savory Spaghetti
To enhance the flavor of plain pasta, add some sugar to the salted water when boiling.

Chicken Salad Brings Cool Refreshment

THE SEASON helps determine how much time is spent in the kitchen. A clear summer day tempts even the most avid cooks to minimize time there.

This menu will give you plenty of time to garden, swim or enjoy a host of other outdoor activities. Its cool and creamy components will provide a welcome chill on a scorching day. Truly, though, it's a refreshing meal any time of year.

The menu was created in our test kitchen using tried-and-true recipes from three seasoned cooks. You can put together this complete meal—including dessert—in 30 minutes or less.

Dijon Chicken Salad is a tasty combination from Raymond Sienko of Hawleyville, Connecticut. "This is, by far, my most requested recipe," he says. "In addition to the traditional grapes, this chicken salad also features sweet apricots."

Buttermilk Rosemary Muffins have a delicate herb flavor that's special alongside any entree. Here, it complements the chicken salad especially well. The recipe is from Debbie Smith of Crossett, Arkansas, who suggests using fresh rosemary for best flavor.

Butterscotch Parfaits, from Judi Klee of Nebraska City, Nebraska, are pretty confections that are impossible to turn down. "Change the pudding flavor to suit your tastes," suggests Judi.

— ⛳ ⛳ ⛳ —

Dijon Chicken Salad

      4 cups cubed cooked chicken
      1 cup sliced celery
      1 cup seedless green grapes, halved
      1 cup seedless red grapes, halved
  1/4 cup chopped dried apricots
  1/4 cup sliced green onions
  3/4 cup mayonnaise
      2 tablespoons honey
      1 tablespoon Dijon mustard
  1/2 teaspoon salt
  1/8 teaspoon pepper
Lettuce leaves
  1/2 cup sliced almonds

In a bowl, combine the first six ingredients. In a small bowl, combine the mayonnaise, honey, mustard, salt and pepper; mix well. Stir into chicken mixture. Cover and refrigerate until serving. Serve on a lettuce-lined plate. Sprinkle with the almonds. **Yield:** 6 servings.

— ⛳ ⛳ ⛳ —

Buttermilk Rosemary Muffins

2-1/4 cups all-purpose flour
      2 tablespoons sugar
      1 tablespoon baking powder
      2 teaspoons minced fresh rosemary *or* 3/4 teaspoon dried rosemary, crushed
  3/4 teaspoon salt
  1/2 cup plus 1 tablespoon shortening
  3/4 cup buttermilk
  1/4 cup butter *or* margarine, melted

In a large bowl, combine the first five ingredients. Cut in shortening until mixture resembles coarse crumbs. Stir in buttermilk just until moistened (mixture will be dry). Fill greased muffin cups two-thirds full; brush with butter. Bake at 400° for 10-13 minutes or until a toothpick comes out clean. Cool for 5 minutes before removing from pan to a wire rack. Serve warm. **Yield:** 1 dozen.

— ⛳ ⛳ ⛳ —

Butterscotch Parfaits

✓ Uses less fat, sugar or salt. Includes Nutritional Analysis and Diabetic Exchanges.

      2 cups cold milk
      1 package (3.4 ounces) instant butterscotch pudding mix
    18 vanilla wafers, coarsely crushed
      1 carton (8 ounces) frozen whipped topping, thawed
      6 maraschino cherries, optional

In a mixing bowl, beat milk and pudding mix for 2 minutes or until thickened. In six parfait glasses, alternate layers of pudding, wafer crumbs and whipped topping. Garnish with a cherry if desired. Refrigerate until serving. **Yield:** 6 servings. **Nutritional Analysis:** One serving (prepared with skim milk, instant sugar-free pudding mix and light whipped topping and without cherries) equals 194 calories, 289 mg sodium, 2 mg cholesterol, 25 gm carbohydrate, 4 gm protein, 7 gm fat, 0 fiber. **Diabetic Exchanges:** 2 starch, 1/2 fat.

Reel in Raves with A Fast Fish Dinner

WHEN cooler days signal the start of the pre-holiday season, even dedicated cooks can't always spend as much time in the kitchen. There's just too much to do and not enough time to do it.

That's when hearty, fast-to-fix meals like this one come in handy. Ready to serve in just 30 minutes, the menu here combines recipes from three great cooks who know what it's like to be pinched for time.

Fish with Cream Sauce is the easy entree to prepare when you want something nutritious and quick for your family.

"Even people who don't like fish enjoy this satisfying dish," says Tiffany Taylor of St. Petersburg, Florida, who shares the recipe. "A sour cream sauce complements the mild-flavored fish."

Garlic Green Beans get a boost from onions and garlic. "Their fresh flavor comes shining through," says Jane Walker of Dewey, Arizona.

Pear Sundaes are perfect for an uncommon dessert that's fresh and fast. Says Len Harkness of Pacifica, California, "These sweet caramel pears over ice cream are easy, special and delicious." For a different flavor, substitute canned peaches.

— 🝙 🝙 🝙 —

Fish with Cream Sauce

8 slices bread, cubed
1/2 cup butter *or* margarine
1/2 cup all-purpose flour
1 teaspoon salt
1/8 teaspoon pepper
1-1/2 pounds fresh *or* frozen sole, haddock *or* grouper fillets, thawed
1 cup milk
1-1/2 cups (12 ounces) sour cream

In a large skillet over medium heat, toast bread cubes in butter until golden brown; set aside. In a large resealable plastic bag, combine the flour, salt and pepper. Add fish, one fillet at a time; shake to coat. Place in a greased 13-in. x 9-in. x 2-in. baking dish. Slowly pour milk over fillets. Bake, uncovered, at 400° for 15-20 minutes or until fish flakes easily with a fork. Spoon sour cream over the fillets. Top with the reserved bread cubes. Bake 5 minutes longer or until heated through. **Yield:** 6 servings.

Garlic Green Beans

✓ Uses less fat, sugar or salt. Includes Nutritional Analysis and Diabetic Exchanges.

2 pounds fresh *or* frozen green beans, cut into 1-inch pieces
1 medium onion, finely chopped
2 garlic cloves, minced
1 tablespoon olive *or* vegetable oil

Place beans in a saucepan and cover with water; bring to a boil. Cook, uncovered, for 8-10 minutes or until crisp-tender. Meanwhile, in a skillet, saute onion and garlic in oil until tender. Drain beans; add to onion mixture. Cook and stir for 2-3 minutes or until heated through. **Yield:** 6 servings. **Nutritional Analysis:** One serving equals 78 calories, 10 mg sodium, 0 cholesterol, 13 gm carbohydrate, 3 gm protein, 2 gm fat, 2 gm fiber. **Diabetic Exchanges:** 2-1/2 vegetable, 1/2 fat.

— 🝙 🝙 🝙 —

Pear Sundaes

2/3 cup packed brown sugar
1/4 cup butter *or* margarine
1 teaspoon ground cinnamon
1 can (29 ounces) pear halves
Vanilla ice cream

In a saucepan, combine brown sugar, butter and cinnamon. Cook and stir over medium heat for 5 minutes or until butter is melted. Drain pears, reserving 1/2 cup juice (discard remaining juice or save for another use). Add pears and reserved juice to saucepan; cook 8-10 minutes longer or until heated through. Serve warm over ice cream. **Yield:** 6 servings.

The Freshness of Spices

Generally, whole spices stay fresh up to 2 years, ground spices about 6 months.

When fresh, most spices have a bright, rich color and strong aroma when you open the container. If either the color or aroma seems weak, discard the spice and purchase a new bottle.

Meals on a Budget

These six economical meals prove you can still serve your family good food at a good price.

POCKETBOOK PLEASERS. Clockwise from upper left: Flavorful Meat Loaf, Noodles Florentine and Lemon Graham Freeze (p. 290); Brisket for a Bunch, Cabbage Tossed Salad and Apple Fritter Rings (p. 282); Sausage Pancakes, Cinnamon Breakfast Bites and Hot Fruit Compote (p. 284); Seasoned Swiss Steak, Onion Mashed Potatoes and Apple-Berry Streusel Bars (p. 286).

Feed Your Family for $1.59 a Plate!

EVEN AT today's prices, you and your family can eat well without spending a king's ransom.

With its vibrant colors and tasty sauces, this dinner looks rich. The fact that it wasn't expensive can be your little secret. The three great cooks who created the meal estimate the total cost at just $1.59 per setting.

Applesauce Pork Chops, from Elaine Anderson of Aliquippa, Pennsylvania, are fast, easy and delicious.

Sunny Carrot Sticks have a lightly sweet sauce with a delicate orange flavor. The recipe comes from Wendy Masters of Grand Valley, Ontario.

Glazed Butter Cookies are suggested by Dorothy Jennings of Waterloo, Iowa, who notes they aren't just for Christmastime.

"I bake these cookies all year, changing cookie cutters for various occasions," says Dorothy.

—— ☕ ☕ ☕ ——

Applesauce Pork Chops

    4 **rib pork chops (1/2 inch thick)**
    2 **tablespoons vegetable oil**
    1 **large red apple**
1-1/2 **cups applesauce**
    1 **cup water**
  1/4 **cup chopped onion**
    1 **tablespoon Worcestershire sauce**
  1/2 **teaspoon garlic powder**
  1/2 **teaspoon salt**
  1/4 **teaspoon pepper**
    1 **package (6 ounces) chicken-flavored wild rice mix**
    2 **teaspoons cornstarch**
    1 **tablespoon cold water**

In a skillet over medium-high heat, brown pork chops in oil on both sides; drain. Cut four thin wedges from apple; set aside. Peel and chop remaining apple. Add chopped apple, applesauce, water, onion, Worcestershire sauce, garlic powder, salt and pepper to skillet. Cover and simmer for 30-35 minutes or until meat juices run clear. Meanwhile, prepare rice according to package directions. Remove pork chops and keep warm. Combine cornstarch and cold water until smooth; stir into apple mixture. Bring to a boil; cook and stir for 2 minutes. Return chops to skillet and heat through. Serve with rice. Garnish with reserved apple wedges. **Yield:** 4 servings.

—— ☕ ☕ ☕ ——

Sunny Carrot Sticks

    1 **pound carrots, julienned**
    1 **tablespoon brown sugar**
    1 **teaspoon cornstarch**
  1/4 **cup orange juice**
    2 **tablespoons butter *or* margarine**

Place carrots and a small amount of water in a saucepan; cover and cook until tender. Meanwhile, in another saucepan, combine brown sugar and

cornstarch. Stir in orange juice until smooth. Bring to a boil; cook and stir for 2 minutes or until thickened and bubbly. Stir in butter. Drain carrots; top with orange juice mixture and toss to coat. **Yield:** 4 servings.

Glazed Butter Cookies

1/2 cup butter (no substitutes), softened
3/4 cup sugar
  1 egg
3/4 teaspoon vanilla extract
1-3/4 cups all-purpose flour
1/2 teaspoon baking powder
1/4 teaspoon salt

GLAZE:
  1 cup confectioners' sugar
  1 tablespoon milk
Red, green and yellow liquid *or* paste food coloring

In a mixing bowl, cream butter and sugar. Beat in egg and vanilla. Combine dry ingredients; gradually add to the creamed mixture. Cover and chill for 1 hour or until easy to handle. On a lightly floured surface, roll out to 1/8-in. thickness. Cut with 2-1/2-in. cookie cutters. Place 1 in. apart on ungreased baking sheets. Bake at 350° for 8-10 minutes or until lightly browned. Cool on wire racks. In a small bowl, combine confectioners' sugar and milk until smooth. Stir in food coloring. Lightly brush onto cooled cookies. Let stand until glaze is set, about 10 minutes. **Yield:** 3 dozen.

Feed Your Family for 94¢ a Plate!

YOU DON'T hear the slogan "change back from your dollar" anymore at restaurants, but you can still feed your family at home for under a buck a plate.

This well-rounded meal is tasty, wholesome and much more satisfying than fast food.

The menu was compiled from three great cooks who each shared one of their family's favorite recipes. The result is a meal that costs just 94¢ per serving.

Brisket for a Bunch makes tender slices of beef in a delicious au jus. Dawn Fagerstrom of Warren, Minnesota suggests the recipe. To easily get very thin slices, chill the brisket before slicing, then reheat in the juices.

Cabbage Tossed Salad is a fun and interesting cross between a green salad and a coleslaw with a tangy dressing. The recipe is recommended by Marilyn Katcsmorak from Pleasanton, Texas.

The recipe for Apple Fritter Rings is an old-fashioned treat that comes from Bernice Snowberger of Monticello, Indiana.

— ♟ ♟ ♟ —

Brisket for a Bunch

   1 beef brisket* (2-1/2 pounds), cut in half
   1 tablespoon vegetable oil
1/2 cup chopped celery
1/2 cup chopped onion
3/4 cup beef broth
1/2 cup tomato sauce
1/4 cup water
1/4 cup sugar
   2 tablespoons onion soup mix
   1 tablespoon vinegar
  12 hamburger buns, split

In a large skillet, brown the brisket on all sides in oil; transfer to a slow cooker. In the same skillet, saute celery and onion for 1 minute. Gradually add broth, tomato sauce and water; stir to loosen the browned bits from pan. Add sugar, soup mix and vinegar; bring to a boil. Pour over brisket. Cover and cook on low for 7-8 hours or until meat is tender. Let stand for 5 minutes before slicing. Skim fat from cooking juices. Serve meat in buns with cooking juices. **Yield:** 12 servings. ***Editor's Note:** This recipe is for fresh beef brisket, not corned beef.

— ♟ ♟ ♟ —

Cabbage Tossed Salad

✓ Uses less fat, sugar or salt. Includes Nutritional Analysis and Diabetic Exchanges.

   5 cups chopped iceberg lettuce
   2 cups chopped cabbage
   2 cups chopped red cabbage
   2 celery ribs, chopped
   3 green onions with tops, sliced
1/2 cup vinegar
1/4 cup vegetable oil
4-1/2 teaspoons sugar
3/4 teaspoon salt, optional

1/4 teaspoon pepper
1/4 teaspoon garlic powder

In a large bowl, toss the lettuce, cabbage, celery and onions. In a small bowl, whisk together the remaining ingredients. Pour over salad and toss to coat. Chill for 30 minutes before serving. **Yield:** 12 servings. **Nutritional Analysis:** One serving (prepared with sugar substitute equivalent to 4-1/2 teaspoons sugar and without salt) equals 54 calories, 14 mg sodium, 0 cholesterol, 3 gm carbohydrate, 1 gm protein, 5 gm fat, 1 gm fiber. **Diabetic Exchanges:** 1 fat, 1/2 vegetable.

Apple Fritter Rings

1 egg
2/3 cup milk
1 teaspoon vegetable oil
1 cup all-purpose flour
2 tablespoons sugar
1 teaspoon baking powder
Dash salt
5 large tart apples
1-1/2 cups vegetable oil
1/4 cup sugar
1/2 teaspoon ground cinnamon

In a bowl, beat egg, milk and oil. Combine flour, sugar, baking powder and salt; stir into the egg mixture until smooth (batter will be thick). Peel, core and cut apples into 1/2-in. rings. In an electric skillet or deep-fat fryer, heat oil to 375°. Dip apple rings into batter; fry, a few at a time, until golden brown. Drain on paper towels. Combine sugar and cinnamon; sprinkle over hot fritters. Serve warm. **Yield:** about 2 dozen.

Feed Your Family for $1.46 a Plate!

PANCAKES are a traditional breakfast favorite, but they can be served any time of day. Steaming 'cakes with syrup and a warm fruit salad can help start your morning or take the chill out of a cold evening.

This flavorful meal is from three frugal cooks who estimate the total cost at just $1.46 per setting.

Sausage Pancakes are a hearty entree from Barbara Downey of Preston, Iowa. "These fluffy pancakes are an easy way to fill up the kids before school or anytime," she says.

Ruth Hastings of Louisville, Illinois recommends Cinnamon Breakfast Bites, scrumptious treats with a sweet, crispy coating.

Hot Fruit Compote is a gently spiced salad that's perfect for any season. "It's such a pretty way to use canned fruit," says Helen Austin of Grand Rapids, Ohio.

Beverage choices could include hot tea or coffee, cold fruit juices or milk, and mineral water.

—— 📑 📑 📑 ——

Sausage Pancakes

    2 cups all-purpose flour
    2 teaspoons baking powder
    1 teaspoon salt
1/2 teaspoon baking soda
    2 eggs
    2 cups sour milk*
    2 tablespoons vegetable oil
    1 pound bulk pork sausage, cooked and
       drained
1-1/2 cups pancake syrup

In a bowl, combine the flour, baking powder, salt and baking soda. In another bowl, beat the eggs, milk and oil. Stir into dry ingredients just until moistened. Fold in sausage. Pour batter by 1/4 cupfuls onto a lightly greased hot griddle. Turn when bubbles form on top of pancakes. Cook until second side is golden. Serve with syrup. **Yield:** 6 servings. ***Editor's Note:** To sour milk, place 2 tablespoons white vinegar in a 2-cup measuring cup. Add milk to measure 2 cups.

Cinnamon Breakfast Bites

1-1/3 cups all-purpose flour
    1 cup crisp rice cereal, coarsely crushed
    2 tablespoons plus 1/2 cup sugar, *divided*
    3 teaspoons baking powder
1/2 teaspoon salt
1/4 cup butter-flavored shortening
1/2 cup milk
    1 teaspoon ground cinnamon
1/4 cup butter *or* margarine, melted

In a bowl, combine the flour, cereal, 2 tablespoons sugar, baking powder and salt; cut in shortening until mixture resembles coarse crumbs. Stir in milk just until moistened. Shape into 1-in. balls. In a bowl, combine cinnamon and remaining sugar.

Dip balls in butter, then roll in cinnamon-sugar. Arrange in a single layer in an 8-in. round baking pan. Bake at 425° for 15-18 minutes or until a toothpick comes out clean. **Yield:** 6 servings (2-1/2 dozen).

🍵 🍵 🍵

Hot Fruit Compote

1 can (20 ounces) pineapple chunks, drained
1 can (15-1/4 ounces) sliced peaches, drained
1 can (15-1/4 ounces) apricot halves, drained
1 can (15-1/4 ounces) pear halves, drained
1/4 cup maraschino cherries
1 cup orange juice
1/3 cup packed brown sugar
1/4 teaspoon ground cinnamon
4 whole cloves
1/8 teaspoon ground mace
Dash salt

In a 2-1/2-qt. baking dish, combine the pineapple, peaches, apricots, pears and cherries; set aside. In a small saucepan, combine the remaining ingredients. Bring to a boil over medium heat; pour over fruit. Bake, uncovered, at 350° for 25-30 minutes or until bubbly. Discard cloves. Serve warm. **Yield:** 6 servings.

Feed Your Family for $1.40 a Plate!

IF YOU'RE looking for comfort food that won't put an uncomfortable crunch in your pocketbook, here's the menu for you.

This meat-and-potatoes meal comes from three experienced cooks who know what their families like. You will like that it costs only $1.40 per setting.

Seasoned Swiss Steak combines tender beef and vegetables in a gravy that melds tomato, brown sugar and mustard. The recipe comes from Edna Hoffman of Hebron, Indiana.

Golden caramelized onions add a rich taste to Onion Mashed Potatoes, says Darlene Markel of Sublimity, Oregon.

With her Apple-Berry Streusel Bars, Jane Acree of Holcomb, Illinois proves that inexpensive meals can include a scrumptious dessert. With fruity filling and nutty topping, these attractive bars taste like they cost a pretty penny!

— 🍴 🍴 🍴 —

Seasoned Swiss Steak

1/4 cup all-purpose flour
1 tablespoon ground mustard
1 teaspoon salt, *divided*
1/4 teaspoon pepper, *divided*
1-1/2 pounds boneless round steak (about 1 inch thick), cut into serving-size pieces
2 tablespoons vegetable oil
1 cup diced carrots
1/2 cup chopped onion
1/2 cup chopped green pepper
1 tablespoon brown sugar
1 tablespoon Worcestershire sauce
1 can (14-1/2 ounces) diced tomatoes, undrained
1/4 cup cold water

Combine the flour, mustard, 1/2 teaspoon salt and 1/8 teaspoon pepper; set aside 2 tablespoons for gravy. Rub remaining flour mixture over steak. Pound with a meat mallet to tenderize. In a skillet, brown steak in oil. Transfer to a greased 2-1/2-qt. baking dish. Top with carrots, onion, green pepper, brown sugar and Worcestershire sauce. Pour tomatoes over all. Cover and bake at 350° for 1-1/2 to 2 hours or until meat and vegetables are tender. Transfer meat and vegetables to a serving dish; keep warm. Strain pan juices into a measuring cup; add water to measure 1 cup. In a saucepan, combine reserved flour mixture with cold water until smooth. Whisk in pan juices. Bring to a boil; cook and stir for 2 minutes or until thickened. Add remaining salt and pepper. Serve over steak. **Yield:** 6 servings.

— 🍴 🍴 🍴 —

Onion Mashed Potatoes

4 medium potatoes, peeled and cubed
1 small onion, thinly sliced
1 teaspoon sugar
2 tablespoons butter *or* margarine

1/2 cup warm milk
1/2 teaspoon salt
1/8 teaspoon pepper
Minced fresh parsley, optional

Place potatoes in a saucepan and cover with water; bring to a boil. Cook until very tender, about 20-25 minutes. Meanwhile, in a skillet over low heat, cook onion and sugar in butter until golden, stirring frequently. Drain and mash the potatoes. Add the milk, salt and pepper. Stir in the onion mixture. Garnish with parsley if desired. **Yield:** 6 servings.

🍷 🍷 🍷

Apple-Berry Streusel Bars

2-1/2 cups plus 2 tablespoons all-purpose flour, *divided*

2 cups old-fashioned oats
1-1/4 cups sugar
2 teaspoons baking powder
1 teaspoon ground cinnamon
1 cup butter *or* margarine, melted
3 cups thinly sliced peeled tart apples
1 jar (12 ounces) raspberry preserves
1/2 cup finely chopped walnuts

In a mixing bowl, combine 2-1/2 cups flour, oats, sugar, baking powder and cinnamon. Beat in butter just until moistened. Set aside 2 cups for topping. Pat remaining oat mixture into a greased 13-in. x 9-in. x 2-in. baking pan. Bake at 375° for 15 minutes. Meanwhile, toss apples with remaining flour. Stir in the preserves; spread over hot crust to within 1/2 in. of edges. Combine nuts and reserved oat mixture; sprinkle over fruit mixture. Bake 30-35 minutes longer or until lightly browned. Cool completely before cutting. **Yield:** 4 dozen.

Feed Your Family for $1.59 a Plate!

LOOKING to trim the amount of your family budget devoted to grocery shopping? This menu will help.

The frugal yet flavorful meal here is from three terrific cooks who estimate the total cost at just $1.59 per setting.

This complete, satisfying meal is chock-full of nutritious vegetables—even the bread and cake. So if you have a fussy eater who refuses veggies, you can sneak in one or two...and get compliments at the same time! Really.

"Skillet Chicken Supper is a hearty main dish," says Marlene Muckenhirn of Delano, Minnesota. "It's gently spiced with a tasty vegetable medley." Frozen mixed vegetables can be used instead of peas.

Cheddar Corn Bread, suggested by Terri Adrian of Lake City, Florida, pleases a crowd with its moist texture and big corn flavor.

The recipe for delicious and penny-pinching Chocolate Potato Cake has been handed down for generations in the family of Charlotte Cleveland from Hobbs, New Mexico. Don't be surprised when members of your family ask for an extra piece.

— ☕ ☕ ☕ —

Skillet Chicken Supper

1/2 **cup all-purpose flour**
1/2 **teaspoon garlic powder**
1/2 **teaspoon pepper**
  1 **broiler/fryer chicken (3 to 4 pounds), cut up**
  2 **tablespoons vegetable oil**
1-3/4 **cups water, *divided***
1/2 **cup soy sauce**
1/2 **teaspoon dried oregano**
  3 **medium red potatoes, cut into 1-inch chunks**
  3 **large carrots, cut into 1-inch pieces**
  3 **celery ribs, cut into 1-inch pieces**
  1 **package (10 ounces) frozen peas**

In a resealable plastic bag, combine flour, garlic powder and pepper. Add chicken, one piece at a time, and shake to coat; set the remaining flour mixture aside. In a large skillet, cook chicken in oil until browned on all sides; drain. Combine 1-1/4 cups water, soy sauce and oregano; pour over chicken. Add vegetables. Bring to a boil; reduce heat. Cover and simmer for 30-40 minutes or until chicken juices run clear. Remove chicken and vegetables; keep warm. Combine reserved flour mixture and remaining water until smooth; add to the cooking juices. Bring to a boil; cook and stir for 2 minutes or until thickened. Serve with the chicken and vegetables. **Yield:** 6 servings.

— ☕ ☕ ☕ —

Cheddar Corn Bread

  2 **packages (8-1/2 ounces *each*) corn bread/muffin mix**
  2 **eggs, beaten**
1/2 **cup milk**
1/2 **cup plain yogurt**
  1 **can (14-3/4 ounces) cream-style corn**
1/2 **cup shredded cheddar cheese**

In a bowl, combine the corn bread mix, eggs, milk and yogurt until well blended. Stir in the corn and cheese. Pour into a greased 13-in. x 9-in. x 2-in. baking dish. Bake at 400° for 18-22 minutes or until a toothpick inserted near the center comes out clean. Cut into squares. Serve warm. **Yield:** 12 servings.

— 🏆 🏆 🏆 —

Chocolate Potato Cake

- 1 **cup butter-flavored shortening**
- 2 **cups sugar**
- 2 **eggs,** *separated*
- 1 **cup mashed potatoes**
- 1 **teaspoon vanilla extract**
- 2-1/2 **cups all-purpose flour**
- 1/2 **cup baking cocoa**
- 2-1/2 **teaspoons baking powder**
- 1/2 **teaspoon** *each* **ground allspice, cinnamon, cloves and nutmeg**

- 3/4 **teaspoon salt**
- 1 **cup milk**

MOCHA FROSTING:
- 1/3 **cup butter** *or* **margarine, softened**
- 2-2/3 **cups confectioners' sugar**
- 2 **tablespoons baking cocoa**
- 1/4 **teaspoon salt**
- 3 **tablespoons strong brewed coffee**

In a mixing bowl, cream shortening and sugar. Add the egg yolks, one at a time, beating well after each addition. Add potatoes and vanilla; mix well. Combine the dry ingredients; add to the creamed mixture alternately with milk. In a small mixing bowl, beat egg whites until soft peaks form; fold into batter. Pour into a greased and floured 10-in. fluted tube pan. Bake at 325° for 1 to 1-1/4 hours or until a toothpick inserted near the center comes out clean. Cool for 10 minutes before removing from pan to a wire rack. In a small bowl, combine frosting ingredients until smooth. Frost cooled cake. **Yield:** 16 servings.

Feed Your Family for $1.38 a Plate!

THE PRICE won't be the first thing that pops into your head when you see the home-style menu we've put together here.

No, you'll be thinking about how good it sounds or how it would satisfy your family on a crisp autumn day. When you do get around to tallying up the cost, you'll feel a smile spread across your face. It's only $1.38 per setting for this trio of dishes shared by three country cooks.

Flavorful Meat Loaf is a firm, hearty loaf with a distinctive taste, thanks to soy sauce and ginger. "This is one recipe I rely on for a satisfying, inexpensive meal," says Sharon Hancock of Belleville, Ontario.

Noodles Florentine is a favorite recommended by Marcia Orlando of Boyertown, Pennsylvania. "With this recipe, you get noodles and a nutritious vegetable in one tasty casserole," Marcia notes.

For a cool, economical treat, try Lemon Graham Freeze from Barbara Husband of Dorchester, Wisconsin. "This light, pleasantly tart dessert is convenient since you make it ahead of time," says Barbara.

—— ☕ ☕ ☕ ——

Flavorful Meat Loaf

✓ Uses less fat, sugar or salt. Includes Nutritional Analysis and Diabetic Exchanges.

    1 medium carrot, shredded
  1/4 cup chopped onion
    2 tablespoons soy sauce
    1 teaspoon tomato paste
    2 garlic cloves, minced
  1/4 teaspoon ground ginger
  1/8 teaspoon crushed red pepper flakes
Pepper to taste
  1/2 pound ground beef
  1/2 pound ground pork

In a bowl, combine the first eight ingredients. Add beef and pork; mix well. Shape into a loaf in an ungreased shallow baking pan. Bake at 350° for 45-50 minutes or until meat is no longer pink and a meat thermometer reads 160°; drain. Let stand for 10 minutes before slicing. **Yield:** 4 servings. **Nu-**

tritional Analysis: One serving (prepared with light soy sauce and 1 pound of lean ground beef instead of beef and pork) equals 215 calories, 353 mg sodium, 41 mg cholesterol, 5 gm carbohydrate, 24 gm protein, 10 gm fat, 1 gm fiber. **Diabetic Exchanges:** 3 lean meat, 1 vegetable.

—— ☕ ☕ ☕ ——

Noodles Florentine

    5 cups uncooked medium egg noodles
    2 tablespoons butter *or* margarine
    2 tablespoons all-purpose flour
    1 cup milk

1 package (10 ounces) frozen chopped
    spinach, thawed and well drained
1/4 teaspoon ground nutmeg
Salt and pepper to taste
1 cup (4 ounces) shredded Swiss cheese

In a large saucepan, cook noodles in water until tender. In another saucepan, melt butter; stir in flour until smooth. Gradually add milk. Bring to a boil; cook and stir for 2 minutes or until thickened. Stir in the spinach, nutmeg, salt and pepper. Drain noodles. Add to spinach mixture; toss gently to coat. Transfer to a greased shallow 2-qt. baking dish; sprinkle with cheese. Cover and bake at 350° for 20 minutes or until heated through. **Yield:** 4 servings.

Lemon Graham Freeze

1 can (5 ounces) evaporated milk
1/2 cup sugar
2 tablespoons lemon juice
4 drops yellow food coloring, optional
6 whole graham crackers

Place milk in a mixing bowl; add beaters to bowl. Freeze for 25-30 minutes or until soft crystals form around edges of bowl. Beat milk until stiff peaks form. Gradually add sugar, lemon juice and food coloring if desired; mix well. Place five graham crackers in an ungreased 11-in. x 7-in. x 2-in. dish; pour milk mixture over crackers. Crush remaining graham cracker and sprinkle over top. Cover and freeze until firm. **Yield:** 6 servings.

Getting in the Theme of Things

You'll find everything you need to plan a special event right here: theme-related menus, fresh decorating ideas and fun-for-all activities.

CELEBRATION STATION. Clockwise from upper left: Teddy Picnic Is Bearly Any Fuss (p. 296), Welcome to My Pineapple Palace (p. 304), Elegant Tea Honors a Bride-to-Be (p. 300) and Snowy Brunch Warms Hearts in a Flurry (p. 294).

Snowy Brunch Warms Hearts in a Flurry

By Renae Moncur, Burley, Idaho

DAUGHTER JONI was not able to come home for the holidays one year, so I planned a trip to see her in sunny California...and I took along a bit of our Idaho winter!

All the trimmings to set a Snowman Brunch table were packed in my suitcase, along with recipes for a festive meal of Warm-You-Up Sausage Quiche, Snowball Peaches, Melt-in-Your-Mouth Pecan Rolls and Frosty's Fruit Slush.

I started to serve theme meals years ago as a special treat for our growing family. Now that the children

are adults, I still plan a theme meal whenever we get together, whether at our home or theirs.

For the wintry brunch, our centerpiece consisted of two jovial snow people standing beside a little evergreen tree sparkling with miniature lights and surrounded by tiny gaily wrapped packages.

For effect, I sprinkled artificial snow on the tree and all around the base. At each place, I set a votive candle inside cute hard-candy rings I'd purchased and decorated with lace ribbon, bows and small bells.

I placed a snowman magnet next to every plate, hung a candy cane on the rim of each glass and brought paper plates and napkins with a bold snowman design.

I kept the menu simple. Warm-You-Up Sausage Quiche is chock-full of sausage and cheesy flavor. The pretty Snowball Peaches have a cream cheese filling sweetened with apricot preserves.

Bite-size Melt-in-Your-Mouth Pecan Rolls start with handy refrigerated crescent rolls. Finally, Frosty's Fruit Slush is lovely and refreshing.

The weather outside was far from frightful, but my snowy theme brought color, fun and a taste of home to the southern branch of our family.

— 🍴 🍴 🍴 —

Warm-You-Up Sausage Quiche

This flavorful dish sparked with spicy sausage and peppers got a reception that was anything but chilly!

  1 **pound bulk mild pork sausage**
1/4 **pound bulk hot pork sausage**
 12 **eggs**
  2 **cups (16 ounces) small-curd cottage cheese**
  3 **cups (12 ounces) shredded Monterey Jack cheese**
  1 **cup (4 ounces) shredded mozzarella cheese**
1/2 **cup all-purpose flour**
1/2 **cup butter *or* margarine, melted**
  1 **teaspoon baking powder**
  2 **cups sliced fresh mushrooms**
3/4 **cup finely chopped onion**
  1 **can (4 ounces) chopped green chilies, drained**
Grated Parmesan cheese, optional
Green and sweet red pepper strips, optional

In a large skillet over medium heat, cook sausage until no longer pink; drain. In a large mixing bowl, beat eggs, cheeses, flour, butter and baking powder. Stir in mushrooms, onion, chilies and sausage. Transfer to two greased 9-in. round baking dishes (dishes will be full). Sprinkle with Parmesan cheese if desired. Bake at 375° for 33-38 minutes or until a knife inserted near the center comes out clean. Garnish with pepper strips if desired. **Yield:** 2 quiches (6-8 servings each).

— 🍴 🍴 🍴 —

Snowball Peaches

Peach halves took on a festive look for our snowman brunch when I mounded a fruity cream cheese mixture in them.

  2 **packages (3 ounces *each*) cream cheese, softened**
  2 **tablespoons apricot preserves**

  1 **cup pineapple tidbits, drained**
  3 **cans (15-1/4 ounces *each*) peach halves, drained**
Leaf lettuce
Fresh mint, optional

In a small mixing bowl, beat the cream cheese and preserves until blended. Stir in pineapple. Place peaches cut side up on a lettuce-lined serving platter; fill with cream cheese mixture. Garnish with mint if desired. **Yield:** 15 servings.

— 🍴 🍴 🍴 —

Melt-in-Your-Mouth Pecan Rolls

When you don't have the time to make a yeast dough from scratch, these "quickie sticky buns" are great.

1/2 **cup packed brown sugar**
1/2 **cup butter *or* margarine, softened**
1/4 **cup corn syrup**
  2 **tubes (8 ounces *each*) refrigerated crescent rolls**
2/3 **cup chopped pecans**
1/4 **cup sugar**
  1 **teaspoon ground cinnamon**

In a small bowl, combine brown sugar, butter and corn syrup. Spread in two greased 8-in. square baking pans; set aside. Unroll each tube of crescent roll dough into a rectangle; seal seams and perforations. Combine pecans, sugar and cinnamon; sprinkle over dough. Roll up, jelly-roll style, starting with a long side; seal edge. Cut each roll into 16 slices. Place cut side down in prepared pans. Bake at 375° for 13-17 minutes or until golden brown. Cool in pans for 1 minute before inverting onto serving plates. **Yield:** 32 rolls.

— 🍴 🍴 🍴 —

Frosty's Fruit Slush

With its peachy color, this beverage looks as great as it tastes. A tiny candy cane makes the perfect garnish.

  2 **cups frozen peach slices**
  2 **cans (5-1/2 ounces *each*) apricot *or* peach nectar**
  1 **can (6 ounces) frozen orange juice concentrate, thawed**
  2 **liters lemon-lime soda, chilled**

In a blender, combine peaches, nectar and orange juice; cover and process until smooth. Pour into ice cube trays. Freeze for 3-4 hours or until firm. Remove from freezer 30 minutes before serving. For each serving, place 2-3 cubes into each glass. Add soda; stir to dissolve cubes. **Yield:** 10-12 servings.

Teddy Picnic Is Bearly Any Fuss

By Sue Schuller, Brainerd, Minnesota

CHOOSING a theme for a baby shower was easy after my friend told me she was decorating her baby's room with teddy bears. I dreamed up a teddy bear picnic!

My table was set with a cheerful red checked gingham cloth. Toy stuffed bears surrounded a main course that was fun to look at—a Sandwich Bear.

With it, I served Bear's Picnic Veggie Dip, Beary Cute Cookies and Teddy Carrot Bars.

Door prizes in teddy bear gift bags were awarded to those who found a teddy bear sticker on the bottom of their picnic plates. The mother-to-be and shower guests were full of compliments…and I thoroughly enjoyed preparing the festive dishes for the gathering.

This theme picnic could be adapted for a child's birthday or to delight teddy bear lovers of any age!

—— 🍲 🍲 🍲 ——

Sandwich Bear

The chubby bear is formed using round bread and rolls filled with meats, cheese and seasoned spread.

   1 **package (8 ounces) cream cheese, softened**
   1 **cup mayonnaise**
   1 **tablespoon prepared mustard**
1/4 **cup chopped green onions**
   1 **unsliced round loaf of bread (1 to 1-1/2 pounds and 10 inches)**

6 **unsliced rolls (one 5 inches and five 3-1/2 inches)**
3/4 **pound thinly sliced deli ham**
1 **cup (4 ounces) shredded cheddar cheese,** *divided*
3/4 **pound thinly sliced deli turkey**
Leaf lettuce, optional
2 **large pitted ripe olives**

In a mixing bowl, beat cream cheese until light and fluffy. Stir in mayonnaise, mustard and onions. Slice bread and rolls one-third from the bottom of each. Carefully hollow out tops of bread and rolls, leaving a 1/2-in. shell. Spread cream cheese mixture on cut sides. Fill loaf with ham and half of the cheddar cheese. Fill the rolls with turkey and remaining cheese. Replace all tops. To assemble bear, place loaf on lettuce if desired on a large board. Place 5-in. roll on top for head and four small rolls for paws. Cut the remaining small roll in half for ears. Use one olive for nose. Cut remaining olive in half; secure with a toothpick for eyes. Cover and refrigerate up to 2 hours. **Yield:** 16 servings.

———— 🍵 🍵 🍵 ————

Bear's Picnic Veggie Dip

A colorful array of vegetables served with this delicious dip added appealing finger food.

1 **cup mayonnaise**
1 **cup (8 ounces) sour cream**
1 **envelope vegetable soup mix**
1 **package (10 ounces) frozen chopped spinach, thawed and squeezed dry**
1 **can (8 ounces) water chestnuts, drained and chopped**
Assorted raw vegetables

In a bowl, combine mayonnaise, sour cream and soup mix. Stir in spinach and water chestnuts. Cover and refrigerate for at least 2 hours. Serve with vegetables. **Yield:** 3 cups.

———— 🍵 🍵 🍵 ————

Beary Cute Cookies

I like to make fun foods but don't care to spend time fussing. I used candy for the bears' features.

3/4 **cup shortening**
1/2 **cup sugar**
1/2 **cup packed brown sugar**
1 **egg**
1 **teaspoon vanilla extract**
2 **cups all-purpose flour**
1 **teaspoon salt**
1/2 **teaspoon baking soda**

Additional sugar
30 **miniature milk chocolate kisses**
60 **miniature M&M baking bits**

In a mixing bowl, cream shortening and sugars. Beat in egg and vanilla; mix well. Combine the flour, salt and baking soda; gradually add to creamed mixture and mix well (dough will be crumbly). Set aside about 1/2 cup of dough for ears. Shape remaining dough into 1-in. balls; roll in additional sugar. Place 3 in. apart on ungreased baking sheets. Flatten to about 1/2-in. thickness. Roll reserved dough into 1/2-in. balls; roll in sugar. Place two smaller balls about 1 in. apart touching each flattened ball (do not flatten smaller balls). Bake at 375° for 10-12 minutes or until set and edges are lightly browned. Remove from oven; immediately press one kiss and two baking bits into each cookie for nose and eyes. Cool for 5 minutes before removing from pans to wire racks to cool completely. **Yield:** 2-1/2 dozen.

———— 🍵 🍵 🍵 ————

Teddy Carrot Bars

I was sure to point out to the mother-to-be that these moist, yummy bars include two jars of baby food!

1-1/4 **cups all-purpose flour**
1 **cup sugar**
1 **teaspoon baking soda**
1 **teaspoon ground cinnamon**
1/2 **teaspoon salt**
1 **jar (6 ounces) carrot baby food**
1 **jar (6 ounces) applesauce baby food**
2 **eggs**
2 **tablespoons vegetable oil**
CREAM CHEESE FROSTING:
1 **package (3 ounces) cream cheese, softened**
1 **teaspoon vanilla extract**
2 **to 2-1/2 cups confectioners' sugar**
1 **to 3 teaspoons milk**
24 **miniature teddy bear-shaped cinnamon graham crackers**

In a mixing bowl, combine flour, sugar, baking soda, cinnamon and salt. Combine baby foods, eggs and oil; add to dry ingredients just until blended. Pour into a greased 13-in. x 9-in. x 2-in. baking pan. Bake at 350° for 20-25 minutes or until a toothpick inserted near the center comes out clean. Cool completely. Cut into bars. For frosting, in a mixing bowl, beat the cream cheese and vanilla until smooth. Gradually add confectioners' sugar. Add enough to milk to achieve desired consistency. Place a dollop of frosting on each bar; top with a teddy graham cracker. **Yield:** 2 dozen.

Forecast's Fine for Weather Party

By Ndara Pike, Tempe, Arizona

MY BROTHER TONY loves studying about weather and trying to predict when rain will fall (which is not very often here in the desert!).

For his 18th birthday party, my sister and I planned a menu and decorations with his special interest—and his favorite foods—in mind.

The hearty main course, which we renamed Clouds at Sunset with Pea Soup Fog, is an all-time favorite family recipe from our grandmother.

The "clouds" are a creamy mixture of mashed potatoes and carrots the color of our spectacular Arizona sunsets. Pea Soup Fog is a creamy gravy made of ground beef and peas.

If you squint and use your imagination, the veggies and bean dip we served might remind you of the results of a heavy rainstorm with mudflows. We named it Mud Slide Dip with "storm-damaged" vegetables.

Dessert is the best part of a birthday party, of course.

With fair weather in mind, we created a rainbow and a pot of gold. Sherbet Rainbow provided a refreshing and colorful accompaniment to End-of-the-Rainbow Cake topped with foil-covered chocolate coins.

Our table was set with a sky blue cloth, paper clouds and "partly sunny" plates, made by cutting out orange paper "rays" to beam out from under the plates. Over the table hung a big colorful rainbow umbrella. The party was a chance to soak up the pleasures of a whole world of weather!

❦ ❦ ❦

Clouds at Sunset

Fluffy garlic mashed potatoes and carrots became Clouds at Sunset. They're topped with a gravy of ground beef and peas we called Pea Soup Fog.

4 large potatoes, peeled and quartered
6 large carrots, cut into 1-1/2-inch pieces

2 to 3 garlic cloves, peeled
1/2 cup milk
1/4 cup butter *or* margarine
Salt and pepper to taste
PEA SOUP FOG:
   1 pound ground beef
1/2 cup finely chopped onion
   2 tablespoons cornstarch
1-1/2 cups milk
   1 package (10 ounces) frozen peas, thawed
1/2 teaspoon beef bouillon granules
1/2 teaspoon salt
1/4 teaspoon pepper

Place potatoes, carrots and garlic in a saucepan; cover with water. Bring to a boil. Reduce heat; cover and cook for 20-25 minutes or until vegetables are tender. Drain, reserving 1/2 cup cooking liquid. In a mixing bowl, mash potatoes, carrots and garlic. Beat in milk, butter, salt and pepper until light and fluffy. Set aside and keep warm. Meanwhile, in a skillet, cook beef and onion over medium heat until meat is no longer pink; drain. Add reserved cooking liquid. Combine cornstarch and milk until smooth; stir into meat mixture. Bring to a boil; cook and stir for 2 minutes or until thickened. Stir in peas, bouillon, salt and pepper. Cook for 2-3 minutes or until heated through. Serve over mashed potatoes. **Yield:** 6 servings.

— ☕ ☕ ☕ —

Mud Slide Dip

The sandy color of this zippy bean dip inspired its weather-related name.

   1 medium onion, finely chopped
   2 tablespoons vegetable oil
1/2 cup water
   1 egg
   1 can (15-1/2 ounces) garbanzo beans, rinsed and drained
1-1/2 teaspoons chili powder
1/4 teaspoon salt
1/4 teaspoon garlic salt
1/4 cup mayonnaise
   5 medium carrots, julienned
   2 cups broccoli florets
   2 cups cauliflowerets

In a saucepan, saute onion in oil until tender. Place water, egg and beans in a blender or food processor; cover and process until smooth. Add to onion. Stir in chili powder, salt and garlic salt. Bring to a boil, stirring frequently. Cook and stir for 2 minutes or until thickened. Remove from the heat. When cool, stir in mayonnaise. Chill. Serve with vegetables. Store in the refrigerator. **Yield:** 2-1/3 cups.

Sherbet Rainbow

My brother was delighted with this colorful dessert.

2-1/2 cups lime sherbet, softened
   2 cups orange sherbet, softened
1-3/4 cups raspberry sherbet, softened
3/4 cup lemon sherbet, softened
Whipped topping, flaked coconut and blue liquid food coloring, optional

Line a 9-in. round pan with waxed paper. Firmly press the lime sherbet into a 1-in. ring around edge of pan. Smooth inside of the ring with a metal spatula or butter knife. Immediately form rings with orange and raspberry sherbet. Smooth inside ring; fill in center with lemon sherbet. Freeze overnight or until firm. Loosen edge with a knife. Invert onto a 12-in.-square piece of waxed paper. Remove waxed paper from top of sherbet. Cut in half. Press two halves together, forming a half circle. Smooth rounded edge. Transfer rainbow, cut side down, to a freezer-proof serving platter. Just before serving, spoon whipped topping "clouds" at each end of rainbow. Tint coconut with food coloring; sprinkle over topping. **Yield:** 10 servings.

— ☕ ☕ ☕ —

End-of-the-Rainbow Cake

(Not pictured)

This pretty cake can be served with foil-wrapped chocolate coins to represent the elusive pot of gold.

3/4 cup butter-flavored shortening
1-1/2 cups sugar
   2 eggs
   2 teaspoons vanilla extract
1/4 teaspoon almond extract
2-1/3 cups all-purpose flour
   3 teaspoons baking powder
   1 teaspoon salt
1-1/3 cups milk
Frosting of your choice
Foil-covered chocolate coins, optional

In a mixing bowl, cream shortening and sugar until fluffy. Add the eggs, one at a time, beating well after each addition. Beat in extracts. Combine flour, baking powder and salt; add to creamed mixture alternately with milk. Pour into two greased and floured 8-in. round baking pans. Bake at 350° for 30-35 minutes or until a toothpick inserted near the center comes out clean. Cool for 10 minutes before removing from pans to wire racks to cool completely. Frost between layers and top and sides of cake. Decorate with chocolate coins if desired. **Yield:** 12 servings.

Elegant Tea Honors a Bride-to-Be

By Robin Fuhrman, Fond du Lac, Wisconsin

PLANNING a Victorian shower for a special bride proved to be just my cup of tea. Enchanted by the era, I've decorated my home in Victorian style and collected antique china and clothing from the period. I often give teas in my home.

We chose teatime recipes to delight the eye and the taste buds. The menu included Victorian Iced Tea, Apricot Scones, Curried Chicken Tea Sandwiches and Midsummer Sponge Cake.

The table settings were mixed-and-matched china and silver, pulled together with pretty linens. Centerpieces were simple—a flowered hat or tea set with a few Victorian items. Traditions and quotes from the Victorian era were typed on cards set at each place.

I invite you to use my recipes, your best china (or your mom's or a friend's) and have a wonderful time!

— ▛ ▛ ▛ —

Curried Chicken Tea Sandwiches

I spread this dressed-up chicken salad on bread cut in the shape of a heart.

   2 cups cubed cooked chicken
   1 medium unpeeled red apple, chopped
3/4 cup dried cranberries
1/2 cup thinly sliced celery
1/4 cup chopped pecans
   2 tablespoons thinly sliced green onions
3/4 cup mayonnaise *or* salad dressing

2 teaspoons lime juice
1/2 to 3/4 teaspoon curry powder
12 slices bread
Lettuce leaves

In a bowl, combine the first six ingredients. Combine mayonnaise, lime juice and curry powder; add to chicken mixture and stir to coat. Cover and refrigerate until ready to serve. Cut each slice of bread with a 3-in. heart-shaped cookie cutter. Top with lettuce and chicken salad. **Yield:** 6 servings.

Apricot Scones

Popular served with tea in Victorian days, scones are making a big comeback.

DEVONSHIRE CREAM:
1 package (3 ounces) cream cheese, softened
1 tablespoon confectioners' sugar
1/2 teaspoon vanilla extract
1/4 to 1/3 cup whipping cream
SCONES:
2 cups all-purpose flour
1/4 cup sugar
1 tablespoon baking powder
1/4 teaspoon salt
1/3 cup cold butter *or* margarine
1/2 cup chopped dried apricots
1/2 cup chopped pecans
1 teaspoon grated orange peel
1 cup plus 2 tablespoons whipping cream, *divided*
Jam of your choice

In a small mixing bowl, beat cream cheese, confectioners' sugar and vanilla until fluffy. Gradually beat in enough cream to achieve a spreading consistency. Cover and chill for at least 2 hours. For scones, combine the dry ingredients in a bowl. Cut in butter until mixture resembles fine crumbs. Add apricots, pecans and orange peel. With a fork, rapidly stir in 1 cup whipping cream just until moistened. Turn onto a floured surface; knead 5-6 times. Divide in half; shape each into a ball. Flatten each ball into a 6-in. circle; cut each circle into eight wedges. Place 1 in. apart on an ungreased baking sheet. Brush with remaining whipping cream. Bake at 375° for 13-15 minutes or until a toothpick comes out clean. Serve with Devonshire cream and jam. **Yield:** 16 scones (1 cup cream).

Midsummer Sponge Cake

Attached to ribbons beneath the cake were Victorian charms for the bridesmaids to pull out and keep.

4 eggs
1-1/4 cups sugar
1-1/4 cups all-purpose flour
2 teaspoons baking powder
1/2 cup water
1-1/2 cups cold milk
1/2 teaspoon vanilla extract
1 package (3.4 ounces) instant vanilla pudding mix
2 cups whipped topping
3 tablespoons lemon gelatin powder
1/2 cup boiling water
10 to 12 ribbons with small charms attached
Assorted fresh fruit

In a mixing bowl, beat eggs until light and fluffy. Gradually beat in sugar until light and lemon-colored. Combine flour and baking powder; add to egg mixture alternately with water, beating just until smooth. Pour into a greased and floured 10-in. springform pan. Bake at 375° for 20-25 minutes or until cake springs back when lightly touched. Cool on a wire rack for 1 hour. Carefully run a knife around edge of pan; remove sides. Invert onto a wire rack. Remove bottom of pan; invert cake so top is up. Using a sharp knife, split cake in half horizontally; set aside. For filling, in a mixing bowl, beat milk, vanilla and pudding mix for 2 minutes or until thickened; chill for 10 minutes. Fold in whipped topping. For glaze, dissolve gelatin in boiling water. Add enough cold water to measure 1 cup. Chill for 15 minutes or until slightly thickened. To assemble, place bottom cake layer on a cake plate. Tuck charms under edge of cake. Spread filling over cake; top with second cake layer and fruit. Drizzle with glaze. Chill until serving. **Yield:** 10-12 servings.

Victorian Iced Tea

Pretty and refreshing, this flavored iced tea was well-received at the Victorian-theme shower.

4 individual tea bags
4 cups boiling water
1 can (11-1/2 ounces) frozen cranberry-raspberry juice concentrate, thawed
4 cups cold water
Ice cubes and fresh mint

Place tea bags in a teapot; add boiling water. Cover and steep for 5 minutes. Remove and discard tea bags. Refrigerate tea in a covered container. Just before serving, combine cranberry-raspberry concentrate and cold water in a 2-1/2-qt. pitcher; stir in tea. Serve on ice. Garnish with mint. **Yield:** 10 (1-cup) servings.

Ring in the Olympics with Flair

By Therese Judge, Westminster, Maryland

THE ancient announcement opening the Olympics—"Let the games begin!"—was heard at our home for the commencement of a party for our daughter's 10th birthday, which occurred during the Winter Games.

Tangy and refreshing Mt. Olympus Punch is a fruity blend with just enough fizz to be fun. Gold-Medal Vegetable Dip gets its zip from mustard and Worcestershire sauce. Served with colorful fresh veggies, it makes a popular appetizer or buffet selection for any occasion.

The familiar interlocking rings logo made a tasty statement on Olympic Rings Pizza and Champion Chocolate Cake. I formed the symbol with pepperoni slices on the pizza, which has a thick, tender crust that's easy to shape. Rings of different-colored M&M's gave an "official" look to my dessert.

The table was set with bright blue, red, yellow and green balloons, plastic plates, cups and cutlery.

For a centerpiece, I used an Olympic "torch" made from a paper towel tube and colored tissue paper. Our young "Olympians" carried and passed this torch in a relay race outdoors. They also competed in a tandem ski race on special skis made from scrap wood.

After the races, we made souvenir T-shirts. The girls

used fabric crayons to draw designs that I ironed onto white T-shirts we purchased for them all.

The final "event" was bursting a pinata filled with goodies. Everyone was a winner!

— 🝙 🝙 🝙 —

Mt. Olympus Punch

(Not pictured)

A delightful blend of four fruit juices gives this pleasant punch its cool character.

> **4 cups cranberry juice**
> **2 cups orange juice**
> **2 cups apple juice**
> **2 cans (6 ounces *each*) pineapple juice**
> **2 liters ginger ale**

Chill the juices and ginger ale. Just before serving, combine juices in a punch bowl. Stir in the ginger ale. **Yield:** 4-1/2 quarts.

— 🝙 🝙 🝙 —

Gold-Medal Vegetable Dip

With just enough zip from mustard and Worcestershire sauce, it's a great-tasting accompaniment to an assortment of crisp vegetables.

> **1 carton (8 ounces) softened chive and onion cream cheese**
> **2 tablespoons mayonnaise**
> **1 teaspoon prepared mustard**
> **1/2 teaspoon Worcestershire sauce**
> **1/4 teaspoon salt**
> **1/8 teaspoon pepper**
> **1 to 2 tablespoons milk**
> **Assorted fresh vegetables**

In a mixing bowl, combine the cream cheese, mayonnaise, mustard, Worcestershire sauce, salt and pepper. Add milk until dip achieves desired consistency. Serve with vegetables. **Yield:** 1-1/4 cups.

— 🝙 🝙 🝙 —

Olympic Rings Pizza

The symbolic five rings—made from pepperoni—decorate the yummy homemade pizza.

> **2-1/2 to 3 cups all-purpose flour**
> **1 package (1/4 ounce) active dry yeast**
> **1/2 teaspoon salt**
> **1 cup warm water (120° to 130°)**
> **2 tablespoons vegetable oil**
> **1 can (15 ounces) pizza sauce**
> **4 cups (16 ounces) shredded mozzarella cheese**

> **1 package (3-1/2 ounces) sliced pepperoni**

In a mixing bowl, combine 2 cups flour, yeast and salt. Add water and oil; beat until smooth. Stir in enough remaining flour to form a soft dough. Turn onto a floured surface; knead until smooth and elastic, about 6 minutes. Cover and let rest for 10 minutes. Roll the dough into a 16-in. x 11-in. rectangle; transfer to a greased 15-in. x 10-in. x 1-in. baking pan. Press dough 1/2 in. up the sides of pan. Spread with pizza sauce and sprinkle with cheese. Arrange pepperoni on top in five interlocking circles. Bake at 400° for 20-25 minutes or until crust is lightly browned. **Yield:** 10-12 servings.

— 🝙 🝙 🝙 —

Champion Chocolate Cake

The kids clamored for pieces with the candy, but every bite of this cake is moist and delicious. I marked the circles on the icing with a glass rim to serve as a guide—then filled in with M&M's.

> **1/2 cup butter *or* margarine, softened**
> **2-1/4 cups packed brown sugar**
> **3 eggs**
> **3 squares (1 ounce *each*) unsweetened chocolate, melted and cooled**
> **1-1/2 teaspoons vanilla extract**
> **2-1/4 cups all-purpose flour**
> **2 teaspoons baking soda**
> **1/2 teaspoon salt**
> **1 cup (8 ounces) sour cream**
> **1 cup boiling water**
> **FROSTING:**
> **1/2 cup butter *or* margarine, softened**
> **4 cups confectioners' sugar**
> **1 teaspoon vanilla extract**
> **4 to 6 tablespoons milk**
> **14 to 16 *each* plain blue, yellow, black *or* brown, green and red M&M's**

In a mixing bowl, cream butter and brown sugar. Add eggs, one at a time, beating well after each addition. Beat in chocolate and vanilla. Combine flour, baking soda and salt; add to the creamed mixture alternately with sour cream. Whisk in water until smooth. Pour into a greased 13-in. x 9-in. x 2-in. baking pan. Bake at 350° for 25-30 minutes or until a toothpick inserted near center comes out clean. Cool for 10 minutes; invert onto a wire rack to cool completely. For frosting, combine butter, confectioners' sugar, vanilla and enough milk to achieve spreading consistency. Frost sides and top of cake. With a glass (about 2-1/4-in. diameter), outline five interlocking circles on frosting. Use M&M's in order listed to cover each circle with a single color. **Yield:** 16-20 servings.

Welcome to My Pineapple Palace

By Jo Ann Fox, Johnson City, Tennessee

I STARTED collecting pineapple items when I learned that the pineapple is the symbol of hospitality. Plus, I love the flavor of this versatile tropical fruit. So wouldn't it be fun, I reasoned, to plan a pineapple party?

I had made many pineapple recipes for various occasions over the years, but I had never tried combining several into a complete meal. When I did, it was not only delicious, it was fun!

Baked Ham with Pineapple is an attractive but easy entree to serve company. My recipe has a pleasant sauce of pineapple juice and brown sugar that's poured over the ham and used for basting. Pineapple slices and maraschino cherries make a pretty garnish on top of the succulent ham.

Pineapple tidbits, miniature marshmallows and dried cranberries give my Pineapple Mallow Slaw special-occasion flair. I combined several recipes to come up with this popular side dish.

I also served sweet potatoes with pineapple chutney and gave guests jars of chutney as favors. Wrapped with yellow and green netting and tied with yellow ribbon, the jars even resembled little pineapples!

For dessert, I baked moist, delicious Hawaiian Cake. An acquaintance shared the recipe with me some 20 years ago, and I've used it many times since then. Toasted coconut sprinkled on the cake's wonderful fluffy topping adds another tropical flavor to this pineapple treat.

My entire kitchen is decorated with pineapple accents, which spill over into the dining room. I set the table using plenty of pineapple pieces.

For the fresh fruit centerpiece, I filled a wrought-iron basket with Golden Delicious and Granny Smith apples and placed a whole pineapple on top.

I also used pineapple-shaped candles, serving dishes and salt and pepper shakers, plus salad utensils with carved pineapple handles. My pineapple napkin rings looked very pretty with the pastel yellow tablecloth and napkins.

Of course, you don't need an extensive "pineapple patch" like mine to enjoy this party theme. You can purchase inexpensive pineapple-design paper plates and napkins and many other decorations.

My husband, Bob, is a symbol of hospitality himself! He doesn't cook much, but he loves to put on a chef's outfit and greet guests at the door. I can always count on his help when we entertain.

We had a great evening eating, talking about the pineapple menu and decorations and visiting with friends. Everyone seemed delighted by my tasty tribute to the symbol of hospitality!

———— 🍴 🍴 🍴 ————

Baked Ham with Pineapple

My mom used to bake ham like this. It's a simple recipe that proves the simplest things in life are best!

   1 fully cooked bone-in ham (6 to 8 pounds)
Whole cloves
1/2 cup packed brown sugar
1/4 cup pineapple juice
   1 can (8 ounces) sliced pineapple, drained
   5 maraschino cherries

Place ham in a roasting pan. Score the surface with shallow diagonal cuts, making diamond shapes; insert cloves into the diamonds. Cover and bake at 325° for 1-1/2 hours. Combine brown sugar and pineapple juice; pour over the ham. Arrange pineapple and cherries on the ham. Bake, uncov-

ered, 30-45 minutes longer or until a meat thermometer reads 140° and ham is heated through. **Yield:** 16-20 servings.

———— 🍴 🍴 🍴 ————

Pineapple Mallow Slaw

When I couldn't find a recipe I liked, I created my own. Our guests loved the mixture and commented on its appealing sweet-tart dressing.

   9 cups shredded cabbage
   1 can (20 ounces) pineapple tidbits, drained
1-1/2 cups mayonnaise
   3/4 cup vinegar
   1/2 cup sugar
   3/4 teaspoon salt
   3/4 teaspoon celery seed
   3 cups miniature marshmallows
1-1/2 cups dried cranberries

In a bowl, combine the cabbage and pineapple. In another bowl, combine the mayonnaise, vinegar, sugar, salt and celery seed. Stir into cabbage mixture. Cover and refrigerate for 2 hours. Fold in marshmallows and cranberries 30 minutes before serving. **Yield:** 16-20 servings.

———— 🍴 🍴 🍴 ————

Hawaiian Cake

Every time I take this cake to an event, someone asks for the recipe. It's moist, delicious and easy to make.

   1 package (18-1/4 ounces) yellow cake mix
1-1/4 cups cold milk
   1 package (3.4 ounces) instant vanilla pudding mix
   1 can (20 ounces) crushed pineapple, drained
   1 envelope whipped topping mix
   1 package (3 ounces) cream cheese, softened
   1/4 cup sugar
   1/2 teaspoon vanilla extract
   1/2 cup flaked coconut, toasted

Prepare and bake cake according to package directions, using a greased 13-in. x 9-in. x 2-in. baking pan. Cool. In a bowl, whisk together milk and pudding mix; let stand to thicken. Stir in the pineapple. Spread over cake. Prepare whipped topping mix according to package directions; set aside. In a mixing bowl, beat cream cheese, sugar and vanilla until smooth. Beat in 1 cup whipped topping. Fold in remaining topping. Spread over pudding. Sprinkle with coconut. Cover and refrigerate 3 hours or overnight. **Yield:** 12-15 servings.

Substitutions & Equivalents

Equivalent Measures

3 teaspoons	= 1 tablespoon		16 tablespoons	= 1 cup
4 tablespoons	= 1/4 cup		2 cups	= 1 pint
5-1/3 tablespoons	= 1/3 cup		4 cups	= 1 quart
8 tablespoons	= 1/2 cup		4 quarts	= 1 gallon

Food Equivalents

Grains

Macaroni	1 cup (3-1/2 ounces) uncooked	= 2-1/2 cups cooked
Noodles, Medium	3 cups (4 ounces) uncooked	= 4 cups cooked
Popcorn	1/3 to 1/2 cup unpopped	= 8 cups popped
Rice, Long Grain	1 cup uncooked	= 3 cups cooked
Rice, Quick-Cooking	1 cup uncooked	= 2 cups cooked
Spaghetti	8 ounces uncooked	= 4 cups cooked

Crumbs

Bread	1 slice	= 3/4 cup soft crumbs, 1/4 cup fine dry crumbs
Graham Crackers	7 squares	= 1/2 cup finely crushed
Buttery Round Crackers	12 crackers	= 1/2 cup finely crushed
Saltine Crackers	14 crackers	= 1/2 cup finely crushed

Fruits

Bananas	1 medium	= 1/3 cup mashed
Lemons	1 medium	= 3 tablespoons juice, 2 teaspoons grated peel
Limes	1 medium	= 2 tablespoons juice, 1-1/2 teaspoons grated peel
Oranges	1 medium	= 1/4 to 1/3 cup juice, 4 teaspoons grated peel

Vegetables

Cabbage	1 head	= 5 cups shredded	Green Pepper	1 large	= 1 cup chopped
Carrots	1 pound	= 3 cups shredded	Mushrooms	1/2 pound	= 3 cups sliced
Celery	1 rib	= 1/2 cup chopped	Onions	1 medium	= 1/2 cup chopped
Corn	1 ear fresh	= 2/3 cup kernels	Potatoes	3 medium	= 2 cups cubed

Nuts

Almonds	1 pound	= 3 cups chopped	Pecan Halves	1 pound	= 4-1/2 cups chopped
Ground Nuts	3-3/4 ounces	= 1 cup	Walnuts	1 pound	= 3-3/4 cups chopped

Easy Substitutions

When you need...		Use...
Baking Powder	1 teaspoon	1/2 teaspoon cream of tartar + 1/4 teaspoon baking soda
Buttermilk	1 cup	1 tablespoon lemon juice *or* vinegar + enough milk to measure 1 cup (let stand 5 minutes before using)
Cornstarch	1 tablespoon	2 tablespoons all-purpose flour
Honey	1 cup	1-1/4 cups sugar + 1/4 cup water
Half-and-Half Cream	1 cup	1 tablespoon melted butter + enough whole milk to measure 1 cup
Onion	1 small, chopped (1/3 cup)	1 teaspoon onion powder *or* 1 tablespoon dried minced onion
Tomato Juice	1 cup	1/2 cup tomato sauce + 1/2 cup water
Tomato Sauce	2 cups	3/4 cup tomato paste + 1 cup water
Unsweetened Chocolate	1 square (1 ounce)	3 tablespoons baking cocoa + 1 tablespoon shortening *or* oil
Whole Milk	1 cup	1/2 cup evaporated milk + 1/2 cup water

Cooking Terms

HERE'S a quick reference for some of the cooking terms used in *Taste of Home* recipes:

Baste—To moisten food with melted butter, pan drippings, marinades or other liquid to add more flavor and juiciness.

Beat—A rapid movement to combine ingredients using a fork, spoon, wire whisk or electric mixer.

Blend—To combine ingredients until *just* mixed.

Boil—To heat liquids until bubbles form that cannot be "stirred down". In the case of water, the temperature will reach 212°.

Bone—To remove all meat from the bone before cooking.

Cream—To beat ingredients together to a smooth consistency, usually in the case of butter and sugar for baking.

Dash—A small amount of seasoning, less than 1/8 teaspoon. If using a shaker, a dash would comprise a quick flip of the container.

Dredge—To coat foods with flour or other dry ingredients. Most often done with pot roasts and stew meat before browning.

Fold—To incorporate several ingredients by careful and gentle turning with a spatula. Used generally with beaten egg whites or whipped cream when mixing into the rest of the ingredients to keep the batter light.

Julienne—To cut foods into long thin strips much like matchsticks. Used most often for salads and stir-fry dishes.

Mince—To cut into very fine pieces. Used often for garlic or fresh herbs.

Parboil—To cook partially, usually used in the case of chicken, sausages and vegetables.

Partially set—Describes the consistency of gelatin after it has been chilled for a small amount of time. Mixture should resemble the consistency of egg whites.

Puree—To process foods to a smooth mixture. Can be prepared in an electric blender, food processor, food mill or sieve.

Saute—To fry quickly in a small amount of fat, stirring almost constantly. Most often done with onions, mushrooms and other chopped vegetables.

Score—To cut slits partway through the outer surface of foods. Often used with ham or flank steak.

Stir-Fry—To cook meats and/or vegetables with a constant stirring motion in a small amount of oil in a wok or skillet over high heat.

Guide to Cooking with Popular Herbs

HERB	APPETIZERS SALADS	BREADS/EGGS SAUCES/CHEESE	VEGETABLES PASTA	MEAT POULTRY	FISH SHELLFISH
BASIL	Green, Potato & Tomato Salads, Salad Dressings, Stewed Fruit	Breads, Fondue & Egg Dishes, Dips, Marinades, Sauces	Mushrooms, Tomatoes, Squash, Pasta, Bland Vegetables	Broiled, Roast Meat & Poultry Pies, Stews, Stuffing	Baked, Broiled & Poached Fish, Shellfish
BAY LEAF	Seafood Cocktail, Seafood Salad, Tomato Aspic, Stewed Fruit	Egg Dishes, Gravies, Marinades, Sauces	Dried Bean Dishes, Beets, Carrots, Onions, Potatoes, Rice, Squash	Corned Beef, Tongue Meat & Poultry Stews	Poached Fish, Shellfish, Fish Stews
CHIVES	Mixed Vegetable, Green, Potato & Tomato Salads, Salad Dressings	Egg & Cheese Dishes, Cream Cheese, Cottage Cheese, Gravies, Sauces	Hot Vegetables, Potatoes	Broiled Poultry, Poultry & Meat Pies, Stews, Casseroles	Baked Fish, Fish Casseroles, Fish Stews, Shellfish
DILL	Seafood Cocktail, Green, Potato & Tomato Salads, Salad Dressings	Breads, Egg & Cheese Dishes, Cream Cheese, Fish & Meat Sauces	Beans, Beets, Cabbage, Carrots, Cauliflower, Peas, Squash, Tomatoes	Beef, Veal Roasts, Lamb, Steaks, Chops, Stews, Roast & Creamed Poultry	Baked, Broiled, Poached & Stuffed Fish, Shellfish
GARLIC	All Salads, Salad Dressings	Fondue, Poultry Sauces, Fish & Meat Marinades	Beans, Eggplant, Potatoes, Rice, Tomatoes	Roast Meats, Meat & Poultry Pies, Hamburgers, Casseroles, Stews	Broiled Fish, Shellfish, Fish Stews, Casseroles
MARJORAM	Seafood Cocktail, Green, Poultry & Seafood Salads	Breads, Cheese Spreads, Egg & Cheese Dishes, Gravies, Sauces	Carrots, Eggplant, Peas, Onions, Potatoes, Dried Bean Dishes, Spinach	Roast Meats & Poultry, Meat & Poultry Pies, Stews & Casseroles	Baked, Broiled & Stuffed Fish, Shellfish
MUSTARD	Fresh Green Salads, Prepared Meat, Macaroni & Potato Salads, Salad Dressings	Biscuits, Egg & Cheese Dishes, Sauces	Baked Beans, Cabbage, Eggplant, Squash, Dried Beans, Mushrooms, Pasta	Chops, Steaks, Ham, Pork, Poultry, Cold Meats	Shellfish
OREGANO	Green, Poultry & Seafood Salads	Breads, Egg & Cheese Dishes, Meat, Poultry & Vegetable Sauces	Artichokes, Cabbage, Eggplant, Squash, Dried Beans, Mushrooms, Pasta	Broiled, Roast Meats, Meat & Poultry Pies, Stews, Casseroles	Baked, Broiled & Poached Fish, Shellfish
PARSLEY	Green, Potato, Seafood & Vegetable Salads	Biscuits, Breads, Egg & Cheese Dishes, Gravies, Sauces	Asparagus, Beets, Eggplant, Squash, Dried Beans, Mushrooms, Pasta	Meat Loaf, Meat & Poultry Pies, Stews & Casseroles, Stuffing	Fish Stews, Stuffed Fish
ROSEMARY	Fruit Cocktail, Fruit & Green Salads	Biscuits, Egg Dishes, Herb Butter, Cream Cheese, Marinades, Sauces	Beans, Broccoli, Peas, Cauliflower, Mushrooms, Baked Potatoes, Parsnips	Roast Meat, Poultry & Meat Pies, Stews & Casseroles, Stuffing	Stuffed Fish, Shellfish
SAGE		Breads, Fondue, Egg & Cheese Dishes, Spreads, Gravies, Sauces	Beans, Beets, Onions, Peas, Spinach, Squash, Tomatoes	Roast Meat, Poultry, Meat Loaf, Stews, Stuffing	Baked, Poached & Stuffed Fish
TARRAGON	Seafood Cocktail, Avocado Salads, Salad Dressings	Cheese Spreads, Marinades, Sauces, Egg Dishes	Asparagus, Beans, Beets, Carrots, Mushrooms, Peas, Squash, Spinach	Steaks, Poultry, Roast Meats, Casseroles & Stews	Baked, Broiled & Poached Fish, Shellfish
THYME	Seafood Cocktail, Green, Poultry, Seafood & Vegetable Salads	Biscuits, Breads, Egg & Cheese Dishes, Sauces, Spreads	Beets, Carrots, Mushrooms, Onions, Peas, Eggplant, Spinach, Potatoes	Roast Meat, Poultry & Meat Loaf, Meat & Poultry Pies, Stews & Casseroles	Baked, Broiled & Stuffed Fish, Shellfish, Fish Stews

General Recipe Index

This handy index lists every recipe by food category, major ingredient and/or cooking method, so you can easily locate recipes to suit your needs.

APPETIZERS & SNACKS
Cold Appetizers
Garlic-Mushroom Appetizer, 21
Lemon-Curry Deviled Eggs, 197
Dips
Avocado Taco Dip, 24
Bear's Picnic Veggie Dip, 297
Fiesta Crab Dip, 11
✓Garden Salsa, 18
Gold-Medal Vegetable Dip, 303
✓Herbed Cheese Dip, 19
Hot Corn Dip, 16
✓Layered Fiesta Dip, 20
Microwave Salsa, 63
Mud Slide Dip, 299
Pepperoni Pizza Dip, 13
Peppery Black Bean Salsa, 58
Ruby-Red Pretzel Dip, 11
✓Salsa Guacamole, 12
Southwestern Star Dip, 11
Taco Appetizer Platter, 27
Tangy Texas Salsa, 9
Hot Appetizers
Bacon-Cheese Appetizer Pie, 26
Cheesy Olive Snacks, 27
Cheesy Sausage Stromboli, 52
Chili Cheese Tidbits, 19
Clam-Ups, 8
Corn Bread Pizza Wheels, 25
Crab Triangles, 17
Crisp Potato Skins, 8
Crunchy Cheese Nibblers, 9
Puffs with Honey Butter, 17
Raspberry Glazed Wings, 14
Sesame Chicken Wings, 15
Spicy Hot Wings, 14
Taco Party Wings, 15
Taco Plate for Two, 200
Treasure-Filled Apples, 20
Vegetable Tortilla Stack, 27
Wontons with Sweet-Sour
   Sauce, 12
Zesty Chicken Wings, 14
Snacks
Caramel Popcorn Balls, 23
✓Chili Popcorn, 23
Corny Chocolate Crunch, 22
Cranberry Popcorn Bars, 23
Oat Snack Mix, 17
Roasted Mixed Nuts, 20
✓Tortilla Snack Strips, 17
Spreads
Christmas Cheese Ball, 10
Festive Apple-Cheese Log, 25

Layered Vegetable Cheesecake, 24
Mushroom Liver Pate, 11
✓Sweet Onion Cheese Spread, 12

APPLES
Apple-Berry Streusel Bars, 287
Apple Bread Pudding, 152
✓Apple Cabbage Slaw, 220
Apple Cinnamon Muffins, 110
Apple Cream Pie, 243
Apple Fritter Rings, 282
Apple-Ham Grilled Cheese, 55
Apple-of-Your-Eye Cheesecake, 172
Applesauce Pork Chops, 280
Apple Snack Cake, 148
Autumn Apple Tart, 156
✓Baked Apples, 170
Caramel Apple Bites, 126
Cheddar Apple Pizza, 145
Chunky Rhubarb Applesauce, 69
Festive Apple-Cheese Log, 25
Hot Cranberry Cider, 18
Pecan Apple Pie, 144
Sweet Potato Apple Salad, 242
Treasure-Filled Apples, 20

APRICOTS
✓Apricot Chicken, 204
Apricot-Filled Cookies, 124
Apricot Glazed Chicken, 196
Apricot-Nut Drop Cookies, 132
Apricot Pecan Tassies, 131
Apricot Scones, 301
Creamy Apricot Pie, 140
Fruit Salad with Apricot Dressing, 40
✓Warm Apricot Chicken Salad, 32

ASPARAGUS
✓Cream of Asparagus Soup, 48
Creamy Herb Dressing, 64
Fiddlehead Soup, 50
Rosemary Asparagus, 62
Stir-Fried Asparagus, 271

AVOCADOS
Avocado Chicken Casserole, 86
Avocado Citrus Toss, 41
Avocado Orange Salad, 200
Avocado Taco Dip, 24
✓Baked Seafood Avocados, 89
Mandarin Avocado Toss, 33
✓Salsa Guacamole, 12

BACON
Bacon and Chive Waffles, 113
Bacon 'n' Egg Lasagna, 106
Bacon Breadsticks, 246
Bacon-Cheese Appetizer Pie, 26
Classic Red Beans and Rice, 194
Country Turnip Greens, 217
Fabulous Fettuccine, 63
Lazy Pierogi Bake, 106
Tossed Spinach Salad, 35

BANANAS
Banana Chiffon Cake, 148
Banana Cream Cheesecake, 176
Banana Crepes, 174
Banana Ice Cream, 158
Banana Split Brownie Pizza, 160
Caramel Banana Sundaes, 152
Frosted Banana Bars, 189
Fruity Banana Freeze, 30

BARLEY *(see Rice & Barley)*

BARS & BROWNIES
Almond Pie Bars, 128
Apple-Berry Streusel Bars, 287
Chewy Peanut Butter Bars, 129
Chocolate Mint Brownies, 130
Chocolate Oat Squares, 190
Coconut Granola Bars, 132
Frosted Banana Bars, 189
Fudgy Toffee Bars, 192
Honey Peanut Squares, 124
Orange Slice Bars, 131
Pear Custard Bars, 133
Shortbread Lemon Bars, 124
Spiced Pumpkin Bars, 125
Teddy Carrot Bars, 297

BASIL
✓Basil Bean Salad, 34
Basil Cream Chicken, 100
Basil Parmesan Shrimp, 38
Basil Parsley Pesto, 65
Cream of Basil Soup, 52
Pesto Pizza, 98
Tomato-Basil Drop Biscuits, 117

BEANS
Baked Beans
Roundup-Day Beans, 185
Sweet 'n' Sour Beans, 183

✓ Recipe includes Nutritional Analysis and Diabetic Exchanges

✓ Recipe includes Nutritional Analysis and Diabetic Exchanges

✓ Recipe includes Nutritional Analysis and Diabetic Exchanges

✓ Recipe includes Nutritional Analysis and Diabetic Exchanges

✓ *Recipe includes Nutritional Analysis and Diabetic Exchanges*

✓ Recipe includes Nutritional Analysis and Diabetic Exchanges

✓ *Recipe includes Nutritional Analysis and Diabetic Exchanges*

✓ Recipe includes Nutritional Analysis and Diabetic Exchanges

✓ Recipe includes Nutritional Analysis and Diabetic Exchanges

✓ Recipe includes Nutritional Analysis and Diabetic Exchanges

Alphabetical Recipe Index

*This handy index lists every recipe in alphabetical order
so you can easily find your favorite recipes.*

✓ Recipe includes Nutritional Analysis and Diabetic Exchanges

D

E

F

G

H

I

J

K

✓ *Recipe includes Nutritional Analysis and Diabetic Exchanges*

✓ Recipe includes Nutritional Analysis and Diabetic Exchanges

✓ Recipe includes Nutritional Analysis and Diabetic Exchanges